VOICES FROM THE MARGINS: FRESH PERSPECTIVES ON AN INTRODUCTION TO

SOCIOLOGY

Edited by Chandra Ward

Kennesaw State University

cognella®
academic publishing

Bassim Hamadeh, CEO and Publisher

Michael Simpson, Vice President of Acquisitions

Jamie Giganti, Managing Editor

Miguel Macias, Graphic Designer

Zina Craft, Acquisitions Editor

Monika Dziamka, Project Editor

Natalie Lakosil, Licensing Manager

Mandy Licata, Interior Designer

First published in the United States of America in 2015 by Cognella, Inc.

Printed in the United States of America

ISBN: 978-1-63189-299-8 (pbk) / 978-1-63189-300-1 (br)

www.cognella.com   800-200-3908

CONTENTS

SECTION III: CLASS, RACE, GENDER, AND SEXUALITY

SECTION IV: SOCIAL INSTITUTIONS: FAMILY, WORK, EDUCATION, RELIGION, AND HEALTH

SECTION V: THE ENVIRONMENT AND SOCIETY

ACKNOWLEDGMENTS

I would like to take this time to acknowledge the academicians who have inspired this work, as well as my own development as a sociologist. The works of bell hooks and Patricia Hill-Collins have been indispensable to me, both personally and professionally. Their works encouraged the direction of this book. As a former student "from the margins," I was always inspired by these women and hoped to bring the voices and experiences of those of us not written about—unless problematized—from the margins to the center.

Amber Deane, one of my best friends and colleagues, deserves my thanks for her camaraderie and support throughout my graduate and professional career.

To Georgia State University faculty Erin Ruel, Dawn Baunach, and Deirdre Oakley, thank you for your professional and personal support.

My utmost gratitude goes to Elisabeth Sheff for her continued support, encouragement, and kindness throughout this process and throughout every step of my life.

I would also like to thank my family and friends for their continued love and support.

Finally, I would like to thank Cognella Publishing for this opportunity!

INTRODUCTION

The contents of this reader were inspired by the title of one bell hooks's classical reads, *Feminist Theory: From Margin to Center*. In her own words, hooks (1984) describes the margins as being "part of the whole but outside the main body." The text centers the ideas and lived experiences of those groups which have traditionally been marginalized, both inside and outside of sociology. Issues of race, gender, and ability status have been virtually nonexistent from the reading and research of early theorists comprising the discipline's canon. These are oversights of the privileged to focus on White, middle-class males in the construction of a social science about society.

This text is a departure from mainstream introductory sociology texts. It is 21st-century sociology for 21st-century students. The text is a collection of readings reflecting the voices and issues of issues of a postmodern American society—one where multiple subjectivities are increasingly emergent. Comprised primarily of the lived experiences of those outside the margins such as women of color, women, sexual minorities, and people with disabilities, included also are discussions of the Internet, a place where society spends an increasing amount of its time, and readings on the environment. The issues and perspectives presented in this reader speak to what is relevant for today's and tomorrow's student, keeping them engaged in the ever evolving and relevant discipline of sociology.

Voices from the Margins: Fresh Perspectives on an Introduction to Sociology, is a collection of readings that survey the landscape of sociological concepts. It is meant to supplement mainstream introductory courses, by introducing students to contributors to the discipline who are not represented in introductory sociology textbooks. As an introductory text, you will find the sections contain topics that correspond to most texts used in introduction to sociology college courses. However, where this reader departs from its introductory companion texts is its intersectional perspective and incorporation of the emerging subdiscipline, digital sociology. Though you will find a section on gender and race, for example, that does not mean gender and/or race are absent from the rest of the text. This text is a reflection of the fact that we do not take our identities off anywhere. Our particular social locations are carried with us, and the readings in this text weave our identities throughout each topic covered. Nothing in society exists in isolation. The constructed identities we carry with us impact every facet of our lives, and that is reflected in this reader. The research and narratives of American "Others" are centered, where traditionally they have been silenced or given attention in specialty sections in the back of texts that can be easily overlooked or skipped if an instructor so chooses.

A BRIEF OVERVIEW OF THE READER

The reader is divided into five main sections: Sociology—Who, What, and How; Self—Culture, Socialization, and Deviance; Class, Race, Gender, and Sexuality; Social Institutions; and the Environment and Society. The first section, Sociology—Who, What, and How, gets at the questions of "what is sociology?" and "who does sociology, and how do they do it?" It does so by including readings from sociologists like W. E. B. Du Bois, whose ideas were not included in the sociological canon for much of the discipline's existence. The section includes sociologists whose identities, backgrounds, or ideas would not have placed them anywhere near the canon awhile back. These readings get us to take a look at the margins, but this time they occupy the center of our sociological imaginary.

The next section, Self, Culture, Socialization, and Deviance, includes readings from these four sociological areas. It is in this section that the reader is introduced to digital sociology. The Internet constitutes its own culture, which we construct and which helps construct us. The remaining readings in this section cover construction of the self. This includes how family helps to construct our sense of self, as well as how we see ourselves through others. The lens through which we see ourselves is constructed through social interaction and varies with the meanings society inscribes on our bodies. In the readings, these bodies are nonwhite and disabled. How do they experience the construction of self, being aware of the dominant culture, yet simultaneously aware of another culture of which they are a part?

The third section consists of readings discussing class, race, gender, and sexuality. Class is discussed in the context of Mexican Americans in Los Angeles. The discussion of race departs from traditional discussion that is dominated by the disparities between blacks and Whites. Here, I include readings interrogating whiteness and its role in race. Race scholarship is replete with research on nonwhites; however, we sometimes neglect the fact that Caucasian is a race. There are several readings here that problematize whiteness and its role in producing and reproducing race relations. There are similar readings included in the discussion on gender that focus on subordinated masculinities. The section concludes with readings on subordinate sexualities.

The fourth section covers a range of social institutions: family, work, education, religion, and health. In keeping with the theme of this book, the readings begin with exploring familial constructions not featured in NBC's and ABC's fall television lineup. The section continues with readings on work and the economy, again revisiting the Mexican American communities studied by Daniel Dohan, elite education, the breaking and creating of social bonds within religion, and health as a social construct.

The final section, a small one, is on the environmental society. This section comprises two readings by Robert Bullard, the father of studies on environmental racism. Integrating several sociological concepts such as race, space, and inequality, these readings familiarize the reader on the subject and how to apply the concept of environmental racism to the biggest natural disaster of this century in America, Hurricane Katrina.

Each section contains discussion questions about the readings to help critically engage the student with the material.

REFERENCES

hooks, bell. *Feminist Theory: From Margin to Center*. Boston: South End Press, 1984.

SECTION I

Sociology—Who, What, and How?

This section introduces the reader to sociology. The readings featured here get at the questions of not only what is sociology, but who are sociologists, and how do they do sociology? With its positivist origins, sociology has long embraced the idea of the objective social researcher to arrive at social "truth." Early on, implicit in this assumption is that one's social identity is absent from these observations, denying the importance of the researcher's social location, as well as the subject's social location in the multiple social realities within which we live. To consider those questions, we begin with the first reading, "Beyond the Double Bind: W.E.B. Du Bois and the Gift of Second Sight." This reading discusses and presents some of the work and contributions of the sociologist whose name is featured in the title, W. E. B. Du Bois. Du Bois, the first African American sociologist, the first sociologist to study "the Negro," and the first theorist on race, is today considered a prominent member of the discipline's classical canon. However, he and his work have long been marginalized within the discipline of sociology. He himself is a figure that asks us to ponder, "who is a sociologist?" "what counts as theory?" and "who is worthy of being studied?" Du Bois rejected biological theories of race, prominent within science during his day. Instead, he applied what is now considered a sociological perspective to race and the social conditions of African Americans, focusing on the impact of social institutions and historical context shaping the conditions of individuals. As a member of "the Negro race," Du Bois was able to add a unique perspective to studying African Americans by coining the phrase "double consciousness" as the lens through which this oppressed group experienced life. When we place our own assumptions and perspectives of the world onto another population, we not only come up with erroneous results, but reinforce inequality among marginalized populations whose conditions well-intended social scientists may sincerely seek to help advance.

Patricia Hill-Collins builds upon the foundation laid by Du Bois in *Black Feminist Thought: Black Feminism, Knowledge and Power*. Black feminist thought, like other similar concepts such as intersectional and standpoint theory, analyzes how multiple dimensions like race and gender "mutually construct one another as unjust systems of power" (Hill-Collins, 2012: 19). This framework has been instrumental in centering the taken-for-granted, lived experiences of those with multiple marginalized identities, especially black women. The concept emerged out of a response to the failure of mainstream feminist and antiracist discourses to acknowledge the multiple marginalized identities of women of color. The essentialist categories contained within hegemonic discourses "render invisible the experiences of the more marginalized members of that category" (Yuval-Davis, 2006: 195). Hill-Collins (2000, 2009) suggests that this is one of many ways in which power works to make hegemonic knowledge and discursive practices appear as "common sense" or "universal," while simultaneously discounting and concealing other ways of knowing and practices.

Patricia Hill-Collins's article, "Going Public: The Sociology That Had No Name," is a response to former American Sociological Association (ASA) president Michael Burawoy's speech on public sociology. Burawoy (2005) defines the purpose of public sociology as bringing "sociology into dialogue with audiences beyond the academy, an open dialogue in which both sides deepen their understanding of public issues."

Conflict theorists such as C. Wright Mills believe that sociologists should not just theorize about social change, but be active participants in it. Being an active participant in social change is what sociologists from W. E. B. Du Bois to Patricia Hill-Collins and others in this section have done with their intellectual prowess. For years, it has been people from the margins like women of color, who have done work in their communities, fighting for equality without the formal recognition and credibility of an academic discipline. I liken it to instances where you have been doing something all along, then a more "reputable" public person comes along and "discovers" it and gives it a name with a specific meaning. You sit there thinking, "Hey, I was doing that all this time before it was called such-and-so." Hill-Collins responds to the call by Burawoy advocating for public sociology challenging whether or not its "naming" and subsequent "institutionalization" into the discipline will help or hurt its cause and its practitioners.

In the reading included here, Hill-Collins asks "which sociological worthies would make the cut to be included on the required reading list and which would be left outside to stare at a closed door." This article represents contemporary debates within the discipline regarding its direction and focus, as well as the multiple marginal knowledges brought to the discipline by both its practitioners and the public.

The section ends with an interview with sociologist Victor Rios and his experiences interviewing inner-city black and Latino male youth. In his interview, Rios discusses how his particular social location informs his research and role as a sociologist, as well as methodological issues experienced while in the field studying his population. Rios is a former gang member from Oakland who now studies the community among which he lived and the circumstances from which he escaped. This reading brings together other readings within this section, where marginalized folks use their opportunity of education to bring the voices, lives, and perspectives of Others from the margin to the center of sociological thought.

DISCUSSION QUESTIONS

1. Explain what Hill-Collins means by black women's outsider-within location? How does an outsider-within location create new angles of vision on oppression?
2. How does Hill-Collins's black feminist thought build upon the "double-consciousness" of W. E. B. Du Bois?
3. Do you share Hill-Collins's concern about public sociology "going public?"
4. Does a policy of inclusion and expansion of the margins undermine the validity or integrity of sociological thought?
5. How does the social location of Victor Rios help him gain access to the population he studies?
6. How does "diversity" help sociology as a discipline?

REFERENCES

Burawoy, Michael. "American Sociological Association Presidential Address: For public sociology" (2004). *American Sociological Review*, 2005, Vol. 70, Issue 1, 4–28.

Hill-Collins, Patricia. *Black Feminist Thought: Knowledge, Consciousness and the Politics of Empowerment*. London: Harper-Collins, 2000.

_____. "Looking Back, Moving Ahead: Scholarship in Service to Social Service." *Gender & Society* 26(1) (2012): 14–22.

Yuval-Davis, Nira. "Intersectionality and Feminist Politics." *European Journal of Women's Studies* 13(3) (2006): 193–209.

GOING PUBLIC

DOING THE SOCIOLOGY THAT HAD NO NAME

By Patricia Hill Collins

For years, I have been doing a kind of sociology that had no name. With hindsight, the path that I have been on seems clear and consistent. In the early 1970s, as a teacher and community organizer within the community schools movement, I did some of my best sociology, all without publishing one word. For six years, I honed the craft of translating the powerful ideas of my college education so that I might share them with my elementary school students, their families, my fellow teachers, and community members. My sociological career also illustrates how the tensions of moving through sociology as a discipline as well as engaging numerous constituencies outside sociology shaped my scholarship. This impetus to think both inside and outside the American sociological box enabled me to survive within the discipline. Early on, I recognized that I needed to create space to breathe within prevailing sociological norms and practices. I wrote "Learning from the Outsider Within: The Sociological Significance of Black Feminist Thought" to create space for myself as an individual, yet that article simultaneously generated dialogues with a broad range of nonsociologists (Collins 1986). Similarly, writing *Black Feminist Thought* (Collins 2000) for social theorists, for sociologists, for feminists, and for ordinary people—in particular, African American women whose lives I hoped to influence—was an exercise in the energy that it takes to engage multiple audiences within one text. When colleagues tell me how much the ideas in that one book have traveled, I realize the importance of connecting scholarship to broader audiences. With hindsight, I see how important my years spent working in the community schools movement have been to my subsequent sociological career.

Over the years, my personal engagement in speaking with multiracial, multiethnic audiences from many social class backgrounds, citizenship categories, genders, sexualities, and ages has taught me much. As a professor, discussing my ideas with diverse groups at colleges, universities, community centers, academic conferences, and social activist arenas has improved my scholarship. Take, for example, how different audiences engaged the ideas in *Black Sexual Politics* (Collins 2004). Writing a book is one thing—talking with different groups of people about what I had written was an entirely different experience. My generic lecture title, "Introduction to *Black Sexual Politics*," fails to capture the wide range of talks that I actually delivered. The African American community residents in Tulsa, Oklahoma, who came out to their local public library to hear the version of the talk that I prepared for them had different reactions than the college students and faculty on the beautiful campus of the University of California, Santa Barbara, who encountered the same ideas, yet in a vastly different format. At times, I had to fall back on pedagogical skills honed during my days teaching seventh- and eighth-grade students, the case when I addressed a lively group of African American and Latino high school students in Louisville, Kentucky. How different their reactions were to the ideas in *Black Sexual Politics* than those of the audience at the feminist bookstore in Cambridge, Massachusetts. The list goes on. I realize how diverse American society is, let alone how rich the tapestry of global cultures and experiences outside U.S. borders. Writing for and speaking with multiple publics has been challenging, but also worthwhile.

Despite this history, I initially found Michael Burawoy's ideas about public sociology unnerving (this volume). I certainly like Burawoy's model and think that it interjects a much-needed breath of fresh air into some increasingly stale sociological debates. At the same time, I'm not completely comfortable with it. Apparently, I had been *doing* public sociology without even knowing it. Moreover, I was not alone. Despite my inability to classify them as public sociologists, many other sociologists had also made the decision to "go public."

On the one hand, I should be happy that the type of sociological practice that has so long preoccupied me is now gaining recognition. What has long been "out" now has a rare invitation to attend the party within American sociology, which has not been particularly inclined to changing its ways. Most certainly individual sociologists have been at the forefront of many progressive issues, yet they do not constitute the center of the discipline of American sociology. On the other hand, I question whether this new visibility for public sociology is inherently good for practitioners of public sociology as well as for public sociology itself. What are the potential challenges that accompany Burawoy's gutsy move?

WHAT'S IN A NAME?

One challenge facing public sociology concerns the way in which naming it will help or hurt its practitioners. Is naming public sociology inherently beneficial? Most people assume that institutionalizing public sociology will be a good thing. Naming public sociology should help legitimate it within the discipline. Perhaps. Yet as mental patients, escaped slaves, runaway brides, and prisoners remind us, institutionalization need not be good for everyone. It all depends on where you stand. Once a set of practices is named, and thereby placed in its classificatory cell within an institution, those practices can become even more difficult to do. In this spirit, I wonder how discussions about public sociology will assist sociologists who currently practice public sociology? We assume that naming will elevate the status of current practitioners, but it may instead install a permanent and recognizable underclass that now carries the stigmatized name of public sociology. Stated differently, will doing public sociology emerge as a new form of tracking within the discipline?

As an ideal type, public sociology seems glamorous. Yet who actually does this kind of sociology? Current practitioners of public sociology are typically not housed in premier institutions, nor do many of them come from privileged groups. I suggest that individuals who are most likely to commit to public sociology have had experiences that provide them with a distinctive view of social inequality. African Americans, Latinos, new immigrant groups, women, working-class and poor people, lesbian, gay, bisexual, and transgendered (LGBT) people, and others who remain penalized within American society and their allies may gravitate toward a sociology that promises to address social issues that affect the public. If not predisposed before entering sociology, individuals from these groups and their allies may develop a public sociology perspective as a result of their sociological graduate training.

Many graduate students choose sociology because they are attracted to the vision of an until-now-unnamed public sociology that they encounter in their undergraduate classrooms. Most do not enter graduate programs to become professional or policy sociologists. For many, graduate training resembles a shell game—they look under one shell for the public sociology prize that they anticipated; yet when they pick up the shell, nothing is there. The real prizes, they are told, lie under the remaining three shells of professional, policy, and, to a lesser extent, critical sociology. They are pressured to choose among types of sociology and to leave behind the idealism of public sociology and the "you'll-never-get-a-job-if-you-keep-that-up" stance of critical sociology. Fortunately, my graduate training differed. I was encouraged to be an independent thinker, and I took my professors at their word. My own path within sociology certainly reflects this predisposition to focus on the recursive relationship between doing and naming.

I often wonder how I managed to carve a path for myself by doing a sociology that had no name. For me, this is not a new question, but rather one that has shaped my entire career. Being an African American woman in overwhelmingly white and male settings, as well as carrying my working-class background into situations that routinely privilege the cultural (and actual) capital of middle-class families, has been frustrating yet immensely helpful. I am used to not belonging, to being stared at as the one who must introduce myself to yet another sociological clique at the American Sociological Association (ASA) in order to put my colleagues at ease. Because I belong to groups that garner less value within American society, I hold ideas about democracy, social justice, color blindness, feminism, and a long list of social practices that differ from those of the mainstream. I stand in a different relationship to power relations, and as a result, I hold a distinctive standpoint on those relations. Being committed to principles that are larger than myself has not been easy. I am the one who has been denied jobs for which I am qualified because I do not do the kind of sociology that is valued. Doing public sociology either will make you strong or might kill you. Would naming the kind of sociology that I have been doing have made these struggles any easier?

Perhaps. Yet at the same time, being classified under the banner of public sociology may foster a kind of sociological ghettoization, primarily because those who gravitate toward public sociology may already hold subordinate status within the discipline itself. Public sociology can thus become a convenient tool for getting African Americans, Latinos, women, community college teachers, and the like to do the service work of the profession, this time not just spreading sociology's mission to students, or serving on endless committees because their "perspective" should be represented, but also by explaining sociology to multiple publics. In this endeavor, would time remain to "do" public sociology in its most robust form? Or would a legitimated public sociology be reduced to a service arm of the discipline, with the "real" sociology of professional sociology still holding sway? Is public sociology a "sociology of and for the Others," namely, all those people who cannot make it within other ideal types of sociology? If so, then the irony of having those who have struggled so mightily to become sociologists serve as the public face of sociology, with the sociological center remaining intact, becomes especially poignant.

Beyond this issue of how legitimating public sociology via naming it might not necessarily help its current practitioners, the act of naming might also shift the very mission of this kind of sociology. I envision the spirit of public sociology as resembling historian Robin D. G. Kelley's notion of a "radical imagination"; or the tenets of "magical realism" invoked by Lani Guinier and Gerald Torres as part of their project to transcend the limits of current thinking about race and democracy; or even sociology's own C. Wright Mills's clarion call for a new "sociological imagination" (Kelley 2002; Guinier and Torres 2002; Mills 1959). In my own work, I draw upon these ideas via the concept of visionary pragmatism within African American women's oppositional knowledge, a creative tension that links visions for a better society and pragmatic strategies of how to bring it about (Collins 2000).

Public sociology resembles these activities. It constitutes a constellation of oppositional knowledges and practices. If American society were just and fair, if the American public were fed, clothed, housed, educated, employed, and healthy, there would be no need for public sociology. Its very existence speaks to the need to *oppose* social injustice yet also to be proactive in creating a democratic and just public sphere. Naming public sociology strives to enhance the stature of these oppositional knowledges and practices by carving out spaces within the boundaries of an established discipline in ways that legitimate the public sociology that already exists and, perhaps, catalyze more. Naming aspires to redefine public sociology as no longer being a subordinated, submerged way of doing sociology and seeks to elevate its stature.

Yet, in the American context, making the shift from outsider to insider knowledge may change the ethos of public sociology. Ironically, despite good intentions, naming public sociology may step on existing land mines of defining the purpose and practices of oppositional knowledge as well as the social location of insiders and outsiders who produce such knowledge. Naming public sociology, and thereby opening the doors to the valid question of defining its distinguishing features, can catalyze endless debates about boundary making. A subtle shift can easily be made from doing an unnamed, messy, and thus incorrigible public sociology to talking about public sociology in ways that shrink its possibilities. Public sociology can easily become yet another fad, a nugget of commodified knowledge that privileged sociologists can play at just as a cat toys with a mouse. What comforting procrastination—one remains ethically honorable by paying lip service to public sociology while never having to take a stand by actually doing it. I can see it now—legions of dissertations analyzing the contributions and failures of public sociology versus dissertations that *do* public sociology. Better yet, what would the "Introduction to Public Sociology" course look like? Which sociological worthies would make the cut to be included on the required reading list and which would be left outside to stare at a closed door?

WHAT'S IN *THIS* NAME?

Another challenge confronting public sociology concerns its chosen name. Is this a good time for the discipline of sociology to claim the term *public*? Is this the best name for this work, even as we persist in doing it? After over two decades of sustained assault on public institutions in the United States, throwing in one's lot with the sinking ship of anything "public" may seem suicidal. Let's just paint a big target on sociology, some professional and policy sociologists could argue; sociology will become viewed as a field for losers.

In the United States, the privatization of public power seems ubiquitous (Guinier and Torres 2002). In the 1980s and 1990s, social policies dramatically reconfigured the meaning of *public* generally and the social welfare state as the quintessential public institution. Current efforts to privatize hospitals, sanitation services, schools, and other public services and attempts to develop a more private-sector, entrepreneurial spirit in others by underfunding them—public radio, public television, subcontracting specific services via competitive bidding—illustrate this abandonment and derogation of anything public. Deteriorating schools, health care services, roads, bridges, and public transportation, resulting from public failure to fund public institutions, speak to the erosion and accompanying devaluation of anything deemed "public." In this context, *public* becomes reconfigured as anything of poor quality, marked by a lack of control and privacy—all characteristics associated with poverty. This slippage between lack of privacy, poor quality, and poverty affects the changing meaning of *public*.

Much of this push toward privatization in the United States has covert yet powerful racial undertones. When African Americans and Latinos among others gained expanded rights, individuals and groups with power increasingly abandoned public institutions. Take, for example, the legacy of the 1954 *Brown* decision that outlawed racial segregation in public education. Thurgood Marshall, Derrick Bell, and other civil rights activists had no way to anticipate how a new color-blind racism would effectively stonewall school integration initiatives. The early trickle away from public schools by middle-class white parents who founded private white academies so that their children need not attend racially integrated public schools opened the floodgates of white flight from public institutions of all sorts. Public schools, public health, public transportation, and public libraries are all now devalued in the face of market-based policies that say "privatization will shield you from rubbing elbows with the public." These new social relations signal a distinct reversal—the public sphere becomes a curiously confined yet visible location that increases the value of private services and privacy itself. Public places become devalued spaces containing Latinos, poor people, African Americans, the homeless, and anyone else who cannot afford to escape. In this context, privacy signals safety; control over one's home, family, and community space; and racial homogeneity—all qualities that can be purchased if one can afford them. This version of privatization dovetails with Lani Guinier and Gerald Torres's notion of the privatization of power. If private spaces are better, then shouldn't private entities run the public itself?

In this political context, naming this sociology *public* sociology inherits this history and these social issues. What does it mean for sociology to claim to be for and about the public at this historic moment? Will this be perceived as sociology for the dispossessed, the displaced, and the disadvantaged? Despite Burawoy's efforts to generate much-needed dialogue that is designed to reinvigorate sociology, I suspect that those currently privileged within professional, critical, and/or policy sociology will express far less enthusiasm for an increased emphasis on public sociology than the internal integrity of doing public sociology might suggest. Following public sociology into the realm of the public raises too many uncomfortable questions about the discipline of sociology's merit, value, purpose within contemporary American society. Currently, the term *public* invokes neither populist nor democratic sensibilities. Rather, it means *popular* (as in popular versus high culture) and, more ominously, inferior. Let the diverse public in and your discipline suffers. Let public sociology in and your scholarship deteriorates. Is sociology ready for that?

I certainly hope so. The social justice sensibilities of public sociology constitute one of its defining features. Caring about the public, seeing all of the others not as devalued entities that one must "mentor" or "help" but rather as potential partners for the betterment of society itself provides a core vision or ethos for this kind of work. People want ideas that matter both to them and within society itself. Public sociology suggests a recursive relationship between those inside the profession and people who are engaged in efforts to understand and challenge prevailing social inequalities that now characterize an increasingly devalued public. In this regard, if public sociology is unprepared to jump into the controversies that surround the term *public,* then this may not be the best name for it.

CAN WE ALL GET ALONG?

A third distinctive challenge confronts public sociology in the United States. Now that public sociology has a name, when it comes to its relationship with professional, critical, and policy sociology, I wonder, can we all get along? American sociologists familiar with the circumstances that catalyzed the 1992 riots in Los Angeles might remember these words from motorist Rodney King. King's videotaped beating by members of the Los Angeles police department was shown around the world. The court decision that exonerated the police also catalyzed several days of rioting, when Angelenos burned down entire city blocks because they couldn't envision living in Los Angeles the way it was. The media loved to broadcast King's query, "Can we get along?" His plea reified American assumptions that talking things through will yield a fair solution for everyone, that better evidence yields stronger public policy, and that if we just put our heads together and let rational minds prevail, we should be able to solve this mess.

However, can it ever be this simple? I have great difficulty imagining a mahogany conference table with representatives of the Los Angeles police force, African American, Latino, and Korean grassroots community groups, mayoral staff, the Los Angeles chamber of commerce, church folks, representatives of the Justice for Janitors and Bus Riders unions, and other members of the Los Angeles community putting aside their differences with an "oops-let's-try-this-again" mentality. Most of us would recognize that the historical power relations in Los Angeles that created many of these groups in the first place make such a scenario unbelievable. The groups themselves are involved in a continually shifting mosaic of hierarchical relationships with one another—sometimes they operate as friends, other times as enemies, and often they have little knowledge of what the others are actually doing. Despite my incredulity about such a meeting, if it did occur, at least the people around that conference table would recognize that the knowledge they brought to the mahogany conference table grew directly from the power relations that got them there. They would know that they could not achieve a new vision for Los Angeles without taking power differentials among themselves into account, let alone among those segments of the public that did not get invited to the meeting.

I wonder whether sociologists would have the same sensibility, if they even saw the need for such a meeting in the first place. Burawoy's four-cell typology gives the impression of parallelism among professional, policy, critical, and public sociology, yet it is important to reiterate that Burawoy proposes a Weberian *ideal-type* framework. These four types have never been nor are they expected to be equal to one another. Therein lies the problem. Unless sociology itself expands (the old Reagan policy of creating a bigger pie so that public sociology can cut a piece), creating space for public sociology means taking away from the space of the other three. Will they move over to make room at the mahogany table? Or do professional, policy, and critical sociology see public sociology as the interloper in a game of musical chairs?—because they occupied the three subdisciplinary seats when the music stopped, poor public sociology is left permanently standing.

This is the rub—in the U.S. context in the post–World War II period, professional and policy sociology have exercised imperial authority within American sociology in ways that obscure public sociology. One would think that critical sociology resists these impulses, but when it comes to the privatization of power, practitioners of critical sociology promise more than they deliver. Critical sociology often talks a good game, yet when it comes to the types of institutional change required to let in sufficient numbers of the unruly public, the intellectual blinders of many progressive sociologists keep them from delivering the goods. For example, the ideas of color blindness and gender neutrality that underpin conservative agendas of the Right seem eerily similar to arguments on the left that race and gender-based identity politics basically destroyed a progressive, class-based politics. They too long for a color blindness and gender neutrality that will uphold a class-based agenda. Yet this failure to engage race and gender as a route to rethinking social class has limited critical sociology's contributions as a vibrant force within American society. Just as it took Hurricane Katrina in 2005 to jolt the American public into seeing the realities of race and class in the United States, so too were critical sociologists caught off guard.

As the sociological pie shrinks, in large part because the demonization of the public outside sociology occurs via race- and gender-based bashing of large segments of the American population, fighting over crumbs within the discipline mimics behaviors that are as American as apple pie. Professional and policy sociology have well-established constituencies and do make important contributions. Critical sociology may have long contested the ideas of professional and policy sociology, yet it too has its well-established constituencies who can be just as resistant to a fully actualized public sociology as their well-heeled counterparts. Why should any of these three ideal sociological types cede territory to the upstart of public sociology, especially one that may contain disproportionate numbers of less desirable people? Given the derogation of anything public in the American setting, public sociology faces an uphill battle in finding its place at the sociological table.

WHY DO PUBLIC SOCIOLOGY?

Given these challenges, why would anyone willingly choose public sociology? When I've shared Michael Burawoy's typology of professional, policy, critical, and public sociology as four ideal types of sociology with some of my students, or even simply summarized its ideas, their eyes light up. There's the aha factor at work—"Public sociology is the kind of sociology we want to do," they proclaim. They resonate with the name *public sociology.* Wishing to belong to something bigger than themselves, they know implicitly that doing public sociology constitutes intellectual labor placed in service to broader ethical principles. They are drawn to the concept of a reenergized public where every individual truly does count. By positioning itself in solidarity with ethical principles of democracy, fairness, and social justice, public sociology seemingly offers a path away from provincial careerism and back toward the sociological imaginations that many students felt they needed to check at the graduate school door.

Yet the inevitable questions that come next speak to their pragmatic concerns. "Where do I go to study it? Do the top sociology programs offer a degree in it? Can I get a job doing it?" they query. Moving quickly through the preliminaries and homing in on the promises of mentoring and role modeling, they shift to the next set of questions: "How did you come to do public sociology?" they ask. "You appear to be successful. Can you teach me how to become a public sociologist?"

I don't fault the students. Their questions stem from the disjuncture between one set of promises within American sociology to place the tools of sociology in service to solving social problems and actual sociological practices that must attend to the realities of car loans and mortgage payments. Unlike students of the past, contemporary students are much more cognizant of the fact that the bill will come due one day. So they feel pressured to choose wisely. Professional and policy sociology may position them to better pay off their student loans—what can critical sociology deliver, or worse yet, public sociology? They confront the contradiction of wishing to garner the moral capital of supporting social justice initiatives without taking personal risks such as having articles rejected from top journals or being denied their dream job. Can one truly work for social justice from the comfort of a cushy job with tenure? Derrick Bell labels this impetus "ethical ambition" and offers reassurances to his readers that it is possible to be ethical and successful at the same time (Bell 2002). I sincerely hope that he is right, but I also know that the vast majority of people who actually do public sociology receive few perks and even less praise.

I suspect that people work at public sociology for very much the same reasons that some individuals become dancers, actresses, singers, painters, or poets—training for their craft may be part of their passion, but they would find a way to dance, act, sing, paint, or write even if no one paid them. The ardor of artists provides a template for the passion for social justice that many sociologists bring to their intellectual work. American pragmatism and its grand entrepreneurial spirit strive to stamp out this passion for justice, raising the question of whether there is even any room for public sociology sensibilities within American sociology anymore. Yet visitors from other national sociological traditions at the 2004 ASA meeting on public sociology remind us that public sociology not only exists but also holds a much larger place in their sociological vision than it does in the United States. It may be more difficult to see public sociology here, in the center of a major world power, but the stakes are too high not to.

When I look back and try to map my involvement in public sociology, I realize that, as with love, I found it in unlikely places. For example, I love social theory—no secret there. But with hindsight, I recognize that the reason that I so appreciated early sociological theorists is that they all seemed to be doing public sociology, or at least that is the way I was introduced to their work. Despite our current efforts to objectify, deify, freeze, and squeeze Karl Marx, Max Weber, Georg Simmel, Émile Durkheim, W. E. B. DuBois, and other classical social theorists into ossified boxes of their "most important contributions that you will need to know in order to get a job," I read the works of these theorists as public sociology. I remain inspired by their commitment to bring the tools of sociology to bear on the important issues of their time. The public need not have been their direct audience—given literacy rates of the late nineteenth and early twentieth centuries, few could read their work—yet so much of what they did was on behalf of bettering the public. They talked to one another because they wanted to understand and better society.

Contemporary American sociology has moved away from this kind of energy and excitement. Yet because public sociology demands that we consider the major issues of the day and that we bring tools of sociological analysis and empirical research to bear on them, it promises to breathe new life into sociological theory as well as the discipline overall. Despite the challenges facing public sociology, as well as the difficulties that I have encountered in my career doing it, I would choose it all over again. At this point in my career, what we call it matters less to me than knowing that I am not alone in choosing this path.

BEYOND THE DOUBLE-BIND

W. E. B. DU BOIS AND THE GIFT OF SECOND-SIGHT

By Charles Lemert

Today, early in the 2000s, after a century in the shadows, W. E. B. Du Bois (1868–1963) is recognized for what he truly was—not simply the first great African American social thinker but one of the twentieth century's most prominent social scientists, writers, and public figures. Born more than a decade after Durkheim and Freud, and four years after Weber, Du Bois outlived them all—both in the number of his years and in the range of his contributions to a theory of race in the modern age. Not only did Du Bois live productively into the 1960s, when much of the classic era's confusion as to the contradictions of the modern world was coming slowly into the open. He was, unlike few of any age, a political force in the shredding away of such naïve modernist ideals as the unity of all humankind and the pledge of human progress.

Du Bois defied modernity's blindness to its own duplicity in producing the very racial differences it then used unscrupulously to manufacture the comforts attendant to its false sense of brilliance. Yet, strikingly, his earliest writings of the 1890s, while brilliant, were not the most remarkable of his social critiques of the modern era. Much like Freud, Du Bois's social thinking belonged to two eras—separated by the disastrous effects of the war of 1914 and its aftermath through the Depression of the 1930s and the war of the 1940s. Where Freud, after 1920, turned to his stark theory of the conflicting drives for building-up and tearing-down of social relations, Du Bois, in the 1920s, would turn to an ever more stark interpretation of racial and social differences as a consequence of the systematic evil of modern capitalism in the West. But also, as Freud's grand book of 1900, *The Interpretation of Dreams*, was a daring, if optimistic, essay introducing his bold interpretation of the human unconscious, so too Du Bois's great book of 1903, *The Souls of Black Folk*, was a stern, but optimistic, appraisal of the possibilities ahead for racial progress. The difference may be that, while Freud changed his mind within essentially the same theoretical scheme, Du Bois changed his theoretical approach altogether. But this is a story for a later time. Had Du Bois not changed at all he would still be honored today for the originality of his theory of the Negro social self—a theory that was, in effect, a fresh way of conceiving the double-bind of modern man.

Of Our Spiritual Strivings

After the Egyptian and Indian, the Greek and Roman, the Teuton and Mongolian, the Negro is a sort of seventh son, born with a veil, and gifted with second-sight in this American world,—a world which yields him no true self-consciousness, but only lets him see himself through the revelation of the other world. It is a peculiar sensation, this double-consciousness, this sense of always looking at one's self through the eyes of others, of measuring one's soul by the tape of a world that looks on in amused contempt and pity. One ever feels his twoness,—an American, a Negro; two souls, two thoughts, two unreconciled strivings; two warring ideals in one dark body, whose dogged strength alone keeps it from being torn asunder.

The history of the American Negro is the history of this strife,—this longing to attain self-conscious manhood, to merge his double self into a better and truer self. In this merging he wishes neither of the older selves to be lost. He would not Africanize America, for America has too much to teach the world and Africa. He would not bleach his Negro soul in a flood of white Americanism, for he knows that Negro blood has a message for the world. He simply wishes to make it possible for a man to be both a Negro and an American, without being cursed and spit upon by his fellows, without having the doors of Opportunity closed roughly in his face.

This, then, is the end of his striving: to be a co-worker in the kingdom of culture, to escape both death and isolation, to husband and use his best powers and his latent genius. These powers of body and mind have in the past been strangely wasted, dispersed, or forgotten. The shadow of a mighty Negro past flits through the tale of Ethiopia the Shadowy and of Egypt the Sphinx. Through history, the powers of single black men flash here and there like falling stars, and die sometimes before the world has rightly gauged their brightness. Here in America, in the few days since Emancipation, the black man's turning hither and thither in hesitant and doubtful striving has often made his very strength to lose effectiveness, to seem like absence of power, like weakness. And yet it is not weakness,—it is the contradiction of double aims.

—W. E. B. Du Bois, *The Souls of Black Folk* (1897/1903)

"Of Our Spiritual Strivings"—these undoubtedly are the most famous lines Du Bois ever wrote. They may also be among the most treasured and quoted lines by any social theorist of any time or place. The words first appeared in a magazine article in 1897, the same year as Durkheim's *Suicide*, and the year before Gilman's *Women and Economics*. It is seldom remarked that Du Bois took up, in very different ways, the main ideas of both Durkheim and Gilman—the disturbing effect of social conflict in the modern world and the distinctive differences of people of a differing social standpoint. Conflict and difference animate Du Bois's famous theory of the American Negro's double consciousness.

When in 1897 Du Bois published "Of Our Spiritual Strivings," as the lead essay in his 1903 masterpiece *The Souls of Black Folk*, a new day dawned in American culture. Du Bois had composed an idea that would come to stun the assumptions of Enlightenment rationality that "the human" is an essential and universal fact.

That idea was, of course, the double-consciousness of the American Negro, conveyed by the plural effect in the title, *souls*. While others of that day were struggling with the problem of social differences, and Charlotte Gilman was among those who dared to state it forthrightly, no one before Du Bois put the general notion of social differences as a historical fact of modern social life. Plus which, he expressed the double-consciousness idea with a poetic beauty that put the lie to the then still prevalent belief that the American Negro was incapable of literary genius. It would be some time before Du Bois's concept of the American Negro as both American and Negro, both at once, beyond reconciliation, would fully dawn on the sleepy white world. The dawning would begin in the Harlem Renaissance of the 1920s, in which Du Bois played a leading role, and would then come to full light after the cultural revolutions of the 1960s. When beauty and truth are hidden in the shadows, their discovery, long after the fact of their first appearances, can cause a commotion—shame among those who should have recognized the truth, excitement among those

> **Negro,** a term derived from the Portuguese word for *black*, which has suffered deterioration into racial epithets like *nigger*; Du Bois, however, sought to claim it as a term of respect and dignity by insisting that Negro be spelled with a capital *N*.

> **Double-consciousness,** sometimes referred to as Du Bois's twoness doctrine of the American Negro; commonly viewed as a subtle, poetic theory of the distinctive social-psychological circumstances of Black Americans who were (and still are) descendants of Black Africa, for which they have been stigmatized, but more deeply, Americans, from which they are excluded; in time, theorists began to see that though the twoness of the Negro American is historically acute, the idea of double-consciousness applies generally to most, perhaps all, people if the obvious differences of racial and ethnic backgrounds are factored in.

who saw their importance to an understanding of social things. Hence, now, the enthusiasm for Du Bois's *The Souls of Black Folk*—a book still scantily read beyond the famous lines in the first essay. Yet, these lines stand on their own, as a tribute to the refinements of early social theory.

The idea is so powerful that many want to know from where Du Bois got it. "*One ever feels his twoness,—an American, a Negro; two souls, two thoughts, two unreconciled strivings; two warring ideals in one dark body, whose dogged strength alone keeps it from being torn asunder.*" Leaving aside the fact that he was perfectly capable of inventing it on his own, the most likely sources were two. One, almost surely, was William James (1842–1910), his friend and teacher at Harvard who in *Principles of Psychology* (1890) had written about the social self in which "a man has as many selves as there are people who recognize him." Du Bois's formulation is very close: "*double-consciousness, this sense of always looking at one's self through the eyes of others, of measuring one's soul by the tape of a world that looks on in amused contempt and pity.*" Just as important, however, were the cues Du Bois may have taken from German idealism, the philosophy widely taught in Germany when he studied in Berlin. Idealism was one of the philosophies that had influenced Max Weber, who, after his visit to the United States and Du Bois in the summer of 1904, would offer to sponsor a translation of *The Souls of Black Folk* in Germany. Idealism, as then practiced in Germany, was itself a kind of philosophical double-consciousness insofar as it emphasized the split between mind and body that necessarily established the two as factors in human consciousness. This theme worked itself out, of course, in the larger program of cultural science (*geisteswissenschaft*) of which Weber was a proponent. To believe that the cultural is distinct from the natural is to see human behavior as, again, doubly motivated, but also split. But even more, in the particulars of Weber's iron-cage figure of speech lay the elements of his larger double-bind riddle of modernity. If modern rational order was simultaneously the best historical hope for human progress *and* a cage that entrapped the human spirit, then Weber's social theory was, if not an explicit double-consciousness theory of the modern self, at least a major contribution to the classic understanding of modernity's dilemma—that with the good in modernity came the bad, leaving modern society torn between two horns.

Thus, it is evident that Du Bois, who was to some degree familiar with Weber's thinking and certainly influenced by German idealism, had been in his youth a theorist of the double-bind. Yet, he was also much more. In contrast to Weber, Du Bois in *The Souls of Black Folk* in 1903 was anything but gloomy and vexed. This no doubt because he was young, but also because by the end of the nineteenth century a highly educated Negro intellectual had every reason to believe that progress was in the offing. He had personally made important strides—from an impoverished childhood in rural Massachusetts to graduate education in Europe and a Harvard doctorate, with more, much more, still to come. He was already a significant race-man—a distinctive social role in the African American community. Within a decade of the publication of *Souls* Du Bois would be the undisputed race-man in America, a calling one can hardly respond to without some hope of real progress. So, those who read beyond the famous lines see that, bleak though they may be, they also convey a clear sense of the American Negro's capacity to be "a co-worker in the kingdom of culture." This was not, however, a rhetorical gesture so much as a well-thought-through principle of Weber's social theory. In contrast to other social theories of the double self, even those of William James, Du Bois's was both historical and sociological. The American Negro was, first and foremost, a global figure: "After the Egyptian and Indian, the Greek and Roman, the Teuton and Mongolian, the Negro is a sort of seventh son, born with a veil, and gifted with second-sight in this American world." Born, yes, under the veil of the color line, but also gifted with the power of second-sight. In this idea Du Bois's literary powers strengthened his social and historical theory. The veil, a metaphor rooted in African American folk culture, is of course imposed by the dominant white culture to hide the Negro. But those behind the veil possess the strange power of seeing those who dare not look at them. This gift of second-sight is a foundational principle of early American Negro culture as it would be for race politics in the twentieth century. To be able to see the cultured ways of those too frightened to regard you is to possess the power of knowledge of social things that, in this case, whites could not face.

> **Race-man,** a popular expression now used somewhat less commonly by African Americans, referring to individuals who devote their lives to work for the uplift of the race.

Thus it is that Du Bois was far less riddled with doubt than was Weber, and far more historically exact than was James. He was indeed a theorist of the double-bind of the modern world but instead of taking the contradiction as a perplexing existential puzzle of a general and abstract culture, Du Bois affirmed the power of Negro culture that arises precisely from the experience of exclusion and racism. When the oppressed grasp the power of second-sight, they turn knowledge and culture into a weapon in the struggle for progress. Du Bois's theory of the second-sight of the doubly-conscious is a kind of cryptorevolutionary theory. Later, after the war of 1914, Du Bois would take an ever more materialist and radical, if not quite Marxist, stance. The seeds of what would come in later years were already present in his early commitments to the revolutionary power of culture. His was not a revolution that would await that conjuncture when the oppressed would cause the collapse of modern capitalist culture. Marx's workers would revolt only when their chains were bound tight to the point of death. Du Bois's American Negro would revolt in the work of cultural and political progress. Not the same thing at all of course. Not, even in the long run, a formulation that Du Bois could live with as in time things got worse, not better, for the American Negro. But it was, at least, a historical materialism of an ironic sort—one in which disciplined cultural work would lead to racial uplift, which, of course, means most of all economic progress.

Du Bois in 1903, thus, was a double-bind theorist who was not himself bound by the ties of modern culture. For him, at the time, the structural change in America would come when the Negro fulfilled his potential as a co-worker in the kingdom of culture and, to be sure, economic life.

BLACK FEMINIST THOUGHT

BLACK FEMINISM, KNOWLEDGE, AND POWER

By Patricia Hill Collins

BLACK FEMINIST THOUGHT AS CRITICAL SOCIAL THEORY

Even if they appear to be otherwise, situations such as the suppression of Black women's ideas within traditional scholarship and the struggles within the critiques of that established knowledge are inherently unstable. Conditions in the wider political economy simultaneously shape Black women's subordination and foster activism. On some level, people who are oppressed usually know it. For African-American women, the knowledge gained at intersecting oppressions of race, class, and gender provides the stimulus for crafting and passing on the subjugated knowledge of Black women's critical social theory (Collins 1998, 3–10).

As an historically oppressed group, U.S. Black women have produced social thought designed to oppose oppression. Not only does the form assumed by this thought diverge from standard academic theory—it can take the form of poetry, music, essays, and the like—but the *purpose* of Black women's collective thought is distinctly different. Social theories emerging from and/or on behalf of U.S. Black women and other historically oppressed groups aim to find ways to escape from, survive in, and/or oppose prevailing social and economic injustice. For African-American women, critical social theory encompasses bodies of knowledge and sets of institutional practices that actively grapple with the central questions facing U.S. Black women as a collectivity. The need for such thought arises because African-American women as a *group* remain oppressed within a U.S. context characterized by injustice. This neither means that all African-American women within that group are oppressed in the same way, nor that some U.S. Black women do not suppress others. Black feminist thought's identity as a "critical" social theory lies in its commitment to justice, both for U.S. Black women as a collectivity and for that of other similarly oppressed groups.

Historically, two factors stimulated U.S. Black women's critical social theory. For one, prior to World War II, racial segregation in urban housing became so entrenched that the majority of African-American women lived in self-contained Black neighborhoods where their children attended overwhelmingly Black schools, and where they themselves belonged to all-Black churches and similar community organizations. Despite the fact that ghettoization was designed to foster the political control and economic exploitation of Black Americans (Squires 1994), these all-Black neighborhoods simultaneously provided a separate space where African-American women and men could use African-derived ideas to craft distinctive oppositional knowledges designed to resist racial oppression.

As mothers, othermothers, teachers, and churchwomen in essentially all-Black rural communities and urban neighborhoods, U.S. Black women participated in constructing and reconstructing these oppositional knowledges. Through the lived experiences gained within their extended families and communities, individual African-American women fashioned their own ideas about the meaning of Black womanhood. When these ideas found collective expression, Black women's self-definitions enabled them to refashion African-influenced conceptions of self and community. These self-definitions of Black womanhood were designed to resist the negative controlling images of Black womanhood advanced by Whites as well as the discriminatory social practices that these controlling images supported. In all, Black women's participation in crafting a constantly changing African-American culture fostered distinctively Black and women-centered worldviews.

Another factor that stimulated U.S. Black women's critical social theory lay in the common experiences they gained from their jobs. Prior to World War II, U.S. Black women worked primarily in two occupations—agriculture and domestic work. Their ghettoization in domestic work sparked an important contradiction. Domestic work fostered U.S. Black women's economic exploitation, yet it simultaneously created the conditions for distinctively Black and female forms of resistance. Domestic work allowed African-American women to see White elites, both actual and aspiring, from perspectives largely obscured from Black men and from these groups themselves. In their White "families," Black women not only performed domestic duties but frequently formed strong ties with the children they nurtured, and with the employers themselves. On one level this insider relationship was satisfying to all concerned. Accounts of Black domestic workers stress the sense of self-affirmation the women experienced at seeing racist ideology demystified. But on another level these Black women knew that they could never belong to their White "families." They were economically exploited workers and thus would remain outsiders. The result was being placed in a curious *outsider-within* social location (Collins 1986), a peculiar marginality that stimulated a distinctive Black women's perspective on a variety of themes (see, e.g., Childress 1986).

Taken together, Black women's participation in constructing African-American culture in all-Black settings and the distinctive perspectives gained from their outsider-within placement in domestic work provide the material backdrop for a unique Black women's standpoint. When armed with cultural beliefs honed in Black civil society, many Black women who found themselves doing domestic work often developed distinct views of the contradictions between the dominant group's actions and ideologies. Moreover, they often shared their ideas with other

African-American women. Nancy White, a Black inner-city resident, explores the connection between experience and beliefs:

> Now, I understand all these things from living. But you can't lay up on these flowery beds of ease and think that you are running your life, too. Some women, white women, can run their husband's lives for a while, but most of them have to ... see what he tells them there is to see. If he tells them that they ain't seeing what they know they *are* seeing, then they have to just go on like it wasn't there! (in Gwaltney 1980, 148)

Not only does this passage speak to the power of the dominant group to suppress the knowledge produced by subordinate groups, but it illustrates how being in outsider-within locations can foster new angles of vision on oppression. Ms. White's Blackness makes her a perpetual outsider. She could never be a White middle-class woman lying on a "flowery bed of ease." But her work of caring for White women allowed her an insider's view of some of the contradictions between White women thinking that they are running their lives and the patriarchal power and authority in their households.

Practices such as these, whether experienced oneself or learned by listening to African-American women who have had them, have encouraged many U.S. Black women to question the contradictions between dominant ideologies of American womanhood and U.S. Black women's devalued status. If women are allegedly passive and fragile, then why are Black women treated as "mules" and assigned heavy cleaning chores? If good mothers are supposed to stay at home with their children, then why are U.S. Black women on public assistance forced to find jobs and leave their children in day care? If women's highest calling is to become mothers, then why are Black teen mothers pressured to use Norplant and Depo Provera? In the absence of a viable Black feminism that investigates how intersecting oppressions of race, gender, and class foster these contradictions, the angle of vision created by being deemed devalued workers and failed mothers could easily be turned inward, leading to internalized oppression. But the legacy of struggle among U.S. Black women suggests that a collectively shared, Black women's oppositional knowledge has long existed. This collective wisdom in turn has spurred U.S. Black women to generate a more specialized knowledge, namely, Black feminist thought as critical social theory. Just as fighting injustice lay at the heart of U.S. Black women's experiences, so did analyzing and creating imaginative responses to injustice characterize the core of Black feminist thought.

Historically, while they often disagreed on its expression—some U.S. Black women were profoundly reformist while more radical thinkers bordered on the revolutionary—African-American women intellectuals who were nurtured in social conditions of racial segregation strove to develop Black feminist thought as critical social theory. Regardless of social class and other differences among U.S. Black women, all were in some way affected by intersecting oppressions of race, gender, and class. The economic, political, and ideological dimensions of U.S. Black women's oppression suppressed the intellectual production of individual Black feminist thinkers. At the same time, these same social conditions simultaneously stimulated distinctive patterns of U.S. Black women's activism that also influenced and was influenced by individual Black women thinkers. Thus, the dialectic of oppression and activism characterizing U.S. Black women's experiences with intersecting oppressions also influenced the ideas and actions of Black women intellectuals.

The exclusion of Black women's ideas from mainstream academic discourse and the curious placement of African-American women intellectuals in feminist thinking, Black social and political theories, and in other important thought such as U.S. labor studies has meant that U.S. Black women intellectuals have found themselves in outsider-within positions in many academic endeavors (Hull et al. 1982; Christian 1989). The assumptions on which full group membership are based—Whiteness for feminist thought, maleness for Black social and political thought, and the combination for mainstream scholarship—all negate Black women's realities. Prevented from becoming full insiders in any of these areas of inquiry, Black women remained in outsider-within locations, individuals whose marginality provided a distinctive angle of vision on these intellectual and political entities.

STUDYING BLACK AND LATINO YOUTH

By Victor Rios

1 *Your book, Punished: The Criminalization of Inner City Youth, is drawn from the three years you spent shadowing African American and Latino youth in Oakland. What led you to consider a comparative analysis of youth experiences? What did you learn about punishment experienced by youth from different racial and ethnic backgrounds?*

Comparing the experiences of young Blacks and Latinos happened organically. I grew up in Oakland in a traditionally black neighborhood that had recently experienced a large influx of Latinos. By the time I came of age, I noticed that Blacks and Latinos in my neighborhood encountered very similar experiences with domestic, street, and state violence. As I began my study I decided I wanted to understand how these young people made sense of these experiences. In my fieldwork I learned that race, of course, does matter, that Black youths often face more dire consequences and heavier criminalization. Moreover, Black and Latino youth respond in very similar ways to punishment, they resist it, they embrace it, or they find creative ways to survive it.

Scholars have written about the role that race or ethnicity plays in building relationships with respondents in the field and, in how our representations are received in the academy. How did sharing an ethnic background with one group in your study but not the other influence your fieldwork? Was it harder or easier to gain access or build trust with some boys? Do you feel as if your analysis of the experiences of Latino youth is given more "authority" than your analysis of the experiences of Black youth?

Although I brought my own biography to this study, that was not enough to give me the insights I needed to develop conceptualizations for understanding the conditions that marginalized young men from Oakland where facing. Based on my experience of reading theories of crime, delinquency, race, and punishment, I had my own ideas about youth and punishment in Oakland. However, these ideas only applied to me. I needed to go beyond my own experience and talk to people to see if they applied to others more widely. Experience alone did not guarantee entre for me; I had to find other ways to tap into the world of these young people. Some Latino youth never gave me their trust, while some Black youth trusted me right away. The first question in many youth's minds when they first met me where, "Is this guy a cop?" "Is he a probation officer?"

Colleagues have often wanted me to provide them something like a "four food group" analysis of the boys. The expectation has been that I tell a racial story for each group. However, the boys I studied were more complex than this. Some racial differences did exist but their experiences and perspectives had more in common then I expected to find. It is important to accept the fact that many urban neighborhoods in the United States have become multi-ethnic and multi-racial. In my study, this meant that the boys shared a common subculture and understanding of social control that transcended racial common sense. However, I do realize that not being racialized as a Black person, I certainly missed some key insights from individuals that have grown up in the Black experience. I have to be the first to acknowledge that my observation and interviews with Black youth are different than they would if a Black researcher who grew up in Oakland had conducted this study. I believe that after enough time in the field, any researcher, despite their background, could find the general patterns that I uncovered in the field: punitive social control, pervasive punishment, the youth control complex, and the need for a "public relations" approach to social control. However, access to certain interactions, more minute patterns, and specific community knowledge may only be grasped by those who are closest in social position to their participants.

2. In your book, you reveal how your own experiences as a gang-involved youth motivated you to systematically study the punitive social control of inner city youth. You began your research project in 2002 at the age of 24, nearly a decade older than many of the youth in your study. What (if any) similarities and differences did you discover between your experiences and the experience of your respondents?

During my time as an active gang member and juvenile delinquent in the streets of Oakland, 1991 to 1994, I witnessed and experienced punitive social control first-hand. However, by the time I conducted the study, I realized that this punitive social control had become formalized, ubiquitous, and systematic. The era of mass incarceration, beginning in the 1960's with law enforcement's repression of social movement activists, and later in the 1980's with disproportionate minority confinement, having increased the U.S. prison population from 700,000 in the 1970's to 2.2. million in 2002, brought about new forms of governance and laws that targeted crime committed by marginalized populations. By the new millennium, zero-tolerance policies in schools, juvenile justice, and criminal justice institutions had become even more punitive and had embedded themselves in the lives of children growing up in marginalized neighborhoods. In other words, my fieldwork taught me that by 2002, mass incarceration policies and practices had solidified themselves and become deeply embedded in the everyday lives of poor urban youths.

3. *In what ways, if any, do your intersecting identities—Latino, male, highly educated, heterosexual—influence your ability to tell the stories of young Black and Latino men? What challenges do you confront in studying and telling stories about a population and a place that you know well, but are also trying to study systematically? What might you say to those scholars who would argue that you are "too close" to tell an "objective" sociological story? Do you see "objective" and "authentic" as fundamentally different?*

My work is inter-subjective. The stories of the youth in my study are told through my perspective. My personal background and academic training have an influence on what I choose to represent. However, my obligation is to report on patterns, recurring themes, and systematic findings that anyone who spends enough time in this context will uncover. I believe that acknowledging subjectivity and providing solid empirical evidence are not mutually exclusive. Knowing one's social position and shortfalls is the beginning of the knowledge production process. To conduct empirical work that is replicable, I recognize my multiple identities. I then utilize my subjective strengths and identify my objective weaknesses. I believe that being "too close" to my subjects provides me an opportunity to reflect on my biases and to learn to separate my own experience from the objective reality of a new generation.

4. *In your current work, you explore patterns of surveillance among gang-associated Latino youth in Santa Barbara, California—a locale that is, at least on the surface, much different from the distressed urban neighborhoods of Oakland. What led you to this new research project? In what ways does this new project extend or complicate the field research you've completed in Northern California?*

Santa Barbara serves as a great case study because of its race and class disparities. Approximately 30% of the population is Latino and working class and approximately 70% is white and middle or upper class. I was drawn to the Santa Barbara research project because I wanted to see if I could compare "delinquent" Latino youths living in relative deprivation with those living in concentrated poverty. In this way we can understand how punishment, race, class, and gender, are experienced and perceived in different contexts by similar populations.

5. *What role has mentoring played in the development of your career? What are the most important influences (or constraints) on who and how you mentor now?*

Without mentoring I wouldn't be here today. One of my academic mentors was Ronald Takaki, the great historian of multicultural America. He was there to hear me out when I felt that I did not belong and he always talked to me as if I did belong. I believe that the greatest challenge to mentors in academia is the deep belief of disbelief. Many brilliant graduate students find it hard to believe in themselves. I have seen many amazing thinkers drop-out of graduate school. How can we teach students to believe in themselves so that they can accomplish the unbelievable?

How do you teach students to believe that they have a place in the academic world? Are there particular practices, exercises, or conversations that you find most useful?

One of the strategies I have found useful with my students has been to provide them a space of their own. Graduate students and I have organized Friday writing groups where we gather to work on our individual projects. We write for 45 minutes at a time and take 15 minute breaks where we catch up with each other. Another strategy that I have used to mentor graduate students is to involved undergraduates in the research process. This allows the graduate students to serve as mentors to undergraduates and in turn they receive mentoring from me. In the end, we all hold each other accountable for our work.

6. You are married and the father of three, including twin girls. How has fathering of twins, and twin girls, at that, influenced your sociological imagination? Has being a father encouraged new questions, new lines of research, or new ways of seeing the world?

During my first week of graduate school at UC Berkeley I found out that my partner, Rebeca, was pregnant with twins. From that day on I realized that all my academic work had to be efficient. Being a father has taught me to let go of my ideas and questions, to allow myself to make my errors and mistakes public. This has produced a collective effect where colleagues, friends, and critics provide me with early feedback that then allows me to produce work already infused with communal feedback. Of course, I had to let go of my ego a long time ago.

Have your girls, now 10, made you see the women in the communities you studied—or their children—differently? If so, how?

Being a father of girls has given me even more drive to maintain a commitment to feminism. In particular, one of the areas I examine in my studies of boys is the ways in which their masculinity has a negative impact on girls in the community. I have also begun to study how some girls embrace masculinity as a self-defense mechanism. My goal is to identify gender practices in marginalized communities that work towards liberation and egalitarianism. In this way, program and policy recommendations can be shaped around strengthening these practices.

7. You came of age in Oakland after the dramatic shift to mass incarceration. As Meda Chesney This shift occurred on our watch—that is, it happened even as social scientists researched and published extensively on the consequences of these punitive turns. What hope do you have for the impact of your research in this context?

I hope that my research enlightens the public, policymakers, schools, and police to change their perceptions, policies, and practices. That it informs us on how punitive social control has failed and how a new form of social control, one that is more egalitarian and productive can be developed.

You do a good deal of applied sociology in Santa Barbara, where you work and where your current research project is based. Can you explain how your field research informs policy and practice in Santa Barbara specifically?

I have made it my goal to become a public sociologist so that my research findings can influence policy and programs. In recent years, I have used my data to inform and advise local school districts and politicians. For example, in Santa Barbara, where I have conducted work on street-oriented youth, I have worked with the school district to devise a "gang prevention" program and to assess its effectiveness. In addition, I have advised private foundations and city and county offices on developing funding that addresses some of the dilemmas exposed by my research. I also conduct staff development with teachers to discuss "best practices" in motivating "at-promise" students to succeed.

8. *You are a faculty member in a department that includes several senior feminist scholars. What role does feminism play in your scholarship? Has engaging with your colleagues challenged or extended your understandings of gender inequality or intersections of race, gender, and class?*

I feel honored to be part of a department that hosts so many groundbreaking and brilliant feminists. I learned about the libratory power of theory through one of my undergraduate mentors and role models, Elizabeth "Betita" Martinez, a legend in the Chicana/o Movement. I remember reading bell hooks in her course. And the following line always follows me:

"...I found a place of sanctuary in 'theorizing', in making sense of what was happening. I found a place where I could imagine possible futures ... this 'lived' experience of critical thinking, a place where I worked at explaining the hurt and making it go away. Fundamentally, I learned from this experience that theory could be a healing place."

I believe that the feminists in my department, feminists I have studied under, feminists I have read, and feminists in the community, have taught me not just to heal my own personal wounds but to constantly make an effort to help others heal their wounds as well—intellectually, politically, programmatically, and in everyday interaction. My departmental colleagues have played a pivotal role in helping me develop my gender analysis when it comes to studying masculinity. I look forward to developing an even richer gender analysis with the support of my senior colleagues.

9. *You spent the first years of your career teaching in an institution different from the one you are in now. What advice might you have for young urban sociologists about where they can make the best institutional "home."*

At both institutions where I have taught I have said that I believe that I landed my dream job. The private liberal arts university, University of San Francisco, where I first taught, expected faculty to be committed to its students. I have always felt a deep passion for teaching and mentoring, so I fit in well at USF. My undergraduate students and I would march into marginalized neighborhoods and conduct "community development" programs supported by the university. This gave me an opportunity to teach my students about opportunity, privilege, and reflexivity, and to help young people with job skills, educational information, or youth violence prevention.

When I was offered the UC Santa Barbara job, I thought to myself, "Now I have to publish or perish. My teaching won't be taken into account." However, I have found that teaching at a research 1 university has provided me the opportunity to teach beyond the classroom. Being from a Research-1 university has opened up publication, speaking, and media opportunities that may not have been possible at a smaller university.

I would tell young urban sociologists to ask themselves, "What kind of teacher am I? Am I a one-on-one, quality time teacher, or do I want to teach at a more global scale?" Either way, I have enjoyed my time at both institutions. To graduate students who are headed for academic jobs, I say, "Whether you end up at a teaching university or a Research-1 university, you picked a great career."

10. What was the worst (or most difficult, or most embarrassing) interview/field encounter you've had?

There have been a few "difficult" field encounters. One of them happened in 2004 in Oakland. I was catching up with some of the boys in the study and I had not seen this group for a few weeks. The three boys I was catching up with, I knew well. A fourth boy—lets call him Tony—walked up to us. I had interviewed Tony once before but I did not know him well. He looked upset, huffing and puffing. He grabbed a C.D. case he was holding in his hand, lifted it high in the air, and slammed it with all his might on the ground. Dozens of clear plastic pieces scattered over an eight feet radius. One of the other boys turned to me and said, "Tony is high man, don't even trip off him." Tony then looked at me in the eyes and said, "What is this snitch doing here?" At this point Tony reached towards his hip and over his XXL sized white t-shirt, sliding what appeared to be a gun to his opposite hip. "I don't like snitches. Snitches are bitches. I should put my thang [gun] down your throat." He reached down to his waist one more time, grabbed the pistol, flashed it in front of my face and put it away. At this point one of the other boys spotted a police car down the street and told Tony to put the gun away. The police car approached us and slowed down. Tony turned around and stared the offi cers down. Then he walked away. Th e officers got out of the car and asked the other three boys and I to turn around. Tony, meanwhile, continued to walk away. I was caught in a huge dilemma, "Do I tell the cops about Tony and confirm to him that I am a snitch?" I decided to fend for my life and did not say a word.

What did you really want to do for a living? What were you afraid you might end up doing?

I really wanted to become an auto mechanic. A few months before graduating from high school a teacher asked me what I was going to do after high school. I said, "Celebrate by drinking a forty [40 ounce malt liquor bottle] every day for the next two years and then go to school to become a mechanic." I was fortunate to have a teacher who connected with some college student mentors who convinced me that a mechanic could not have as much impact on society as a college educated person. With their support, I applied to college. The rest is history but I still love working on old cars. It helps me relieve my stress when I get anxious about tenure. During college, I feared that one day I would end up working for the "Man." Some might argue that my fears were certainly realized.

What's the study you never pursued, but always wanted to?

I have always wanted to study everyday acts of resilience among marginalized populations. How do everyday people navigate insurmountable obstacles? What skills do those people who survive these obstacles hone? The study would be a comparative ethnography conducted in different parts of the globe where ordinary people are found to accomplish extraordinary acts. How does social efficacy operate in even the most marginalized communities?

SECTION II

Self, Culture, Socialization, and Deviance

When you think of culture, what exactly is it that comes to mind? Do you think of the likes and dislikes of the particular culture or cultures you inhabit? Do you think of material culture or nonmaterial culture such as symbols and unspoken values? Do the values and norms of cultures you inhabit ever conflict and contradict one another? What about the Internet, a pervasive part of our lives? When you are online, do you think you are consuming culture? Culture is everything. It is everything around us, from mobile devices to texting to unspoken assumptions of how things should be or should not be. We produce culture, while simultaneously, culture and cultural meanings are imposed upon us. The readings in this section explore a variety of aspects of culture, from the meaning we attach to cultural artifacts such as tattoos and our role in cultural reproduction via socialization.

In the next two readings, we see how family, the primary agent of socialization, shapes our individual identities and sense of self. Family does not consist of a uniform identity, but is concurrently shaped by race, class, gender, and ethnicity. Extending classical explanations of the construction of self, Espiritu's article and the ones following offer examples of how the self is constructed through a myriad of factors such as race, ethnicity, gender, and disability status.

Each of us is socialized differently through our families, depending upon our social location. Espiritu's "We Don't Sleep Around Like White Girls Do: Family, Culture, and Gender in Filipina American Lives" offers us a look into the meaning of sex through a specific cultural lens: young Filipina American women straddling their place in two cultures at once. The reading reveals how the construction of self can be a tool of empowerment, as well as a strategy of resistance against meanings imposed by the dominant culture onto the lives of those who fall outside of the norms of this culture. The dominant culture can marginalize the identities of those who do not conform to the norms and values of its culture. As a strategy of resistance, a counter narrative can be produced by those outside the dominant culture providing a source of agency in transcending an otherwise subordinated Othered identity.

As the title indicates, "The Microsystem Level: The Continuing Influence of Childhood Socialization on Adult Masculinity" by Elizabeth A. Mansley, focuses on how men are socialized from their childhoods and the perceived effects of early socialization on their adult lives and selves. Mansley looks at various agents of socialization from childhood such as family of origin, peers, and neighborhood, as well as exposure to violence in shaping one's masculinity. In addition to the agents of socialization, the intersections of race, class, and gender are implicated in childhood socialization and its effect on masculinity in adulthood. This is important, because like family, masculinity is not monolithic. Hegemonic masculinity is the highest level of masculinity and exists in relation to and is measured against what it is not: a female, a boy, homosexual, poor, and a nonwhite race and ethnicity. It is argued that those who do not embody the highest level of masculinity find other avenues in which to assert power such as violence, for example. This concept will be explored further in the next section.

The next reading relates to constructions of self and identity management. We all engage in forms of identity management every day. Whether we go on a job interview, a first date, or attend a family function, we engage in practices to manage how we think others will perceive us. We generally hope to manage our identity in a way that leaves people with positive impressions of ourselves. Gerianne Merrigan's "Negotiating Personal Identities Among People With and Without Identified Disabilities: The Role of Identity Management" explores how persons with disabilities engage in identity management and negotiation, especially with those who are not disability identified. Having an already stigmatized identity of being disabled, having a body that does not conform to the dominant culture's norm, this reading addresses how those with a visible disability negotiate and manage how they are seen by those without an observable disability.

Another reading having to do with the body is Eve Shapiro's "Focus on Tattooing and Masculinity." The reading chronicles the shifting deviant identity and meaning surrounding tattoos. Tattoos are a type of symbolic culture. The tattoo itself has meaning, regardless of the personal meaning of an individual's tattoo, meaning that has changed over time and space, like many other cultural artifacts. Tattoos carry larger cultural meaning, sometimes deviant, sometimes a ritualized norm within a particular culture. Shapiro examines how the meanings of tattoos have been constructed since their introduction into Western society, how their meaning has shifted over time, and how they have been associated with different forms of masculinity throughout modern history.

Deviance and the subsequent stigma associated with it can come in many forms. Deviance can come in the form of behavior, attitudes, and characteristics that one can embody, which can either be achieved or ascribed. Regardless, deviance is not an inherent wrongdoing, but rather is a product of the negative reactions of a judging audience. In our society, many react negatively to government assistance, specifically the kind received by the poor. In "Making Welfare Stigma," Daniel Dohan looks at how the stigma of welfare is applied and negotiated among residents he interviewed in two barrios in Southern California. Being a recipient of welfare in the United States has become an increasingly stigmatizing status to occupy. And it is arguably even more stigmatizing for black and brown folks who utilize this form of government assistance because of dominant narratives in the media of who receives welfare and who are the deserving versus the undeserving poor. In this reading, Dohan examines the meaning ascribed to welfare use in two Mexican American communities in Southern California and uncovers the process by which these communities applied a stigmatizing status to welfare to their own members.

DISCUSSION QUESTIONS

1. Based on the reading "We Don't Sleep Around Like White Girls Do: Family, Culture, and Gender in Filipina American Lives," discuss the positives and negatives of preserving cultural ideas about Filipina American women.
2. Why is it important to consider the issue of identity for people with disabilities, in addition to considering image?
3. Do you think tattoos on men and women are still interpreted differently? Why?
4. How might the pain involved in the tattooing process impact the meaning ascribed to individual tattoos and tattooing?

"WE DON'T SLEEP AROUND LIKE WHITE GIRLS DO"

FAMILY, CULTURE, AND GENDER IN FILIPINA AMERICAN LIVES

By Yen Le Espiritu

Focusing on the relationship between Filipino immigrant parents and their daughters, this essay argues that gender is a key to immigrant identity and a vehicle for racialized immigrants to assert cultural superiority over the dominant group. In immigrant communities, culture takes on a special significance: it forms not only a lifeline to the home country and a basis for group identity in a new country but also a base from which immigrants stake their political and sociocultural claims on their new country (Eastmond, 1993, p. 40). For Filipino immigrants, who come from a homeland that was once a U.S. colony, cultural reconstruction has been especially critical in the assertion of their presence in the United States—a way to counter the cultural Americanization of the Philippines, to resist the assimilative and alienating demands of U.S. society, and to reaffirm to themselves their self-worth in the face of colonial, racial, class, and gendered subordination. Before World War II, Filipinos were barred from becoming U.S. citizens, owning property, and marrying Whites. They also encountered discriminatory housing policies, unfair labor practices, violent physical encounters, and racist as well as anti-immigrant discourse (Cordova, 1983; Jung, 1999; Scharlin & Villanueva, 1992; Sharma, 1984). While blatant legal discrimination against Filipino Americans is largely a matter of the past, Filipinos continue to encounter many barriers that prevent full participation in the economic, social, and political institutions of the United States (Azores-Gunter, 1986–87; Cabezas, Shinagawa, & Kawaguchi, 1986–87; Okamura & Agbayani, 1997). Moreover, the economic mobility and cultural assimilation that enables White ethnics to become "unhyphenated Whites" is seldom extended to Filipino Americans (Espiritu, 1994). Like other Asians, the Filipino is "always seen as an immigrant, as the 'foreigner-within'; even when born in the United States" (Lowe, 1996, p. 5). Finally, although Filipinos have been in the United States since the middle of the 1700s and Americans have been in the Philippines since at least the late 1800s, U.S. Filipinos—as racialized nationals, immigrants, and citizens—are "still practically an invisible and silent minority" (San Juan, 1991, p. 117). Drawing from my research on Filipino American families in San Diego, California, I explore in this essay the ways racialized immigrants claim through gender the power denied them by racism.

My epigraphs, statements by a Filipina immigrant mother and a second-generation Filipina daughter, suggest that the virtuous Filipina daughter is partially constructed on the conceptualization of White women as sexually immoral. This juxtaposition underscores the fact that femininity is a relational category, one that is co-constructed with other racial and cultural categories. These narratives also reveal that women's sexuality and their enforced "morality" are fundamental to the structuring of social inequalities. Historically, the sexuality of racialized women has been systematically demonized and disparaged by dominant or oppressor groups to justify and bolster nationalist movements, colonialism, and/or racism. But as these narratives indicate, racialized groups also criticize the morality of White women as a strategy of resistance—a means of asserting a morally superior public face to the dominant society.

By exploring how Filipino immigrants characterize White families and White women, I hope to contribute to a neglected area of research: how the "margins" imagine and construct the "mainstream" in order to assert superiority over it. But this strategy is not without costs. The elevation of Filipina chastity (particularly that of young women) has the effect of reinforcing masculinist and patriarchal power in the name of a greater ideal of national/ethnic self-respect. Because the control of women is one of the principal means of asserting moral superiority, young women in immigrant families face numerous restrictions on their autonomy, mobility, and personal decision making. Although this essay addresses the experiences and attitudes of both parents and children, here I am more concerned with understanding the actions of immigrant parents than the reactions of their second-generation daughters.

CONSTRUCTING THE DOMINANT GROUP: THE MORAL FLAWS OF WHITE AMERICANS

Given the centrality of moral themes in popular discussions on racial differences, Michele Lamont (1997) has suggested that morality is a crucial site to study the cultural mechanisms of reproduction of racial inequality. While much has been written on how Whites have represented the (im)morality of people of color (Collins, 1991; Hamamoto, 1994; Marchetti, 1993), there has been less critical attention to how people of color have represented Whites. Shifting attention from the otherness of the subordinate group (as dictated by the "mainstream") to the otherness of the dominant group (as constructed by the "margins"), this section focuses on the alternative frames of meaning that racially subordinate groups mobilize to (re) define their status in relation to the dominant group. I argue that female morality—defined as women's dedication to their families and sexual restraint—is one of the few sites where economically and politically dominated groups can construct the dominant group as other and themselves as superior. Because womanhood is idealized as the repository of tradition, the norms that regulate women's behaviors become a means of determining and defining group status and boundaries. As a consequence, the burdens and complexities of cultural representation fall most heavily on immigrant women and their daughters. Below, I show that Filipino immigrants claim moral distinctiveness for their community by representing "Americans" as morally flawed, themselves as family-oriented model minorities, and their wives and daughters as paragons of morality.

FAMILY-ORIENTED MODEL MINORITIES: "WHITE WOMEN WILL LEAVE YOU"

In his work on Italian immigrant parents and children in the 1930s, Robert Anthony Orsi (1985) reports that parents invented a virtuous Italy (based on memories of their childhood) that they then used to castigate the morality of the United States and their U.S.-born or -raised children. In a similar way, many of my respondents constructed their "ethnic" culture as principled and "American" culture as deviant. Most often, this morality narrative revolves around family life and family relations. When asked what sets Filipinos apart from other Americans, my respondents— of all ages and class backgrounds—repeatedly contrasted close-knit Filipino families with what they perceived to be the more impersonal quality of U.S. family relations. In the following narratives, "Americans" are characterized as lacking in strong family ties and collective identity, less willing to do the work of family and cultural maintenance, and less willing to abide by patriarchal norms in husband/wife relations:

> American society lacks caring. The American way of life is more individual rather than collective. The American way is to say I want to have my own way. (Filipina immigrant, 54 years old)

> Our [Filipino] culture is different. We are more close-knit. We tend to help one another. Americans, ya know, they are all right, but they don't help each other that much. As a matter of fact, if the parents are old, they take them to a convalescent home and let them rot there. We would never do that in our culture. We would nurse them; we would help them until the very end. (Filipino immigrant, 60 years old)

> Our [Filipino] culture is very communal. You know that your family will always be there, that you don't have to work when you turn eighteen, you don't have to pay rent when you are eighteen, which is the American way of thinking. You also know that if things don't work out in the outside world, you can always come home and mommy and daddy will always take you and your children in. (Second-generation Filipina, 33 years old)

> Asian parents take care of their children. Americans have a different attitude. They leave their children to their own resources. They get baby-sitters to take care of their children or leave them in day care. That's why when they get old, their children don't even care about them. (Filipina immigrant, 46 years old)

Implicit in negative depictions of U.S. families as uncaring, selfish, and distant is the allegation that White women are not as dedicated to their families as Filipina women are to theirs. Several

Filipino men who married White women recalled being warned by their parents and relatives that "White women will leave you." As one man related, "My mother said to me, 'Well, you know, don't marry a White person because they would take everything that you own and leave you.'" For some Filipino men, perceived differences in attitudes about women's roles between Filipina and non-Filipina women influenced their marital choice. A Filipino American navy man explained why he went back to the Philippines to look for a wife:

> My goal was to marry a Filipina. I requested to be stationed in the Philippines to get married to a Filipina. I'd seen the women here and basically they are spoiled. They have a tendency of not going along together with their husband. They behave differently. They chase the male, instead of the male, the normal way or the traditional way is for the male to go after the female. They have sex without marrying. They want to do their own things. So my idea was to go back home and marry somebody who has never been here. I tell my son the same thing: if he does what I did and finds himself a good lady there, he will be in good hands.

Another man who had dated mostly White women in high school recounted that when it came time to marry, he "looked for the kind of women" he met while stationed in the Philippines: "I hate to sound chauvinistic about marriages, but Filipinas have a way of making you feel like you are a king. They also have that tenderness, that elegance. And we share the same values about family, education, religion, and raising children."

The claims of family closeness are not unique to Filipino immigrants. For example, when asked what makes their group distinctive, Italian Americans (di Leonardo, 1984), Vietnamese Americans (Kibria, 1993), South Asian Americans (Hickey, 1996), and African Americans (Lamont, 1997) all point proudly to the close-knit character of their family life. Although it is diffcult to know whether these claims are actual perceptions or favored self-legitimating answers, it is nevertheless important to note the gender implications of these claims. That is, while both men and women identify the family system as a tremendous source of cultural pride, it is women—through their unpaid housework and kin work who shoulder the primary responsibility for maintaining family closeness. As the organizers of family rituals, transmitters of homeland folklores, and socializers of young children, women have been crucial for the maintenance of family ties and cultural traditions. In a study of kinship, class, and gender among California Italian Americans, di Leonardo argues that women's kin work, "the work of knitting households together into close, extended family ties," maintains the family networks that give ethnicity meaning (1984, p. 229).

Because the moral status of the community rests on women's labor, women, as wives and daughters, are expected to dedicate themselves to the family. Writing on the constructed image of ethnic family and gender, di Leonardo argues that "a large part of stressing ethnic identity amounts to burdening women with increased responsibilities for preparing special foods, planning rituals, and enforcing "ethnic" socialization of children" (1984, p. 222). A 23-year-old Filipina spoke about the reproductive work that her mother performed and expected her to learn:

> In my family, I was the only girl, so my mom expected a lot from me. She wanted me to help her to take care of the household. I felt like there was a lot of pressure on me.

It's very important to my mom to have the house in order: to wash the dishes, to keep the kitchen in order, vacuuming, and dusting and things like that. She wants me to be a perfect housewife. It's diffcult. I have been married now for about four months and my mother asks me every now and then what have I cooked for my husband. My mom is also very strict about families getting together on holidays, and I would always help her to organize that. Each holiday, I would try to decorate the house for her, to make it more special.

The burden of unpaid reproductive and kin work is particularly stressful for women who work outside the home. In the following narrative, a Filipina wife and mother described the pulls of family and work that she experienced when she went back to school to pursue a doctoral degree in nursing:

The Filipinos, we are very collective, very connected. Going through the doctoral program, sometimes I think it is better just to forget about my relatives and just concentrate on school. All that connectedness, it steals parts of myself because all of my energies are devoted to my family. And that is the reason why I think Americans are successful. The majority of the American people they can do what they want. They don't feel guilty because they only have a few people to relate to. For us Filipinos, it's like roots under the tree, you have all these connections. The Americans are more like the trunk. I am still trying to go up to the trunk of the tree but it is too hard. I want to be more independent, more like the Americans. I want to be good to my family but what about me? And all the things that I am doing. It's hard. It's always a struggle.

It is important to note that this Filipina interprets her exclusion and added responsibilities as only racial when they are also gendered. For example, when she says, "the American people they can do what they want," she ignores the differences in the lives of White men and White women—the fact that most White women experience similar competing pulls of family, education, and work.

RACIALIZED SEXUALITY AND (IM)MORALITY: "IN AMERICA ... SEX IS NOTHING"

Sexuality, as a core aspect of social identity, is fundamental to the structuring of gender inequality (Millett, 1970). Sexuality is also a salient marker of otherness and has figured prominently in racist and imperialist ideologies (Gilman, 1985; Stoler, 1991). Historically, the sexuality of subordinate groups—particularly that of racialized women—has been systematically stereotyped by the dominant groups. At stake in these stereotypes is the construction of women of color as morally lacking in the areas of sexual restraint and traditional morality. Asian women—both in Asia and in the United States—have been racialized as sexually immoral, and the "Orient"—and its women—has long served as a site of European male-power fantasies, replete with lurid images of sexual license, gynecological aberrations, and general perversion (Gilman, 1985, p. 89). In colonial Asia in the 19th and early 20th centuries, for example, female sexuality was a site for colonial rulers to assert their moral superiority and thus their supposed natural and legitimate right to rule. The colonial rhetoric of moral superiority was based on the construction of colonized Asian women as subjects of sexual desire and fulfillment and European colonial women as the paragons of virtue and the bearers of a redefined colonial morality (Stoler, 1991). The discourse of morality has also been used to mark the "unassimilability" of Asians in the United States. At the turn of the 20th century, the public perception of Chinese women as disease-ridden, drug-addicted prostitutes served to underline the depravity of "Orientals" and played a decisive role in the eventual passage of exclusion laws against all Asians (Mazumdar, 1989, pp. 3–4). The stereotypical view that all Asian women were prostitutes, first formed in the 1850s, persisted. Contemporary American popular culture continues to endow Asian women with an excess of "womanhood," sexualizing them but also impugning their sexuality (Espiritu, 1997, p. 93).

Filipinas—both in the Philippines and in the United States—have been marked as desirable but dangerous "prostitutes" and/or submissive "mail-order brides" (Egan, 1996; Halualani, 1995). These stereotypes emerged out of the colonial process, especially the extensive U.S. military presence in the Philippines. Until the early 1990s, the Philippines, at times unwillingly, housed some of the United States' largest overseas air force and naval bases (Espiritu, 1995, p. 14). Many Filipino nationalists have charged that "the prostitution problem" in the Philippines stemmed from U.S. and Philippine government policies that promoted a sex industry—brothels, bars, and massage parlors—for servicemen stationed or on leave in the Philippines. During the Vietnam War, the Philippines was known as the "rest and recreation" center of Asia, hosting approximately 10,000 U.S. servicemen daily (Coronel & Rosca, 1993; Warren, 1993). In this context, all Filipinas were racialized as sexual commodities, usable and expendable. A U.S.-born Filipina recounted the sexual harassment she faced while visiting Subic Bay Naval Station in Olongapo City:

> One day, I went to the base dispensary.... I was dressed nicely, and as I walked by the fire station, I heard catcalls and snide remarks being made by some of the firemen.
>
> ... I was fuming inside. The next thing I heard was, "How much do you charge?" I kept on walking. "Hey, are you deaf or something? How much do you charge? You have a good body." That was an incident that I will never forget. (Quoted in Espiritu, 1995, p. 77)

The sexualized racialization of Filipina women is also captured in Marianne Villanueva's short story "Opportunity" (1991). As the protagonist, a "mail-order bride" from the Philippines, enters a hotel lobby to meet her American fiancé, the bellboys snicker and whisper *puta* (whore)—a reminder that U.S. economic and cultural colonization in the Philippines always forms a backdrop to any relations between Filipinos and Americans (Wong, 1993, p. 53).

Cognizant of the pervasive hypersexualization of Filipina women, my respondents, especially women who grew up near military bases, were quick to denounce prostitution, to condemn sex laborers, and to declare (unasked) that they themselves did not frequent "that part of town." As one Filipina immigrant said,

> Growing up [in the Philippines], I could never date an American because my dad's concept of a friendship with an American is with a GI. The only reason why my dad

wouldn't let us date an American is that people will think that the only way you met was because of the base. I have never seen the inside of any of the bases because we were just forbidden to go there.

Many of my respondents also distanced themselves culturally from the Filipinas who serviced U.S. soldiers by branding them "more Americanized" and "more Westernized." In other words, these women were sexually promiscuous because they had assumed the sexual mores of White women. This characterization allows my respondents to symbolically disown the Filipina "bad girl" and, in so doing, to uphold the narrative of Filipina sexual virtuousness and White female sexual promiscuity. In the following narrative, a mother who came to the United States in her 30s contrasted the controlled sexuality of women in the Philippines with the perceived promiscuity of White women in the United States:

> In the Philippines, we always have chaperons when we go out. When we go to dances, we have our uncle, our grandfather, and auntie all behind us to make sure that we behave in the dance hall. Nobody goes necking outside. You don't even let a man put his hand on your shoulders. When you were brought up in a conservative country, it is hard to come here and see that it is all freedom of speech and freedom of action. Sex was never mentioned in our generation. I was 30 already when I learned about sex. But to the young generation in America, sex is nothing.

Similarly, another immigrant woman criticized the way young American women are raised: "Americans are so liberated. They allow their children, their girls, to go out even when they are still so young." In contrast, she stated that, in "the Filipino way, it is very important, the value of the woman, that she is a virgin when she gets married."

The ideal "Filipina," then, is partially constructed on the community's conceptualization of White women. She is everything that they are not: she is sexually modest and dedicated to her family; they are sexually promiscuous and uncaring. Within the context of the dominant culture's pervasive hypersexualization of Filipinas, the construction of the "ideal" Filipina as family oriented and chaste can be read as an effort to reclaim the morality of the community. This effort erases the Filipina "bad girl," ignores competing sexual practices in the Filipino communities, and uncritically embraces the myth of "Oriental femininity." Cast as the embodiment of perfect womanhood and exotic femininity, Filipinas (and other Asian women) in recent years have been idealized in U.S. popular culture as more truly "feminine" (i.e., devoted, dependent, domestic) and therefore more desirable than their more modern, emancipated sisters (Espiritu, 1997, p. 113). Capitalizing on this image of the "superfemme," mail-order bride agencies market Filipina women as "'exotic, subservient wife imports' for sale and as alternatives for men sick of independent 'liberal' Western women" (Halualani, 1995, p. 49; see also Ordonez, 1997, p. 122).

Embodying the moral integrity of the idealized ethnic community, immigrant women, particularly young daughters, are expected to comply with male-defined criteria of what constitute "ideal" feminine virtues. While the sexual behavior of adult women is confined to a monogamous, heterosexual context, that of young women is denied completely (see Dasgupta & DasGupta, 1996, pp. 229–231). In the next section, I detail the ways Filipino immigrant parents, under the rubric of "cultural preservation," police their daughters' behaviors in order to safeguard their sexual innocence and virginity. These attempts at policing generate hierarchies and tensions within immigrant families—between parents and children and between brothers and sisters.

THE CONSTRUCTION(S) OF THE "IDEAL" FILIPINA: "BOYS ARE BOYS AND GIRLS ARE DIFFERENT"

As the designated "keepers of the culture" (Billson, 1995), immigrant women and their behavior come under intense scrutiny both from men and women of their own groups and from U.S.-born Americans (Gabaccia, 1994, p. xi). In a study of the Italian Harlem community from 1880 to 1950, Orsi reports that "all the community's fears for the reputation and integrity of the homes came to focus on the behavior of young women" (1985, p. 135). Because women's moral and sexual loyalties were deemed central to the maintenance of group status, changes in female behavior, especially that of growing daughters, were interpreted as sins of moral decay and ethnic suicide and were carefully monitored and sanctioned (Gabaccia, 1994, p. 113).

Although details vary, young women of various groups and across space and time—for example, second-generation Chinese women in San Francisco in the 1920s (Yung, 1195), U.S.-born Italian women in East Harlem in the 1930s (Orsi, 1985), young Mexican women in the Southwest during the interwar years (Ruiz, 1992), and daughters of Caribbean and Asian Indian immigrants on the East Coast in the 1990s (Dasgupta & DasGupta, 1996; Waters, 1996)—have identified strict parental control on their activities and movements as the primary source of inter-generational conflict. Recent studies of immigrant families also identify gender as a significant determinant of parent-child conflict, with daughters more likely than sons to be involved in such conflicts and instances of parental derogation (Gibson, 1995; Matute-Bianchi, 1991; Rumbaut & Ima, 1988; Woldemikael, 1989).

Although immigrant families have always been preoccupied with passing on their native culture, language, and traditions to both male and female children, it is daughters who have the primary burden of protecting and preserving the family. Because sons do not have to conform to the same image of an "ideal" ethnic subject as daughters do, they often receive special daily privileges denied to daughters (Haddad & Smith, 1996, pp. 22–24; Waters, 1996, pp. 75–76). This is not to say that immigrant parents do not place undue expectations on their sons; rather, these expectations do not pivot around the sons' sexuality or dating choices. In contrast, parental control over the movement and action of daughters begins the moment they are perceived as young adults and sexually vulnerable. It regularly consists of monitoring their whereabouts and forbidding dating (Wolf, 1997). For example, the immigrant parents I interviewed seldom allowed their daughters to date, to stay out late, to spend the night at a friend's house, or to take an out-of-town trip.

Many of the second-generation women I spoke to complained bitterly about these parental restrictions. They particularly resented what they saw as gender inequity in their families: the fact that their parents placed far more restrictions on their activities and movements than on those of their brothers. Some decried the fact that even their younger brothers had more freedom than they did: "It was really hard growing up because my parents would let my younger brothers do what they wanted but I didn't get to do what I wanted even though I was the oldest. I had a curfew and my brothers didn't. I had to ask if I could go places and they didn't. My parents never even asked my brothers when they were coming home." As indicated in the following excerpt, many Filipino males are cognizant of this double standard in their families:

My sister would always say to me, "It's not fair, just because you are a guy, you can go wherever you want." I think my parents do treat me and my sister differently. Like in high school, maybe 10:30 at night, which is pretty late on a school night, and I say I have to go pick up some notes at my friend's house, my parents wouldn't say anything. But if my sister were to do that, there would be no way. Even now when my sister is in college already, if she wants to leave at midnight to go to a friend's house, they would tell her that she shouldn't do it.

When questioned about this double standard, parents generally responded by explaining that "girls are different":

I have that Filipino mentality that boys are boys and girls are different. Girls are supposed to be protected, to be clean. In the early years, my daughters have to have chaperons and curfews. And they know that they have to be virgins until they get married. The girls always say that is not fair. What is the difference between their brothers and them? And my answer always is, "In the Philippines, you know, we don't do that. The girls stay home. The boys go out." It was the way that I was raised. I still want to have part of that culture instilled in my children. And I want them to have that to pass on to their children.

Even among self-described Western-educated and "tolerant" parents, many continue to ascribe to "the Filipino way" when it comes to raising daughters. As one college-educated father explains,

Because of my Western education, I don't raise my children the way my parents raised me. I tended to be a little more tolerant. But at times, especially in certain issues like dating, I find myself more towards the Filipino way in the sense that I have only one daughter so I tended to be a little bit stricter. So the double standard kind of operates: it's all right for the boys to explore the field but I tended to be overly protective of my daughter. My wife feels the same way because the boys will not lose anything, but the daughter will lose something, her virginity, and it can be also a question of losing face, that kind of thing.

Although many parents discourage or forbid dating for daughters, they still fully expect these young women to fulfill their traditional roles as women: to marry and have children. A young Filipina recounted the mixed messages she received from her parents:

This is the way it is supposed to work: Okay, you go to school. You go to college. You graduate. You find a job. *Then* you find your husband, and you have children. That's the whole time line. But my question is, if you are not allowed to date, how are you supposed to find your husband? They say "no" to the whole dating scene because that is secondary to your education, secondary to your family. They do push marriage, but at a later date. So basically my parents are telling me that I should get married and I should have children but that I should not date.

In a study of second-generation Filipino Americans in Northern California, Diane Wolf (1997) reports the same pattern of parental pressures: Parents expect daughters to remain virgins until marriage, to have a career, and to combine their work lives with marriage and children.

The restrictions on girls' movement sometimes spill over to the realm of academics. Dasgupta and DasGupta (1996, p. 230) recount that in the Indian American community, while young men were expected to attend faraway competitive colleges, many of their female peers were encouraged by their parents to go to the local colleges so that they could live at or close to home. Similarly, Wolf (1997, p. 467) reports that some Filipino parents pursued contradictory tactics with their children, particularly their daughters, by pushing them to achieve academic excellence in high school but then "pulling the emergency brake" when they contemplated college by expecting them to stay at home, even if it meant going to a less competitive college or not going at all. In the following account, a young Filipina relates that her parents' desire to "protect" her surpassed their concerns for her academic preparation:

> My brother [was] given a lot more opportunity educationally. He was given the opportunity to go to Miller High School that has a renowned college preparatory program but [for] which you have to be bussed out of our area. I've come from a college prep program in junior high and I was asked to apply for the program at Miller. But my parents said "No, absolutely not." This was even during the time, too, when South-side [the neighborhood high school] had one of the lowest test scores in the state of California. So it was like, "You know, mom, I'll get a better chance at Miller." "No, no, you're going to Southside. There is no ifs, ands, or buts. Miller is too far. What if something happens to you?" But two years later, when my brother got ready to go on to high school, he was allowed to go to Miller. My sister and I were like, "Obviously, whose education do you value more? If you're telling us that education is important, why do we see a double standard?"

The above narratives suggest that the process of parenting is gendered in that immigrant parents tend to restrict the autonomy, mobility, and personal decision making of their daughters more than that of their sons. I argue that these parental restrictions are attempts to construct a model of Filipina womanhood that is chaste, modest, nurturing, and family oriented. Women are seen as responsible for holding the cultural line, maintaining racial boundaries, and marking cultural difference. This is not to say that parent-daughter conflicts exist in all Filipino immigrant families. Certainly, Filipino parents do not respond in a uniform way to the challenges of being racial-ethnic minorities, and I met parents who have had to change some of their ideas and practices in response to their inability to control their children's movements and choices:

> I have three girls and one boy. I used to think that I wouldn't allow my daughters to go dating and things like that, but there is no way I could do that. I can't stop it. It's the way of life here in America. Sometimes you kind of question yourself, if you are doing

what is right. It is hard to accept but you got to accept it. That's the way they are here. (Professional Filipino immigrant father)

My children are born and raised here, so they do pretty much what they want. They think they know everything. I can only do so much as a parent.... When I try to teach my kids things, they tell me that I sound like an old record. They even talk back to me sometimes ... . The first time my daughter brought her boyfriend to the house, she was eighteen years old. I almost passed away, knocked out. Lord, tell me what to do? (Working-class Filipina immigrant mother)

These narratives call attention to the shifts in the generational power caused by the migration process and to the possible gap between what parents say they want for their children and their ability to control the young. However, the interview data do suggest that intergenerational conflicts are socially recognized occurrences in Filipino communities. Even when respondents themselves had not experienced intergenerational tensions, they could always recall a cousin, a girlfriend, or a friend's daughter who had.

SANCTIONS AND REACTIONS: "THAT IS NOT WHAT A DECENT FILIPINO GIRL SHOULD DO"

I do not wish to suggest that immigrant communities are the only ones in which parents regulate their daughters' mobility and sexuality. Feminist scholars have long documented the construction, containment, and exploitation of women's sexuality in various societies (Maglin & Perry, 1996). We also know that the cultural anxiety over unbounded female sexuality is most apparent with regard to adolescent girls (Tolman & Higgins, 1996, p. 206). The difference is in the ways immigrant and nonimmigrant families sanction girls' sexuality. To control sexually assertive girls, nonimmigrant parents rely on the gender-based good girl/bad girl dichotomy in which "good girls" are passive, threatened sexual objects, while "bad girls" are active, desiring sexual agents (Tolman & Higgins, 1996). As Dasgupta and DasGupta write, "the two most pervasive images of women across cultures are the goddess and whore, the good and bad women" (1996, p. 236). This good girl/bad girl cultural story conflates femininity with sexuality, increases women's vulnerability to sexual coercion, and justifies women's containment in the domestic sphere.

Immigrant families, though, have an additional strategy: they can discipline their daughters as racial/national subjects as well as gendered ones. That is, as self-appointed guardians of "authentic" cultural memory, immigrant parents can attempt to regulate their daughters' independent choices by linking them to cultural ignorance or betrayal. As both parents and children recounted, young women who disobeyed parental strictures were often branded "nonethnic," "untraditional," "radical," "selfish," and "not caring about the family." Female sexual choices were also linked to moral degeneracy, defined in relation to a narrative of a hegemonic White norm. Parents were quick to warn their daughters about "bad" Filipinas who had become pregnant outside marriage. As in the case of "bar girls" in the Philippines, Filipina Americans who veered from acceptable behaviors were deemed "Americanized"—as women who have adopted the sexual mores and practices of White women. As one Filipino immigrant father described "Americanized" Filipinas: "They are spoiled because they have seen the American way. They go out at night. Late at night. They go out on dates. Smoking. They have sex without marrying."

From the perspective of the second-generation daughters, these charges are stinging. The young women I interviewed were visibly pained—with many breaking down and crying—when they recounted their parents' charges. This deep pain, stemming in part from their desire to be validated as Filipina, existed even among the more "rebellious" daughters. One 24-year-old daughter explained:

> My mom is very traditional. She wants to follow Filipino customs, just really adhere to them, like what is proper for a girl, what she can and can't do, and what other people are going to think of her if she doesn't follow that way. When I pushed these restrictions, when I rebelled and stayed out later than allowed, my mom would always say, "That is not what a decent Filipino girl should do. You should come home at a decent hour. What are people going to think of you?" And that would get me really upset, you know, because I think that my character is very much the way it should be for a Filipina. I wear my hair long, I wear decent makeup. I dress properly, conservative. I am family oriented. It hurts me that she doesn't see that I am decent, that I am proper, and that I am not going to bring shame to the family or anything like that.

This narrative suggests that even when parents are unable to control the behaviors of their children, their (dis)approval remains powerful in shaping the emotional lives of their daughters (see Wolf, 1997). Although better-off parents can and do exert greater controls over their children's behaviors than do poorer parents (Kibria, 1993; Wolf, 1992), I would argue that all immigrant parents—regardless of class background—possess this emotional hold on their children. Therein lies the source of their power: As immigrant parents, they have the authority to determine if their daughters are "authentic" members of their racial-ethnic community. Largely unacquainted with the "home" country, U.S.-born children depend on their parents' tutelage to craft and affirm their ethnic self and thus are particularly vulnerable to charges of cultural ignorance and/or betrayal (Espiritu, 1994). Despite these emotional pains, many young Filipinas I interviewed contest and negotiate parental restrictions in their daily lives. Faced with parental restrictions on their mobility, young Filipinas struggle to gain some control over their own social lives, particularly over dating. In many cases, daughters simply misinform their parents of their whereabouts or date without their parents' knowledge. They also rebel by vowing to create more egalitarian relationships with their own husbands and children. A 30-year-old Filipina who is married to a White American explained why she chose to marry outside her culture:

> In high school, I dated mostly Mexican and Filipino. It never occurred to me to date a White or Black guy. I was not attracted to them. But as I kept growing up and my father and I were having all these conflicts, I knew that if I married a Mexican or a Filipino, [he] would be exactly like my father. And so I tried to date anyone that would not remind me of my dad. A lot of my Filipina friends that I grew up with had similar experiences. So I knew that it wasn't only me. I was determined to marry a White person because he would treat me as an individual.

The few available studies on Filipino American intermarriage indicate a high rate relative to other Asian groups. In 1980, Filipino men in California recorded the highest intermarriage rate among all Asian groups, and Filipina women had the second-highest rate among Asian American women, after Japanese American women (Agbayani-Siewert & Revilla, 1995, p. 156).

Another Filipina who was labeled "radical" by her parents indicated that she would be more open-minded in raising her own children: "I see myself as very traditional in upbringing but I don't see myself as constricting on my children one day and I wouldn't put the gender roles on them. I wouldn't lock them into any particular way of behaving." It is important to note that even as these Filipinas desired new gender norms and practices for their own families, the majority hoped that their children would remain connected to Filipino culture.

My respondents also reported more serious reactions to parental restrictions, recalling incidents of someone they knew who had run away, joined a gang, or attempted suicide. A Filipina high-school counselor relates that most of the Filipinas she worked with "are really scared because a lot of them know friends that are pregnant and they all pretty much know girls who have attempted suicide." A 1995 random survey of San Diego public high schools conducted by the Federal Centers for Disease Control and Prevention (CDC) found that, in comparison with other ethnic groups, female Filipino students had the highest rates of seriously considering suicide (45.6%) as well as the highest rates of actually attempting suicide (23%) in the year preceding the survey. In comparison, 33.4% of Latinas, 26.2% of White women, and 25.3% of Black women surveyed said they had suicidal thoughts (Lau, 1995).

CONCLUSION

Mainstream American society defines White middle-class culture as the norm and whiteness as the unmarked marker of others' difference (Frankenberg, 1993). In this essay, I have shown that many Filipino immigrants use the largely gendered discourse of morality as one strategy to decenter whiteness and to locate themselves above the dominant group, demonizing it in the process. Like other immigrant groups, Filipinos praise the United States as a land of significant economic opportunity but simultaneously denounce it as a country inhabited by corrupted and individualistic people of questionable morals. In particular, they criticize American family life, American individualism, and American women (see Gabaccia, 1994, p. 113). Enforced by distorting powers of memory and nostalgia, this rhetoric of moral superiority often leads to patriarchal calls for a cultural "authenticity" that locates family honor and national integrity in the group's female members. Because the policing of women's bodies is one of the main means of asserting moral superiority, young women face numerous restrictions on their autonomy, mobility, and personal decision making. This practice of cultural (re)construction reveals how deeply the conduct of private life can be tied to larger social structures.

The construction of White Americans as the "other" and American culture as deviant serves a dual purpose: It allows immigrant communities both to reinforce patriarchy through the sanctioning of women's (mis)behavior and to present an unblemished, if not morally superior, public face to the dominant society. Strong in family values, heterosexual morality, and a hierarchical family structure, this public face erases the Filipina "bad girl" and ignores competing immoral practices in the Filipino communities. Through the oppression of Filipina women and the denunciation of White women's morality, the immigrant community attempts to exert its moral superiority over the dominant Western culture and to reaffirm to itself its self-worth in the face of economic, social, political, and legal subordination. In other words, the immigrant community uses restrictions on women's lives as one form of resistance to racism. This form of cultural resistance, however, severely restricts the lives of women, particularly those of the second generation, and it casts the family as a potential site of intense conflict and oppressive demands in immigrant lives.

THE MICROSYSTEM LEVEL

THE CONTINUING INFLUENCE OF CHILDHOOD SOCIALIZATION ON ADULT MASCULINITY

By Elizabeth A. Mansley

"I knew violence from where I grew up. It is all that there was. If you didn't know how to fight, then you were going to get beat up. Everyone, even every woman, has to protect themselves. It ain't no one's job but your own to take care of you" (Johnny, 21 year old White man).

In an Ecological Nested Model, the first level is the Microsystem (Bronfenbrenner 1977), and it is comprised of an individual's perspective on their childhood experiences, family of origin, childhood socialization and role models. In reference to this study, this level of ENM will explore the men's exposure to violence as a child, the presence/absence of a father figure, and various experiences of childhood socialization including tendency to fight, experiences with bullying and views on education. In every interview that I conducted, the men devoted considerable time to discussing their childhood and their relationships with their mothers and fathers. This detailed discussion of childhood socialization occurred in interviews with men from "good" families and in interviews with men from "troubled" families. These distinctions come from the men's accounts and are conceptually similar to Anderson's description of decent and street families (Anderson 1999). The consistency with which the men discussed their childhood experiences and their tendency to use examples from the past as contributing to current behavior lends credence to the importance of analysis of the Microsystem level.

NEIGHBORHOOD DURING CHILDHOOD[1]

> "The violence was around the corners. My parents didn't allow us to go around the corners. We could only go to the store and back. That's how it was. It was violence all around … two blocks up was a drug corner, five blocks up there were Whites and they were prejudiced. You couldn't travel through the area. If you go downward, it was the gangs. It was like we were trapped" (Tyrone, 35 year old Black man).

Forty percent of my sample described the neighborhood that they grew up in as violent, crime ridden and poverty stricken.[2] These neighborhoods, the Badlands, had lasting consequences for the men. In the Badlands, the men were encouraged to use violence to handle conflict. They were socialized to believe that the police could not be trusted, that friends and girlfriends would betray them and that employing violence was necessary to prevent future conflict. Violence outside the home has been linked to predicting the severity of future intimate partner violence (Sonis and Langer 2008). These individuals often employ a masculine persona that emphasizes toughness and independence as a reaction to extreme structural constraints. The men are governed by "a set of prescriptions and proscriptions, or informal rules, of behavior organized around a desperate search for respect that governs public social relations, especially violence" (Anderson 1999:9). The socially disadvantaged men that I interviewed verbalized this emphasis on survival.

> "There was a lot of violence and a lot of drugs. And from time to time you have to fear for your safety. There were people who were getting shot in broad daylight. Living that way does something to you. It turns you hard. It has to or else you don't survive" (Julian, 24 year old Black man).

Predominantly, men from the Badlands were Black men (14 men out of 20) and were among the youngest in my sample (average age of 26). These men were the most likely to have no relationship with their fathers, to drop out of high school before graduation, to have a history of substance abuse, to have a criminal record and to work in low paying jobs or lack employment altogether. While these men did not "excuse" their behavior because of their upbringing, they were the most likely to conceptualize intimate partner violence as just another form of violence.

Conversely, sixty percent of my sample describes their childhood homes as being found in "good" neighborhoods. For these men, their neighborhood was given much less attention during the interviews. Lives in these neighborhoods, the Highlands, were relatively peaceful. The only violence the men were regularly exposed to was at home or on television. Men from the Highlands were predominantly White, reported positive relationships with their fathers, graduated from high school and have no criminal record other than a history of intimate partner violence.

EXPOSURE TO VIOLENCE AS A CHILD

One of the most widely accepted risk markers for instances of intimate partner violence is exposure to violence as a child (Pollack 2004; Thio 2006). Intergenerational transmission of violence theory originated as an attempt to explain instances of child abuse. Initially, the theory argued that individuals who were exposed to violence during their childhood have an increased risk to grow up and become child abusers (see for example, Straus, Gelles and Steinmetz 1980). The theory went through many evolutions as research was undertaken to address its simplistic theoretical foundation. Initial criticism challenged that most child-abuse victims do not grow up and become abusers (Kaufman and Ziegler 1993; Peterson 2000; Rein 2001). Further being a victim of child abuse could contribute to an individual's likelihood to engage in violence in a variety of relationships, not solely a parent-child relationship (Kantor and Jasinksi 1998; Tjaden and Thoennes 2000). The theory was further developed by insights arguing that witnessing abuse as a child, not necessarily being the victim of abuse will contribute to likelihood of violent behavior. Finally, research informed by gender role socialization insights revealed that the consequence of witnessing childhood violence is influenced by gender resulting in women's increased likelihood to become victims of violence and men's increased likelihood to become perpetrators of violence (Thio 2006). This theory however, has received additional criticism. Some research suggests that witnessing childhood abuse can lead to a survivor's commitment to never allow violence to exist in his/her home (for a review, see Belknap 2007).

Consistent with previous research, 28% (14 men) of my sample admitted to being abused as a child or to witnessing their fathers abuse their mothers. Of that 28%, ten men (20% of the sample) admitted that they were physically abused by either their mother, their father or both parents[3]. The men who admitted to being abused or to witnessing abuse came from all social classes and from both racial/ethnic categories. Eight of the ten men who admitted to being physically abused were White men and were raised in working class homes (4 of 8) or middle class homes (4 of 8). These eight men grew up in the Highlands. The two Black men who described themselves as previous victims of child abuse were both from poverty stricken homes or grew up in the Badlands. Only one White man in my sample identified his abuser as his mother. One Black man said that both his parents were abusive. All of the other men who revealed that they were abused claimed to be abused by their fathers/stepfathers only.

> "My family was bad. I grew up bad. My father used to beat me. I got hit and beat up all the time. He would come home from work just to beat me or my mom" (Michael, 30 year old White man).

Important differences by class (and consequently by race) in how the men evaluated the abuse during their childhood were revealed. For the men who were raised in middle class homes in the Highlands, being abused as a child and/or witnessing their mothers being abused seemed to be more influential. For these men, this was the only form of violence that they described being consistently exposed to. Consequently, for the middle class men who had an abusive childhood, the men describe this abuse as being a primary contributor to their own use of violence against their wives/girlfriends.

> "In my house, I was conditioned to beat my wife. I saw my dad hit my mom. I saw it everyday. What does everybody expect would happen? I am a smart guy. I saw that it got my dad what he wanted. Why wouldn't I use it to get what I want?" (Matt, 24 year old White man).

"It's definitely messed up. I used to get mad at my mom for not leaving him and now I am mad at my girl for leaving me for hitting her. It's like, my dad taught me that nothing bad would happen if I did hit her" (Bill, 33 year old White man).

Since these men saw the past abuse as extremely significant in their own behavior, they were angered by their perception that the program directors refused to see the abuse as a contributing factor in their own violence. While these above quotes can be dismissed merely as excuses for their own behavior, it is important to acknowledge the batterer's perceptions. If a batterer considers childhood abuse as a contributing factor, then that factor needs to be addressed. As long as that rationalization remains, the men can fall back onto this reasoning as justification for future abusive behavior.

"He (the program director) refuses to let me talk about how the abuse affected me. He acts like I want to pretend none of it's my fault. It's not that. I just think that I wouldn't have hit her (his wife) if my dad hadn't hit my mom all the time. I know that ultimately it's my fault, but I was hurt by what my dad did too" (Marty, 41 year old White man).

"Every time, I sit down in group treatment or in a psychiatrist's office I think 'Gee, thanks Dad'. You really start getting weird when that kind of stuff is going on to you. You get to where at the slightest provocation, you might just fire off at somebody and mess her up" (Marc, 44 year old White man).

Unlike the middle class White men who were abused or witnessed abuse, the working class White men[4] were slightly less likely to describe the abuse as one of the most contributing factors in their own violence. These men were more likely to witness other forms of violence in their neighborhood and only talked about the impact that a childhood history of abuse had in passing.

"Yeah, I guess if I think about it then I get mad. My dad shouldn't have hit me. But I got hit by other people too. Should I think that it is all of their faults that I am this way? At the end of the day, I am the one that hit my girlfriend. It don't matter what else happened" (Jason, 25 year old White man).

Similar to the working class White men who had a history of childhood abuse, the Black men who were abused downplayed the significance of the abuse in explaining their own violence. These men from the Badlands, were the most likely to have been exposed to multiple forms of violence in their neighborhood and in their homes. For them, the systemic nature of violence was apparent. No one particular form of violence was seen as more significant that any other form as contributing to their violence.

"Yeah my dad hit me and he hit my mom. He also hit other guys. He was violent because you gotta be violent to protect your turf. Niggas are gonna try to hate. Black women are going to try to hate worst of all. You gotta stand up and defend yours or else someone else is going to take it. You gotta defend yours against anyone even a woman, who tries to disrespect you" (Dewitt, 28 year old Black man).

Unlike their White middle-class counterparts, the Black men in my sample were more likely to reveal a criminal history that included the use of violence against multiple people, not just their intimate partners. Similar to Black women (Bliss et al. 2008; Nash 2000; Richie 1995) these men may have felt a pressure to deny the extent of the abuse they suffered or witnessed in an attempt to protect the image of Black families.

> R: Yeah, I was abused by my daddy. There ain't no way that I would talk about it in group. Those guys already think all Black dads are bad or not around. I don't want to give them another reason to think that.
> I: By those guys, do you mean the White men in group?
> R: Them and the director. They all think that (Okezie, 26 year old Black man).

The previous comment illustrates that some of the men in my sample perceived a racial tension during group treatment sessions. The White men who were abused or witnessed abuse felt that the other men, Black men in particular, are denying the impact of childhood abuse.

> "I just don't believe them. They are trying to pretend that having your daddy hit you doesn't hurt anymore that having some other guy hit you. But it does hurt more. It hurts a lot more" (Marc, 44 year old White man).

> "I think that the other guys who saw their mothers get abused won't admit how much it matters. I don't know if it is because they don't want to hate their dads or because they want to look good in front of (program director's name)" (Marty, 41 year old White man).

In contrast, the Black men reported feeling that the White men are trying to use a history of violence during childhood as an excuse.

> "I am so sick of hearing about their daddies hitting their moms. It don't make what they are doing ok. They need to talk about why *they* (emphasis by interviewee) are doing it" (Dewitt, 28 year old Black man).

Consistent with previous literature, my research did uncover that exposure to violence as a child contributes to instances of intimate partner violence. However, that contribution is mitigated by race and class differences. For men in the middle class, violence in their family of origin was often the only form of violence, other than violence portrayed in the media, that they were consistently exposed to during childhood. Therefore, this violence was seen as significant and then men felt that it did substantially contribute to their own use of violence against their partner.

For the Black men who were abused or who witnessed their mothers being abused, the importance of this violence as an explanatory factor in their violence was considerably less than for the White middle class men. For the Black men living in poverty and growing up in the Badlands, violence is systemic and they are exposed to multiple forms of violence in home, in school and in the neighborhood. They saw child abuse or the abuse of their mother as just another instance of violence. Perhaps, these men have been desensitized to violence due to the overexposure. The lower number of Black men who acknowledged abuse in the family of origin is telling. Perhaps these men are protecting the image of Black families and want to downplay violence in the home, or perhaps these men would not define certain behaviors as abusive given the prevalence of violence in their lives. Black men and women who are successful are often encouraged to present the black community in a positive way (Anderson 1999; Bliss et al. 2008). This pressure to "behave in ways that would reflect well on the race" could serve to silence Black men about their abuse in their families (Anderson 1999:180).

Finally, the White working class men can be seen as a middle ground between the White middle class men and the Black poor men. Their experiences in some ways mirror the White middle class men. The childhood violence is seen as a factor but not given the same preeminence that the White middle class men assign to the violence. They also mirror the experiences of the Black poor men because they are more likely to be exposed to multiple forms of violence throughout their childhood. These differences illustrate important differences in the role of childhood violence by race and class.

ABSENCE OF A FATHER FIGURE

Another strong predictor of intimate partner violence is family disruption, with previous research indicating a strong positive relationship between instances of family disruption and likelihood of intimate partner violence (see for example, Sampson and Lauritsen 1994; Smith and Jarjoura 1988). This relationship has proven especially significant for Black families (Cazenave and Straus 1990). Cazenave and Straus (1990) found that for Black families, the lower the number of years living in the neighborhood, increased number of children, and increased number of non-nuclear family members living in the household contributed to an increased likelihood of intimate partner violence. Poor Black families, especially female-headed households, are disproportionately concentrated in inner city areas (Sonis and Langer 2008; Wilson 1987). These communities are the most affected by the shift from an industrial economy to a service economy. The loss of manufacturing jobs has heavily influenced Black men. This structural unemployment has led to severe disruptions for Black families (Hampton, Carrillo and Kim 1998; Wilson 1987). Men in these communities are encouraged to adopt a hyper-masculine persona to compensate for their inability to demonstrate masculinity through their role of provider (Williams 1998).

The presence of a high number of female-headed households in inner city communities has lasting impact for many of the men in my sample. Several men grew up as boys who did not know their father. Thirty-eight percent of the men in my sample (19 men), reported little or no contact with their father during their childhood. The majority of men who reported not knowing their fathers were from the lower class or the Badlands (79%) and were disproportionately Black men (84%). For the men in my sample, the lack of a relationship with his father was often a source of shame and anger.

> "I never knew my father. It's like I am so mad because he could have done better. I am going to do better. For my son, he is going to have it all. I don't care if I have to rob and

kill. He is going to have it all. He got it all now. I ain't never had that as a kid" (Felix, 24 year old Black man).

In addition to feelings of shame and anger, the men reported the lack of a father figure provided them with more opportunities to engage in criminal/violent behavior due to a lack of parental supervision.

"My mom was working all the time so I had a lot of free time to do whatever I pleased. I went to the streets and got into trouble" (Felix, 24 year old Black man).

Many of the men who had relationships with their fathers, even if those relationships were not positive, felt that a father was needed to successfully raise a son.

"Little boys need a man around to grow up to be a man. They really need a father figure around. Moms can't raise boys to be men. They need someone to emulate. On the streets, it's the wrong guy" (Joe, 38 year old Black man).

"I wish that there were more fathers there. I watch the neighborhood. I know where they fathers are at ... they dead, on drugs or in jail. There were some good fathers out there, but not with this younger generation. We need more men to take care of their responsibility. The mothers are frustrated and letting them run wild and that is what happening. The mothers are frustrated because there is no father around. When I was young, we all ate together, went to church together, spent time together. That is how I was raised and we need more of that. If the father is not involved, the mother is frustrated and letting her kids run wild. That is from what I see and hear all the time" (Daniel, 28 year old Black man).

Men raised in female-headed households were more likely to have childhoods characterized by residential instability. These men moved several times during their youth. These frequent moves required adjustments to a new school and a new neighborhood. For many of the men, these new environments increased the likelihood that they would employ violence. Further, these moves reflected the boy's lack of control to prevent residential moves. Employing violence to create successful masculine personas can possibly be seen as the boys' attempts to obtain some measure of control in their new environment.

"I grew up everywhere. I went to ten different schools before I finished eighth grade. Each time we moved, I had to establish myself in the neighborhood. I had to fight all the time because I had to keep proving that I was tough" (Julian, 24 year old Black man).

In addition to increased likelihood of childhood violence, these men were the least likely to have sustained and relationships from childhood. Thus, these men were the most likely to report serious difficulties in establishing trust. These men had learned a childhood lesson of mobility. When their adult relationships experienced difficulties, these men often revealed that they would leave the relationship. These men had also learned that employing violence would garner respect. Insights gained from social learning theory would argue that these men's child-hood experiences could contribute to the likelihood to use violence in their intimate relation-ships to secure respect.

> R: No, I don't have a lot of friends. You need to really know someone to consider them a friend. I moved a lot. I never got to make friends.
> I: How do you think that affects you now?
> R: I guess it makes me more likely to leave when things get bad. I don't see any reason to stay. There is always somewhere else that you can go (Jevon, 28 year old Black man).

According to the men in my sample, the biggest consequence of not having a father was the lack of guidance. If the men got into trouble, they had nowhere to turn for advice or for help. Previous research has indicated that the presence of a working father can provide their children more employment opportunities when the children grow up (Anderson 1999). Increased levels of viable employment are theorized to decrease poor men's use of intimate partner violence (Staples 1982; Williams 1998).

> "You need resources to survive. If I want to get myself together, I have no one to go to. My dad, uncles, older brothers, they are all locked up. It's all that I know" (Earl, 27 year old Black man).

> "These guys they have to learn it on their own. They have no men in their lives teach-ing them what to do. By the time they get in trouble, it's too late" (Adam, 49 year old Black man).

Men who grow up without fathers often attribute their lack of a "decent daddy" role model as a contributing factor in marital discord (Anderson 1999). Black men were slightly more likely than White men to mention that fathers were necessary for raising sons. An important difference by age emerged when examining the Black men's answers. Fifteen Black men discussed the importance of a man's presence for young boys, however 80% of the aforementioned Black men were men who were at least 30 years old. The younger Black men (under 30 years of age) were much less likely to discuss the necessity of fathers.

The men raised two factors that could mitigate the impact of an absent father. The first factor was the presence of a strong mother. Of the nineteen men who did not know their fathers, fifteen men credited their strong mothers as the most positive influence in their lives. White men and Black men from the Badlands were equally as likely to credit their mothers for their impact.

> "My dad wasn't there, but my mom was. She was my queen. My mom was strong and she kept all of us in line. She didn't need nobody to survive. I learned that from her" (Stephon, 29 year old Black man).

"I guess that I could have gotten into a lot of bad stuff growing up where I did. My mom was the reason that I finished high school. She was tough. She didn't let me mess up. She was like my mom and dad both. Without her, I would be in jail or dead by now" (Joey, 24 year old White man).

This heroic conceptualization of their mothers has impact for intimate partner violence. The women in their lives are often seen as failing to live up to the standard that men's mothers set.

"My girl is nothing like my mom. There is no way that my mom would do half the stuff that she did. Don't get me wrong. There is no way that my mom would think that it was ok to hit a girl. But that said, she would definitely see my baby's momma as nowhere near as good as she was" (Stephon, 29 year old Black man).

The second factor was the presence of alternate role model. The Black men were more likely to discuss finding someone in their immediate or extended family or someone who resides in the neighborhood to act like a surrogate father. These men were often referred to as "old-heads". The presence of old heads is often seen as a positive adaptation by the African American community to the lack of fathers (Anderson 1994; Payne 2006).

"You can find somebody to step up and fill in. There are old heads in every neighborhood. You just gotta find them" (Issac, 35 year old Black man).

"My father was never around. There was men on the block that knew my mother's father. They was the ones that stood up and took me to the baseball games. They were the ones that kept me from going in the wrong direction. They picked up the slack. My grandfather had to take care of a ton of kids. We never talked about it, but I could visibly see that this is what a man is supposed to do" (Burton, 41 year old Black man).

The importance of "old heads" in the inner city community is being undermined and their roles co-opted by "bad heads" (Anderson 1999). Due to continuing structural inequality, "bad heads" offer increased access to financial resources. Therefore, the men living in poverty often adopt male role models that espouse violence, control and intimidation.

For the White men, this surrogate father was most likely to be a stepfather. Unlike the positive relationships that the Black men described with old heads, for the White men these relationships were often a negative influence. Stepfathers seemed unable to fill the void of a biological father and were often a source of abuse, resentment and anger.

"My stepfather was abusive. I ran away from home from ages12-15. I stayed away until I was 15, until I was old enough to defend my mom and to defend myself. I got caught up in it" (Dwayne, 30 year old White man).

"I hated having a stepfather. He was always trying to be my dad and that was never going to happen. I hated to see him and my mom together. I used to just wish that my dad was still living with us" (Luke, 27 year old White man).

Perhaps stepfathers were perceived more negatively than "old heads" because stepfathers lived with the men. As a live in parent, stepfathers were more able to exert discipline and serve as controlling influences in the men's lives than non-residential "old heads" were.

PRESENCE OF A FATHER FIGURE

Since previous research revealed that high levels of family disruption increase the likelihood of intimate partner violence, the presence of a father could serve as preventive factor. Thirty-one men in my sample grew up with the father consistently present in their lives, even if there was a divorce. In fact, five men (10%) in the sample revealed that they were primarily raised by their fathers. Except for the men who revealed that they had experienced abusive childhoods, the relationships that men described with their fathers were mostly positive, but a present father often served as a disciplinary figure that exerted a steadying influence or a source of strict control. American culture has a historical tendency of relying on fathers to perform as the disciplinarians responsible for the most serious breaches of household rules and thus administering the harshest punishments (Rotundo 1993).

> "I was raised by my pop. He was a disciplinarian. He's the one who came after us when we did wrong. We had to keep good grades. We had to cook, clean and iron our clothes. We had to work. That's pretty much how I was raised. My father taught us about respect. Disrespect was not an option in our family. My thing was always that I was afraid of my pop finding out. I didn't have a lot of run-ins with the law until later in life" (Ron, 35 year old Black man).

> "When I was younger, I know that I feared my dad. He was like so strict. I was a total momma's boy. I ain't gonna lie. When I was three, he had taught me to read, write and do math. I credit him for making me as smart as I am. I could have been dumb if it wasn't for him. Growing up where I am from, I could have gotten into a lot of bad things if it wasn't for him. I give him credit for that" (Nathan, 23 year old Black man).

> "My dad was the one who made me do the right thing. I was afraid to let him down by messing up. If it hadn't been for him, I would have gotten into a lot more trouble when I was a kid" (George, 40 year old White man).

These men were the most likely to be raised in homes that employed traditional gender role schemas. Their mothers were responsible for the majority of childcare and housework, while their fathers were the primary breadwinners. The result of seeing discipline as a "man's job" has consequences for the men in their own intimate relationships and parental roles which will be discussed in later chapters.

In addition to discipline, fathers were also important sources of information on fighting techniques and resisting bullying. Forty percent of the men identified their fathers as their primary instructors on how to fight. Further, their fathers instilled in them the requirement to stand up for yourself physically when challenged.

"My dad showed me stuff when I was younger. He told me that you have to stand up, that you can't let people push you around" (Johnny, 21 year old White man).

"Men gotta be able to protect themselves. You learn that as a boy. My dad beat me for running from a fight. He said that men don't run. If I am going to get hurt then so is somebody else" (Isaac, 35 year old Black man).

Employing physicality when challenged has lasting impact on these men. One could argue that this childhood lesson followed the men into adulthood by condoning and conditioning the use of violence against women for challenging their masculinity.

For all the men in my research, their fathers provided models about masculinity. For the men who described positive relationships with their fathers, this model of masculinity was often an idealized version of fatherhood that they were failing to obtain. For the men who described negative relationships or no relationships with their fathers, these models were the antithesis of how they wanted to behave as fathers. A "decent daddy" is conceptualized as a man who supports his family and rules his household (Anderson 1999). "He is in charge of his family and has the respect of his woman and children; in exchange, he provides for them" (Anderson 1999:182). There are consequences for men defining fatherhood in these terms. The desire to control can often result in the use of violence against an intimate partner. This model of manhood can be seen as a contributing factor in the likelihood to employ intimate partner violence.

FIGHTING DURING CHILDHOOD

Men who grew up in the Badlands were more likely to describe themselves as boys who fought a lot. For these men, fighting provided many things: a source of social validation, an emotional release and insurance against being forced into future fights.

"When I was a kid, I thought that all that I had was my rep. If I lost face, it was just like losing my life. You gotta do what it takes to protect yourself. If you had a good rep, then everyone respected you" (Jake, 33 year old Hispanic man).

Social validation because of physical prowess is consistent with previous research. In what Katz (2006) refers to as the "tough guise" and Majors and Billson (1992) term the "cool pose", men in economically disadvantaged areas (the Badlands) develop a masculine persona that emphasizes toughness and the ability to intimidate. Payne's research (2006) with street-oriented men revealed that a central task to assure a successful masculine identity is obtaining respect and avoiding disrespect. This type of masculinity also relies on demonstrating exploitive and emotionally distant relationships with women.

Men who grew up in the Badlands also obtained an emotional release by fighting.

"Sometimes you're violent so that you don't have to think. It keeps you from having to think about other stuff in your life. If you stop to think, that is when you get hurt. There are no emotions and no time to think in fighting" (Nathan, 23 year old Black man).

"Fighting can be a way to release. If you hurt someone else, then you can let your own pain out" (Joey, 24 year old White man).

Men who grew up in the Badlands were taught to abide by a traditional gender script where men are not allowed to be emotional. The only acceptable emotion is anger and fighting provided a means to release the unacceptable emotions of pain, fear and disappointment disguised as the acceptable emotion of anger.

Finally, for men from the Badlands, fighting was seen as necessary and preventive. They reported that they had no choice about fighting. They fought mostly because they had to. If they were not willing to fight, then they would be subject to further instances of violence.

"To be a man, you don't want to be viewed as weak. You always want to be seen as strong. It is as simple as that. It is just how it is. Even though you know you don't have to be violent to be a man, there are so many more people who don't know it and you have to deal with them. I am not proud of my fighting. It's just the way that I had to be to make it" (Johnny, 21 year old White man).

Conceptualizing fighting as a necessity and not as a choice is the main difference between how men from the Badlands and men from the Highlands viewed fighting during childhood.

Unlike men from the Badlands, men (mostly White) who grew up in the Highlands view fighting as a choice. They described childhood fights as events they willingly engaged in. These fights were seen as conscious choices and thus imbued with much more significance. Men who grew up in the Highlands would describe childhood altercations in much greater detail, explaining motivations for fights and describing the outcomes of each these fights.

"So, I fought because I was in a bad mood and I gave people attitude hoping that they would want to put their hands on me. Sometimes that would happen. I actually don't think that I can count how many times that I have been in a fight. I am proud of it because fighting would make me feel a little bit better. Fighting was a release. Before I fought, I was the most nervous person in the world, but afterward because I would win, then I would feel a lot better" (Christian, 33 year old White man).

Men from the Highlands tended to fight less often than men who grew up in the Badlands. Fighting with peers often took the form of bullying. Men from the Highlands would routinely describe themselves as bullies and report high levels of personal satisfaction in their ability to intimidate and thus control others. Further, men from the Highlands were more likely to describe themselves as the initiators of the fight. Unlike in the Badlands, fighting was not seen as necessary and did not obtain a high amount of social validation but did secure a large degree of personal satisfaction. Previous research has shown that boys tend to use fighting and bullying as a means to release pain or stress (McGuffey and Rich 1999). The demands of hegemonic masculinity encourage boys to engage in behavior that draws attention to themselves (Bird 1996). Deriving personal satisfaction from intimidation and controlling others has obvious impact for intimate partner violence. Bullying other children taught these men that power and control could be obtained through intimidation.

ATTITUDES TOWARDS EDUCATION

Men's attitudes towards education are important for treatment of intimate partner violence. Amenability to treatment is a reflection of how the men approach education (see chapter seven). Further, increased levels of men's education serve as a deterrent to likelihood of engaging in intimate partner violence (Aldarondo et. al 2002). Higher levels of education result in higher income status and increased occupational prestige, which decreases likelihood of intimate partner violence (Baca Zinn and Eitzen 2005).

The men's attitudes towards education could be divided into three general types: favorable, unfavorable and indifferent. Twenty-eight percent of the men (14 men) described their overall impressions of school as positive. The majority of these men were from the Highlands (10 men out of 14) and a slight majority of the men were White (9 out of 14). Four men who were raised in the Badlands also had a favorable view of school. These four men were all Black. Fifty-six percent of the men had a negative attitude towards school. A slight majority of these men came from the Badlands and were Black (16 out of 28 men). The remaining twelve men who didn't like school were from the Highlands and were White or Hispanic. Finally, sixteen percent of my sample had attitudes towards school that could best be described as indifferent. All of these men were from the Highlands (8 men) and were White.

Positive attitudes toward school were often the result of doing well in school or from seeing school as an escape from the turbulence of the community. White men from the Highlands were the most likely to describe school as a positive experience due to their own personal successes.

"Of course, I liked school. I did really well. My good grades got my parents to let me do anything that I wanted" (Marc, 44 year old White man).

The men from the Badlands that liked school described school as an escape. This escape functioned in two ways. On the one hand, school was seen as a location where the men did not have to worry about being hurt. It provided eight hours when the men did not have to focus on violence and instead could relax.

"School was like paradise. Nobody messed with you. The only thing that you had to worry about was getting schoolwork done. Compared to worrying about getting beat up or killed in the streets, school was the best" (Eric, 35 year old White man).

School was also seen as an escape by providing the means to leave the Badlands and gain access to the Highlands.

"It was really important to my family that I did well in school. They always said that I was the smart one and that I could go to college and get to leave the hood" (Okezie, 26 year old Black man).

Negative attitudes towards education were attributed to school being seen as boring, as a breeding ground for violence, as a site of racism and failing to provide answers for any of the problems that they face in everyday life. The men from the Highlands who did not like school explained their animosity as the result of boredom. They described school as required and serving no purpose in their lives. These men often did well in school but derived no pleasure from their success.

The men from the Badlands who did not like school were much more nuanced in their reasoning. The main reason that the men from the Badlands gave for disliking school was that the school was a site of racial inequality that failed to address the lived experiences of young Black men.

> "I loved learning. I got really disappointed in school in the 9th grade. The school that I went to when I was little was in a White neighborhood. In 8th grade, they gave us business books that they gave me in the Black school in 11th grade. That turned me off from school. I seen racism for the first time kick me in the face" (Jamal, 55 year old Black man).

> "I think that the violence all starts with schools. There are no men, especially no men of color. Only women around ... school doesn't bring them reality ... It's hard to go to school where everyone is fighting and the teacher is sleeping. What's the point?" (Montee, 29 year old Black man).

> "You don't learn nothing in school. You learn more in the streets" (Joey, 24 year old White man).

The men's indifferent attitudes were all explained by viewing school as boring and thus un-fulfilling. The men who described school as boring often performed poorly but attributed their scholastic failure to the boredom inspired by an inadequate instructor/curriculum. Poor school performance has lasting consequences for intimate partner violence. Poor grades often resulted in dropping out of high school or choosing not to pursue college. Men with lower levels of education tend to be employed in lower paying jobs. Lower educational attainment and lower job status are often seen as risk factors for engaging in intimate partner violence (Anderson 1997; Baca Zinn and Eitzen 2005).

THE MEN'S VIEWS OF TODAY'S YOUTH

The continued impact of childhood socialization was evidenced when the men discussed the difference between their upbringing and "these kids today". A common theme that emerged in interviews with all Black men and White men who were raised in the Badlands was a condemnation of kids today. These men routinely contrasted their childhood behavior with the reckless and more dangerous violent behavior found in inner cities today. No matter how bad things were in the Badlands growing up, things are much worse now. Even the few Black men who grew up in the Highlands denounce the actions of inner city youths. These condemnations addressed three common themes: children have a damaged concept of time; children are not punished or forced to accept consequences for bad behavior and the increased likelihood to use guns instead of fists in fights.

The criticism that most men made about kids today involved children's inability to plan for the future. Many men in my sample felt that violence is more prevalent today because of a sense of fatalism: children expect to die before they reach adulthood. They will therefore engage in more risky behaviors during late childhood and early adolescence.

> "It's sad to me because they are so young and they are actually killing each other. To live to be twenty-six is old to them. Twenty-six is old so they do all they do at the young age. I seen a young kid who was ten smoking a cigarette like he was grown. Their time is messed up. They don't have no love. I grew up in the love zone. I grew up in the 1950s. The change came for us, but it didn't come for the newer generation. They didn't get it. If you read a book and skip the whole middle part and go to the end, that is what they did. They don't have no love. No compassion. The violence in their lives is normal to them. They grew up with that kid and they grew up together and now they are going to kill each other. Its normal for them" (Marvin, 62 year old Black man).

This acceleration into adulthood is consistent with previous research. Payne (2006) argues that inner-city youths are pressured to skip being a teenager in order to fiscally provide for their families' needs. These youths are more likely to engage in sexual behavior at an early age and to drop out of high school to get a job (Anderson 1999; Payne 2006).

> "It was totally fun. We got to be kids and have fun. Today, in this city it is not like that for brothers" (Walter, 42 year old Black man).

The second criticism of kids today involved the lack of perceived consequences for children's misbehavior.

> "That's another thing that don't happen now. Back then, you got your ass beat if you said something back. I can remember times that my grandmother would whip me for talking back. I dare not tell my dad, because he would beat me too. Being brought up that way, I knew consequences. *Kids today don't know consequences anymore.* I wasn't brought up to be sitting here (in treatment). Kids are like a sponge and kids today are being brought up to be sitting here" [emphasis added by interviewee] (Walter, 42 year old Black man).

This lack of punishment was the reason that the older Black men provided for the younger Black men's lack of success in treatment. It is interesting to note that even the younger Black men distanced themselves from kids today. Their own behavior is minimized by stressing the worse behavior of youth. Further, they stated that their amenability to treatment is evidenced by the fact that they were "raised better."

The final criticism men raised was the observation that children now employ guns to solve conflicts that previously would have been solved through fist fights.

> "It was just a lot of misbehaving. I don't think that kids were like killing each other. There was a lot of fights that were fist fights. This neighborhood was fighting this

neighborhood. Not like it is now. Now people don't fight no more. They just use guns. They won't fight each other. They just kill each other. That is what I see as different than when I was growing up" (Joe, 38 year old Black man).

I: Has the neighborhood gotten worse in your opinion?

R: It's the same to me. It is more violent in a way. I don't know like, I know like my generation as opposed to young buys who are growing up now. We probably would rumble or fight first, but they just go to straight grabbing guns.

I: How old are you?

R: I am twenty-three. To them, I am considered old. They are young boys because they were seventeen and in high school (Nathan, 23 year old Black man).

The increased likelihood to employ weapons was symbolic of the increased capacity of violence necessary to assure masculinity. Previous research has demonstrated that men and boys in the inner-cites are required to intensify their displays of public masculinity in order to obtain social validation (Katz 2006; Payne 2006). Increased likelihood to employ firearms could have lethal consequences for intimate partner violence.

All of the Black men regardless of class status and the White men who were in the lower class found it necessary to differentiate themselves from "kids today". Their own use of violence against women and against other men pales in their comparison to the violence of youth. The tendency to distinguish themselves from kids was present even in the men who were ages 18–25. Clearly, age is a factor that influences masculine identity and is a topic that must be addressed in studying intimate partner violence.

NOTES

1. … I differentiate between men who grew up in working class, middle class and upper class neighborhoods (The Highlands) and men who grew up in poverty (The Badlands). These names came from the respondent's self-description of their neighborhood.

2. While I briefly discuss the impact of neighborhood of origin here, greater attention will be devoted to the impact of neighborhood of current residence on IPV in a later chapter. Living in The Badlands or The Highlands characterizes men's responses/attitudes towards various social institutions including the criminal justice system, work, and education.

3. It is important to note that I did not ask any of the men specifically if they were abused. Rather, the men were asked what their relationship with their parent(s) was like and were asked to describe how they remember their parents' relationship. Since I did not ask the men specifically if they were abused, it is possible that more men were abused and chose not to reveal that abuse.

4. Although both middle class and working class men grew up in the Highlands, I distinguished between working class homes and middle class homes to better reflect more nuanced social class differences in the data.

NEGOTIATING PERSONAL IDENTITIES AMONG PEOPLE WITH AND WITHOUT IDENTIFIED DISABILITIES

THE ROLE OF IDENTITY MANAGEMENT

By Gerianne Merrigan

The 1990 passage of the Americans With Disabilities Act (ADA) focused national attention on disability issues in the United States. It also provided a historical marker for the disability civil rights movement, which has gained prominence in particular disability communities like Deaf culture and in able and disabled populations more generally (Barnartt, 1996; Long-more, 1995; Scotch, 1988). The ADA broadened the U.S. legal definition of disability considerably, and 43 million persons now fit in the category "Americans with disabilities" (Burnett & Paul, 1996), Furthermore, the ADA gave people with disabilities a bigger role in negotiating their own reasonable accommodations.

Today, people with and without identified disabilities have the opportunity to negotiate disability-related identity issues in their relationships, groups, and organizations. This selection focuses on the specific contributions of identity-management theory (Cupach & Imahori, 1993) to understanding some ways that people with and without identified disabilities negotiate personal identities. Conflicts arise when the identities held by people with disabilities violate the images others hold of them, or vice-versa. The interactions that result from incompatible identities and images often lead to face-threatening actions for one or more parties.

The first section of this selection introduces some of the specific, identity-related problems people with disabilities face when interacting with those who have no identified disability. The next two sections describe identity-management theory (IMT) as a way of addressing these problems, first by detailing the ways participants' cultural identities are cued in the relationship, and second by describing IMT's three-phase model of developing intercultural relationships. The final section outlines some possible ways to anticipate and resolve potential identity conflicts in interactions between people with and without disabilities.

(DIS)ABILITY-RELATED IDENTITY PROBLEMS[1]

Identity is a self-conception, one's theory about oneself (Cupach & Imahori, 1993). Identity management is accomplished for self-benefit. Impression management describes interlocutors' attempts to influence the images others hold of them (Tedeschi & Reiss, 1981). In this way, the identity of a person with a disability is not isomorphic with the images held of that person by others.

In this section, four identity-related problems are posed, each related to (dis)ability and identity. Goffman's influential (1963) *Stigma: Notes on the Management of Spoiled Identity* aptly characterized the first of these problems. Goffmao used *stigma* to mean "an undesired differentness," and he specifically listed "abominations of the body, the various physical deformities" as a source of stigmatization. Goffman called "those who do not depart negatively from the particular expectations at issue" *normals* (p. 5). Three additional problems discussed in this section arise from the persistent application of the stigma model, including face-threats, inadequate and incompetent support, and a lack of cultural cohesion among people with disabilities and between those with and without disabilities.

Stigmatizing Disability

The first identity-related problem for people with disabilities is that most disability research has been conducted under the medical pathology model, in which the definition of disability is rooted in health-related disease or defect (Silvers, 1994). This model reflects a conceptualization of relationships between disabled patients and abled health-care professionals, who know what is best for people with disabilities (Fine & Asch, 1988; Scotch, 1988). Rose (1995) and others have pointed out that the medical pathology model of disability is the source of many cultural conflicts about people with disabilities because it stigmatizes people with disabilities as defective and abnormal.

Bishop's (1986) study of the effects of training on verbal and nonverbal behavior and Sharkey and Stafford's (1990) study of turn-taking cues among congenitally blind adults are examples of communication research informed by this pathology model of disability. The researchers start with the assumption that blind people are unable to communicate competently, due to lack of sight, and then suggest that training may help blind people accommodate their behavior to appear competent in sighted terms.

MacLean and Gannon's (1995) research comparing two scales that measure attitudes of nondisabled people toward people with disabilities further illustrates the relationship of the pathology and stigma models: The authors identify as "highly problematical" their finding that the Interaction with Disabled Persons Scale (IDP) measures not only "discomfort" but also "sympathy" toward people with disabilities. They assert that discomfort underlies a negative attitude toward people with disabilities. Unfortunately, the responsibility of minimizing that discomfort usually falls on people with disabilities (cf. Royse & Edwards, 1989). In fact, Braithwaite and Labrecque (1994) identified seven strategies "persons with visible physical disabilities can use to manage the discomfort of ablebodied persons with whom they interact" (p. 289), such as modeling or using humor. Although such suggestions may help to produce more comfortable interactions for everyone involved, the need for such accommodations is most often prioritized from the perspective of the "whole" or "able" person, in what Silvers (1994) called the "tyranny of the normal" (p. 154).

Face-Threats

Brown and Levinson's (1978) anthropological treatise on the phenomena of politeness behavior provided a theoretic framework for the second (dis)ability-related identity problem, face-threats. Face is a communicator's claim to be seen as a certain type of person: Positive face refers to the desire to be liked and respected (Brown & Levinson, 1978). Lim and Bowers (1991) separated these two needs into fellowship and competence face, respectively. Negative face refers to a person's desire to be autonomous, or to avoid being intruded on (Brown & Levinson, 1978; Lim & Bowers, 1991).

Braithwaite's (1991) title, "Just How Much Did That Wheelchair Cost?" captured one instantiation of the sort of privacy violations, or autonomy face-threats, that are endemic to living with a visible disability. Her study of how privacy boundaries are managed by people with disabilities showed how central face-needs are to establishing personal identity. Braithwaite (1996) extended her argument by analyzing how individuals' identification with health, stigma, and cultural models of disability affected their personal identities. Her development of disability as a cultural category showed how face-threats can be negotiated via cultural competence and need not be essential to interactions between those with and without identified disabilities.

Johnson and Hammel (1994) transcribed in-depth interviews with nine people with spinal cord injuries and analyzed these participants' use of alignment actions, the accounts, disclaimers, and excuses interlocutors employ to present their behavior in culturally acceptable terms (Scott & Lyman, 1968; Stokes & Hewitt, 1976). By their nature, therefore, alignment efforts can be used to locate face-threats, or potential face-threats, Johnson and Hammel analyzed patterns of aligning actions used by the speakers, and concluded that self-disclosure and social critique were two forms of culturally suspect conduct among people with disabilities. When people with disabilities engage in this conduct, they risk threatening their interlocutor's face, so that self-disclosure and social critique become confined to in-group interactions among people with disabilities.

Incompetent and Inadequate Support

The third identity-related problem is the receipt of incompetent or inadequate social support by people with disabilities. Hart and William's (1995) participant-observation study of interactions between ablebodied instructors and physically disabled students in U.S. college classrooms induced "four predominant roles assumed by instructors who teach students with disabilities, including the avoider, the guardian, the rejecter, and the nurturer" (p. 144). Of these roles, only the nurturer's way of relating to students with disabilities was positive and enhanced their educational experience. In contrast, "guardian" teachers gave students with disabilities special intellectual and physical roles that resulted in lower performance expectations for the students. The teachers' attempts to address fellowship face, or belonging, actually threatened the students' competence face. Fine and Asch (1988) published a similarly discouraging report on the state of instructors' interactions with disabled students.

Cultural Cohesion

The fourth identity-related problem is one of cultural cohesion. People with disabilities have to address tensions between group cohesion within their disability-community and integration with nondisabled members of their mainstream cultural group(s).[2] For the past 4 years at San Francisco State University (SFSU), I have worked with a class designed to train students with disabilities in the Americans With Disabilities Act. Each semester, after the training was completed, I interviewed the students involved and asked this question: "What was the most rewarding aspect of the project for you?" The following response, from a student with learning disabilities, addressed the challenges of cultural cohesion:

> Meeting others with disabilities and learning more about their problems and not being so focused on my own. This helped me realize the global importance of the disability movement and that I needed to be more outspoken and responsive to the needs of others. ... In the past, I had interned with the Association for Retarded Citizens (ARC), and only saw clients as "them" or only saw their "otherness." I now realize that attitude kept me from connecting with them. ... This class has helped me understand the disability community needs to become united in order to give local, state, federal, and global equality. (I-P-2)[3]

Although this student explicitly addressed the problem of cultural cohesion with the disability community, his comments also implicated the other three disability-related identity problems discussed in this section, stigma, face-threats, and inadequate support. The next two sections show how Cupach and Imahori's (1993) IMT can help to address these problems. First, the distinction between cultural and relational identities is explicated and three cultural identity cues are explored. Then, the IMT's three-phase model of intercultural relationship development is presented.

IMT:CULTURALVERSUS RELATIONAL IDENTITIES

Cupach and Imahori (1993) conceptualized self-concept as having two facets: cultural identity and relational identity. Relational identity includes the cultural identities of both partners, as when two people from different national origins marry. Similarly, a relationship between someone with a disability and someone with no identified disability includes both partners' separate cultural identities as disabled and nondisabled.[4]

However, the partners' individual cultural identities become more and less situationally salient within the relationship, in part, due to the dynamics of three relational phases: (a) trial and error, (b) enmeshment, and (c) renegotiation. According to Cupach and Imahori (1993), these three phases are sequential necessities in developing intercultural relationships. IMT shows how conflicting cultural identities can threaten actors' competence, autonomy, and fellowship face, and prevent their relationship identity from developing beyond the initial trial-and-error phase. Competence, autonomy, and fellowship face needs exist in dialectic tension with one another and are cued by the scope, salience, and intensity of the participants' cultural identities. Therefore, before we can explore the phases of developing intercultural relationships, the tensions among these face needs and identity cues must be examined in detail.

Scope

The first cultural identity cue described by Cupach and Imahori (1993) is scope, which refers to the number of people who potentially share an identity. For example, scope may account for the ease of in-group communication among deaf people at Gallaudet, where most students, faculty, and staff use sign language. Similarly, Berkeley, California, is the home of the Independent Living Movement in the United States and a place of residence for many people with disabilities. Wheelchair users report that they are stared at less and interacted with more effectively in Berkeley than in other U.S. cities. This may be due to the sheer number and presence of people with visible disabilities: There is comfort in being among similar others, access to necessary services is improved, and the novelty effect of disability is lessened.

Salience

The second cultural identity cue, salience, refers to the relevance of one's cultural identity in a given situation or relationship (Cupach & Imahori, 1993). The fact that I see and my friend does not see becomes more relevant when we travel to areas we have not visited before, compared with negotiating familiar settings. Within a relational identity, the salience of a disability identification may be both diminished as novelty wears off and heightened as the stresses of living without walking, seeing, or breathing independently become progressively more apparent (see the third cultural identity cue, intensity, in the following section).

Furthermore, the salience of some cultural identities may be more flexible than that of a disability identity, which significantly affects daily living activities. For example, some people with nonvisible disabilities like alcoholism, HIV, or some learning disabilities, or who have low-level impairments like a mild hearing loss, can pass as able (Goffman, 1963), even within a relational identity. One blind student who had completed two 15-week classes in my department informed me, after our semester ended, that she had an identified learning disability in addition to being blind. She said she chose not to disclose the learning disability to me because, "that is just too complicated for professors to deal with" (O-P-11). She saw her learning disability as less salient. She felt she could cope with it on her own, whereas the blindness was more obvious and required more direct, apparent forms of accommodation such as carrying a cane and audio-taping lecture notes.

Salience is further highlighted in the following interview quotations from students who completed the ADA training program at SFSU. To one student, the campus was a more *salient* setting for ADA training than were small businesses: "I thought that more attention might be focused on changing campus attitudinal barriers rather than concentrating on 'other' organizations around the Bay Area" (I-P-2). Another student summarized, "Being able to implement this knowledge in my life and career will be the real value of the course to me" (I-P-9). Contrast his perception of the program's "real value" with a third student's view: "The most rewarding aspect for me was being able to have the opportunity to educate others about the ADA" (I-P-8). It is likely a matter of personal identity, rather than cultural category membership, that explains why the salience of the program was so different for these three students.

Intensity

The third cultural identity cue, intensity, "refers to the strength with which a particular aspect of the person's identity is communicated" (Cupach & Imahori, 1993, p. 10). For example, the legal and political aspects of disclosing one's disability in competitive situations like those necessitated by employment and higher education make voluntary self-disclosure of the disability an indicator of intense cultural identification. Likewise, immediate disclosure of one's disability, particularly when the disability is not directly relevant to the present interaction, may communicate that the disability is an intense aspect of an individual's cultural identity. Given the potential costs of disclosure and the option to pass or blend in, a person must identify strongly with their disability to disclose it voluntarily and immediately.

However, obvious markers like wheelchairs, respirators, and white canes can make a disability salient for the nondisabled novice observer, even when it is not an intense cultural identity cue for the person with the disability. People with disabilities are expected to take the perspective of the novice observer and empathize with his or her discomfort, or suffer the consequences of continual identity conflicts in which the disability is framed as more intense or more salient than desired. Obviously, the option to blend in, or pass as able (Goffman, 1963), is constrained for those with visible disabilities, at least during face-to-face interaction. That is one reason computer-mediated communication (CMC), is being lauded as a status-leveling technology by the disability community. With CMC, people with disabilities can interact without revealing their physical state (cf. Eckhouse & Maulucci, 1997; Matthews & Reich, 1993). It may be that CMC advantages people with disabilities by allowing them to manage the rate at which others develop an impression of them and their disability, whereas the impressions gained almost instantaneously during a face-to-face meeting make the disability cues too salient and too intense (see Walther, 1993).

IMT: DEVELOPING INTERCULTURAL RELATIONSHIPS

Cepach and Imahori (1993) theorized that the cultural identity cues of scope, salience, and intensity must be negotiated at each phase of the developing intercultural relationship. This section explores IMT's three relationship phases in detail, and demonstrates how competence, autonomy, and fellowship face needs exist in dialectic tension with one another at each phase.

Phase I: Trial and Error

The initial phase of an intercultural relationship is characterized by the parties' separatebut-salient cultural identities, and as such, challenges the participants to negotiate fellowship, or belonging needs, in balance with autonomy, or separateness, needs (Lim & Bowers, 1991). "A competent relationship emphasizes fellowship face when it is appropriate for the partners to be connected and autonomy face when it is crucial for the partners to be independent" (Cupach & Imahori, 1993, p. 128). Autonomy and independence have been highly valued in U.S. culture and in the disability rehabilitation field, and people with visible disabilities regularly experience being offered assistance when it is neither wanted nor needed; such offers threaten the competence and autonomy face of the person with disabilities, implying that he or she cannot function effectively and cannot be left safely alone.

On the other hand, disabled people who rely on others for assistance are judged as maladaptive or worse if they are seen as electing aid over functioning independently. For example, a person with multiple sclerosis or cerebral palsy might use a wheelchair because it affords greater mobility, in time and distance, than walking with crutches. However, if this person rises suddenly from a seated position and walks across the room, observers are likely to feel surprised and somehow offended. In fact, the observer's competence face has been threatened by the wheelchair rider's expectancy-violation. The sanction for such a face-threat often is to blame the victim, assigning him a less-than-pure motive for failing to behave in the expected fashion. Those with identified disabilities are expected to be independent, but only to a limited degree. If they are seen as too independent, their disability identity may be called into question.

The dialectic between autonomy and fellowship face may be the most salient and difficult tension to manage in intercultural relationships between able and disabled people. For example, leaders of the disability civil rights movement at Gallaudet University made substantive contributions to the development of the ADA and many seek its protection, at the same time attempting to isolate their disability-specific deaf culture (O-S-4). Deaf people's autonomy face needs, in this case, promoted their in-group cohesion, while their fellowship face needs encouraged integration with other disability groups. These conflicting needs make cohesion generally difficult between those with and without disabilities, in part because explicit discussion of potentially conflicting face needs is itself face-threatening. It may only be feasible after the relationship enters the enmeshment phase, when shared rules for discussing such delicate issues have emerged.

Phase II: Enmeshment

Cupach and Imahori's (1993) second phase of intercultural relationship development is enmeshment, in which both partners' separate cultural identities are joined by developing shared rules and symbols. In a January 1995 class at SFSU, I was seated next to a hearingimpaired student I had met in another context, but with whom I was not well acquainted. During our break in the class, he apologized for "sssh-ing" me during the lecture, when I had made a side comment. He said he "was having trouble hearing me and the lecture at the same time." This student reads lips and wears a hearing aid. When I responded by apologizing for not recognizing the problem before he pointed it out to me, he replied that I was, "one of about five people that he could lip-read or otherwise understand when they whisper" (O-P-3). This disclosure of a difference that I saw as positive, between our relationship and the relationships he had with most hearing people, confirmed my autonomy and fellowship face simultaneously. In our subsequent interactions in that class and in other contexts, we have been able to negotiate turn-taking and body orientation more-or-less seamlessly, and to the extent this happens successfully, our shared relational identity is each time confirmed.

Similarly, interlocutors in highly interpersonal, intercultural relationships in which one or both partners has a disability (e.g., a married couple) develop integrated rules systems; sometimes, the needs of the partner with the disability predominate, and at other times, the needs of the nondisabled partner predominate. Taking turns happens in all relationships, and is more of a distribution of justice than a true integration of the partners' separate identities. However, Cupach and Imahori (1993) do not address what happens when relational parties' perceptions of their interactions differ. A nondisabled person might leave an interaction with a person with a disability feeling that he or she has behaved competently, and the disabled person may feel that the nondisabled person has been inappropriate or ineffective. The two people may never even know that their perceptions differed. For example, because of rules accommodation, rather than actual coorientation, students with disabilities may never tell me, a nondisabled professor, that I have behaved incompetently. Accommodation, rather than true coorientation, is not addressed by Cupach and Imahori's second phase, relational enmeshment.

Phase III: Renegotiation

Cupach and Imahori's (1993) third phase extends beyond the developmeet of an enmeshed relational identity based on symbolic and rule convergence: "Competent interculteral interlocutors use their narrowly defined but emerging relational identity from the second phase as a basis for renegotiating their separate cultural identities" (p. 127). In this phase, interactants realize a "truly integrated relationship" (p. 127). They evaluate one another's separate cultural identities positively and regard themselves differently for having participated in that intercultural relationship.

Cupach and Imahori (1993) asserted that renegotiation of individual cultural identities allows more competent management of the dialectical tensions between competence, autonomy, and fellowship face needs. Consider a prevalent face-threat to people with visible disabilities—being stared at in public settings. For people with visible disabilities, staring may be a particularly salient face-threat, based on the inherent dialectic tension between competence and autonomy face. In the case of a temporary disability, autonomy face-threats may be more easily tolerated, because both parties know the face-threat is temporary. However, for someone with a permanent disability, the autonomy face-threat cannot be tolerated indefinitely, due in part to the burden of continuously educating disability-ignorant people.

SOLUTIONS FOR (DIS)ABILITY-RELATED IDENTITY PROBLEMS

Cupach and Imahori's (1993) IMT shows how people from different cultural identities can negotiate the face-threats inherent in their relationships, and go on to develop enmeshed relational identities and renegotiate their separate cultural identities. This section presents three possible solutions for identity-related problems among those who seek to develop (dis) ability intercultural relationships.

Emphasize Relational identities Over Cultural Identities

To emphasize relational identities means becoming aware of cues like scope, salience, and intensity—perceptual cues that can help to identify others' preferred identities, rather than one's own impression about who they are. Emphasizing relational identities also means treating people and relationships as unique, not as reliable representatives of any cultural category or categories. It means experimenting with the trial-and-error phase if we have had little experience with disability, and it means taking the risks needed to enmesh oneself in this intercultural communication. After all, errors are a requisite cost of initial intercultural interactions, despite the inherent threats they pose to fellowship face. If incompetence, paradoxically; is necessary along the road to competent, enmeshed intercultural relationships, perhaps short-term, local risks in each individual interaction are exchanged for long-term attitudinal change and development. Finally, emphasizing relational identities means renegotiating one's own self-concept as a result of these interactions.

Relating to others interpersonally, seeing others as "persons first" (Braithwaite, 1996) rather than through category memberships, is desirable and helps us appreciate one another as individuals with complex identities comprised of multiple categories. At a policy or societal level, however, where "people with disabilities are handicapped by attitudes toward them" (Hart & Williams, 1995, p. 151), the dilemma of separate or blended identities is not so easily resolved. Political identification with a cultural category leads to collective power, which is also desirable for those involved in the disability civil rights movement.

Anticipate Face-Needs and Learn to Repair Face-Threats

The second possible solution, face-work related to the salience of a disability, may be more a matter of interpersonal support than of mere cultural knowledge (Cupach & Imahori, 1993). The desire to support another's face by including him or her (fellowship), or by respecting his or her abilities (competence) can help interlocutors anticipate and avoid face-threatening acts. When face-threats do occur, apologies can help repair the damage (Scott & Lyman, 1968).

Some actions that are face-threatening in the trial-and-error phase can be face-supporting in the enmeshment or renegotiation phase of a relationship. For example, when I tease my friend about her mobility problems related to a childhood ankle injury, I support her competence and autonomy face simultaneously. The same verbal and nonverbal messages probably would be seen as face-threatening in an obligatory relationship; but when a friend singles a friend out as unique because she belongs to a particular group, cultural identity becomes salient in a complimentary way. This can and does backfire, of course, when interlocutors misjudge their level of friendship and receptivity to autonomy face support. From a neutral, unknown, or a negative relational partner, attempts to support autonomy face (i.e., uniqueness) and fellowship face (i.e., belonging) are more likely to be seen as face-threatening.

That the perception of face-threat or degree of threat rests with the disabled person in intercultural relationships is generally assumed (Silvers, 1994). A threat to autonomy or fellowship face is perhaps the most difficult face-threat to repair, especially if the parties fail to recognize what is causing the offense. For example, Adler and Rodman (1991) pointed out that reciprocal, voluntary self-disclosure is most effective in developing interpersonal relationships. Too much self-disclosure, too soon, or disclosures that are not reciprocated, threaten competence face. Yet, people with disabilities often are asked to disclose private information in medical and social settings in which nonreciprocal self-disclosure marks them as belonging to a special category, that is, disabled (Braithwaite, 1991; Thompson, 1982). This requested disclosure also threatens their fellowship face. The disabled person who seems reticent to disclose in great breadth or depth, or nonreciprocally, often is labeled as ill-adjusted or noncompliant. Ironically, that labeling amounts to an additional face-threat.

Allow the Paradox of Cultural Cohesion

A third possible solution to identity-related problems between people with and without identified disabilities is to actively embrace the paradox between cohesion within and across these distinct cultural groups. Those who seek to develop intercultural relationships need to recognize that bonding with similar others, or ingroup members, is as valuable as are interactions with those who are different from oneself, or outgroup members.

One student in the ADA project addressed the tension between cohesion and integration with nondisabled people after conducting a consultation with a campus student-services office: "When I told the lady behind the counter what a wonderful difference the changes made, and how pleased I was, she enthusiastically replied that the office staff is also very pleased with the changes. As a result of the modifications they also have more space and feel more comfortable" (O-P-1). This participant had cerebral palsy, and she walked with crutches or used a wheelchair. Her comment suggested cohesion and fellowship with the ablebodied staff members through expressed identification with similar values, in this case, for space and comfort.

However, the lure of cohesion, or fellowship face, may lead interlocutors to threaten one another's competence or autonomy face. For instance, ingratiating may be used to support another's competence face by giving compliments. Asking questions that promote disclosure of information about the other also may be used to support fellowship face. Both moves threaten autonomy face by freezing the other's cultural identity as a person with disability, thereby blocking other aspects of his or her identity from being realized in that interaction. The face-threat comes in trying to relate interpersonally but in the process locking onto cultural category differences (Cupach & Imahori, 1993). Similarly, highlighting differences when merging identities is desired can be counterproductive. Inferring that another cannot enact any role outside his or her (autonomous) cultural identity threatens both fellowship and competence face. Cupach and Imahori (1993) noted that balancing these dialectic tensions may only work across multiple encounters, so that episodic incompetence is repaired in the long run.

Gradual implementation of the ADA has exacerbated the fundamental tension between inclusion and respect regarding people with disabilities at work. Some attention to fellowship face in the form of "everyone here is equal" can come at the expense of competence face for the person with disabilities. Avoiding conflict, or "helping" a disabled person keep the job—in other words, inclusion on bases other than competence—eventually becomes a violation of fellowship face, and communicates lack of respect through deceit. However, addressing competence face-needs does threaten fellowship face, in some cases, to the point of relational dissolution.

There are no easy answers. Intercultural competence is a matter of individual and relational adaptation after an initial trial-and-error phase, and presumably, with the accumulated wisdom of multiple intercultural relationships over time (Cupach & Imahori, 1993). Relying on the broad category of "disability knowledge" will not help one interact effectively with an individual disabled person.

DISCUSSION QUESTIONS

1. What is the difference between a person's identity and image?
2. Why is it important to consider the issue of identity for people with disabilities, in addition to considering image?
3. Discuss the scope, salience, and intensity of your own cultural identity in your relationship with one other person (e.g., your significant other). How does your cultural identity impact this relationship?
4. For the relationship you identified in Question 3, Identify the relationship stage you have reached with this person: Are you "enmeshed" in a relational identity? Have you experienced renegotiation of self?
5. What [dis]ability identity problems have you experienced? What solutions have you tried? Describe your experiences.

REFERENCES

Adler, R., & Rodman, G. B. (1991). *Understanding human communication* (4th ed.)-New York: Holt, Rinehart, & Winston.

Barnartt, S. N. (1996). Disability culture or disability consciousness? *Journal of Disability Policy Studies, 7*(2), 1–19.

Bishop, V. (1986). Effects of training on non-verbal and verbal behaviors of congenitally blind adults. *Journal of Visual Impairment and Blindness, 73,* 1–9.

Braithwaite, D. O. (1991). "Just how much did that wheelchair cost?": Management of boundaries by persons with disabilities. *Western Journal of Communication, 55,* 254–274.

Braithwaite, D. O. (1996). "I am a person first": Different perspectives on the communication of persons with disabilities. In E. B. Ray (Ed.), *Communication and disenfranchisement: Social health issues and implications* (pp. 257–272). Mahwah, NJ: Lawrence Erlbaum Associates.

Braithwaite, D. O., & Labrecque, D. O. (1994). Responding to the Americans with Disabilities Act: Contributions of interpersonal communication research and training. *Journal of Applied Communication Research, 22,* 287–294.

Brown, P., & Levinson, S. (1978). Universals in language usage: Politeness phenomenon. In E. N. Goody (Ed.), *Questions and politeness: Strategies in social interaction* (pp. 56–97). Cambridge, U.K.: Cambridge University Press.

Burnett, J. J., & Paul, P. (1996). Assessing the media habits and needs of the mobility-disabled consumer. *Journal of Advertising, 25*(3), 47–59.

Cupach, W. R., & Imahori, T. T. (1993). Identity management theory: Communication competence in intercultural episodes and relationships. In R. L. Wiseman &. J. Koester (Eds.), *Intercultural communication competence* (pp. 112–131). Newbury Park, CA: Sage.

Eckhouse, R. H, & Maulucci, R. A. (1997). A multimedia system for augmented sensory assessment and treatment of motor disabilities. *Telematics and Informatics, 14,* 67–82.

Fine, M., & Asch, A. (1988). Disability beyond stigma: Social interaction, discrimination, and activism. *Journal of Social Issues, 44,* 3–21.

Goffman, E. (1963). *Stigma: Notes on the management of spoiled identity.* Englewood Cliffs; NJ: Prentice-Hall

Hart, R. D., & Williams, D. E. (1995). Ablebodied instructors and students with physical disabilities: A relationship handicapped by communication. *Communication Education, 44,* 140–154.

Johnson, G., & Hammel, J. (1994). *The negotiation of identity by persons with disability: The role of alignment actions.* Paper presented at the annual meeting of the Western States Communication Association, Portland, OR.

Johnson, G., & Albrecht, T. (1996). Supportive structures for people with disabilities: Smoothing or smothering the way? In E. B. Ray (Ed.), *Communication and the disenfranchised* (pp. 433–447). Mahwah, NJ: Lawrence Erlbaum Associates.

Lim, T., & Bowers, J. W. (1991). Face-work: Solidarity, approbation, and tact. *Human Communication Research, 17,* 415–450.

Longmore, P. (1995, September/October). The second phase: From disability rights to disability culture. *Disability Rag,* 4–11.

MacLean, D., & Gannon, P. M. (1995). Measuring attitudes toward disability: The interaction with disabled persons scale revisited. *Journal of Social Behavior and Personality, 10,* 791–806.

Mathews, J. T., & Reich, C. F. (1993). Constraints on communication in classrooms for the deaf. *American Annals of the Deaf 138,* 14–18.

Rose, H. M. (1995). Apprehending deaf culture. *Journal of Applied Communication Research, 23,* 156–162.

Royse, D., & Edwards, T. (1989). Communicating about disability: Attitudes and preferences of persons with physical handicaps. *Rehabilitation Counseling Bulletin, 32,* 203–209.

Scotch, R. K. (1988). Disability as the basis for a social movement: Advocacy and the politics of definition. *Journal of Social Issues, 44,* 159–172.

Scott, M. B., & Lyman, S. W. (1968). Accounts: The use of alignment actions. *American Sociological Review, 33,* 46–62.

Sharkey, W. R, &. Stafford, L. (1990). Turn-taking resources employed by congenitally blind conveners. *Communication Studies, 41,* 161–182.

Silvers, A. (1994). "Defective" agents: Equality, difference, and the tyranny of the normal. *Journal of Social Philosophy, 25,* 154–175.

Stokes, R., & Hewitt, J. P. (1976). Aligning actions. *American Sociological Review, 41,* 838–849.

Tedeschi, J. J., &. Reiss, M. (1981). Verbal strategies in impression management. In C. Antaki (Ed.), *The psychology of ordinary explanations of social behavior* (pp. 271–309). New York: Academic Press.

Thompson, T. L. (1982). Disclosure as a disability-management strategy: A review and conclusions. *Communication Quarterly, 30,* 196–202.

Walther, J. (1993). Impression development in computer-mediated interaction. *Western Journal of Communication, 57,* 381–398.

NOTES

1. The brackets in "[dis]ability" are used here to heighten the reader's awareness of the political nature of this term. The prefix "dis-" means "the opposite of " (Webster's New World Dictionary, 2nd ed.); but in fact, many [dis]abilities are defined more by social and cultural biases about a particular ability than by the lack (or limitation) of the ability, per se. For example, some deaf people do not consider themselves [dis]abled. They simply cannot hear.

2. I believe strongly that people with and without disabilities share this burden. However, when people with no identified disability fail to seek out cohesion with disabled people, it becomes the responsibility of people with disabilities, if they seek the benefits of effective in-and out-group relationships (see Johnson & Albrecht, 1996, for a more detailed discussion of this issue).

3. Each quotation taken from the ADA training project at SFSU was coded to identify the data source (i.e., S = survey; O = observation; or I = interview) and speaker's role (i.e., P = participant; S = staff member), while protecting confidentiality and anonymity. Each speaker was assigned an identification number so that quotes from a single speaker can be identified by the reader. For example, the code "S-S-l" indicates a quote taken from survey data, by staff member 1).

4. The students enrolled in the ADA class demonstrated symbolic convergence around the terms *disabled* and *disability community,* and rejected the term *handicapped.*

FOCUS ON TATTOOING AND MASCULINITY

By Eve Shapiro

Tattooing is an increasingly prevalent form of intervention into the body in North America. As a technology—it is after all a clear intervention into the natural body—tattooing has changed very little over the past several thousand years. Save for one significant innovation in the late 1890s when the tattoo machine was created, the principles and basic methods have remained the same. Tattoos are created by inserting ink (natural or synthetic) under the dermis layer of skin using needles (which historically could be made of a variety of materials such as shells, bone, quills, and metal). Because tattoos are pictorial and/or word images literally written on the body, they alter the embodied landscape of individuals. In addition, because of the body-identity connection assumed in contemporary body ideologies, these inscriptions are assumed to have significance for the individual (Giddens 1991). Yet, the social meaning of tattoos has changed drastically over the past 150 years, and these changes have concurrently shaped the meaning and import of tattoos for individuals. Tattoos are part of a historical process of continual redefinition and negotiation of gendered terms, especially within the context of masculine identities.

In contemporary North American society tattoos are viewed as meaningful acts of identity building on personal expression. For example, television shows such as *Miami Ink* on The Learning Channel document acts of narrative identity formation, often profiling the personal stories behind a client's tattoo. Because of these expectations individuals are called on to narrate the meaning of a tattoo for themselves and others and they do so using the social scripts available (Kosut 2000). Sociologist Mary Kosut elaborates on this relationship and explains that,

Although tattooing is a way to construct one's body and self in one's own desired image, it is also a phenomenon that reflects cultural influences. An important characteristic of the tattoo as a form of communication is that it largely "speaks" through non-verbal transmission.

(2000: 80)

The stories individuals tell about their tattoos are the product of both the internal self and embodied experience and are shaped by the dominant beliefs and scripts of the day. Personal and societal meaning-making about tattoos comes from the interaction of a number of social forces: dominant ideologies for bodies and gender, social scripts for acceptable bodies and identities, technologies of tattooing, and the bodies and identities of individuals within a group or society.

An example of this complex play of forces is tattoos within gangs (a particular social context with its own social scripts for behavior). Gang tattoos take highly regimented forms as a way of communicating to others an individual's personal experiences within the group, such as their history of violence, loss of loved ones, and sense of loyalty. Each element of the tattoo holds a range of meanings, depending on its location on the body and the symbols contained therein.

In different eras social scripts for tattooing in North America have labeled bodies as beautiful or deviant, military or criminal, aristocratic or working-class. Tattoos have been used by individuals as accessories, badges, and to symbolize among many other things social status, rites of passage, community affiliations, personal triumphs and tragedies, racial, ethnic, political, sexual, and gender identities. Tattoos have also been deeply gendered; scripts for men's and women's tattoos have distinct forms and conventions in North America as well as in many other cultures that practice tattooing. Examining tattooing as a gendered technology reveals a lot about how gendered bodies and identities are in dynamic relationship to new technologies and social scripts.

Tattooing dates back to 6000 B.C.E. and has been present in many cultures around the world. Early European explorers came into contact with tattooing practices among the Moors (North African peoples) as well as within indigenous communities in Central and South America and on the Pacific Islands. Tattooing was not adopted by European explorers until the mid-eighteenth century, however, when sailors and merchants began acquiring tattoos during their travels. The practice became more widespread in the West after Captain James Cook named the practice and brought several natives from the South Pacific back to Europe with him. As trade and colonization accelerated, tattooing was increasingly practiced in Europe and the North American colonies. Simultaneously increased contact with Japan in the late nineteenth and early twentieth centuries introduced Westerners to classic Japanese tattoo art, a much more artistic and graphic style than that which dominated in Europe and North America. During this time tattooing was almost exclusively practiced on men. Even though women in other societies such as the Ainu of Japan practiced tattooing, in the West, tattooed women were extremely marginalized.

Tattoos themselves carried with them information about man's trade—adventurer, merchant, rebel, or sailor—and in the process reinforced the meaning tattoos had within the society. Because the men who donned tattoos in the 1800s were from a social stratum associated with radical politics and social non-conformity, these characteristics came to be associated with tattoos as well. In other words, tattoos conveyed ideas not only of the specific gendered and classed identity of the subject but also his social and political affiliations. For these very reasons men who were free thinkers, radicals, and outlaws embraced the tattoo and its associations; it is this mutually constitutive process that is at the heart of how new technologies reshape bodies and identities in conversation with other social forces.

For a brief period of time (from the late 1800s to early 1900s) the European gentry was enamored with tattoos. While it had been the purview of sailors (by choice) and criminals (by force), tattoos became all the rage among upper classes in these few decades. A number of European royalty were tattooed including Prince Waldo-mar of Denmark, Grand Duke Alexis of Russia, Queen Olga of Greece, and King Oscar of Sweden (DeMello 2000; Fisher 2002; Sanders 1989). This trend was part of a larger fascination with all things "native" and "primitive" sparked by the expanding European colonization of Pacific and American lands. It was in the midst of this tattooing fad that the practice came to North American White communities (it was prevalent among some indigenous groups long before then). Both wealthy men and some women were tattooed but these tattooing practices and motifs differed from one another, just as they differed from the prevailing lower-class styles and customs. These differences were the product of differences in social scripts and embodied identities available to men and women of different social classes.

Tattoos were employed by elite individuals to inscribe markers of aristocratic status on the body. An article that appeared in the *Boston Morning Journal* in 1897 emphasizes the very classed nature of the tattoo fad of the late 1800s:

> Have you had your monogram inscribed on your arm? Is your shoulder blade embel-
> lished with your crest? Do you wear your coat-of-arms graven in India Ink on the
> cuticle of your elbow? No! Then, gracious madame and gentle sir, you cannot be *au
> courant* with society's very latest fad—the tattooing fad. It has just reached New York
> from London and Paris. It may develop into a mania.
>
> ("The Tattooing Fad" 1897)

By emphasizing its European roots and suggesting that individuals inscribe their crest or mono-gram, the article makes clear that this type of tattoo was associated with both cosmopolitan fashions and aristocratic genealogies in the late 1800s.

By the early 1900s tattooing had once again become highly contested and over the next sev-eral decades lost social status and became associated with marginal subcultures. This shift was due in part to the increased access working-class individuals had to tattooing with the advent of the electric tattoo machine; the more accessible tattoos were, the less elite they became (Fisher 2002). In 1891 the tattoo machine was patented by Samuel O'Reilly and this made the tattooing process more efficient while less costly and painful. In addition, at the turn of the century, a number of criminologists began to hypothesize that tattoos were proof of criminal intent or propensity. While forced tattooing of prisoners in Europe had fallen out of fashion, criminal connotations persisted and voluntary tattooing was seen as proof of deviance. At the same time public health campaigns linked tattooing to sexually transmitted diseases; some doctors went as far as to claim that tattoos were external representations of pathology and deviant proclivities. According to criminologists the tattoo was a stigmata of as-yet uncommitted crimes, and accord-ing to medical experts the tattoo was a symptom of as-yet undiagnosed disease.

This connection between tattoos and both mental and physical pathology has carried over into some current social science and medical research and into popular culture (Armstrong and Murphy 1997; Braithwaite et al. 1999; Koch et al. 2005). These enduring legacies continue to shape the meaning of tattoos and the social scripts that govern their gendered embodied significance. For example, tattoos are often used in literature and film as shorthand for a man's shady past, questionable character, or ill intent and a woman's lack of femininity or morality. In the 1951 Tennessee Williams' play *The Rose Tattoo* (made into an eponymous film in 1955), the main character's husband, a truck-driver who smuggles contraband, has a rose tattooed on his chest. When he is shot and killed by the police, his wife discovers not only his illegal activities but also his adultery. By the play's end, the tattoo in the play's title symbolizes the husband's double deceptions.

By the mid twentieth century, tattooing was most common among young military and working-class men in North America, and primarily featured military, death, and pinup imagery. Small tattoos were often used like badges to mark significant events, and the tattooing session itself was one such event. Surviving the pain of tattooing is viewed as evidence of machismo or manliness, and it is this willingness to accept the pain that has historically situated tattooing as a rite of passage for men (often at puberty or adulthood) within a variety of cultures world-wide (Janssen 2005). Many of the qualities defined as central to masculinity within dominant social scripts, including bravery, endurance, and immunity to pain, are qualities tested in the act of acquiring a tattoo. These qualities are available to men regardless of social class and historically tattoos were a way for lower class men to compensate for their compromised masculinity. Because many of the socially sanctioned markers of masculinity (e.g. a high paying job, material wealth, and social power) were out of reach for poor men, they drew on tattooing and its related masculine social scripts to bolster their sense of manhood (Halnon and Cohen 2006).

In the West this has been particularly true within military groups. Tattooing in the military is a longstanding practice. The first professional tattooist in the United States was Martin Hildebrand who traveled around during the American Civil War tattooing both Union and Confederate soldiers in what was likely the first widespread use of tattoos by soldiers. Hildebrand's tattoos were primarily political and patriotic images that made explicit for which side, North or South, the soldier fought (Govenar 2000). The practice of tattooing in the armed forces continued to be widespread into the twentieth century, according to tattooist Charlie Wagner, profiled in the *New York Times* in 1943: "Fighting men want to be marked in some way or another. High-class fellas, too—men from West Point and Annapolis. Sailors used to be my big customers, but now it's soldiers" (Cumming 1943: 38).

Today, different branches of the military claim particular symbols, tattoo locations, and rituals so that the whole experience, from the act of getting the tattoo (which symbolizes bravery) to the images inscribed (symbolizing dedication to the group) connect an individual to his military "brothers." For example, the U.S. Marines often have a blade and skull tattooed onto their left shoulder while Navy sailors use an anchor. Sociologists Coe, Harmon, Verner, and Tonn interviewed military college cadets and found that for these men getting a tattoo was a social bonding act done in groups and used to mark their membership in the community (Coe et al. 1993). Both the cost and the pain of the tattoo were sources of pride and the men's sense of masculinity.

Similarly, research suggests that tattooing is a significant social practice within other men's groups and communities in North America (DeMello 2000). Tattoo scholar Janine Janssen argues that, for many men:

> A tattoo is not only a form of establishing an identity (e.g. as a sailor or biker), there is also a relationship between tattoos and male bonding. By wearing a specific tattoo they can show each other and the rest of the world what kind of men they are (e.g. gang members or soldiers). Not only the final result—the tattoo—but also the process of "inscribing" the body can be a manner for expressing one's masculinity.
>
> (Janssen 2005: 185)

Not only do they select a single design in common, these men will have their tattoos done as a group, suggesting a ritualistic quality to the tattoo process. Examples like this illustrate how the technology of tattooing, informed by the social norms and scripts of an era, has been used in the service of gendered body and identity work (Phelan and Hunt 1998). In North America masculinity has intertwined with tattooing in a variety of ways including in its historical legacy and enduring social meanings, in the process of acquiring a tattoo, its location, and the imagery it contains.

In the post-World War II political and social climate that stressed conformity to White middle-class values, tattoos were increasingly disparaged. By mid-century tattooing had been taken up by prison and motorcycle gangs and came to symbolize violent, rebellious masculinities. The historical legacy of tattooing links the act to archetypical masculinities, however (e.g. sailors, soldiers, Popeye, and the Marlboro man). Even though tattoos were held in distaste in the 1950s, their connection to idealized masculine figures in these advertisements created a tattoo craze. For example, in the 1950s and 1960s Marlboro cigarette ads featured cowboys, musclemen, and suave debonair men with Marlboro eagle tattoos on their hands (Fisher 2002). Concurrently, the conventionalized form of these tattoos, drawn from media or trademark imagery, tended to reinforce dominant paradigms of masculinity, such as rugged independence and physical strength. It was only in the midst of the 1970s' social change movements that tattooing began to be revived as an acceptable form of bodily manipulation. In this era of anti-establishment attitudes and rejection of authority, the tattoo was reclaimed, and many counter-culture musicians and celebrities sported highly visible tattoos. The tattoo was burnished with rock-and-roll glamor.

Since then both the number of individuals soliciting tattoos and the stigma associated with the practice have shifted considerably. A recent national survey conducted by the Pew Research Center estimated that 36 percent of the U.S. population between the ages of 18 and 25 and 40 percent between 26 and 40 had at least one tattoo. Estimates for Canada are similar (Hawkes, Senn, and Thorn 2004). Not only is this figure a large proportion of the North American population, but it points to a dramatic increase in the use of this particular body technology; in the same survey only 10 percent of individuals between 41 and 64 years old reported ever getting a tattoo (Pew Research Center for People and the Press 2007). Charting the same generational shift, survey data from the early to mid-1990s estimated that fewer than 3 percent to 10 percent of the U.S. population had a tattoo, while a 2006 survey found that 24 percent of individuals under 50 had one (Armstrong and Murphy 1997; Laumann and Derick 2006).

A more detailed analysis highlights how these changes are also deeply gendered. Historical data points to a dramatic disparity in rates of tattooing between men and women. The stigma attached to tattooed women has been much stronger than that attached to men. In one 1950s account of tattoo culture, for example, tattooist Samuel Steward recounted that he personally refused to tattoo women unless they were 21, married, and had permission from their husbands (Steward 1990)! Certainly not all tattooists were this blatantly sexist, but statistics do suggest that women accounted for a small minority of tattoo clients up until the 1970s. Even by the late 1990s Copes and Forsyth estimated that while between 10 percent and 20 percent of men in the United States were tattooed, only 7 percent of women were (Copes and Forsyth 1998). In contrast several surveys conducted in the early 2000s found no significant differences in rates of men and women clientele; women were requesting tattoos at rates even with those of men (Laumann and Derick 2006; Pew Research Center for People and the Press 2007).

The increasing parity between men and women tattoo-ees does not erase, however, the gendered aspects of tattooing or the particular function tattoos continue to play in relation to masculinity. A number of scholars have documented how tattoos on men and women are interpreted in vastly different ways boosting masculinity while threatening femininity (Hawkes, Senn, and Thorn 2004). There are also significant differences in the placement and imagery of tattoos between men and women. For example, while women are more likely to situate a tattoo on a part of the body that is easily covered, men often select a highly visible area that is associated with male secondary sexual characteristics, such as biceps and forearms (Fisher 2002: 100). Th e imagery in men's tattoos is also often chosen to represent masculine traits including toughness, individuality, and braveness. The scale of men's tattoo designs is usually large too. In their study of young British men Rosalind Gill, Karen Henwood, and Carl McLean found that men turned to tattooing in part as an effort to publicly stake claim to particular identities (Gill, Henwood, and McLean 2005). In a historical moment when men's bodies are under increasing scrutiny but, simultaneously, men are not supposed to care about their looks, body work is fraught with tension for men. Young men "must simultaneously work on and discipline their bodies while disavowing any (inappropriate) interest in their own appearance" (Gill, Henwood, and McLean 2005: 38). As a result of these constrained social scripts for acceptable masculinity, Gill, Henwood, and McLean argue that young men make sense of tattoos as identity and community-focused endeavors. Moreover, they found that the available social scripts for young men's masculinity were so limited that although all the young men interviewed espoused personal reasons for getting a tattoo, their narratives were surprisingly uniform.

Drawing together this range of scholarship makes evident how the technology of tattooing has been both shaped by and influential in social scripts for masculinity and individuals' embodied experiences. Sociologist Paul Sweetman summarized that:

> As corporeal expression of *the self,* tattoos and piercings might thus be seen as instances of contemporary *body projects* (Shilling 1993): as attempts to construct and maintain a coherent and viable sense of self-identity through attention to the body and, more particularly, the body's surface (Featherstone 1991).
>
> (Sweetman 1999: 53)

As body projects, tattoos carry with them legacies of social signification about men, masculinity, and social class. Whether upper-class men in the 1900s tattooing their elite lineage, or 1850s sailors charting their travels, tattoos have been purposefully used by men to establish and reinforce their manhood. These legacies, built out of dominant ideologies about the gendered body and self, have in turn shaped the use of this technology by different groups of men over time.

DISCUSSION QUESTIONS

1. How might the pain involved in the tattooing process impact the meaning ascribed to individual tattoos and tattooing?
2. How does the development of tattoo removal procedures impact the meaning behind tattooing as a practice?
3. Think about other forms of bodily modification, either permanent or temporary, practiced by men in the United States today. How is masculinity defined by these practices? Has the meaning of these practices changed over time? Is the meaning different for different groups of people?

MAKING WELFARE STIGMA

By Daniel Dohan

n the United States, public assistance is uncommon yet controversial, its economic impact joined by its symbolic significance.[1] Originally intended to support a narrowly defined group of "deserving" Americans, such as workers injured on the job and the children of widows, public aid has increasingly gone to people Americans think of as "undeserving," such as working-age men and never-married mothers.[2] This use of aid concerns Americans who fear that the availability of aid may act as a perverse incentive that encourages the able-bodied to shirk work or the morally sound to eschew marriage.[3]

What I have shown so far about public aid in the barrios addresses parts of this controversy. Aid in the barrios did not tempt residents away from their jobs or entice them to avoid marriage. Barrio residents came to rely on public aid as a result of bad luck and tragedy, as I showed in Chapter 8, not as a result of calculations of economic self-interest. Residents did not see aid reliance as a sensible way to make do or get ahead economically, and they did not see aid as a reasonable alternative to a steady job or stable marriage.

Even if aid did not constitute a perverse economic incentive, however, it could have negative social and cultural consequences of other kinds. Means testing can isolate and disempower aid recipients; recipients can constitute a negative role model to others; and public largesse to the "undeserving" appears to violate cardinal American norms and values of self-reliance and individual responsibility.[4] The concern, in short, is that even if aid does not constitute a perverse incentive to reject mainstream culture, it could nevertheless foster a troubling isolation between cultural orientations in low-income communities and those of mainstream America.

In this chapter, I focus on this concern by analyzing the role of public aid in everyday social and cultural life in the barrio. I address several questions. How did welfare requirements affect interpersonal relationships in the barrios? Did welfare use by some negatively affect everyone?

If public aid, *prima facie,* violates cultural norms and values of self-reliance and personal responsibility, how did this affect barrio culture as a whole?

To address these questions, I describe the meanings of public aid among the residents I knew in the low-income barrios. I focus in particular on how these meanings organized themselves into subcultures that informed residents' behavior and outlook toward welfare. In my experience during fieldwork, barrio residents championed ideals of self-sufficiency and personal responsibility, but in everyday interactions and conversations residents constructed the meaning of "self-reliance" and "personal responsibility" in different ways. At times, they saw "selfreliance" and "personal responsibility" as strict standards of behavior to be applied to everyone all the time. According to this view, welfare was universally unacceptable, and residents who subscribed to this view expressed a Manichaean disapproval of aid and aid recipients. At other times, residents applied the norms of "self-reliance" and "personal responsibility" more flexibly. They recognized that some forms of public aid received by some people under certain circumstances were understandable and even acceptable; framed this way, welfare stigma was selectively applied and open to contestation.

In the particular structural circumstances of Guadalupe and Chávez barrios, the meanings of welfare organized themselves into subcultures with their own dynamics and their own influence on everyday life. In Guadalupe, where relatively few residents had suffered the bad luck and tragedy that led to welfare reliance, the universal and Manichaean view of welfare prevailed. In Chávez many residents had the misfortune to end up reliant on aid, and selective and contested meanings of self-reliance and personal responsibility commonly held sway. I see these differences in welfare cultures in the two barrios as an exemplar of how culture actually works in everyday life—of subcultures in action. In this chapter I lay to rest fears that receiving aid undermined the values of residents in the low-income barrios by carefully examining how residents in Guadalupe and Chávez used their culture to make sense of aid receipt in everyday life. I document a lot of variation in how residents made sense of aid receipt. This variation reminds us that culture is not a static set of values and norms but rather a dynamic set of behaviors, talk, habits, and orientations. Differences in how barrio residents used and made sense of public aid reveal culture operating in everyday life, not a troubling isolation from mainstream norms and values.

UNIVERSAL STIGMA

Most of the residents I knew in the barrios viewed public aid the way Americans are supposed to view aid—as wrong under any circumstances. They expressed this view in confidential comments about family, friends and neighbors who received public aid as well as in direct confrontations with aid recipients. Even when recipients turned to aid during a time of temporary economic dislocation or following a major disruption in income generation, many barrio residents remained steadfast in their belief that welfare use remained unacceptable and unexplainable.

Confidential or behind-the-back comments often provided the opportunity to criticize welfare receipt and recipients. Without the recipient there to explain him- or herself, reasonable explanations of aid receipt could be quickly dismissed and discounted, as the following conversations in Guadalupe barrio illustrate. The conversations took place in July 1994, when I joined Rosa, Chela, Verónica, and Carmen—the heart of the *convive* group—at a children's play date they had arranged in a Guadalupe park.

José Mendoza is going to drop me off at the park on his way to work. In the car, he tells me that work has been slow recently. He's gone home at 6:00 every day this week, so he's losing two to three hours of wages a day. "A lot of people are on vacation right now. So that means that no one is putting in new orders." At the park, the *convive* ladies are gathered around a shady picnic table with a clear view of their children in the sandy play area. José greets them, and when Rosa asks why he isn't working he tells her how slow work has been. He leaves a few minutes later to resume his trip to work.

When José is out of earshot, Rosa turns to Chela and says that she saw José down at the food bank the other day. "They gave him some money to buy food at Lucky's [supermarket]," she says disapprovingly. "About $100 a month. It wasn't the first time. I don't know how long he's been getting it but it has been a while." Chela looks surprised, and shaking her head remarks, "*De veras?*" with a disapproving click of her tongue.

Rosa and Chela's comments illustrate a truism in both Guadalupe and Chávez: when recipients were not present to explain themselves, residents felt free to ignore the context of aid receipt. Rosa and Chela knew that José had turned to the food bank when forces beyond his control had reduced his wages. Moreover, Rosa knew José and his family well, and she knew the long hours his entire family worked in low-wage jobs. Experience could have told her that José's use of assistance would be brief—as it was—and that he would soon make ends meet through work—he did so by obtaining false papers. Had José remained at the park, he could have corrected the impression that Rosa created of his aid receipt. But by the time Rosa spoke her mind about his aid receipt, José was already on his way to work.

The barrio residents I knew expressed particular suspicion about recipients who relied on aid as a primary source of income or received aid for long periods of time. Later that same July afternoon, I walked with the women and their children from the park toward the apartment buildings where most of them lived, and the group passed by Señora Lupe's house. Someone asked where the *señora* was that day, and Rosa said that last night her son had been in an accident—maybe a broken arm—and she was at home taking care of him. Verónica looked annoyed. "What I don't understand," she said. "Is why can't her husband take care of him? He's home all day anyway." Nodding her head in agreement, Carmen said that when the group met at Señora Lupe's house a few weeks earlier, her husband seemed perfectly fit—remember how he had chased the kids all over the backyard that day? Raising her voice above the noise of the traffic, she said, "It is a disgrace for them to get welfare. He needs to leave the house and get back to work."

In Chávez barrio, where more residents relied on public aid, private gossip about aid recipients arose frequently and sometimes unexpectedly, as it did one Monday night in the back seat of my car. I was driving toward Chávez with Marco, a twenty-one-year-old father, and Ben, whose fiancée was at that moment six months pregnant. Marco missed his daughter, whom he had seen infrequently in recent weeks, and he blamed his girlfriend. "She's a real bitch," he said, referring to his daughter's mother. "She don't get along with her mom but she still won't call me up when she needs a baby-sitter. She'll just leave her with whoever." Ben replies that when his child is born, he's not going to have any problems like that because he will spend lots of time with his child. "That's what you say now," counters Marco.

"But just wait until the baby's here. You watch what happens. That's what happened to me. I was taking care of the baby. Then, she decides she wants to get on aid. So, now she just stays at home all day doing nothing. She says she can't go to school even because there's no one to look after the baby. But she won't even let me see her, and she won't let her mom. She's just lazy. She wants to stay home and do nothing all day. You'll see what happens. It's not so easy."

In both Guadalupe and Chávez, gossip about aid recipients ranged from the disapproving side comments that Chela and Rosa leveled against José to Verónica and Marco's personal attacks on recipients' motivations and behavior. Confidential comments reflected an atmosphere of Manichaean disapproval of aid in both barrios, and they provided ready opportunities for residents to express disapproval toward recipients. At the same time, the Guadalupe and Chávez residents I spent time with did not confine their criticism of aid receipt to behind-the-back gossip; they also confronted recipients publicly and personally.

Gary, the Chávez GA recipient I introduced in the last chapter, regularly found himself encountering criticism over his welfare use. Gary was personable and popular—someone who spent a lot of time in the public places of Chávez and seemed to know everyone in the projects. He usually went out of his way to exchange greetings and pass some time with groups hanging out on the street, but he also cultivated and maintained friendships with many residents who preferred to have nothing to do with street life or the gang. During fieldwork in Chávez, I spent time with Gary in the shooting galleries and in groups of beer-drinking Elm Street members as well as at meetings of activist community leaders and at church events sponsored by the Chávez *señoras*. People in each of these groups told me that Gary made positive contributions to the community by keeping an eye on neighborhood children in the Chávez gym, for example, or contributing to the food bank and other community-based projects.

Despite these wide-ranging friendships and positive evaluations, Gary did not escape stigma that stemmed from his receipt of aid and lack of a job, as I saw one spring afternoon at a church gathering we attended. The gathering had been called to organize an upcoming performance of Native American dances. The church and housing authority had donated a small amount of funds as well as some in-kind support for the performance, and I was curious to see how the organizing committee would allocate these scarce resources. Most of the people at the meeting that day were the Chávez women who organized and controlled the food bank. Gary sat quietly through discussions about the event date, publicity, whether to invite the local priest to open the dances with a prayer, and whether to try to raise a little money for the community center by setting up a barbeque and selling hamburgers and hot dogs. Finally, the co-organizers asked for volunteers to help out on the day of the event by asking residents to move their cars from the parking lot near the community center, setting out trash barrels, helping at the barbeque, and picking up detritus. Gary raised his hand to volunteer, and the co-organizers appeared ready to welcome his help. But one of the other members of the organizing committee objected. The people who volunteer for this event, she pointed out, represent the community. Do we want someone who is unemployed and receiving aid to do that? Isn't there someone else who can help out? Some others on the organizing committee agreed that it might be better if Gary were not involved and if the volunteers came from the planning committee. Gary did not object, and the organizers decided against his participation.

I left the church with Gary when the meeting ended and we chatted about how things had turned out. He said that he was not happy that the committee would not let him take part, but he also understood their perspective. They did not want someone like him out there representing the community, maybe representing the community before the priest. The organizers preferred to represent themselves. He could still go to the event—they couldn't stop that—and probably someone wouldn't show up and he would find something to do if he wanted to.

Public confrontations such as Gary experienced at the church meeting were also common at the Guadalupe job-training center, where nearly all enrollees received aid from federal, state and local programs. One March afternoon, for example, Henry was taken to task for participating in AFDC.

When ESL (English as a Second Language) class begins today, Vero asks to make an announcement. Max, the instructor, lets her take the floor on the condition that she speak English, but speaking in front of the class makes Vero nervous, and after a few halting English phrases she makes a frustrated gesture in Max's direction and switches to Spanish. She says that next week is the birthday of Judy [a job skills instructor], and she is taking a collection to buy a present.

Henry jokes that he'll contribute a whole book of food stamps, but Vero responds humorlessly. She tells Henry that she's not taking any food stamps. "We're not buying her a present at Lucky's, right? Why do you have food stamps anyway? You make your wife get welfare and then come in here with the stamps that are for her and the baby. That is disgraceful." Max breaks in, also in Spanish, to tell Vero that if she's done he will start class.

Vero did not hesitate to publicly confront Henry about what his use of food stamps and AFDC. In her eyes, it was inappropriate for Henry's wife to receive AFDC, and it was even more inappropriate for Henry to offer *her* food stamps as a gift contribution. His jovial demeanor also inspired Vero's public rebuke. Like other friends and acquaintances of Henry, Vero believed he used AFDC too instrumentally and cavalierly, that he could support his family through legitimate work but that he chose to hustle and rely on welfare instead. They did not know that Henry's participation in AFDC was only instrumental to a point, and Henry did not concede that he saw aid as an unattractive but necessary way to make ends meet given his family's financial circumstances. Rather, he acted as though receiving aid and hustling at the flea market were his preferred means of earning a living. In fact, during the months I spent time with Henry he had repeated bad luck finding a job—several times signing up with firms that could offer only a few months of work or did not pay an hourly wage sufficient to pay the rent for himself, Tanya, and the baby. In the summer of 1994, he finally found steady work and stopped receiving aid. But in March, his friends and acquaintances in Guadalupe knew little about his frustrating job search. As far as Vero and others were concerned, Henry had chosen aid, and this belief sustained the ire of their public criticism.

The appearance of choice tainted how residents viewed Henry's circumstances, but residents who clearly did not choose aid also faced public criticism. Tricia was in her late twenties and had two children, a seven-year-old boy and a four-year-old girl. She had come to Guadalupe from Michoacán to join her husband Luis in 1988. Tricia and Luis were settled migrants who were, according to Tricia, fairly happy with the life they were constructing in San Jose. The couple's daughter was born in the States, and they both received permanent residence, or green cards, in 1991. Luis found steady work for a construction firm, and Tricia cleaned houses part time. Everything changed in early 1993, however, when Luis was arrested. There were multiple stories about what had happened. Some of Tricia's acquaintances said Luis was involved in the drug trade, but Tricia insisted that the police had unfairly detained Luis following a minor altercation simply because he was Mexican. In any case, the courts treated Luis like a drug offender. He was sentenced to two years in jail, and Tricia had to turn to AFDC to support herself and the children. In December 1993, a social worker referred Tricia to the Guadalupe job-training center in hopes of getting her into the workforce.

Like many aid recipients in Guadalupe, Tricia was treated as though her use of welfare constituted fraud. During the time I spent with her, she appeared to be participating according to the spirit of the welfare rules. She attended job-training classes nearly without fail, and she made progress learning English and acquiring job skills. She seemed to want to work, and as it turned out she found a swing-shift position at $8 an hour with one of the Silicon Valley's largest employers in May 1994. While she received aid, however, Tricia's Guadalupe friends suspected that she used welfare inappropriately. Their suspicions came clear one Thursday morning in April. That day, Tricia arrived at the center wearing a black dress instead of her usual jeans and blouse. Paco reported that Luis was coming home on furlough and predicted that Tricia would miss class the next day. During lunch later that same day, Tricia, Paco, Ron and Virginia played dominos, and Virginia asked if it was true about Luis coming home. Tricia said that Luis was coming home for twenty-four hours and that she was going to skip class tomorrow. Her news sent Paco into a quiet celebration of his soothsaying ability, and it prompted Ron to ask for more details about Luis: What did he do? How long was he locked up? You're getting welfare that whole time? The last question touched a nerve.

"No. Why do you think I'm here? I want to get a job," says Tricia, obviously annoyed at Ron's last question. Ron replies, "But how come you just got welfare for a year after he got locked up? You didn't come here looking for a job." Virginia interjects to chastise Tricia: "You should have known Luis was involved with drug selling." Tricia denies to Virginia that Luis had anything to do with drugs, and Ron continues, "I just don't think it is right to give welfare to someone when they break the law. That's not right."

The imprisonment of Tricia's husband was common knowledge, but Ron and Virginia still questioned Tricia's motivation for using AFDC. They wanted assurances from her that she had tried her best to avoid using aid, and they wanted her to explain how she could have left herself vulnerable to aid dependence by starting a family with a criminal.

Ron and Virginia's comments to Tricia—like Guadalupe residents' comments about José, Señora Lupe, and Henry—illustrate the universal stigmatization of aid recipients and the Manichaean unacceptability of aid receipt. Guadalupe residents stigmatized all aid recipients, no matter what the particulars of their economic situation. They stigmatized residents whose participation in aid seemed an active choice, such as Señora Lupe and Henry, and they stigmatized residents whose participation seemed to stem from a misfortune over which they had limited control, as was the case for José and Tricia. Guadalupe residents also saw aid receipt as a moral failure and thus a legitimate object for criticism. They criticized aid in conversations when recipients were out of earshot, such as José and Señora Lupe, and they confronted recipients in public, as Henry and Tricia experienced. In Chávez, some residents experienced a similar stigmatization. Marco found a ready audience for his complaints about his girlfriend's indolence in the back seat of my car, and Gary experienced firsthand how receiving aid colored residents' views of a person's worth and value in the community. In these instances among the persistently poor of East LA, and more generally among the immigrants of San Jose, participation in any welfare program for any reason under whatever circumstances occasioned questioning and suspicion. Aid required explanation, but it was also inexcusable and unexplainable.

Guadalupe residents—some of them with only a few months or years of residence in the United States—embraced a view of welfare use and abuse that closely coincided with the views of U.S. policy makers in Washington, D.C. Like the policy makers, Guadalupe residents regarded aid use as a character flaw at best and a premeditated attempt at fraud at worst. This understanding of aid was nearly universal, and Guadalupe residents were as suspicious of aid use among family or friends as they were of aid use among acquaintances or rivals.

SELECTIVE STIGMA

Residents in Guadalupe and Chávez mostly expressed disapproval of aid, and they regularly stigmatized recipients both confidentially and face to face. This disapproval was not unremitting, however; at times, residents I spent time with in both barrios selectively excused the aid use of family, friends, and neighbors.

Discussions and debates over the propriety of aid receipt reflected the particular aid program in question. Gary's experiences at the church meeting illustrate one truism in Chávez: residents rarely defended GA receipt. Even recipients declined to justify their GA receipt as a way to generate income or as a reasonable response to unavoidable economic dislocation.

On a hot afternoon in July 1995, I am standing near the corner *tienda* when Danny comes up and says hello. I usually spend time with Danny around the shooting gallery, as he is a regular heroin user. Seeing him near the *tienda,* I ask him what he's up to. He says that he's going to go down to the store on Broadway to cash his check. "I just got paid," he says showing me his GA check. "I want to get to Broadway and cash this.... You got a car, right? Give me a ride?" I agree to give him a ride if he's waiting on the corner for me in half an hour when I'm heading out of the projects. Danny says, "Okay, but don't take too long because they're going to close up there."

A half-hour later, Danny is waiting on the corner and gets in for the ten-minute ride from the projects up to the check-cashing store on Broadway. "I woke up this morning, and I thought what am I gonna do today?" he says. "And then I remembered that I had this check, so I could use it to get some beer and stuff." Good thing you got that GA, I say to him. "No, I don't think so," he replies. "I don't like it. It's not enough to live on. I get one eighty something a month, and I can't live on that. I stay with my sister so I get by for a couple weeks but the end of the month is tough .... I'd rather be working. Most definitely. I get some work sometimes—little things for people when I need the money at the end of the month.... But I have trouble keeping a job because of the drinking and drugs and shit. So, I guess GA is better than nothing. But it's not a good thing."

For Danny, as for many residents in Chávez, an awareness of the personal histories and daily rounds of GA recipients made it hard to conceive of GA as "a good thing." In this sense, GA receipt had a relatively fixed and simple meaning in the barrios. GA was part of the experience of substance abuse. The connection between GA and alcoholism or heroin left little reason for residents to discuss whether one recipient "deserved" to receive aid or whether another's aid receipt might somehow constitute "cheating." It seemed painfully obvious why Chávez residents received GA, and this self-evidence meant few residents would even discuss whether a GA recipient should be exempted from welfare stigma.

In contrast to the apparently clear meaning of GA in the lives of people with substance abuse problems, programs such as AFDC or food stamps played a number of relatively varied roles in the complex lives of aid recipients. These varied meanings gave residents more leeway to make and justify selective exceptions to the general rule of universal stigma.

Sometimes, selective exception took place in a "confessional" atmosphere where recipients expressed shame because they used aid and others excused their use. In Chapter 8, I described a gathering in June 1994 where a discussion about California's anti-immigrant Proposition 187 led to "confessions" of aid use by Rosa, Chela, and Doña Lupe. Rosa was ashamed of the food stamps her family used for a year, and she recalled with particular dread taking the stamps out of her purse in public to buy groceries at the local market. Chela recalled how she had been forced to use public aid after her husband left her, and Doña Lupe had recently turned to food stamps to help make ends meet while her husband recovered from an on-the-job back injury. In response to these "confessions," their friends gathered around the table that day offered supportive comments that in effect absolved the three recipients—and Rosa in particular—of the shame they felt using public assistance.

In Guadalupe, I rarely heard residents excusing or explaining aid use outside the kind of confessional atmosphere such as that at the *convive* group. More typically, residents refused to excuse aid receipt—as the *convive* group itself steadfastly criticized aid recipients at their park play date several weeks after the confessional lunch. In Chávez, on the other hand, residents more frequently conceded that receipt sometimes reflected economic necessity rather than personal impropriety. Welfare receipt *could* arise from circumstances beyond the recipient's control. I listened in on many conversations during which Chávez residents discussed whether a particular family member, friend, or neighbor used public assistance deservedly.

Often, these conversations paralleled stories of how "bad" men could leave women reliant on AFDC and how "good" men could have the misfortune of being unable to provide for their wives and children. For example, their friends in Chávez held different opinions of the aid used by Norma and Beatrice, the two women I introduced in the last chapter. In many ways, both women followed similar pathways to AFDC reliance. For both women, the loss of a male provider—Norma to alcoholism and abandonment, Beatrice to violence and imprisonment—preceded long-term use of AFDC. Explaining how these single mothers ended up on aid, their Chávez friends told morality tales about the shortcomings of absent fathers and husbands. In the case of Norma, friends often depicted her reliance as one of the inevitable problems that stemmed from involvement with a "bad" man, while tales of Beatrice's situation focused on the fact that sometimes a "good" man could not get a break. Chávez residents told similar morality tales about the deservingness of AFDC use by the mothers and wives who remained in the community—tales I heard from the moment I arrived in the barrio.

During my first few weeks in Chávez, it became clear that Norma, Al, and Paul were not getting along with Blanca and Gladis. These residents made up distinct groups that, while polite in public, had few positive things to say in private. At first, I spent more time with Norma and her friends, and I heard from them about the selfish and immoral behavior of their rivals. According to Norma, Blanca had made fraudulent claims on AFDC. Al said that Gladis had included several family members who lived outside Chávez on her lease in order to get a larger apartment. The food bank provided further evidence of the rival group's fraudulent ways, according to Paul. He said that Blanca and Gladis gave food only to their friends inside and outside Chávez, and that this had led to the food bank's cutting off Chávez from the program. The paperwork he had to re-create, as well as the fact that non-Chávez residents expressed surprise when his team of volunteers tried to restrict their entrance to the food bank, appeared to substantiate Paul's version of events. The rivalry between these two groups appeared related to competition over who would serve as official resident representative to the Los Angeles Housing Agency. The story, as I understood it during my first months in the projects, was that Blanca and Gladis had lost their hold on these coveted positions because they had engaged in various kinds of welfare fraud.

But as I became more familiar with daily life in Chávez and began to develop an independent view of income-generating routines based on interactions with a variety of residents, Norma, Al, and Paul's accusations of fraud against Blanca and Gladis began to seem superficial and perhaps even hypocritical. Residents struggling to make ends meet regularly violated the letter of the rules governing AFDC receipt and eligibility.5 Housing authority officials regularly ignored lease violations by pretending not to notice friends and family members sleeping on living room couches or doubling up in bedrooms. If the morality tale about Blanca and Gladis's disenfranchisement had a hypocritical facet, it involved the food bank. The misbehavior that Paul attributed to his rivals seemed hardly different from his own volunteer team's habit of stashing away choice food for themselves, their families, and their friends. And under Paul's supervision, the food bank continued to distribute food to people who did not live in Chávez—just different outsiders than had benefited from Blanca's largesse. Perhaps Blanca's method of allocating food bank resources had differed from Paul's in extent, but it could not have differed much in kind.

Accusations of fraud made by Norma, Al, and Paul against Blanca and Gladis were not simple hypocrisy, however. By accusing Blanca and Gladis of defrauding AFDC and the housing authority, Norma and Al established their own legitimacy to replace the former barrio leaders. By accusing Blanca of abusing the food bank program, Paul used stigma to consolidate his own control over food bank resources. These accusations showed residents of the barrios selectively deploying welfare stigma.

In the contest between Norma, Al, and Paul on one side and Blanca and Gladis on the other, deployed stigma flowed in both directions. One midsummer afternoon, at a time when my circle of relationships in Chávez had expanded to include her, Blanca told me how she and Gladis had been displaced as Chávez's official representatives.

I've retreated to a back room of the housing office, one of the inconspicuous spots I use to write notes, when Blanca comes into the room to ask if I have seen Paul. "I need to talk to him about the food bank," she says, watching me return pen and notebook to my jeans pocket. I say I think he went upstairs, but instead of going upstairs to look for him, Bianca seems inspired by the sight of my notebook to sit down and talk.

"I've been living in Chávez for forty-one years," she says. "I know that there are all kinds of rumors going around about me and my friends—that we don't like Norma or Paul—but there's nothing to that. It is just a vicious thing going around. People say I want to stop the food bank, but that's not true. It all started because I supported Norma and her friends to be representatives when me and Gladis stepped down. I didn't know her then, but I heard she was okay, so I said, okay I'll vote for her, and I told all my friends to vote for her, too. And that's how she got elected. But now that she is representative, all the power is going to her head. She and Al are messing everything up, and now people are coming to me and saying, 'My God, that lady is a witch!' And here I am just trying to make sure that some food goes to the community. She and Al—and now Paul, too, except Paul is too young and doesn't really know what they're doing—they're doing all these horrible things and stealing all the food for themselves.... Now, I go to Santa Margarita to try to get some food to the community, and I find out from people there that Norma has always been like this. I didn't know that before. But she has been cheating on welfare for years—did you know she has a man in that house?"

In our conversation that afternoon, Blanca deployed the stigma of aid against Norma, Al, and Paul in much the same way that Norma and her allies had used it against Blanca herself. Her narrative confirmed the rivalry and enmity between the two groups of residents, and it demonstrated how selective stigma could be invoked in different ways by various players in intrabarrio rivalries and friendships.

In the months following this conversation with Blanca, I heard from both sides of this rivalry, as well as from residents who did not identify with either group, of how different forms of stigma and gossip had provided potent tools for forging and defining lines of political alliance and enmity in Chávez. Several residents confirmed one version of events.

In 1994, when Norma first took over as Chávez representative, she asked Al to take charge of the food bank. A short time later, Blanca spoke with Buddy, a senior member of the Elm Street *varrio*. She told him that she was afraid that Al was ruining the food bank by disrupting relationships with suppliers, keeping food for himself, and distributing food to nonresidents. At the time, Blanca had good relations with Elm Street. During her time as housing authority representative, she had sponsored several community events that members attended and enjoyed, especially an annual Thanksgiving turkey dinner at a local church. At the next Elm Street meeting Buddy reported to other members of the *varrio* that the food bank was in danger and that something had to be done. One group of Elm Street members confronted Al with Blanca's accusations, and from other members Al heard a rumor that this *clika* planned to physically attack him. Fearing for his own safety, Al left Chávez for a few weeks and went to stay with relatives.

In his absence, Norma and Paul intervened on Al's behalf. Norma circulated the rumor that, following her success at getting gang members to confront Al, Blanca had taken to calling herself the "Queen of Elm Street." Blanca understood that this moniker hurt her standing with Elm Street. "It's disrespectful," she explained to me. "And the guys were upset about it. I have no control over Elm Street—they know that. But I had to go and get Buddy to explain it and straighten it out." Buddy successfully restored Blanca's good name in Elm Street, and in the process Paul worked to restore Al's reputation and secure a withdrawal of the threats against him. In the end, Paul garnered *varrio* support to head the food bank himself as part of a compromise that allowed Al to safely return to Chávez.

SUBCULTURES IN ACTION

Few Americans generate income by participating in public assistance; even in low-income neighborhoods, the number of welfare users rarely approaches the number of residents who earn their income through other means. But because welfare receipt is seen to violate core societal values of personal responsibility and self-reliance, even small amounts of welfare use generate concern. Aid receipt may be seen as socially isolating poor people from the nation's mainstream institutions. Many believe that welfare recipients subscribe to cultural orientations that foster dependence, and it is troubling that this "culture of dependence" might undermine the work ethic of all residents in the low-income community. For policy makers, these concerns have proved a powerful lever to push welfare programs in new directions. The end of AFDC and the introduction of TANF represent a fundamental shift in the goals of the American welfare system: from supporting the economically vulnerable to making all Americans economically self-sufficient. Ethnography provides the means to examine the cultural consequences of welfare use and assess to what extent concerns about dependence reflect the cultural reality of welfare in low-income communities.

At first glance, attitudes toward welfare in Guadalupe and Chávez appeared to confirm policy makers' fears that aid receipt undermines core American values. In Guadalupe, where few received aid, residents appeared firm in their belief that no matter what the circumstances, welfare was an unacceptable way to generate income—an orientation I call here universal stigma. Their principled belief appeared to pay off in self-reliance, as few residents traveled down the pathway to aid reliance. In Chávez, on the other hand, residents appeared to waver in their cultural commitment to the ideals of personal responsibility and self-reliance. They roundly and consistently impugned GA receipt, but their resolve weakened when it came to AFDC and in-kind local aid programs. Moreover, when Chávez residents did condemn aid receipt, it appeared to occur in hypocritical expressions of intrabarrio *chisme* and in the service of local politics rather than as an expression of a genuine belief in its impropriety. Chávez residents regularly excused the aid use of friends and allies while invoking welfare stigma to discredit the character of rivals and enemies. Was this cultural capriciousness one reason that welfare receipt was more common in the housing projects of Los Angeles than in the immigrant barrios of San Jose?

Policy makers fear that poor people living in places like Chávez endorse self-reliance selectively because welfare has diluted this ideal in their community—a simple and direct model of the relationship between public aid and cultural orientations. A brief comparison of aid receipt and welfare cultures in Guadalupe and Chávez appears to offer support for this simple model. But closer examination of how residents used welfare and deployed welfare stigma day by day reveals several problems with this simple model and suggests a more subtle and complex understanding of the relationship between aid use and cultural ideals.

Day to day, barrio residents constructed the meaning of reliance through their talk about and behavior toward family, neighbors, and local institutions. They declared that some people had achieved self-reliance and that others had fallen short. They celebrated those they saw as overcoming barriers to achieve self-reliance, and they criticized others who appeared to have succumbed to the temptations of irresponsibility. Residents applauded or condemned local institutions such as churches, job centers, local aid programs, and community leaders depending on their assessment of whether they helped or hindered residents in their efforts to stand on their own two feet. These cultural construction projects contrast sharply with the policy maker model. In that model, poor people either embrace or reject ideals of self-reliance, and their attitudes toward welfare is a relatively stable part of their personal and community cultural orientations. In day-to-day reality, in contrast, barrio residents ruminated over the meaning of self-reliance and personal responsibility; they argued about the circumstances which justified their abandonment—such as in reaction to disrespectful treatment from a hostile boss; and they tirelessly debated who was living up to these ideals, who was falling short, and why. The first way in which the simple policy maker model falls short of day-to-day reality in the barrios, therefore, is in failing to recognize that barrio residents construct local welfare cultures. Fears of poor people simply abandoning mainstream ideals once and for all misrepresents how culture operates in everyday life.

The policy maker model misrepresents not only how culture operates but also how every-day conditions in the barrios shape local cultural orientations. Cultural construction projects in the barrios often began with the same notions of personal responsibility and self-reliance that, in the policy makers' simple cultural models, pervade other U.S. communities. These ideals make up the locally available cultural materials in the barrios too. Residents criticized each other as lazy or undeserving precisely because these ideals were pervasive. They alleged that political rivals failed to measure up to these behavioral benchmarks because these cul-tural ideals retained their power to tarnish reputations, sway opinion, and influence action. The policy maker model fails to recognize the enduring power of mainstream ideals in the low-income barrios.

Where ideals thrive matters. In the low-income barrios, these ideals thrived in a social environment of economic need. Welfare cultures of Guadalupe and Chávez reflected the con-crete reality of urban poverty as much as they did the abstract American ideals of personal responsibility and self-reliance. Differences in the concrete reality of poverty in Guadalupe and Chávez produced markedly different cultural constructions around welfare. On the one hand, greater poverty in Chávez meant more welfare stigma because more residents used aid to generate income. On the other hand, welfare stigma in Chávez had a different quality than its counterpart in Guadalupe. Compared to Guadalupe residents, with their Manichaean views of welfare, Chávez residents more frequently excused aid or acknowledged the circumstances at-tending receipt. They paid closer attention to the shades of gray in welfare recipients' economic circumstances. Family, friends, and neighbors, it was understood, used welfare for different rea-sons. Welfare had multiple meanings, and the stigma associated with welfare could take myriad forms. Chávez residents skillfully deployed these meanings in everyday life. Like the residents of Guadalupe, Chávez residents knew what welfare in America was *supposed* to mean, and in some circumstances Chávez residents invoked these meanings of welfare. But Chávez residents also adeptly shaped and manipulated the meaning of welfare in light of local circumstances and personal desires and interests.

Regular interactions with aid and aid recipients shaped how Chávez residents thought about self-reliance through a process of cultural proliferation—not isolation, withdrawal, or rejection. Simply put, Chávez residents had *more* ways to make sense of aid receipt than residents in Guadalupe. Chávez residents were more skilled manipulators of welfare stigma and more adept users of the culture surrounding welfare than residents in Guadalupe. This is not surprising. Guadalupe residents had less experience with the dynamics of the U.S. welfare system and its peculiar significance in American society. As they become more familiar with these meanings, we might expect the immigrants of Guadalupe to become more comfortable using culture in ways that would match their local circumstances and further their personal interests. We might expect them to become more skilled at deploying cultural content as they acquired a nuanced sense of self-reliance and personal responsibility in the U.S. context and abandoned the simple rules that define these concepts. Comparing welfare stigma in Guadalupe and Chávez shows how stigma is not simply a cultural construction but an institutional means for managing the use of welfare in everyday life.

SECTION III

Class, Race, Gender, and Sexuality

This section includes readings that cover aspects of identity that have been constrained by structural inequality. Not only that, but they are categories whose justification for inequality has been based on biological explanations of inferiority. The Age of Enlightenment and Reason saw a quest for scientific knowledge like never before. The need to classify, name, define, and order our world is not reserved to the natural world, but could be extended to the social. In answering questions of the day, thinkers did just that, and in doing so created classifications for different human characteristics. Those doing the naming centered themselves as the pinnacle of knowledge and culture, while everyone else was ordered lower down on the human evolutionary scale. Similar to the natural sciences, early social scientists believed that human conditions were a natural and essential outcome of the characteristics of the person. So, for instance, early criminologists associated urban decay and crime with poor immigrants. Instead of looking at social conditions to help explain their assumptions, they looked for differences in skull sizes to help them explain urban crime. Human variation was seen as the innate cause of the plight of the oppressed and the explanation for their oppressor's success. Africans were biologically predisposed to be slaves. Women were biologically seen as inferior to men, and therefore meant to be the property of men like their children. People are poor because they are lazy, something intrinsic to their being. Heterosexuality is natural, and any sexual expression which deviates from that is unnatural. Laws were created to reinforce these ideas, and these laws helped to construct reality.

These identities are also ways in which society organizes us differentially from one another, justifying some groups to have greater access to power and resources than others. These are class, race, gender, and sexuality. While many of the readings in this section focus on one aspect such as race more than another, they all intersect and intertwine with these categories. Consistent with an intersectional perspective, class, race, gender, and sexuality are mutually constituted identities, none of which can exist in isolation or should be studied that way. They overlap, constructing the multiple subjectivities by which we navigate our daily lives.

This section begins with another reading from Daniel Dohan; it discusses how poverty is both situated and structured within the barrios he studied in Southern California. In "The Price of Poverty," Dohan describes how residents made ends meet and attempted upward mobility. He also examines the local institutions created out of the particular circumstances: the intersections of immigration status, language barrier, and status as a source of cheap labor unique to these communities.

In the discussion of race, whiteness itself as a race is oftentimes whited out. Race is that which is not White, in effect Othering nonwhites. However, more recently, whiteness itself has come under scrutiny and has been highlighted as not only a race, but a powerful social institution like that of a patriarchy. Much of the discussion on race found here is the opposite of most of our "common-sense" understanding of race, where race is anything but White. The first two of the three readings on race interrogates whiteness, its construction, and position within the racial hierarchy. Informed by Omi and Winant's racial formation theory, Steve Garner's "Whiteness as Contingent Hierarchies: Who Counts as White and Why" discusses the creation and historical evolution of the racial category "White" and whiteness as a social institution.

In another reading on whiteness, we are asked to look beyond the traditional and myopic definitions of racism and understand the subtle ways in which it is perpetuated and enacted in everyday life. Many believe we live in a color-blind society, where race no longer is relevant.

Since the post–civil rights era—and more importantly and recently with the election of a black president—we have entered what many proclaim to be a post-racial society. As a result, individuals who make up our social institutions may not feel the need to enforce certain legislation for equality or to maintain a diverse workplace. The idea of a color-blind society simply ignores and dismisses how deeply rooted sexism and racism are in our social institutions. It assumes that a couple of decades of legislation, not necessarily enforced, reverses and wipes away centuries of overt discrimination and segregation. Color-blind racism gladly absolves society of the reality, persistence, and complexity of racism and sexism. It allows Whites and men to have the idea that they know what is and is not sexist or racist better than the oppressed. Even if something is identified as such, since we live in a post-racial society and women have made so many gains, sexism and racism are innocuous, and the offended are invalidated due to their oversensitivity. "Passivity in Well-Meaning White People" by Barbara Trepagnier discusses the subtle ways usually "color-blind" White people perpetuate racism by examining their position of detachment and role of passivity when a bystander to racist incidents.

The problem with subscribing to the color-blind society ideology is that it denies the lasting effects of institutionalized racism. Racism is still alive and well today, but even if it were not, color blindness erases the daily impact institutionalized racism has on nonwhites even today. One of the biggest culprits of present-day inequality is in housing discrimination. The discussion of the lasting effects of racism would not be complete without a look at the roles that housing discrimination and residential segregation have played in the lives of African Americans in the United States. Andrew Wiese does this in "The House I Live In: Race, Class, and African-American Suburban Dreams in the Postwar United States." This reading examines the role of housing discrimination in the continued legacy of residential and wealth inequality between blacks and Whites. This legacy is responsible for the wealth gap that persists between blacks and Whites and a myriad of life chances that are determined by the neighborhood you live in.

In the next set of readings, we focus our attention to gender. Gender is virtually absent from the classical mainstream sociological canon, having been largely overlooked by male theorists, while female theorists were ignored or "written out" during the construction of what is now considered classical sociological theory (Lengermann and Niebrugge, 1998: 11). When classical social theory does deal with gender, it is most often contained firmly within the domain of family sociology (Engels, 1978 [1942]). Modern theorists looked more closely at gender, building on their predecessors' theories to analyze the uses and implementation of gender. As the dominant theorist of his day, the functionalist Talcott Parsons was instrumental in promoting the prevailing perspective on gender at the time—role theory—in the social sciences. Role theory is a perspective where gender is viewed as a naturally occurring role within the nuclear family, as well as outside the family. Roles are described as instrumental for men, which make them natural breadwinners, and expressive for women, explaining their nurturing nature (Parsons & Bales, 1953). The theory situates gender within a biological essentialist framework that conflates gender with sex and conceptualizes them as naturally occurring binary oppositional categories. In other words, using role theory, Parsons treats gender as a naturalized and immutable expression of biological sex (Parsons & Bales, 1953).

Both the essentialist and social constructionist perspectives shape not only how we view and study gender, but also how we understand the social inequality embedded in gender definition and categorization. Parsons's sex role theory understands the inequalities of gender to originate in biological sex differences. These differences are interpreted as a function of the naturally oc-curring roles men and women are socialized into in our society. As passive recipients of gender roles, men and women function best, Parsons theorizes, in a binary oppositional fashion and within a heterosexual framework. For Parsons, these differences between men and women are foundational to explanations and perhaps justifications for inequality between the sexes. Male and female roles are different, though complementary, especially in family life. The different roles occupy different functions and statuses in society that are not necessarily equal, nor do they necessitate equality.

In sharp contrast to (and even outright rejection of) Parsonian views of gender as an innate, fixed, and essential human trait, West and Zimmerman provide a symbolic interactionist and constructivist perspective of gender. In other words, what may be perceived as a natural social phenomenon is the result of historically and culturally specific social meaning, created through social relations and power (Lorber, 1994). What we observe is not what invariably is, but what we create and give meaning to as social beings.

Rather than a static, fixed, immutable entity, gender could be seen as an accomplishment or achievement. The idea that gender is something one *does*—and not something one *is*—revolutionized understandings of how women and men live social lives. West and Zimmerman (1987) argue that gender should be examined as something that is "exhibited or portrayed through interaction, and thus be seen as 'natural' while it is being produced as a socially orga-nized achievement" (West & Zimmerman, 1987: 129). Building upon the preceding work of the symbolic interactionist Erving Goffman, West and Zimmerman unpack what had previously been a taken-for-granted conflation of sex and gender. West and Zimmerman disentangle sexual-ity, sex category, and gender, illustrating the performative relationship between the body and gender (Risman & Davis, 2013). Gender is distinguished as a social signifier of sex genitalia, but has to be correctly performed according to the socially agreed-upon practices that come to be recognized as masculinity and femininity.

Continuing the social constructionist perspective of gender, the first reading, "Gender Roles in Sociocultural and Historical Context" by Marjorie Schweitzer, chronicles the history of gender roles in the 20th century. One of the key aspects of the sociological imagination is using history in order to understand an individual's biography. In this reading, she situates the intersection of race, class, and gender in a historical context. By doing so, the reader can see shifts in gender roles over time, a demonstration of the instability of gender norms and roles. This opens the door to one of the biggest and oldest debates in the discipline and in gender studies—about gender roles and norms situating gender within a biological essentialist framework that conflates gender with sex and conceptualizes them as naturally occurring binary oppositional categories.

As a social space, the Internet, like any other social institution, is gendered. Van Doorn and Van Zoonen shift the discussion of gender online. They explore how gender is negotiated in technological spaces in "Theorizing Gender and the Internet: Past, Present, and Future."

"Gender Presentation in Black and Lesbian Communities" by Mignon Moore explores the different representations of gender among black lesbians, suggesting that the configurations may be somewhat different for them compared to representations of gender in the mainstream White lesbian communities. Gender, race, class, and sexuality are mutually shaping, meaning that "woman" is not a monolithic identity—it is one that is shaped by race, class, and sexuality. Moore's reading highlights the ways gender is performed among black lesbian–identified women.

Similar to the interrogation of whiteness in race studies, masculinity began to be incorporated into part of gender studies. Masculinity takes many forms, with the dominant expression taking the form of hegemonic masculinity. Hegemonic masculinity is hierarchical in nature, subordinating alternative masculinities that do not conform to its standard. Two readings on masculinity address this topic. Robert Heasley explores some of the subordinate masculinities represented among heterosexual males in "Crossing the Borders of Gendered Sexuality: Queer Masculinities of Straight Men." The reading documents the experiences of heterosexual males who challenge and blur the boundaries of heteronormative masculine practices. In another reading on multiple masculinities, "Maintaining Manliness in Later Life: Hegemonic Masculinities and Emphasized Femininities" by Robert Meadows and Kate Davidson, scrutinize the relationship of older men to hegemonic masculinity. In this examination, they explore how an increase in age signals a shift in this relationship for men, situating them in opposition to a youthful, more hegemonic form of masculinity.

Another identity long assumed to be naturally occurring and fixed is sexual orientation—specifically, heterosexuality. In the 1940s, Alfred Kinsey helped create a paradigm shift in how we think of sexuality with his introduction of the Kinsey Scale, based on his research of the sexual behavior of Americans. Until that time, it was assumed that people were either exclusively heterosexual or homosexual, and that those categories were mutually exclusive and binary opposites. What Kinsey found was that in fact, people's sexual practices—regardless of how they personally identify—fall along a spectrum or scale between heterosexual and homosexual. In "Introduction: Thinking Straight," Chrys Ingraham discusses the social construction of heterosexuality and sex categories in general and our role in producing and reproducing these categories.

In discussing sexuality, we are again socialized to think of the able-bodied/disabled binary. The able-bodied person, constructed as a whole, is thought of as someone able to participate in the entirety of life, whereas the disabled body is constructed as broken, one that does not participate in the whole of life, including sex. Thus, the abled-bodied constitutes the normative sexual subject, while the disabled constitutes the nonnormative sexual subject. "Society, Sexuality, and Disabled/Able-bodied Romantic Relationships" by Sally A. Nemeth explores how sexuality is negotiated in disabled/able-bodied sexual relationships. This reading shifts the sexual experiences and perspectives of the disabled from the margins to the center.

REFERENCES

Engels, Friedrich, and Lewis H. Morgan. *The Origin of the Family, Private Property and the State* (p. 110). Moscow: Foreign Languages Publishing House, 1978[1942].

Lengermann, Patricia Madoo, and Gillian Niebrugge. *The Women Founders: Sociology and Social Theory 1830–1930*. Long Grove, IL: Waveland Press, Inc., 1998.

Lorber, Judith. "Beyond the Binaries: Depolarizing the Categories of Sex, Sexuality and Gender." *Sociological Inquiry* 66 (2) (1996):143–159.

Parsons, Talcott, and R. F. Bales. *Family, Socialization and Interaction Process*. Glencoe, IL: Free Press, 1954.

Risman, Barbara J., and Georgiann Davis. 2013. "From Sex Roles to Gender Structure." *Current Sociology Review* 61(5–6) (2013): 733–755.

West, Candace, and Don H. Zimmerman. 1987. "Doing Gender." *Gender & Society* 1 (1987): 125–151.

DISCUSSION QUESTIONS

1. According to the reading *Passivity in Well-Meaning White People*, how does passivity among Whites work against racial equality?
2. Based on *The House I Live In: Race, Class, and African-American Suburban Dreams in the Postwar United States*, how does the history of residential segregation affect the persistence of racial inequality today?
3. How are we socialized to "think straight?"
4. What messages does society give us about sex and people with disabilities? What do these messages, or lack thereof, tell us about how we see the sexuality of the disabled?

THE PRICE OF POVERTY

By Daniel Dohan

P overty exacts its price quietly in Guadalupe. The small houses and treelined streets, even the concrete-slab apartment buildings, do not advertise deprivation. But if you wait until late in the afternoon, you can see the signs of poverty appear. When school lets out, the sidewalks fill with children, mothers, and grandmothers, a hint of the large families in the neighborhood's small houses and apartments. Over the next few hours, driveways and streets, sidewalks and front lawns become choked with cars—another signal of overcrowding and an indicator of how many jobs it requires to sustain each of these Silicon Valley households. My landlady Gloria cobbled together the rent for her three-bedroom house from me and another full-time boarder by providing in-home care to the aged, from her sons' busboy and prep cook jobs in San Jose and San Francisco, and from the occasional odd-job earnings and constant in-kind services of the young *Salvadoreña* who stayed with us for a few months. "You don't need a key," Gloria told me the day after I moved into the house. "Just ring the bell. There's always someone around to let you in."

Travel to Chávez barrio, where the price of poverty announces itself. From the moment you top the hill above the projects and drive down into the complex of identical low-rise buildings, you know you have entered a poor neighborhood. The identical buildings need repair, men hang out on the sidewalk, storefront walls are tagged "Gato," "Stinger," and the ubiquitous Elm Street "ES." I first met Stinger (given name Tomas) and his family, including most of his seven brothers, in the spring of 1995. One of his older brothers told me that of eight boys in the family, four had been shot and one, his youngest brother, had been killed. "He was sitting in the back seat of a car, and someone came up and said, 'Where you from?' and they said, 'Elm Street,' and he started shooting and he hit my brother right in the head." Most of the sons in the family had retired from active gang life. Only Stinger and one other brother remained active, and Stinger was the only one not yet shot. One Sunday morning, I bumped into Tomas's mother as she climbed into a car driven by her husband. She carried flowers, and she told me that they were heading to the cemetery to visit her youngest son. She asked if I had seen Tomas; he had said he wanted to go with her that day. I had not seen him, but could I give him a message? "No message," she said. "Just tell him I love him."

The quiet toils of Guadalupe and the spectacular struggles of Chávez evoke profound and profoundly different reactions for Americans. Poverty in Guadalupe evokes immigrant hopes for socioeconomic mobility and thus represents an understanding of poverty and struggle that resonates in the experiences of early-twentieth-century European Americans and in the imaginations of their descendants. Deprivation in Chávez exemplifies an experience of inter-generational poverty and socioeconomic stagnation that seems to have no parallel outside the deteriorating African American ghettos of the late-twentieth-century Rust Belt. Yet we find reminders of both kinds of poverty in the Mexican American barrios of contemporary California, sometimes even in contiguous neighborhoods. Comparing poverty in Guadalupe and Chávez allows us to better understand what distinguishes the pedestrian price of poverty paid by recent immigrants from the more spectacular price exacted in neighborhoods of persistent poverty. Comparing Guadalupe and Chávez encourages us to speculate about the future of Mexican American poverty and incorporation in the United States, especially in comparison with socio-economically disadvantaged groups such as African Americans. Examining poverty in Chávez and Guadalupe leads us to consider how citizens and policy makers should view barrio poverty and what public policy might do to reduce its price.

SOCIAL INSTITUTIONS AND THE EXPERIENCE OF POVERTY

Poverty unfolds differently in Guadalupe and Chávez—severe overcrowding, relentless work hours, and migration-initiated family separation versus public drug markets, deadly violence, and family breakup. In popular and scholarly thought, these dislocations and hardships re-flect not just different daily experiences of poverty but different kinds of poverty altogether. Popular accounts contrast the mobility and industry of recent immigrants with stagnation and dysfunction in persistently poor communities. Contrasts persist in scholarly work, even though ethnographers have increasingly highlighted the internal divisions among seemingly united recent immigrants as well as the forms of community solidarity in even the most impoverished areas of persistent poverty. My experiences in Guadalupe and Chávez add to an ethnographic record that emphasizes the continuities of experience in diverse low-income communities. Guadalupe and Chávez faced similar deprivation but developed quite different ways of manag-ing it. Examining why similar structural circumstances and individual orientations energized different social institutions helps explain how these different kinds of poverty can exist side by side in the barrios.

Structures of Poverty

Analyzing institutions of poverty in Guadalupe and Chávez highlights important ideas about the relationship between social structure and poverty. Generally, we think of social structure, as

William H. Sewell, Jr., notes, "as primary, hard, immutable, like the girders of a building." In analyses of poverty, this immutable structure often appears to directly determine income-generating possibilities and behaviors in poor communities. Structure exists outside the control of poor people and thus appears to "force" them to adopt certain behaviors. In the most influential statement of this direct relationship between structure and poverty, William Julius Wilson has analyzed deindustrialization's structural relationship to poverty. Deindustrialization, in this view, causes poverty along with social problems such as joblessness, crime, and welfare reliance by making it impossible for residents of low-income communities to find work. My analysis of institutions of poverty in Guadalupe and Chávez suggests that deindustrialization shapes the experience of urban poverty in myriad ways. The relationship between social structure and social dislocations is complex and hard to predict.

Structural circumstances affect poverty not just by causing economic dislocations but also by their effects on the institutions that poor people use to manage those dislocations. The barrio institutions of poverty that help residents find jobs (social networks), generate illegal income (indigenous organizations), and make sense of welfare reliance (subcultures) reflect a variety of structural factors. Social networks that helped residents find jobs reflected the concentration of particular ethnoracial groups in particular kinds of jobs. Illegal organizations that helped residents participate in economic crime recognized the residential differentiation that meant that police crackdowns targeted some neighborhoods more than others. And local subcultures that made sense of welfare reliance took account of the family structure in households that received aid. Race, neighborhood, and family structure thus affected the experience of poverty in the barrios through their influence on social institutions.

Structural circumstances affect poverty in ways that are difficult to predict, owing to the complex relationship between structure and institutions of poverty. Even structural dislocations that have large and seemingly self-evident effects on the poor actually play out in a wide variety of ways in everyday life. Deindustrialization, for example, had quite different effects in Guadalupe and Chávez because residents of the two barrios mobilized social institutions in different ways to manage the problems of disappearing industrial employment. Comparisons between the barrios in general and other kinds of low-income communities also illustrate this point. Industrial plant closings in the Los Angeles Basin affected job opportunities in both the Mexican American barrios of East LA and the African American ghettos of South LA, but the effects of these plant closings worked themselves out quite differently in the two urban areas. Examining the role of institutions of poverty can help explain these different outcomes.

An institutional perspective encourages us to empirically examine how structural change and dislocation shape the experience of poverty. It reminds us that structural circumstances are rarely dire enough to "force" poor people to take particular actions. In a multitude of ways, social structures affect the resources and constraints that affect how poor people actively manage everyday life in conditions of material deprivation. But much of what shapes the daily experience of poverty and much of what makes life different in different kinds of low-income communities hinges on the operations of social institutions of the middle range. To predict and understand how structural change and dislocation shape the world of the urban poor, we must focus on the complex and contingent effects of social institutions.

Individual Orientations

The role of individual orientation, initiative, and volition is one of the most controversial top-ics in studies of urban poverty. Oscar Lewis's culture-of-poverty theory introduces a recurring theme: that individual orientations of the poor are a proper object for social scientific research and that some poor people embrace self-destructive orientations and behaviors. Lewis argued that these orientations and behaviors are rooted in family relations and that they can constitute a self-perpetuating culture. In this reading, culture consists of values and norms that people carry about in their heads as mental abstractions and images. In this sense, the culture of poverty resident in individual mental orientations can "tell" poor people what to do; observ-able behaviors arise fairly directly from individual orientations, initiatives, and volitions. In the wake of Lewis's influential statement of the theory, researchers asked poor people about their desires and aspirations and found that their answers suggested that the culture-of-poverty theory had serious empirical weaknesses. Nevertheless, the theory continues to represent the dominant model for how culture operates in poor communities. For example, researchers who observe differing styles of dress and language in poor communities still worry that these areas are culturally "isolated" from higher-income America—and thus unwittingly invoke a model of culture in which what people do reflects precisely what they think or want.

Outside the domain of urban poverty, scholars commonly speak of culture as a publicly available "web of meanings" or set of habits that people draw upon in the course of everyday life. From this perspective, cultural systems lend order and meaning to people's lives rather than acting as a set of rules telling them what to do. In analyses of urban poverty, the older view of culture—a view still embraced in policy circles—remains influential. Focusing on institutions of poverty encourages cultural analyses that do not invoke the culture-of-poverty theory's prob-lematic view of the relationship between individual volition and observed behavior. Institutional analysis emphasizes that the relationship between culture and poverty is important not because culture tells poor people what to do but because it shapes when and how income generation takes place and poverty is reproduced in low-income communities.

Cultural differences marked everyday economic life in Guadalupe and Chávez with respect to the meaning of money, the operational logic of locally controlled economic organizations, and the interpretation of material deprivation and welfare receipt. In short, culture matters for poverty when institutional arrangements allow it to touch on the relationship between poor people and material resources. Culture matters because social networks shape the meaning of money; because indigenous organizations structure participation in the illegal economy; and when material deprivation means residents cannot avoid public aid and its stigma. In each of these cases, culture shapes poverty not through a quiet "telling" of poor people what to do but in public forums where members of the community—the poor people who live there as well as outsiders ranging from relatives in a different country to police who patrol the streets to ethnographers conducting research—broadcast, discuss, and debate the honor, elegance, and ef-fectiveness of various income-generating activities. Differences in income-generating activities do not stem from the cultural isolation of poor communities, nor does cultural distinctiveness in low-income communities usually create poverty. The institutional perspective emphasizes that the currency and legitimacy of cultural perspectives on income generation reflect real conditions in the low-income community. In particular, income-generating cultures reflect connections between particular poor communities and family, employers, and politicians who may live and work in distant neighborhoods, states, or nations.

IS THERE A MEXICAN AMERICAN "UNDERCLASS"?

Questions about how culture and structure matter in poverty came to a head in debates over the so-called urban "underclass"—a debate that generated as much heat as light. In the early 1980s, journalists and conservative scholars depicted the "underclass" as a group with a self-destructive culture, as evidenced by their embrace of welfare, drugs and alcohol, crime, and single parenthood. By the mid-1980s a more liberal alternative perspective, championed by Wilson, maintained that social problems in "underclass" neighborhoods reflected the disappearance of work, not a dysfunctional lifestyle choice. Examining the "underclass" question focused a substantial amount of scholarly and policy maker attention on the contemporary experience of urban poverty but produced few new insights into the condition. The term *underclass* was imprecise, pejorative, and distracting; the debate's "culture versus structure" framework failed to generate theoretical epiphanies; and the debate focused narrowly on the African American experience in Rust Belt ghettos rather than examining the diverse experiences of poverty among all ethnoracial groups, including Mexican Americans. Chávez appears to be home to an "underclass"—which is to say that some residents struggled with severe or intergenerational deprivation and with problems including unemployment, welfare reliance, crime and violence, and family breakup. Guadalupe appears free of these troubles. Can we speak of a Mexican American "underclass"? What are we saying when we call a neighborhood "underclass"? Over time, might the quiet immigrant poverty of Guadalupe become the spectacular "underclass" poverty of Chávez?

Underclass is a pejorative and imprecise code word for poverty in neighborhoods dominated by hustling. Hustling thrives in some Mexican American barrios, including Chávez, as it does in certain African American ghettos, such as Chicago's Robert Taylor Homes. Hustling does not arise mechanically from a dysfunctional culture, nor does it surface spontaneously from the constraints of social structure. It represents one sensible economic strategy for people struggling to satisfy high expectations for success in an environment of poor opportunities. Chávez residents' cultural worlds emphasized palpable material success, including conspicuous consumption; labor markets in East LA provided opportunities to work, but workers usually understood that these opportunities offered few prospects for success. The situation in Guadalupe differed because transnational networks allowed residents to deemphasize local consumption in their definitions of economic accomplishment. In Guadalupe, as in other immigrant communities, overwork represented a reasonable pathway toward economic goals that were objectively more modest.

Hustlers use crime and welfare to generate income. The label *under-class* highlights the stigma we attach to these activities while it minimizes the income they generate. The label implies that hustling is an isolated and unneeded economic strategy, while the debate focuses on whether it arises from the dysfunctional preferences of individuals or from a breakdown of the economy. Hustling and what some might label an "underclass" existed in Chávez but not in Guadalupe, but not because of simple differences in residents' economic preferences or because of differences in economic possibilities in the barrios of East LA compared to San Jose. Chávez residents did not *want* to generate income through crime and welfare, nor did a breakdown in the economy *force* them to do so. A variety of local institutions made crime a reasonable way to generate income in both communities, but we would never apply the label *under-class* to crime in Guadalupe because of the particular laws that residents violated. Neither Guadalupe nor Chávez residents condoned welfare receipt, but the ubiquity of deprivation in Chávez encouraged residents there to be more flexible in their condemnation.

Calling people who engage in hustling and the communities where they live "underclass" implies that they stand apart from and beneath U.S. mainstream society. Examining how Chávez residents use crime and welfare to generate income reveals hustling's foundations in mainstream institutions—in residents' embrace of mainstream culture's measures of economic success and their position in the least desirable sectors of the mainstream job structure. Like most Americans, Chávez residents valued financial independence and conspicuous consumption. They could demonstrate financial independence by living on one's own in private housing—thus demonstrating independence from parents and the state. Conspicuous consumption meant having one's own car, at least occasionally dressing up in fashionable clothing, and having cash on hand to treat friends and relatives to a meal at the local *taquer'a* or McDonald's. Attaining success was a challenge, however, because of structural characteristics of the mainstream job market. Few local jobs provided decent wages and security—a benefit for mainstream employers and a reflection of local and national political arrangements. In these circumstances, hustling and the local institutions that supported hustlers allowed residents to continue to strive toward the goals of mainstream culture despite the constraints of mainstream structure.

Guadalupe residents also faced slim opportunities on the job market, and they sought local institutional support to manage the problems that resulted. In contrast to the Chicanos of Chávez, however, Guadalupe's immigrants did not embrace mainstream American expectations of economic success. As a result, the kinds of institutional solutions they adopted to manage job market problems led them to overwork rather than to hustle. Though Guadalupe could never be mistaken for an "underclass" neighborhood, the job market created problems there as it did in Chávez. Household routines had to accommodate long hours of work at low wages, undocumented workers had to find secure methods of meeting employers or obtaining *chuecos,* and mainstream cultural expectations were held in check only as long as residents could sustain vibrant connections with communities in Mexico. Guadalupe residents forged ties with existing San Jose institutions such as job markets, local schools, and barrio neighborhoods. They maintained their distance from others, including the peculiar materialism of American consumer society. These institutional arrangements changed slowly and incrementally, for example, when settlement snuck up on long-staying residents, and they changed quickly and dramatically, as when the passage of California's anti-immigrant Proposition 187 galvanized *Mexicano* interest in citizenship and other political institutions. In Guadalupe, a different—and less destructive—set of institutions provided solutions to the problems associated with work.

Hustling and overwork both used local institutions to solve dilemmas rooted in low-wage labor markets. Both economic strategies helped residents address problems related to lousy jobs, and neither erased the problems those jobs created. Lousy jobs—and the resource deprivation that accompanies them—inevitably exacted a price in both low-income communities. In many ways Chávez residents paid a higher price, but neither institutional solution was perfect or painless. Applying the pejorative term *underclass* to the institutional solution that dominated in Chávez—as well as in other low-income urban areas such as Rust Belt ghettos—reflects the cultural orientations of scholars and policy makers. Residents in Chávez and in Rust Belt ghettos similarly applied pejorative terms to overworkers, seeing them as slaves, suckers, or sellouts.

Focusing on institutions leads us to examine how different low-income communities are culturally and structurally integrated into the United States rather than to examine whether the "underclass" is culturally deviant or structurally disenfranchised. Low-income areas are not places separate or apart from mainstream America. Loïc Wacquant argues that these communities are properly understood as a particular social institution within U.S. society. Is there a Mexican American "underclass"? Of course not. There are, however, many Mexican American communities caught between the rock of cultural expectations and the hard place of low-wage jobs. Poor people try to solve this problem, and their solution is to devise and energize local institutions that allow them to make do with resources that are available. Rather than label and condemn some of these institutional solutions as typifying an "underclass," we would do better to examine what sorts of institutions can do a better job at resolving problems generated by low-wage jobs and considering how to encourage and sustain those institutions.

PUBLIC POLICY AND THE PRICE OF POVERTY

Even as they argue over whether structure or culture is more important, policy makers subscribe to a fundamentally similar model of poverty. In day-to-day politics, disagreements about structure versus culture—with liberals supporting structural arguments and conservatives sympathetic to cultural ones—obscure this fundamental consensus. The consensus is that poverty reflects a lack of social mobility, that social mobility is the antidote to poverty, that mobility should occur in the space of a generation or so, and that mobility is facilitated by a good job in the legitimate economy. Disagreements about why poor people are immobile do not threaten this fundamental consensus.

My analysis of barrio life suggests that institutions of poverty facilitate income generation even as they impede mobility. In some situations, small changes in institutions of poverty can substantially increase their potential to support income generation as well as upward mobility. In other situations, institutions of poverty can be a more significant barrier to mobility than structural dislocations or cultural deficits.

The fundamental dilemma confronting residents of both Guadalupe and Chávez was neither a structural disappearance of work nor a cultural disinclination to seek mobility through work. It was, rather, that available jobs paid so poorly that participating in work could not be counted on to produce upward mobility. Everyday economic life in Guadalupe and Chávez revolved around the institutional solutions that residents embraced to resolve this dilemma. In Guadalupe, they resolved it by using local institutions to redefine the rewards of low-wage jobs. In Chávez, residents turned to alternative income-generating institutions ranging from the illicit economy to the public aid system. Neither of these institutional solutions, however, provided a sure path out of poverty for barrio residents.

In Guadalupe, the institutional solution supported overwork, the key to which was maintaining the migrant's inflated view of the dollar. Those who subscribed most fully to overwork lived in abysmal conditions in San Jose so that they could send as many dollars as possible home to Mexico, and they crossed and recrossed the border to get relief from the difficult conditions of daily living in the States and to maintain connections and keep abreast of investments at home. These practices maintained ties to Mexico and sustained the cultural orientation that low-wage jobs in the States were valuable. But these practices also precluded socioeconomic advancement in the United States. Even if employers were happy to hire a hard-working immigrant who really believed $5 an hour was a good wage, they were unlikely to promote an employee who regularly left the job for weeks at a time or whose living situation did not promote the acquisition of English. Thus, overwork could serve as a barrier to mobility.

Not surprisingly, overwork broke down for many residents of Guadalupe. Many migrants left Guadalupe barrio permanently—exhausted, frustrated, and disgusted by life in the States. Others embarked on the path to U.S. settlement. They began to raise families and to devote less time, money, and attention toward practices that renewed links with Mexico. They sent smaller remittances less frequently, they took fewer and shorter trips to visit family, and they began to spend more time in social situations where people did not speak fluent Spanish. Something in the life circumstances of these residents disturbed the institutional solution of overwork. Landing a steady job could encourage a circular migrant to move family from Mexico to the States, or a fight with relatives in Mexico could interrupt remittance sending. Frequently, overwork broke down slowly and incompletely—for example, when family members in Mexico joined an already overcrowded household in Guadalupe. New arrivals meant new ties to people in Mexico. At the same time, new arrivals meant greater demands on U.S. household resources and a reduction in migrants' ability to sustain ties through remittance sending.

In even the best of circumstances, therefore, Guadalupe residents found that overwork could perpetuate poverty rather than facilitate upward mobility. This happened in different ways for recent migrants and for more settled migrants. Recent migrants inspired by the value of their dollars in Mexico threw themselves into low-wage work. But lousy jobs were worthwhile only as long as migrants maintained their ties to Mexico, and maintaining ties to Mexico could disrupt work routines in the States enough to preclude upward mobility out of lousy jobs. This was the price of poverty exacted by overwork among recent migrants in Guadalupe. More settled migrants frequently found themselves economically immobilized by a precarious social balancing act. Migrant success attracted family and neighbors to move north, and isolated migrants often welcomed their company. But new arrivals also strained resources. Earnings that might have supported upward mobility—moving to a larger house or a better neighborhood, for example—might instead be devoted to sponsoring more migration. Some settlers withdrew support from migration chains and devoted resources to their own mobility, but this meant paying a price in social isolation. Thus, institutions of poverty exacted a price from settlers who were forced to chose between mobility and isolation.

In Chávez, residents resolved the dilemma of low-wage work through hustling, an institutional solution that exacted a heavy price. Residents who embraced hustling risked arrest, incarceration, and violence in the illicit economy, and they endured stigmatization and a constant scramble for economic survival in the welfare economy. Nevertheless, residents embraced hustling because they believed it provided a better chance of economic success than low-wage work. The evidence for this belief came from three sources. First, there was the reality of life on the low-wage labor market. Chávez residents, unable to take advantage of a transnational perspective on the dollar's value, felt sure that devoting oneself to a low-wage job was a definite and certain economic dead-end. Second, there were some people who earned decent money through participation in the illicit economy and by taking advantage of welfare. Stories of long-term success through crime or welfare were often apocryphal and rarely well documented. But there was plenty of evidence—in the clothes, cars, and furniture of barrio residents—that drug sales or AFDC could bring short-term success. The final piece of evidence was that many residents who participated in crime or welfare seemed to find a way to garner eventual success, even if that success did not take place within the confines of the illicit or welfare economy. Elm Street affiliation, for example, seemed to open doors to some highly coveted jobs that paid decently, and some welfare participants could find good jobs through programs targeted to move them into the labor force. Thus, although participating in the institutions that supported hustling carried grave risks, it also seemed to increase participants' chances of enjoying long-lasting success.

Public policy may be able to affect the extent to which institutions of poverty impede and facilitate upward mobility among the poor. Policy makers might recognize that low-wage jobs do not necessarily represent the first step on the ladder of upward mobility, nor does migrants' willingness to take these jobs and natives' rejection of them indicate a difference in devotion to the work ethic or a difference in job availability. The dynamics of low-wage working among immigrants and natives reflect the operations of different institutions of poverty. Too often, however, the effects of these institutions are interpreted as evidence that immigrants and natives have different and immutable cultural orientations or that they live in different and incompatible structural circumstances. Policy makers would do better to seek out ways to strengthen the operations of institutions of poverty that encourage upward mobility.

Public policy can also shape the extent to which institutions of poverty exact a price from the poor in everyday life. That is, aside from whether an institution of poverty encourages upward mobility, these institutions play an enormous role in everyday life in low-income communities. Policy makers may sometimes find themselves in a position where they have little leverage to alter how institutions of poverty shape mobility. For example, the dilemmas surrounding migration and low-wage work in Guadalupe barrio are driven by international social dynamics that may lie beyond policy makers' ability to control. Relationships between the Elm Street gang and local police in Chávez bring into play legal issues that tend to tie policy makers' hands. However, even in these cases, policy makers may have a substantial ability to alter the price that these institutions exact from the poor in everyday life. Public policies that support a safe and decent workplace, that encourage a focus on rehabilitation rather than punishment in law enforcement, and that emphasize income support rather than fraud prevention in public assistance will all serve to lower the price of poverty in everyday life.

Policy makers worry that policies that reduce the price of poverty will affect the poor in untoward ways. They are concerned that increasing the minimum wage, for example, may have an adverse effect on structural circumstances by increasing unemployment. They are concerned that less punitive criminal justice or more generous welfare will harm poor people's cultural orientations. My sense is that this focus on structural and cultural factors is misplaced.

Institutions of poverty are complex combinations of structure and culture. The only certainty is that lowering the price of poverty, if done properly, will improve the everyday quality of life among the poor and reduce the amount of social suffering that they endure.

If we as a society decide to change our institutions of poverty, the task will not be easy. It will require enormous energy, skillful politicking, and good luck. Institutions are, after all, durable arrangements of structure and culture, and they resist change. But if we take our goal to ameliorate poverty, it is essential that we moderate those institutions that exact its price.

WHITENESS AS CONTINGENT HIERARCHIES

WHO COUNTS AS WHITE AND WHY

By Steve Garner

WHAT IS THE POINT OF USING 'WHITENESS' AS AN ANALYTICAL TOOL?

So far we have observed that whiteness has been conceptualized in a number of complementary ways. In this chapter I will focus on the idea that in addition to a set of borders between people categorized as 'white' and 'non white', there is another set of internal borders produced by racialization. In other words, there are socially observable degrees of whiteness between the groups that seem to be unproblematically white. Examples here include Southern, Central and Eastern European immigrant groups, Jews, Gypsy-Travellers/Roma, as well as the numerous and important divisions based on class, gender, sexuality, region, etc., identified in the literature on both America and Britain (Hartigan 2005, Nayak 2003, Daniels 1997). The reader may well be experiencing trepidation about the extent to which we are encroaching onto other areas of work. We already have concepts like 'anti-semitism', 'sexism' and 'homo phobia'. Class divisions are already covered in other literatures. Considering that European migrants are white anyway, how is this to do with 'race'? Isn't it ethnicity, another area abundantly, if not excessively, analyzed already? I do not want to be proscriptive. There are plenty of perspectives that can bring fruitful analyses to bear on these identities and social hierarchies, and using the whiteness problematic is one of them. However, I hope to convince you of its utility through the use of three of the broad areas of study dealt with in the literature: immigration into America in the nineteenth and early twentieth century (the 'inbetween peoples' thesis); the 'White Australia' policy (1901–1972); and the related ideas of 'white trash' in America, and the working class in the UK.

Before we look at those case studies, I want to provide a brief outline of the history of 'white' as a racial identity, in order to put them into perspective. We have to keep in mind that we are dealing with social interpretations of physical and cultural phenomena, and these interpretations can change over time and place, reflecting the political, economic and cultural distinctiveness of the context.

WHERE DID WHITENESS COME FROM?

Primarily we have looked so far at the intersection of white ness and its Others, those racialized identities created by white world's military, commercial and ideological domination of the globe since the sixteenth century. That is the story of how Europeans simultaneously created white-ness and otherness as collective identities. Although from the vantage point of the twenty-first century, the terms 'white' and 'black' seem to go without saying, these words have not always been used to identify human beings. Indeed use of the term 'white' to describe people dates back only to the sixteenth century. At that time however it was one of a range of labels, and not the one most frequently used. Religion, nation, and social class were all deployed more than color. The literature on the period from 1500 to the end of the seventeenth century arrives at a rough consensus: the co-existence of religious labels of identity; 'Christian' and 'heathen' in the American colonies (Jordan 1968, Frederickson 1988) rendered color distinctions redundant until slaves began to convert to Christianity. Elsewhere in the New World, V.S. Naipaul (1969) notes that after the slave revolt in Berbice (then in Dutch Guiana, South America) in 1764, the dead were divided up in official reports neither as 'black' and 'white', nor even as 'slave' and 'free', but as 'Christians' and 'heathens'.

Slavery is now irrevocably linked in popular understandings of history to the transatlantic slave trade and its institutions in the Americas, with Africans as its principal population. However, vital to the development of whiteness is the acknowledgement that in the Anglophone colonies, it was the end of the seventeenth century before the status of 'free' and 'unfree' labor cor-responded perfectly to European and African workers respectively. This is because in the earlier days of colonization, white indentured laborers (1) were employed before, and then alongside Africans. When these indentured laborers became numerically inferior due to their access to land ownership after indentureship, then the numbers of enslaved Africans started to rapidly over take them. So it was around the last decade of the seventeenth century that the only unfree laborers were Africans. There were free Blacks as well as free white laborers, and it is at this point that we see the emergence of colony-level legislation against voting rights for Blacks; 'race' mixing; and the introduction of restrictions on property ownership for Black people. We can thus start the clock of 'whiteness' as an explicit legitimized collective identity in North America and the Anglophone Caribbean from around that point. This was clearly not a historical coincidence. The sixteenth and seventeenth centuries was the period when Europeans were beginning to encounter people from Africa, the Americas and Asia on an ongoing basis, and notice the obvious if cosmetic physical differences between groups alongside the cultural ones.

In the period between then and the mid nineteenth century, the idea that some people's identities were 'white' came to be attached to the new ways of understanding mankind that developed out of the Enlighten ment (Eze 1997). Th ese understandings were enshrined in elite scientific discourse as empirically provable racial differences explaining cultural, political and technological inequalities. While earlier eras had noted that physical appearance, climate and culture differed from place to place, there was no sustained intellectual effort to link these in a coherent philosophy of difference. This changed during the Enlightenment. Climate, it was argued, determined physical appearance, and in turn these determined the capacity of different people to evolve, that is, toward the goal of European norms. However, the mainstream discourse fixed the relationship of climate to civilizational capacity: only those living in temperate climates, that is, white Europeans, could properly attain the heights of civilization, and the others trailed behind. Versions of this logic appeared throughout the eighteenth and early nineteenth centuries. By the mid nineteenth century, this was no longer up for discussion, but was itself the basis for further discussion.

Indeed, as racial science and philosophy garnered credence, increasingly complex schemas were produced, in which there were subdivisions of whiteness. Notions of Anglo-Saxon supremacy (within the multi-layered 'white race') began to gain intellectual support, bolstered by an amalgam of the press, a network of scientists engaged in somatic measurements (Horsman 1981) and internationally read work. Robert Knox and Joseph Arthur Comte de Gobineau developed the notion that within the white 'race', Anglo-Saxons were particularly capable of civilization in comparison to Celts, Slavs and Latins (2). This hierarchy within a hierarchy is the basis of the thesis developed by US labor historians David Roediger and James Barrett, whose work we shall look at next.

CASE STUDY 1: 'INBETWEEN PEOPLE'?

In a set of influential publications (Roediger 1991, Barrett and Roediger 1997, 2004, 2005), Roediger and Barrett argue that in the period from the 1850s to the 1910s, incoming migrant Europeans were exposed to a situation where the American mainstream racialized values exerted forces that pushed Europeans to claim whiteness for themselves, in order to gain privileged access to resources, and psychological and social capital (Du Bois's 'wages of whiteness')(3). Barrett and Roediger (1997, 2004) maintain two principal and connected points. Firstly, 'Whiteness' is to do with cultural and political power and, secondly, not all those who appear phenotypically white are incorporated equally into the dominant group.

Catholic and Jewish migrants from the various, Southern, Eastern and Central European countries, they argue, were not immediately accepted socially and culturally as white. Differential access to this resource was sought by successive waves of migrants learning the rules of the game, or 'this racial thing', as one of Barrett and Roediger's respondents puts it (1997: 6). They label these groups of less dominant Europeans, who were temporarily disadvantaged in the US context by class and culture, 'inbetween people': not white, but not black either.

Scholarship in dialogue with the writers above has debated the extent to which various ethnic groups such as Jewish- (Brodkin 1994, 1998) and Italian-Americans (Guglielmo and Salerno 2003) can be considered 'white'. These arguments posit some parallels between the Irish and the Italians in America, suggesting that over time they 'became' white. However, there is a counter-argument developed by some historians such as Eric Arnesen (2001) and Tom Guglielmo (2003) that European immigrants did not actually have to 'become' white, relative to

Blacks and Mexicans, for example, and that the 'inbetween people' theory does not withstand scrutiny. I think the key to unravelling this knot are reasonably straightforward. They are to do with understanding the priorities and assumptions of the protagonists. The first thing to realize is that the 'inbetween people' thesis does not claim that Irish, Italian and other European immigrants were really 'black', but that they were literally 'denigrated', that is, likened to black Americans (in terms of civilization and social status), and they temporarily occupied the lowest positions on the economic and social ladder of free labor. This social, occupational and often geographical proximity to Free Blacks gave rise to the imperative for these migrant groups to distance themselves from them. The further they moved from blackness, the closer they got to whiteness. This strategy was executed in some cases through the urban equivalent of ethnic cleansing (Bernstein, 1990; Ignatiev, 1996).

So the point is not to suggest that certain groups of immigrants were not phenotypically white, which is why Tom Guglielmo (2003) correctly identifies 'race' and color as often separate but over lapping criteria in late nineteenth- and early twentieth-century American institutional definitions, but that ideologically and culturally they were indeed considered different and lesser 'white races'. The corollaries of this categorization were not a set of life chances equivalent to those of Blacks, Native Americans or Hispanics, rather the obligation to define themselves as 'white' in a society where that mattered a great deal, whereas in their countries of origin, it had mattered scarcely at all. European immigrants thus 'became' white on arrival in the New World, runs the argument, because they disembarked into a new set of social identities that articulated with those they had brought with them, and one overarching identity was whiteness.

I think this conclusion needs qualification. Not being white, and being black, are two very different things: the Catholic Irish were always salvageable for whiteness in a way that African, Mexican, Asian and Native Americans were not (Garner 2003). This is because legally they were definitely white, in as far as they could become naturalized citizens, and were not treated as imports (Haney-López 1996, Jacobson 1998). The second problem is an interesting one that illustrates a divergence of interpretations of identical material. The protagonists in this debate prioritize different arenas as the source of their claims. On one side, Barrett and Roediger see the cultural domain as the one in which perceptions of 'inbetweenness' are made explicit, while Arnesen and Guglielmo pragmatically see the legal domain as predominant. Whatever people said or did, argue the latter, in law all white people were white. However, this reasoning is open to the criticism that in sociological terms, the law can just as easily be deconstructed as can popular culture: it is not a superior level of discourse. The legal domain, argues Cheryl Harris (1993), was utilized from the nineteenth century to inject scientific rationality into decisions about who belonged to which race: and these decisions had material impacts. Yet the basis of the law was spurious, reliant as it was on unfeasibly accurate records about people's ancestry, and understandings of definitions of 'race' that were not empirically provable. The result of this was that the legal concept of '"blood"' was no more objective than that which the law dismissed as subjective and unreliable (Harris 1993: 1740). Guglielmo (2003), for example, refers to material suggesting that Italians (especially from the South) were subject to the same kind of racializing discourses, placing them at a lower level of civilization vis-à-vis Anglo-Saxons, as were the Irish. Yet it is worth reiterating that 'not white' does not mean 'black'. Even if it did, how can we explain the court ruling referred to by Jacobson (1998: 4) in which an Alabama court found that the State had not proved beyond doubt that a Sicilian woman was white?

Used sociologically, the term 'white' can be interpreted as encompassing non-material and fluid dominant norms and boundaries. Within the white racialized hierarchy were, as Guglielmo rightly points out, a number of 'races'. Indeed, using the distinction between 'white' and 'non white' as a starting point is a legitimate historical argument. In the USA, white migrants were people with rights, while Blacks were property without rights, for example. Yet this approach regards the terms 'white' and 'black' themselves as natural entities or givens, whose existence is then transposed into law. A sociologist however, ought to view these terms and the social relations they cover as part of the puzzle itself, that is, as products of the processes of racialization.

What emerges from this is that there are various contexts: economic, social, legal, cultural, for example, in which meaning is attributed to types of difference. In practice, it is impossible to completely separate these dimensions, but it is useful to start from this basis as a way of thinking through these issues. Moreover, the period covered, around 70 years from the mid nineteenth century to the First World War, enables us to see that understandings of who fits where in the social hierarchies can change. Why this happens when it happens can only be answered by reference to the historical record. We might put forward a few important structural items here, such as the Irish Famine, which altered the complexion of Irish migration to America; the Civil War, Reconstruction and after, which provided the framework both for black/white relations and for the formation of a 'white vote' in American politics; the development of the US economy to a stage which required so many manual workers that the labor supply was exhausted within the country and meant that there was plentiful work available for migrants; the consequent slump at the end of the nineteenth century experienced by Western Europe, which meant that the availability of employment that had absorbed some of the workers from Southern and Eastern Europe was diminished. Place all these together with the framework for understanding difference established by racial science in the nineteenth century, and outlines of the problem we have seen conceptualized, using the shorthand 'inbetween peoples', or the process of 'becoming white', emerge more clearly. Bear in mind that being white was not just about a certain range of phenotypes, but also about claims on culture and values.

CASE STUDY 2: 'WHITE AUSTRALIA'

The Australian colonies were founded, much like the American colonies, as separate entities. Their foundation at the end of the eighteenth century, under the British Crown, proceeded on the legal principle that Australia was empty, uninhabited and unsettled land (*terra nullius*). Thus the white European settlers founded the colonies on the contradictory basis that the Aboriginal populations (now referred to as 'First Australians') did not exist, yet their collective relations with them were, as for the European settlers in North America, frequent and necessary. By the mid nineteenth century, the Australian colonies were absorbing migrant labor from the Pacific Islands, China and India. Between 1901 (when the Commonwealth of Australia became a dominion, with its own federal government) until 1972, Australia's immigration policy was based on the objectives of:

1. Protecting indigenous (i.e. white) labor from competition with Asian and Pacific Island labor, and
2. Preserving an Anglo-Celtic majority in the country.

The term 'White Australia' was coined in 1906, as an assertion of these twin objectives. The point of looking at this policy and the problems it ran into later in the twentieth century is firstly, to highlight both the haziness around who is considered white at a given moment and why; and secondly, to give an idea of some of the contextual, structural considerations that frame such changes within a hierarchy.

'White Australia' then was not a single piece of legislation, but a doctrine underlying an accumulation of laws and practices that restricted immigration from outside the country (except Europe) and excluded foreign nationals within Australia from various benefits and elements of citizenship. The 1901 Commonwealth Immigration Restriction Act (I.R.A) was the first piece of legislation passed by the new Federal Government. Its most well-known features were its provision for a written test in any European language, at the discretion of an immigration officer, to determine a prospective immigrant's fitness for approval; and the categories of person whose entry was prohibited. These were: the physically or mentally ill, categories of criminal other than political prisoner, prostitutes, those living on prostitutes' earnings, and those likely to be a charge on the communal purse (Tavan 2005: 7–8). In addition, various other laws provided for the repatriation of foreigners (Pacific Island Labourers Act 1901), excluded foreigners from voting (Commonwealth Franchise Act 1902; Naturalization Act 1903) and from benefits like pensions (Old-Age and Invalid Pensions Act 1908) and the Commonwealth maternity bonus (1912).

However, to properly understand the compound anxieties about being usurped by foreign labor and facing 'racial contamination', as Labor Party leader John Christian Watson put it during parliamentary debate in 1901, it should be noted that blueprints of White Australia were already embodied in the legislation of the various Australian colonies before they combined to form the Commonwealth of Australia in 1900. Asian and Pacific Islanders had been working in Australia since the first half of the nineteenth century, primarily in the mining and sugar industries respectively. Hostile political agitation as a response to the migration of Indian, Chinese and Pacific Islanders into various parts of the country had led to state governments passing restrictions in a number of waves during the second half of the century. This became particularly intense in the late 1880s. By the end of the century, a model of indirectly discriminatory policies had been introduced. The 1901 I.R.A was therefore the endorsement, on a national level, of a set of practices ongoing across Australia. What was at stake was a conception of Australia as a unique civilization of Europeans encountering and overcoming a natural environment that other Europeans did not have to tame. The combination of whiteness, Britishness and embryonic Australianness that this embodied was most clearly defined in its dealings with First Australians and with the Chinese, not only through the physical differences shorthanded as racial, but the underlying values that Australians saw themselves as having and the other groups as lacking: vitality, industriousness, purity, cleanliness. The idea of geographical vulnerability added urgency to turn-of-the-century Australians' view of themselves as the pioneers of civilization surrounded by potential adversaries. In the prevailing social Darwinist ideological context, they were the spearhead of the white race forced into proximity with lesser races. In the ensuing struggle, they would prevail as the stronger, fitter race (4). This is why although non-Europeans had their uses, mixing with them and allowing them citizenship was seen as counter-productive. Governments did not attempt the mass deportations provided for in the IRA, and particular industries such as pearl diving enjoyed, de facto, special dispensation to employ Pacific Islanders and Chinese, who were seen as 'naturally' more suited to this work. Gwenda Tavan (2005:15) interprets White Australia as a populist and popular device for generating nationalism in a fledgling society. It garnered support from all interest groups despite tensions of gender, class and religion. She goes on to contextualize it as central to the specific form of social liberalism that was the national ideology of the emergent State. This required state intervention to mitigate the excesses of the market, ensure fairer distribution of wealth, and provide minimum living conditions. The cultural homogeneity putatively anchoring this set of values was seen as essential to successfully building a civilization geographically remote from the epicenter of world civilization (Europe). Within this, the labor movement's opposition to the conditions of Kanaka (Pacifi c Island) workers in the sugar industry, on the grounds of their virtual slavery, was not viewed as contradictory to its support for repatriation of the foreign element of the workforce.

Indeed, it was the tropical part of Australia, the Northern Territories, that most exercised elite Australians' minds in the first half of the twentieth century. While the baseline for Australian immigration was to build on British and, to a lesser extent, Irish stock, the idea of 'race' and its relationship to climate and space proved problematic. Simply put, the association of different 'races' with particular types of climate, and with innate characteristics militated against Northern Europeans flourishing in this tropical environment (Anderson 2006). Yet with the departure of the Pacific Islanders in the first decades of the twentieth century, the North required a substitute labor force. The settlement of the North needed not just white supervisors, as had been the case in other tropical areas of colonial expansion, but a tropical white male laboring workforce. Was this a contradiction in terms? Alison Bashford (2000: 255) argues that tropical medicine debated the question, 'Is White Australia possible?' between 1900 and the 1930s. The problem revolved not around white men colonizing other people in the tropics, but 'as colonizers of a difficult and resilient space' (2000: 258). In this debate, First Australians had again been made invisible. The focus was on how whiteness could be adapted to overcome the tropical environment. Indeed, suggestions of how to accomplish this contributed, maintains Bashford, to producing 'an idea that whiteness was not only a characteristic of skin and color, but was also about how one lived, how one arranged one's moment by moment existence in space and time [...] the capacity to live in the tropics had to be learnt in minute, detailed and constant ways' (2000: 266).

At least for those engaged in the public health discourse, the solution was to apply science and rationality to impose order on the environment (Anderson 2006). A more pressing problem for employers in the Queensland and Northern Territories sugar plantations was to remain eco-nomically viable. Here, the niceties of the public health debate were ignored by workers intent on retaining a standard of living promised by the dismissal of competition in the form of Pacific Island labor. Yet in the mid 1920s, migrants from Italy began arriving in their thousands to work on the estates. Th is triggered a hostile campaign led by the Brisbane-based *Worker* newspaper against Italian immigration (Sheills 2006). The Italians occupied a position straddling the lines of whiteness. Offcially categorized as 'white aliens', they became the object of a discourse aimed at presenting them as a threat not just to jobs, but to living standards (being willing to work for lower wages) and the cultural future of Australia (due to their clannishness, corruption, backward civilization and unfitness for vigorous pioneer activity required to settle and develop empty land). By 1925, the Queensland government had set up a Royal Commission to investigate the impact of the increased number of aliens in North Queensland. The Commissioner charged with producing a report made a sharp distinction between Northern and Southern Italians, castigating the latter vis-à-vis their Northern counterparts, for their clannishness, resistance to assimilation and propensity towards crime and violence. He was not alone in thinking this, either in Australia or elsewhere. Italians themselves debated the North–South divide in terms of culture and civilization (Verdicchio 1997), and the characterization of the Sicilians as 'inferior types' represented a boundary line between white and less white aliens.

Indeed, while the 1901 Immigration Act had been primarily aimed at keeping out the Chinese, the second- and third-largest groups of 'prohibited' immigrants (i.e. those refused the right to land in Australia) were Southern Europeans: Maltese and Italians. Distinctions within the 'white race' meant that Latins were lower down the racial pecking order than Anglo-Saxons, Alpines and Nordic peoples. Added to this complication was the reclassification of Axis member nationals (from Bulgaria, the Austro-Hungarian Empire, Germany and Turkey) during World War I as hostile aliens. There was even a temporary internment camp in New South Wales, and bans continued until at least 1923. Between 1912 and 1946 (the period when separate figures on the Maltese were kept), the prevailing practice of immigration officers was to question the right of Southern Europeans to land, even if, as in the case of the Maltese, they had British passports. Perceived racial difference here overrode nationality. In the most well-known case, 208 Maltese were kept out of Australia in 1916 (York 1990) by Melbourne immigration offcials who gave them the dictation test in Dutch: all failed.

What this reveals about the workings of whiteness is its lack of solidity and stability. Even the taken-for-granted visible signs can be misleading, or be irrelevant to those wielding power in precise situations. Cultural and political factors can override the phenotypical ones. Moreover, the capacity to centre problems around whiteness per se can make other people invisible. Despite First Australians living in Northern Territories and Northern Queensland for millennia, public discourse obliterated them from the picture. The land was read through white eyes as 'empty' because it was neither owned according to private land-ownership laws, nor cultivated in ways that made sense in agrarian norms (planting, cultivation and harvest).

The basis for anxiety about shades of whiteness is expressed again through competition, or at least perceived competition, for work and conditions within international labor markets. It is not feasible to extricate the material from the cultural aspects of whiteness if we seek to understand it in its lived context.

CASE STUDY 3: THE RACIALIZATION OF WORKING-CLASS CULTURES

'Abject Whites' in the UK

Ethnographic writing on white racialized identities in the UK has focused disproportionately, as has much of the academic work on class, on working-class men. This can be seen as a reflection of the academy's middle-class composition and of ethnography's colonial heritage. Since Victorian times, middle-class academics and philanthropists have conducted surveys of the poor, the work of Friedrich Engels (1969[1844]), Henry Mayhew (1967[1861]) and Charles Booth (1902) being the best-known examples. The objective of such projects may have been to reform, politicize or evangelize the working classes, but the common strands were the revelation of their failings, and the creation of an inventory of what they did not have. In describing them, researchers drew parallels between them and colonized peoples. Anthony Wohl, on the web resource 'Victorian Web' (5) notes that a number of characteristics were applied by British commentators to the nineteenth-century working classes, Irish immigrants and colonial subjects. They were: unreasonable, irrational, and easily excited, childlike, superstitious (not religious), criminal (with neither respect for private property, nor notions of property), excessively sexual, filthy, inhabited unknown dark lands or territories and shared physical qualities. Wohl has clearly identified an overlap between the language of 'race' and that of class, locating both as being fixed on the body and culture.

The key point to grasp in the discourse on whiteness is that behavior, appearance and culture are linked. There has to be an explanation for why some of the 'race' placed at the top of the hierarchy clearly do not match the criteria established for superiority: bad genes and dysfunctional culture. From this viewpoint, the language and frames used in order to discursively distinguish (or make) classes, class fractions and 'races', are very similar.

This process of negatively evaluating working-class habitus and behavior has become so dominant a discourse that in the post-industrial era of structural un- and underemployment, studies demonstrate that such values have to some extent become internalized. Bev Skeggs (1997) observes that the working-class women she interviews themselves often dis-identify from the working class. They define 'working class' by reference to values they personally do not or no longer have, or to economic predicaments they do not face. Indeed, the age of readily-sanctioned reference to a working-class 'us' appears, outside particular work milieux, to have disappeared from their social world. The anxiety around owning white working-class subject positions can be read as a reflection of white middle- and ruling-class attempts to pathologize and racialize them as an 'underclass'. Although the 'underclass' is rarely used as a sociological term in twenty-fi rst century British scholarship (after intensive use in the late 80s and 90s), parts of the underclass debate map onto groups within the working class who are perceived as lacking in respectability: in the contemporary period these are 'Chavs' (Haywood and Yar, 2005; Nayak, 2003), or more abstractly, in Chris Haylett's (2001) argument, 'abject whites'.

She contends that that sections of a white 'underclass' are constructed in turn-ofthe-century Britain as 'people who are outside/beyond/beneath the nation' (2001: 358). This process involves devaluing social actions carried out by them. The protagonists in the Autumn 1993 'white' riots (in Oxford, Cardiff and Newcastle) 'were not hailed as class revolutionaries or even righteously angered disenfranchised minorities, rather they were an embarrassing sign of what the white working-class poor had become—a disorganized, racist and sexist detritus' (ibid.: 358). Indeed, in the de-unionized post-Fordist landscape, blame for this 'decline' in the working class, is placed on the working class themselves, or at least the poorest sections of it. Over time, argues Haylett, explanations of decline have become increasingly less structural, and more individual, and fixed around pathological working-class masculinities, and backwardness. In short the poor emerge as the exact opposite of the expanding multicultural, cosmopolitan middle classes. Indeed,

Haylett stresses that the identity work accomplished in this discourse is relational, that is the multicultural modern group (the British middle classes) depend on the 'abject unmodern' white working class (ibid.: 365) for their own identity.

This 'power-evasive discourse' (Frankenberg, 1994) is picked up in specific relation to 'race', in for example the work on 'color-blind racism' (Bonilla-Silva, 2002) in the USA. Like minorities, with whom they are often compared, working-class Whites in these narratives are culturally disposed to degeneracy, crime, over-fecundity, fecklessness, etc.

'White Trash' in the USA

Similar themes resonate throughout the new studies and problematization of 'white trash' in the USA (Wray and Newitz 1997, Hartigan 2005, 1999, 1997a, b, Wray 2006). In these accounts, whiteness is significantly mediated by class (Bettie 2000, Gibbons 2004, Morris 2005). The polarized pairing of pro ductiveness–unproductiveness is also central. Hartigan's tracing of the development of the phenomenon of 'white trash' in the USA (2005) demonstrates some interesting points of comparison between 'race' and class on one hand, and the UK and the USA on the other. Using the conclusion of nineteenth-century travel writer James Gilmore (6) he distinguishes between elements of the working class: 'The *poor* white man labors, the *mean* white man does not labor: and labor makes the distinction between them'.

Again, echoes of the underclass debate resonate loudly, with a moral categorization of the working class into productive and unproductive groups: the deserving and undeserving poor. Writing from the 1860s, says Hartigan, evidenced the struggle between those for whom such 'meanness' was in the blood and those who recognized a degree of environmental input. These competing logics developed into the twentieth century. Racial theorist Madison Grant, for example, understood 'white trash' as a combination of natural habitat and bloodlines: to do with sexuality, urbanization and crime, rather than just immigration (Grant 1916). Eugenics discourse stressed the perils of mixing good with bad genes, and responsibility for policing the genetic border. It argued that a host of antisocial and expensive behavior derived from poor family etiquette and practices. The result of this discourse in popular outlets, contends Hartigan, was heightened middle-class awareness of their racial selves, and of threat from below. In the scenarios popularized in the press, the idea of 'racial poisons' dominated discourse, with the weaker blood multiplying faster than the stronger. Gertrude Davenport (the wife of leading eugenicist Charles Davenport) wrote in a popular magazine in April 1914 that 'the greatest menace of imbecility is not that the imbecile may break into our house and steal our silver, or that he might set fire to our barn, but that he may be born of our flesh' (Hartigan 2005: 95).

Similarly, in Winthrop Stoddard's (1922) Freudian fight for civilization taking place within the Self, class status coincides with racial value:

> Let us understand once and for all [he warns] that we have among us a rebel army—the vast host of the inadaptable, the incapable, the envious, the discontented, filled with instinctive hatred of civilization and progress, and ready on the instant to rise in revolt. Here are foes that need watching. Let us watch them (1922: 87).

The overlap with contemporaneous American eugenics discourse on immigrants from Southern and Eastern Europe is very similar to Stoddard's comments here, and underscores the idea that 'race' and class are intimately connected in discourse of hierarchisation. People's culture and behavior is in the blood, these theories argue, and within the dominant 'race' there are those whose culture and behavior is more like those of subordinate races than those of the dominant. The struggle is for the dominant to remain pure and unpolluted, a theme pivotal to discourse on 'race'. The white trash figure then is marked as an excessive body that pollutes others. It displays the innate behavior that both confirms the depths to which the working class has collapsed (so far from work, so far from respectability), and at the same time emphasizes the industriousness and respectability of the middle-class subjects that fill the signifier 'white trash', with meaning.

PLURAL TRAJECTORIES OF WHITENESS

I began this chapter by floating the idea that there are a set of internal borders within the ostensibly homogenous 'white' group, and that these borders are contingent on political, economic and social factors that make them more or less relevant. In this final section, I want to draw out some of the complexity involved in the social relations that white working-class people maintain with minorities in Britain, as illustrated through empirical fieldwork.

Ethnographic fieldwork has illuminated what we could call the 'plural trajectories' of whiteness. In other words, how white people in broadly similar class positions make sense of the social material used to understand 'race' in differing ways. We are going to look briefly at two pieces of British ethnographic fieldwork to demonstrate some aspects of these 'plural trajectories': Katherine Tyler's discussions with residents of a former mining town in the English Midlands (2004), and Les Back's study of young people on the 'Riverview' estate in South London (1996).

Tyler's (2004) inter-generational dialogue among small-town Leicestershire inhabitants shows how personal biographies profoundly shape the ways in which people perceive 'Others'. Among the interviewees, no homogenous representative voice is expressed: white superiority is contested by some, just as it is accepted unthinkingly by more. Identification can take the form of empathy. 'Sarah's' experience of growing up working in her Czech immigrant father's shop gives her empathy with the people working in family-run Asian businesses when she hears criticisms of Asian corner shops, for example (Tyler 2004: 304). Moreover, a person may develop a critical angle through mobility and return. Another of Tyler's respondents, 'Jim', returns to the town after three years at university in a small, more multicultural city. He reports that his recognition and awareness of racism increased dramatically after he was reabsorbed into family circles and heard the types of discourse that he previously listened to uncritically. He can now reflect on the older generation's assumptions and dissect them. When his grandmother died, the house she had lived in was bought by an Asian family, something that his uncles were unhappy about. 'The presence of Asians in the home where they were brought up', paraphrases Tyler (2004: 299), 'signifies an intolerable and unacceptable transformation'. Here we see a crucial element of the mechanism of enacting whiteness. A perceived negative change (in this case the retrospective tainting of the family) is attached to an effect (the Asian buyer) rather than a cause (the grandmother's death, the psychological toll of memories of childhood in that home, the broader global changes that brought the family in question from Asia to Britain).

Inter-generational and gendered differences are also revealed by this study. The older people are generally less reflexive about whiteness and quicker to deploy racialized discourse, as are men as compared to women, many of whom see more positives where the men see only negatives.

There are clearly a number of places to be located ideo logically in the racialization process, which becomes even more evident in the London housing estates where Les Back worked in the early 1990s. Back's (1996) ethnography of youth culture on South London estates suggests that values determine the salient borders of identity, and that culture becomes the 'modality' (following Stuart Hall) through which they are racialized. Black and white youths there put aside sporadic but real differences in order to ally against Vietnamese and Bangladeshi newcomers (1996: 240–241) in what Back terms 'neighborhood nationalism'. This alliance assumes the form of verbal and occasionally physical attacks. While the black youths are well aware that in other circumstances they could, and indeed have been, the victims of such aggression from their white counterparts, in the context of defining membership of the estate, their secular, linguistic and music-based coalition with white youth in 'Riverview' estate appears to predominate. They thus become what Back terms 'contingent insiders' (1996: 240), while their counterparts in 'Southgate' estate seemed to enjoy a qualitatively different relationship with their white peers, who had 'vacated concepts of whiteness and Englishness … in favor of a mixed ethnicity that was shared' (ibid.: 241). So while there is frequently tension, there is also often alliance, through personal relationships drawing on shared knowledge and experiences.

Indeed, a recurrent topic in British ethnographic studies is the heterogeneity and elasticity of the category 'white' in its members' affiliations with black and Asian cultures, to the point where, in some specific contexts, terms such as 'black' or 'white' culture become almost ideal-types (7).

These groups of young people illustrate a paradox that resurfaces elsewhere in British fieldwork. In their survey of shopkeepers in a London borough, Wells and Watson (2005) find that not all those championing 'white values' are white, while some champions of white rights include their black neighbors in their embattled and beleaguered 'we'. In these cases the 'Other' is usually Muslim. Clearly, the power relationships at a personal and local level allow for whiteness to be expanded to incorporate those not phenotypically white beneath its cultural canopy for the enactment of both rhetorical and physical violence. People who are not white can be absorbed into honorary whiteness in particular circumstances, yet this invariably involves othering different groups. In fact this othering appears constitutive of the process of redrawing the boundary of whiteness in terms of values, so that it embraces British black or Asian people, depending on the context. In confirming shared values, the groups that share and do not share them are defined.

CONCLUSIONS: OVERLAPPING HIERARCHIES OF CLASS AND WHITENESS

In previous chapters, I focused on the borders between white and non-white. Here, the concentration has been on the other end of whiteness, between the constituent groups of the white whole. I want to emphasize that these latter borders are contingent, that is, open to political and social change. A group might be considered unproblematically white at one stage in one place, but not in another place at another time. Or, this might change for a specific group in the same place over different periods. Changing economic and social conditions led to different appraisals of who was allowed into Australia and why: what were the criteria? The design and application of the White Australia strategy, as well as the example of the 'inbetween peoples' thesis, are clearly about the parallel boundaries of whiteness; the one separating white from its non-white Other, and those separating the really white from the less so.

While groups such as Jews, Gypsies and immigrants frequently find themselves marginalized within the social relations of 'race', I want to encourage you to think of how the process works in relation to class. We have already noted that for a long time, the way in which membership of classes and 'races' was conceptualized was very similar. One function of the internal borders of whiteness is to isolate a group of Whites as being the sole agents of negative and un-modern behaviors and attitudes, thus removing responsibility for discrimination from the others. As Hartigan concludes:

> 'Part of what the epithet white trash expresses is the general view held by whites
> that there are only a few extreme, dangerous whites who are really racist or violently
> misguided, as opposed to recogniz ing that racism is an institutional problem pervad-
> ing the nation and implicating all whites in its operation' (Hartigan 2005: 118–119).

I am tempted here to paraphrase Orwell, and suggest that in the process of racialization, all Whites are nominally equal, but some are more equal than others. This is true not only of how people express racism, but in the representations of how racism is expressed. The idea of portraying, or representing some groups as not-quite-white is part of the same power imbalance as the one that enables racism to function at a collective level. The discourse of 'race' and class are intimately connected.

Indeed, while racist ideas do abound in the working-class communities studied—although this label is contested in Chicago's Midtown (Kefalas 2003), and Detroit's Corktown and Warrendale (Hartigan 1999)—academics and media professionals play a significant role in creating a selective picture in which only the working class express such ideas and live in segregated neighborhoods. This is not borne out, even by the often questionable opinion poll results. Studies of whiteness in middle-class circles, residential areas or workplaces, or at all, are unfortunately few and far between (8). Whiteness is neither just for the wealthy, nor just the poor. Yet the people who have engaged in defining the desirability of including particular segments of their compatriots in the civilized, right-thinking mainstream have been middle- and upper-class British and Americans.

Moreover, under certain conditions, whiteness (as a dominant set of values and assumptions that make various groups problematic) is not even always only for white people. It is clear from survey research that minorities generally have more sympathy for immigrants and asy lum seekers, and more of them tend to understand racism as structural rather than individually generated (Lamont 2000, Weis and Fine 1996), yet from the examples of Back (1996), Wells and Watson (2005) and Hoggett et al. (1992, 1996) there is enough to suggest that there might occa-sionally be a strategic overlap of values between white and black people that coalesce around defending neigh borhoods, and possibly jobs. Moreover, minorities do engage to a degree with power-evasive discourse such as color-blind racism (Bonilla-Silva, 2002), just as many of Skeggs' respondents defined 'working class' as not them, but somebody else. There is a great deal of complexity on view in the fieldwork done on white working-class communities, and a number of individual biographical pathways that lead people also to be anti-racist. If this work teaches us anything, it is that attitudes cannot be read off simplistically from class positions.

We should recognize throughout that hierarchies are always in the process of construction, deconstruction and reconstruction: nothing is fixed, not even racialized boundaries. The hierarchies I refer to are expressed in terms of patterns of power relations; that is, the power to name, the power to control and distribute resources. While the group defined as 'white' has historically monopolized this sort of power, who counts as 'white' at a given moment and at a given time is far less certain. This requires us to understand political, social, cultural and economic factors as a messy whole, rather than as easily distinguishable and analyzable components: a challenge, but a worthwhile one.

DISCUSSION QUESTIONS

1. What do class and racial identities have in common and what distinguishes them?
2. What role to specific national contexts play in the way class and race get linked and unlinked?
3. When we define our own group, we define another implicitly. What evidence of this emerges from the discussion of class and 'race' here?
4. What does the author mean by '... in the process of racialization, all Whites are nominally equal, but some are more equal than others' in this context?

PASSIVITY IN WELL-MEANING WHITE PEOPLE

By Barbara Trepagnier

D ata presented in the previous chapter demonstrated that silent racism permeates the "not racist" category. In this chapter I argue that the exposure of silent racism renders the "not racist" category meaningless. Readers will see that in addition to hiding silent racism, the "not racist" category conceals passivity regarding race issues. Passivity not only inhabits the "not racist" category but appears to be partly created by the category itself; that is, passivity is often an unintended consequence of the category "not racist."

PASSIVITY

Passivity regarding racism is not well documented in the race literature. The exception is Joe Feagin (2001), who briefl y mentions "bystanders" as a category of white racists that "provide support for others' racism" (p. 140), and who in his work with Hernán Vera and Pinar Batur (2001) suggests that "passivity is a first step in learning to ally oneself with white victimizers against black victims" (p. 49). The latter study deals primarily with passivity in the face of antiblack violence. This follows much of the literature on bystanders, which is based largely on the "anonymous crowd" that colluded with the atrocities of the World War II Holocaust (Barnett 1999: 109). Our interest concerns the passivity of well-meaning white people who collude not with violent acts but with subtle forms of racism.

Ervin Staub (2003), the foremost scholar regarding the bystander role, defines bystanders as people "who are neither perpetrators nor victims" (see Goleman 2003: 29). Bystanders are present in situations where a person or a group is the target of a negative act or statement, whether or not the victim is present at the time. Passivity in bystanders appears to have multiple causes, including alienation from victims, identification with perpetrators, and fear of repercussions. And, although bystanders are neither victims nor perpetrators, their reaction in the situation is important. Passive bystanders differ from "active bystanders" (Staub 2003: 3) in that passive bystanders do nothing in the face of injustice or discrimination; active bystanders interrupt the unjust behavior or discrimination.

Most passive bystanders feel little or no connection to the victim (Barnett 1999). In-group/out-group differentiation may play a part in the passivity of bystanders because it is easier not to come to the aid of people who are in some way outsiders (Staub 2003). Intergroup theory posits that a primary function of groups, or categories, is to enable their members to distinguish themselves from members of other groups. Categorical differentiation is a means of cognitive sorting that facilitates information processing (Brown 2002). The sorting procedure "sharpen[s] the distinctions between categories and, relatedly, blur[s] the distinctions *within* categories" (Brown 2002: 397, emphasis in original). The resulting emphasis on similarities with in-group members and on differences with members of the out-group cause the in-group to be seen positively in comparison to the out-group. According to intergroup theory, differential categorization accounts for members of out-groups being seen in a less positive light than fellow in-group members and helps explain why people are more likely to be passive bystanders when targets of discrimination are different from themselves. Some have critiqued intergroup theory because it tends to make discrimination appear as though it is a natural occurrence and therefore cannot be avoided (see Fiske 1989).

The just world hypothesis may help explain passivity as well. The *just world hypothesis* refers to the idea that victims of injustice get what they deserve. The premise is that people want a world that is orderly and predictable. And if the world is orderly and predictable, it is also just. In order to sustain this belief, people must either come to the aid of victims of injustice or decide that the victims deserve the treatment they receive. Given that out-group members—people that are different in some way—are more likely to be seen as deserving of discrimination than in-group members, people's level of belief in the just world hypothesis is in inverse relation to the degree of empathy held for the group under attack (Staub 1992). The silent racism in people's minds would tend to support the white belief that blacks in some way deserve discrimination.

Another reason some people are passive bystanders is out of loyalty to the person doing the discriminating. Fear of causing embarrassment or anger may discourage interrupting racism, even if the bystander disapproves of the behavior. Shifting from being a passive bystander to an active one takes moral courage (Staub 2003). This is particularly true in situations where a power differential is in play, such as when one's boss tells a racist joke or makes a racist decision. In this case ambivalence (Smelser 1998) is likely to occur, and the decision of whether to intervene will be weighed against the cost of doing so.

The role of bystanders is important because they have a good deal of influence in how a given situation will proceed (Staub 2003). For example, when people make racist statements and bystanders remain passive, the passivity is perceived as collusion with the exposed racist point of view. This perception, right or wrong, empowers people to persist in their racism. By contrast, when bystanders actively interrupt racist statements, the balance of power shifts away from those making racist statements in support of the target group, blacks or other people of color. This means that despite the connotation of the terms "bystander" and "passivity," neutrality is not an option. Doing nothing creates an alliance with the perpetrator, regardless of the bystander's intention (Barnett 1999). In other words, bystanders, by virtue of being present during a racist incident, align either with the target of discrimination by interrupting the discrimination or with the perpetrator by remaining passive.

A final point about the bystander role is in order. The tendency to remain passive in the face of discrimination tends to continue once the pattern is set (Staub 2003). By the same token, taking an active bystander role by interrupting racism may also become easier with practice.

The data discussed in the next section relate to passivity in the participants. The first form of passivity results from feeling estranged from the target of discrimination because of detachment. Two additional sources of passivity emerged in this study, both of which are latent effects of the "not racist" category: apprehension about being perceived as racist, and confusion about what is racist.

Detachment from Race Issues

The "not racist" category distances well-meaning white people from racism by implication: White people who see themselves as "not racist" are unlikely to see their connection to race or racism. Sharon expressed a sense of detachment from race issues several times during the discussion in her group. The first example was in response to the question, "What do you think needs to happen in order for racism to end?" Sharon said, "Racism has no connection to my life." Later, when asked if she had ever been told by someone else, or realized herself, that she had said or done something racist, Sharon again appears detached. She said, "I can't think of anything. I'm sure there must be, but I can't think of anything. It didn't hit me." Sharon would not regard her indifference as problematic in any way. Rather, as she stated, "Racism has no connection to my life." But Sharon's thinking is faulty: we are all intimately connected with issues of race (Frankenberg 1993).

Sharon's detachment from race issues makes her a passive bystander when confronted with others' racism. For example, when asked, "What do you do when you are around someone who has made a racist remark or tells a racist joke?" Sharon responded, "Nothing, usually." The indifference characterized by Sharon is akin to willful blindness, a term used in reference to the perpetrators of white-collar crime such as Ken Lay, the president of Enron. Lay claims no knowledge of criminal behavior that he and others greatly profited from. Similarly, detachment from race matters serves white people who benefit from the racial status quo. Sharon's detachment from race issues is more striking than any other participant's, although others demonstrated disconnections as well. For example, Karen, in Sharon's focus group, also said that she usually does nothing when confronted with others' racism.

Detachment from racism is not limited to people like Sharon, who came to this study accidentally and who knows very little about racism. Penny is more representative of well-meaning white people who are concerned, yet passive. Penny senses that she should interrupt racism, but she openly admits that often she does not. When Penny answered the question about what she does if someone tells a racist joke or makes a racist comment, her answer illustrates passivity. Penny said, "Ideally, I would say, 'I don't laugh at that.' Do I say it? [That] depends on how grounded I'm feeling that day or what my relationship, my role in the group, is …. Then you get into the whole thing about, 'Oh, I didn't say it.' And 'I'm complicit.' It can be quite a conundrum." Penny, unlike Sharon, has good intentions about interrupting racism and feels bad about not doing it. Penny mentions that her role in the group could affect her reaction as a bystander. Bystanders who identify with the perpetrator or inhabit a subordinate role in relation to the perpetrator are less likely to take an active role for fear of disapproval or alienation (Staub 2003).

Vanessa said in response to the question about being around someone telling a racist joke, "I probably just don't laugh," an interesting response because the word "probably" casts her answer as a hypothetical statement rather than a statement of fact. A hypothetical answer instead of a factual one about one's behavior is likely to indicate avoidance of the question, perhaps due to being unsure about how the inquiring party might react. Nevertheless, whether Vanessa "just doesn't laugh" or laughs politely, her answer appears to indicate a measure of detachment.

Racist comments and jokes that go uninterrupted implicate the listener as well as the actor. The only way to not comply with racism when it occurs is to interrupt it. It is not correct to think that racism only occurs in interactions between whites and blacks or other people of color. To the contrary, those interactions may demonstrate less racism than comments that occur between or among white people when no blacks are present. Interrupting racism is as important at these times as it is when blacks are present, primarily because not to do so is perceived by perpetrators as encouragement of their racism.

Unintended Consequences

The "not racist" category appears to produce two unintended consequences: apprehension about being perceived as racist, and confusion about what constitutes racism. Both of these consequences result in passive behavior in white people. Differentiating manifest consequences—those that are obvious and intended—from latent consequences—those that are not obvious and not intended—is important in order to avoid confusion between "conscious *motivations* for social behavior and its *objective consequences*" (Merton 1967: 114, emphasis in original). A failure to distinguish between intended and unintended consequences results in flawed theoretical assumptions.

The putative intended function of the oppositional categories is to distinguish between antiblack racists and well-meaning white people who are presumed not to be racist. The unintended consequence is that the "not racist" category produces passivity, which is manifested in two ways: apprehension about being seen as racist, and confusion about what is racist.

Apprehension About Being Seen as Racist. Everyday rules regarding race matters, known as "racial etiquette" (Omi and Winant 1986: 62), are imbued with myriad meanings regarding race and racial difference that produce apprehension in white people. Several participants said that they felt apprehension about being perceived as racist. Elaine articulated her self-consciousness in dealing with black/white difference when she shared a story about meeting Dorothy, the friend of a friend, at a barbecue. Elaine said, "I opened the door and she's *black*. Oh! And I was just so mad at myself, and embarrassed for thinking that. I mean like, 'Oh, did that show?' Really worrying about it; just never getting past that."

Elaine's surprise that Dorothy was black was only exceeded by her embarrassment about being surprised. Based on her past experience, Elaine expected to see only white people at the barbecue. The racial etiquette that Elaine learned in her "all white" upbringing seems to have left her unsure about how to navigate a social setting that included both whites and blacks. The phrase "Did that show?" indicates that Elaine was afraid Dorothy might have noticed her surprise and interpreted it as racist. Apprehension about being perceived as racist troubled Elaine quite a bit, as evidenced by the comment, "Really worrying about it; just never getting past that." Elaine elaborated her discomfort by explaining how she makes sense of her reluctance to initiate friendships with black women. She said, "I do tend to socialize with people that are like me .... It's comfortable, it's easy, the knowns outweigh the unknowns. I think working against racism includes that fear of offending someone or fear of saying/doing the wrong thing and not being conscious of this .... I'm gonna make a mistake and I don't want to have to worry about that."

Elaine's comments do not imply that she thinks it is right to avoid situations in which she might make a misstep, as in her response to Dorothy. Nevertheless, she acknowledges that she often takes the easier path in developing friendships rather than the path that is more likely to provoke her anxiety about race difference. Her apprehension is important because of its own consequences: a tendency to avoid interactions with people of color. Ironically, as we will see in Chapter 5, having close ties with blacks and other people of color is important in developing race awareness—something that would lessen Elaine's apprehension.

Elaine added, "Racism has such a stigma attached to it that yes, we fear it. We don't want to be associated with [it]—we are not supposed to be making any mistakes." The "not racist" category produces fear of losing one's status as not racist and, in the process, lessens the tendency to question ideas about racism.

Karen made a related point in her group when she said, "I sometimes feel a barrier in approaching black women, in that I feel that they don't want to deal with me, and so I feel like I'm being respectful by keeping my distance, or something. I feel more comfortable letting them make the first move instead of me going over and starting conversations." Karen's reluctance to initiate friendships, or even conversations, with black women so they won't have to "deal with her" may relate to the incident described in Chapter 2 when Karen's black friend, Belle, rebuffed Karen's attempt to order her ice cream for her. Belle had not said why she was upset about the incident, and Karen did not ask. Consequently, Karen assumed it was simply because she was white, not realizing that it was because she had expressed a paternalistic assumption.

Apprehension about being perceived as racist keeps well-meaning white people from finding out more about racism. Anita made this point when she said, "[The] fear of saying anything that's going to label you racist ... you're not really dealing with. Well, is it or isn't it [racist], and why do I feel like that?" Lucy makes a similar point when she says, "Something that gets in my way [of dealing with my own racism] is feeling that I've got to be cool, or good, or maybe it's feeling like I try too hard or I care too much. I think it gets in my way because it prevents me from ... acknowledging that I am human." I think what Lucy means by "acknowledging that [she is] human" refers to the inevitability that she will at times be unwittingly racist. Humans make mistakes, and sometimes those mistakes are because of misconceptions or ignorance regarding racism. The need to be seen by oneself and others as "not racist" hinders becoming more aware of race matters. Moreover, people with low race awareness are not likely to be active bystanders who interrupt others' racism; rather, people with low race awareness are likely to be passive bystanders, encouraging racism.

Loretta also indicated apprehension about being perceived as racist. She said, "People silencing themselves out of the fear of not saying the right thing [means] not being able to talk, and therefore not being able to change. Making actual change may mean making a mistake, saying the wrong thing, and having somebody call you on it and having to own that." Loretta's statement shows insight into the paradox of being unable to discuss racism for fear of being perceived as racist. Loretta's comment also shows insight into the danger of seeing racism as deviant. The original defi nition of *political correctness,* now known as PC, was "internal self-criticism" among liberals (Berube 1994: 94). For example, liberals hoped to raise awareness about biases in language—such as the use of sexist language—because biases in language reinforce biases in society (Hofstadter 1985). Conservatives co-opted the term, mocking liberals by casting political correctness as an attempt to limit the freedom of speech. Today political correctness is widely perceived as destructive, rather than as it was originally intended: an attempt not to be offensive (Feldstein 1997).

Passivity resulting from the apprehension about being perceived as racist is evident in the preceding stories of the well-meaning white women. The fear of being seen as racist paralyzes some well-meaning white people, causing them to avoid meeting and interacting with blacks. This is significant—and ironic—because forming close relationships with blacks and other people of color is the most important step they can take to lessen their apprehension.

Confusion About What Is Racist. Confusion about racism is epitomized by uncertainty and embarrassment and is sometimes related to being apprehensive about being seen as racist. People who see themselves as not being racist often presume that they should know what is racist and what is not, even when they are not sure. Confusion about what is racist is closely related to passivity in that it suppresses action. In the following comments, participants share experiences demonstrating confusion.

Anne spoke of her confusion about whether referring to people as "black" is in itself racist. Anne reported a conversation she had with her mother in reference to a baseball announcer during a New York Yankees game. When her mom asked who announced the game, Anne said that it was Bill White. "My mom asked me, 'Who's Bill White?' I didn't want to say he was black—I thought it would be racist." Anne attempted to avoid using color as a marker for distinguishing among the sports announcers, believing that mentioning his race would have been racist. After describing many details about Bill White—color of hair, size, and so on—Anne could not think of any other way to distinguish him and finally told her mother that he was "the black announcer." This raises an important point of discussion: Was Anne's telling her mother that Bill White was "the black announcer" racist? Was it the same as Ruth, who earlier said she had a bright "black" student in her class? (See Chapter 2.)

I classified Ruth's comment as racist, as did the friend that interrupted it, pointing out that Ruth's reason for mentioning that the student was black was related to the fact that he was bright. However, that is not the case in Anne's situation; saying that Bill White was the black announcer was not related to any negative stereotype but was instrumental in identifying him to her mother.

Some would argue that using "black" as an identifying characteristic is always racist because it reinforces the notion that blacks are racialized and whites are not. This view is called *other-izing* and is thought to marginalize blacks and other minorities. However, sometimes identifying someone as black is pertinent to the context of a situation. To say he was "the black announcer" was not racist in Anne's situation because it was instrumental in that context and in no way reproduced a stereotype about blacks. I agree that white people virtually never use *white* in the same way. Nevertheless, avoiding the word *black* simply because its use is not equivalent to the use of the word *white* seems like faulty logic to me.

While discussing this issue with a black colleague, I was given this response: "Sometimes a person will apologize for saying the word *black* even when it is appropriate to include for clarity. Very often I have had whites apologize for even uttering the word. It's as if, for them, the word *black* is gaining status with *nigger* as a racially sensitive word."

Avoiding the use of *black* because it might be racist results from confusion about what is racist. Using *black* as an identifying characteristic is racist when its use is associated with a racist stereotype or if it is tacked on solely because a person is not white. However, rigidly avoiding *black* unnecessarily when its use would serve a purpose is tantamount to pretending that race does not exist or was not noticed, a prime example of racial etiquette (Omi and Winant 1986).[1]

Anne's reluctance to "utter the word" *black* indicates some hesitation about saying the word at all. Anne may have received a message as a child similar to the one Lisa received from her parents. Lisa said that she was told explicitly not to notice race differences. Lisa said that in addition to telling her "colors don't matter," her parents added, "[but] don't ever say the word *black,* don't say the word *Mexican,* and don't ever refer to a person's color. It's offensive to say those words." Lisa said that when she was ten, she and her family moved into a housing project where she would be in close proximity to black children. Since Lisa would undoubtedly play with black children—her new neighbors—Lisa's parents were perhaps trying to prepare her for that experience. By cautioning Lisa to ignore difference—a difference they also denied was there—Lisa's parents wanted to both protect her from any repercussions they thought might occur from pointing out difference *and* teach her about equality. However, parents' double messages about race and racism can cause confusion in their children in terms of what is and what is not racist. In Anne's case, confusion contributed to her apprehension about being racist, which had a paralyzing effect. Avoiding any mention of race or the word *black* rather than acknowledging one's confusion keeps people from understanding what is and what is not racist.

In a related incident, Penny, who grew up in the 1960s, spoke of asking her mother about a house that looked "different" from the ones in their neighborhood—she said that it was pink and had iron grillwork across the front. Penny stated, "My mother said, 'Oh, that's where Egyptians live.' [My mother] didn't think that I'd ever meet Egyptians, and so it was okay for me to think that Egyptians were different." The logic that Penny attributes to her mother's comment—that it was okay to think that Egyptians were different because it was unlikely that Penny would meet any—indicates the lengths to which Penny's mother went in avoiding a discussion about race difference with her children. Although Penny did not recall receiving an explicit message to "not notice" race, it appears that her mother saw the acknowledgment of difference *itself* as problematic and perhaps racist, a confusion of what is racist and what is not.

Although the reluctance to mention race can be referred to as being colorblind, the instances here do not meet the definition of *color-blind racism*: a racial ideology that "explains contemporary [racial] inequality as the outcome of nonracial dynamics" (Bonilla-Silva 2003: 2). Color blindness derives from a racist ideology that is at times racist but that is not necessarily always racist. The individuals described in this section are only color blind in that they did not want to draw attention to race difference for fear it would be racist to do so. However, I would characterize the reluctance to mention race as confusion about what is racist rather than as racism per se.

Confusion was also evident in Heather's description of an incident that occurred in her high school circle of friends. However, Heather's confusion is not coupled with apprehension. Heather said,

> I just remembered a very good friend of mine in high school who was half black—his dad was black and his mom was white—and he was blond, with blue eyes. There was an incident [in high school] that was really sticky. One of our friends didn't even know that David's father was black, and she made a very bad mistake by telling a joke about a black man and a Jewish man in an airplane—an awful, awful joke that just did not go over [well] .... I think part of it was that [David] was such a blond guy. And his father had a Ph.D. in some hard science and has taught at [a major university]; he was on the faculty and then went to work at a laboratory. [David's] mom is a nurse.

Heather characterized the "sticky" incident as "a mistake" and that the friend telling the racist joke "didn't even know that David's father was black." What seems to be problematic for Heather is that David had inadvertently heard the racist joke, not the fact that the joke was racist. This interpretation is substantiated by Heather's comment that the "mistake" resulted from David being "such a blond guy" whose father has a Ph.D. and whose mother is a nurse. Heather's confusion about what is racist concerning the joke incident is likely to result from her not thinking the incident through, and, as a result, excusing her friend's racism by seeing it as harmless rather than as racist.

Confusion was also evident in a statement Alyssa made in her focus group:

> I think that everyone should be noted for their differences and celebrate their differences, instead of just ignoring, and looking through them and saying, "You know, I don't see color." Because you do [see color]. Everyone sees it. You may not think negatively of it, but when you think of the fact that you notice that a person is black, you think it's something bad. But I don't see that as something being bad—you can celebrate a difference.

The confusion in Alyssa's notion of celebrating difference becomes evident when she states inconsistent views centered on the pronoun *you*: "you may not think negatively of it" and "you think it's something bad." Alyssa seems to notice the apparent contradiction between these two thoughts when she quickly distances herself from the second statement by adding, "*I* don't see it as something bad." The confusion in Alyssa's thinking (that noticing race difference is "good" and that being black is seen as "something bad") presumably remains intact in her thinking, perhaps below her awareness. Holding contradictory beliefs without scrutinizing them may explain how many white people harbor racist thoughts about blacks and other people of color without being aware of it.

Loretta talked about the celebration of difference, but without the confusion exhibited by Alyssa. She said, "We can have a kind of 'feel good' cultural diversity yet not be antiracist. We [can] all talk the same talk, isn't this great, and cultural diversity is great. I [can] go to a food fair and taste [different food] and that's great, on one level. But if the reality is that economically only certain people are getting jobs ... and people of color are getting paid less than white people ... then there is still going to be racism." Loretta does not embrace the celebration of difference uncritically, as Alyssa does. Her critical assessment of the concept exposes the danger of celebrating the different cultural traditions of black and white Americans without acknowledging the history of racial oppression in the United States and the current racial inequality that continues today.

Confusion in well-meaning white people does not produce passivity as directly as detachment from race issues does. Neither does confusion produce passivity in the same sense that apprehension about being racist does, through the avoidance of contact. However, confusion is linked to passivity indirectly in that white people who are confused about racism are not likely to take a stand against it; one must be able to conclusively define an act as racist in order to feel justified in contesting it. Only white people who are clear about the historical legacy of racism in the United States, who understand how institutional racism operates, and who sense their own complicity with a system that benefits them to the detriment of people of color are likely to be active in interrupting racism when they encounter it. In this way, confusion along with detachment and apprehension is the antithesis of antiracism. For this reason, I consider it racist and place it just inside the midpoint toward the less racist end of the racism continuum. See Figure 12.1 for passivity on the racism continuum.

The aforementioned data support the claim that the "not racist" category itself produces several latent effects that bring about passivity in well-meaning white people. Just as silent racism produces institutional racism, passivity produces collusion with racism. Said differently, everyday racism could not stand without the participation and cooperation of well-meaning white people. However, before discussing how silent racism and passivity are key ingredients in the production of institutional racism, there is another topic to consider: possible unintended consequences of replacing the oppositional categories with a racism continuum.

ONE MORE UNINTENDED CONSEQUENCE

Would racism increase if people came to believe that all white people are somewhat racist? This concern—that some whites who now suppress their racist thoughts would presume to have permission to express them—is well founded. We saw this effect in Chapter 2 when Vanessa expressed the racist belief that black Americans are essentially different from white Americans. I questioned Vanessa's point that blacks and whites are inherently different, using the analogy of how supposed inherent gender difference between men and women have traditionally been used as a rationale against change for women. Vanessa responded, "Exactly. I just feel safe in saying this; I've never said it anyplace else. ... As a psychologist, I wouldn't dare say what I said [laughter from several group members], but I really do question what people are so quick to say, that all races have to be equally endowed."

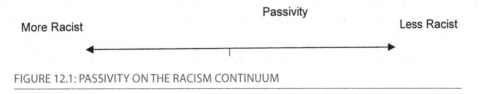

FIGURE 12.1: PASSIVITY ON THE RACISM CONTINUUM

Vanessa acknowledged that she has never voiced the opinion before, and that she "felt safe" in saying in the focus group what she "wouldn't dare say" any place else. The idea raised by Vanessa may exemplify what would result if the sanctions against acknowledging racist thoughts were eliminated. In other words, is expressing suppressed racist thoughts a greater harm than the harm caused by their suppression?

Despite her belief in biological race differences, Vanessa expressed pride in her antiracist heritage when she told about her great-grandparents who helped "slaves escape to the North." Vanessa invokes both racist and antiracist sentiments, shifting between the two. The term *drift* can be used to explain juvenile delinquents' movement between two cultures, "convention and crime" (Matza 1964: 28). Similarly, that the focus groups granted permission to talk about race and racism likely explains Vanessa's "drift" into racism. In her journal entry, Vanessa further explained her statement concerning biological determinism:

> I felt a kind of exhilaration in being able to talk openly about a loaded subject. Also, being with others who seemed to totally share my general [antiracist] attitudes on racism was a pleasure. I soon began to view them all with admiration as the stories came forth. Although I told of attitudes and beliefs the others might not agree with offhand, I had the feeling it was a good place to share them—[I thought] they would be fairly considered.

Vanessa appears to offset her statement about biological determinism by stating that she had never said it "anyplace else," that she "wouldn't dare," and that she felt "safe" in saying it in the focus group. *Neutralization* refers to a set of techniques intended to rationalize or justify delinquent behavior (Sykes and Matza 1957). Vanessa's use of a neutralization technique illustrates her awareness that what she said is not acceptable under normal circumstances. Her statement verifies the concern that removing the "not racist" category and its tendency to silence those in it would increase the expression of racist ideas. However, concern about this effect is based on the dubious assumption that suppressed racism is preferable to overt racism. I maintain that even if statements like Vanessa's increased, the benefit of increasing race awareness would outweigh that consequence because the increased race awareness is essential to decreasing the production of institutional racism. The drift into racism demonstrated by Vanessa should not be reason to dismiss rethinking the oppositional categories; on the contrary, Vanessa's statement is evidence that more open discussion about racism is needed. The expression and discussion of racist ideas would be more conducive to understanding racism than the confusion and apprehension that now govern white people who care about racism but feel paralyzed when faced with it.

In the 1950s, whites who stood up against racism were labeled "deviant"; today, the opposite is true: whites who are overtly racist are labeled "deviant." Labeling theory posits that the process of naming people "deviant" pertains to social rules that define deviance (Becker 1963). The deviance literature states that rules concerning who is deviant (and by implication who is not deviant) are imposed from outside, by moral entrepreneurs. In the case of the labels "racist" and "not racist," however, many white people who see themselves as "not racist" impose the rules on themselves. And yet, if the function of the "racist" category is to identify and therefore punish racists, then racism is sustained by the very social regulation intended to curtail it. Furthermore, the label "not racist" produces passivity in well-meaning white people, the supposed allies of blacks and other people of color. Labels imply essences—ways of being rather than merely ways of acting (Katz 1975). This is particularly true in the case of the racism labels; white racists are perceived as qualitatively different from whites presumed to be "not racist." If all whites are somewhat racist, this distinction is false, serving only to protect silent racism, everyday racism, and institutional racism.

CONCLUSION

Passivity is common in well-meaning white people. It is marked by detachment that produces a bystander effect in white people who find themselves in the face of others' racism. In addition, passivity results from apprehension about being seen as racist and from confusion about what is racist—both unintended but direct effects of the "not racist" category. This chapter's central thesis is that *passivity works against racial equality.* Well-meaning white people who are passive bystanders quietly watch America grow more divided over race issues. Yet, these are not innocent bystanders. They profit from the racial divide; they reap the same advantages received by those performing racist acts that they silently witness. The well-meaning whites who are the least aware of this fact feel little or no discomfort about the situation—they do not recognize the benefits that institutional racism affords them. The well-meaning whites who are detached have a measure of race awareness and feel bad about the situation as well as about their own passivity. Other passive bystanders are apprehensive—afraid to make a move for fear that they may be seen as racist. And still others are confused or misinformed, even though most do not recognize their confusion.

Both silent racism and passivity in well-meaning white people, some of which is produced by the category system, are instrumental in the production of institutional racism, described in the next chapter.

NOTE

1. I would like to thank Glynis Christine and Chad Smith for their conversations regarding this topic.

"THE HOUSE I LIVE IN"

RACE, CLASS, AND AFRICAN AMERICAN SUBURBAN DREAMS IN THE POSTWAR UNITED STATES

By Andrew Wiese

I t took Jim and Ann Braithewaite two years to find a home in the suburbs. After trans-
ferring to Philadelphia in 1957, the family began looking for a house almost immediately. Meanwhile, they rented in "a predominantly Negro neighborhood" in the city. They
dreamed of owning a detached, split-level house with a big yard in the suburbs, which
was common enough for couples with children in postwar Philadelphia. Yet, like thousands of
African Americans, they searched in vain, while white families moved to new suburban homes
with relative ease.

The Braithewaites' struggle exemplified the experience of many African Americans after
World War II. Although the couple was plainly middle class—she was a schoolteacher, he a
mechanical engineer—with a combined income well above the metropolitan average, their race
made them outcasts in the housing market. They answered newspaper ads, contacted real estate
brokers, attended auctions, and made an estimated three hundred phone calls, but they met a
"stone wall" of resistance. "We don't have any split-levels," or "That's already spoken for," brokers
told them. Others were more straightforward: "You're colored, aren't you? I can't do anything for
you," said one. Whatever the reaction, the results were the same. As African Americans, they were
not welcome in any part of Philadelphia's white suburbia.

In "desperation," the Braithewaites recalled, they shifted strategies. With the help of a local
fair-housing organization, they found a vacant lot whose owner was willing to sell. Though they
had reservations about the location because it was "very close to a public school" and near an
existing "Negro neighborhood," they hired a contractor and built a new home, inspecting progress at night, "hoping to prevent the accumulation of resentment" among their new neighbors.
The family took occupancy in October 1959, remaining fearful that "something cataclysmic"
might happen. For "some time" they even avoided standing in front of the picture window. But

the neighborhood remained quiet, thanks in part to the efforts of local Quakers who hosted a meeting to calm the neighbors and stayed with the family on their first night in the house. After months of frustration, the Braithewaites were suburbanites at last.

As a white-collar family, the Braithewaites symbolized a new wave of black suburbanization after World War II. During the 1940s and 1950s, the number of black suburbanites rose from one and a half to two and a half million. Whereas working-class families had dominated the prewar migration to the suburbs, middle-class African Americans—wealthier, better educated, and more likely to hold white-collar jobs than the earlier suburbanites—began moving to suburbs in growing numbers after the war. Bolstered by national economic expansion and the opening of new occupations to African Americans, black family incomes rose. By the mid-fifties, the United States was home to a growing black bourgeoisie and a cohort of economically stable industrial workers whose members had the means to purchase comfortable suburban housing on a greater scale than ever before. As their numbers increased, middle-class families became the predominant suburban migrants by the mid-1950s. These decades represented a period of transition in a century-long process of black suburbanization. Working-class households and communities remained a majority through the mid-1960s, but the momentum had shifted perceptibly toward the nascent middle class.

The Braithewaites' struggle for a suburban home also points to the links between black suburbanization and the making of race and class in the postwar United States. As upwardly mobile African Americans achieved middle-class incomes, occupations, and education, they also expressed a sense of class status through choices about how and where to live. Like millions of postwar Americans, many sought to own modern homes in recognizably middle-class neighbor-hoods. Their suburban dreams emphasized opportunities for children, proximity to jobs and services, leisure-time pursuits, and architecturally uniform residential landscapes. Contrasting in subtle and not-so-subtle ways with the ethic of prewar suburbanites, postwar suburbanization became a means for members of a rising middle class to express and reinforce their newly won social position.

Nonetheless, changes in the palette of black suburban preferences did not connote a lessen-ing of racial distinctions or a "whitening" of the middle class. As racial outsiders in a predomi-nantly white society, families like the Braithewaites could not be ordinary suburbanites even if they wanted. Their unique public experience indelibly shaped the meaning of private places, such as homes and neighborhoods, and it nurtured a distinctive politics related to housing. By achieving widespread suburban living patterns, African Americans asserted their equality and consciously minimized the social distance that whites sought to maintain as a privilege of race. In so doing, they challenged and subverted a central element of the dominant suburban ethos, which was white supremacy. In these ways, suburbanization tended to strengthen migrants' identities as black people even as it reinforced patterns of class stratification among African Americans themselves.

With respect to the wider literature, including the stories of suburbanites like the Braithewaites not only fills out the universe of places in which African Americans made history, it encourages attention to aspects of black life that scholars have not sufficiently explored. Changing the spatial context of analysis from city to suburbs makes it essential to ask, for instance, about African Americans' ideals for home and landscape—questions that have long been the focus of suburban history, but that few scholars have asked about African Americans. The history of black suburbia, too, suggests the importance of housing as an arena of black politics, linking African American social and political history though the politics of housing. Likewise, attention to African American migration and community-building in suburbia demands a fuller accounting of African Americans' relation to space more generally. Their struggles to control it, define it, and reap its advantages were a crucial terrain of black agency, politics, and identity-making throughout the twentieth century. The persistent efforts of whites to deny the same—systematic discrimination against black-occupied space—remained perhaps the most significant barrier to racial equality into the twenty-first century. In making places of their own on the margins of the city, African American suburbanites negotiated not only the hurdles of building homes and communities, but lines of color, class, and power embedded in the world around them.

IMAGES OF HOME

A closer look at African Americans' ideas about housing and landscape after World War II reveals both persistence and change. The clearest indication of continuity between pre- and postwar suburban values was the unswerving appeal of home ownership among African Americans of every social class. Attitude surveys uncovered a widespread inclination among African Americans to own homes of their own and, for many, the wish to buy in the suburbs. A nationwide survey of black veterans in 1947 disclosed that one-third to one-half of veterans in cities such as Philadelphia, Detroit, Indianapolis, Atlanta, Houston, and Baton Rouge hoped to buy or build a home of their own within the next twelve months. A 1948 study of six hundred "middle-income Negro families" in New York City revealed that three-quarters "would like to move to suburban areas and nine-tenths of them preferred to buy their own homes." Approaching the question from a different angle, researchers in Philadelphia asked some fifteen hundred African Americans in 1960 how they would spend a "windfall" of $5,000. More than half reported that they would use the money to buy a new house or pay off an existing mortgage.

Evidence of African Americans' tenacious "demand for home ownership" was apparent in everyday behavior as well. Supported by gains in income and civil liberties, as well as marginal assistance from the federal government, rates of nonfarm home ownership among African Americans climbed from 24 to 39 percent between 1940 and 1960. In the most populous suburban areas, however, the proportion of owners rose from 32 to 51 percent. Home ownership, which had long been a goal among African Americans, remained a fundamental aspiration among black suburbanites after the war.

What home ownership meant to suburbanites, of course, remained a complex matter. As was common before the war, many suburbanites viewed home ownership as the basis for economic security through thrift and domestic production. Prewar patterns of black suburban life endured in a range of working-class suburbs. Suburbanites relished their gardens and fruit trees, and many insisted on keeping livestock. In places such as Chagrin Falls Park, Ohio, the war did little to change the disposition of residents like Clydie Smith, who fondly remembered gardens lush with "pinto beans and collards and black-eyed peas and cabbage and beets and squash and peppers," as well as the sow, called Sookie, that her father kept. Across the continent in Pasadena, California, city officials fought a running battle with black householders who kept chickens and ducks in violation of a local ordinance. In Mt. Vernon, New York, David Doles, who had prospered as a laundry owner in Harlem before moving to the suburbs, extolled self-provisioning as part of an ethic of thrift that included other productive uses of property as well. Recalling that "we used to eat off our place down home" in Virginia, Doles boasted that he planted "more fruit right here in my place in the back yard than some people with a great big place."

This vision was also evident in the popular culture of the period. In her 1958 drama *A Raisin in the Sun*, playwright Lorraine Hansberry used this rustic ethic to symbolize both the endurance and the violation of African Americans' hopes for the urban North. The character Mama, a southerner living in a Chicago tenement, dreams of buying "a little place" with "a patch of dirt," explaining that "[I] always wanted me a garden like I used to see sometimes at the back of the houses down home." The sun-starved plant on her windowsill is as close as she was able to come. In fiction and in real life, the echoes of rural and working-class upbringings reverberated in the choices that migrants made. For as long as they lived, lifeways such as these would shape the environment of hundreds of suburban communities.

Many postwar suburbanites also used their homes as a source of income and an anchor for continued migration by renting rooms to recent migrants and sharing space with kin. Older suburbs, in particular, witnessed intensified multifamily occupancy during the period. In Evanston, Illinois, scores of homeowners converted houses to include rental units. In the streets off Emerson Avenue on the suburb's west side, the number of owners and renters rose simultaneously despite little new construction, indicating that African Americans were buying and converting their own homes to multifamily use. Similar practices affected neighborhoods in East Orange, New Jersey; New Rochelle, New York; and Pasadena and Berkeley, California, where black homeowners capitalized on continued migration by becoming landlords. Though some residents expressed a more restrictive view of domestic space, charging that "overcrowding" would lead to "possible neighborhood deterioration," old settlers offered a foothold for migrants in established communities, while the newcomers provided rental incomes that supported home ownership and upward mobility for a rising class of black proprietors.

Advertisements in the black press indicate that a vision of economic independence through productive use of property remained a marketable option in urban communities through at least the late 1940s. As the war ended, realty companies in Detroit, New York, Chicago, and other cities dusted off old subdivisions and began selling low-cost building lots, much as they had before the war. The *Chicago Defender* advertised homesites for as little as "$10 down" in suburbs such as Robbins, Phoenix, East Chicago Heights, and Maywood, as well as in predominantly black subdivisions within the city such as Morgan Park and Lilydale. New York's *Amsterdam News* pitched building lots in Westbury, Hempstead, Amityville, Hauppauge, and other suburbs where African Americans had lived since the nineteenth century. A 1947 advertisement for "Farm Homesites" in Farmingdale, Long Island, for instance, depicted a small house and outbuildings surrounded by tilled fields and fruit trees, while the text stressed links to the urban economy, highlighting "easy commuting, close to large airplane factory, plenty of employment." Like advertisements published during the Great Migration, these appealed to a working-class, southern aesthetic, describing semirural landscapes, open space, and low-cost property ownership, plus "the opportunity to grow your own food" in proximity to established communities and urban jobs.

Owner-building and other informal construction practices also persisted in blue-collar subdivisions. In Chagrin Falls Park, Ohio, the families of Clydie Smith, William Hagler, and Clara Adams built homes after the war. So, too, did families in suburbs such as Inkster, Michigan; the

American Addition near Columbus, Ohio; and North Richmond, California, where lot owners went "to the lumberyard and bought what they could without access to mortgage loans, and ... put up what they called their home." Advertisements for do-it-yourself house kits, Quonset buildings, and other nontraditional shelters—such as the prefabricated "Port-o-Cottage, the house you have been waiting for"—were common fare in the black press through the late 1940s. As this evidence indicates, home ownership for many black families remained a productive enterprise rooted in the working-class experience; and to the extent that middle-class status was fleeting or uncertain, such practices remained attractive, representing continuity in African American values and lifeways in the postwar suburbs.

In contrast to the thrift-oriented ethos that prevailed in older suburban areas, an increasing number of new suburbanites articulated preferences for housing that reflected norms prevalent across the wider middle class. In a study of black professionals and technical employees in upstate New York, Eunice and George Grier concluded that "little if anything ... distinguishes the requirements of these Negro home seekers from criteria one would expect to find among their middle-class white counterparts." They sought "adequate play space for children, good schools, safety and quiet, good property maintenance, and congenial neighbors of roughly equivalent income and educational background." Not surprisingly, most were "looking for a house of post–World War II vintage in a suburban area." Researcher Dorothy Jayne encountered similar attitudes in 1960 among pioneer families in suburban Philadelphia. Two-thirds of her respondents hoped to buy a single-family home in a "desirable" suburban neighborhood—a third were looking for ranch or split-level models. They described their ideal neighborhoods as "quiet, clean, with well-kept properties," convenient to shopping, with good schools and services and an abundance of "fresh air and green grass." Many indicated that they were willing to pay more to attain these amenities.

Among the expectations of suburban life that many middle-class African Americans shared with their white counterparts was an emphasis on a materially abundant family life in a residential setting removed from the "grind" of paid labor. A glimpse of the ideal lifestyle circulating among middle-class blacks after the war can be seen in the pages of *Ebony* magazine, which appeared on newsstands in 1945 and targeted readers in the aspirant black bourgeoisie. During its first few years, *Ebony* ran regular features publicizing the housing and domestic lifestyles of the nation's black elite. Reporters fawned over "big impressive home[s]," "sumptuous" furnishings, stylish house parties, and the financial success and style that these implied. Many stories featured families who lived in elegant central-city apartments, reflecting the continued concentration of black elites in neighborhoods such as Harlem's Sugar Hill; but an equal number highlighted the owners of detached, single-family homes in suburban or suburban-style neighborhoods.

An *Ebony* feature on the Addisleigh Park neighborhood of St. Albans, Queens, New York, reveals the physical and social environment that many middle-class African Americans idealized in the postwar decades. With its two-story Tudor and Colonial Revival houses, green lawns, and canopy of mature trees, the place merited its description as a "swank suburban neighborhood" or a "suburban Sugar Hill," even though it was located inside the municipal limits of New York City.

Reflecting the importance of landscape as a status marker, the writer highlighted residents' richly appointed housing and abundant greenery. The essay featured more than twenty photographs of tree-shaded homes belonging to such celebrities as Ella Fitzgerald, Roy Campanella, Billie Holiday, Jackie Robinson, and Count Basie, underscoring the affluent surroundings and amenities they enjoyed. "Many home owners have two cars," including "more Cadillacs per block ... than any other like community in the country," the reporter enthused. Captions listed the dollar value of almost every home pictured, suggesting none too subtly the connection between home ownership and wealth, not to mention good taste.

If few *Ebony* readers could afford such luxuries, the article took pains to emphasize Addisleigh Park's down-to-earth social life, which the writer described as "swank without snobbery." According to the reporter, Mercer Ellington mowed his own yard and preferred to "romp with his children on the front lawn," while Illinois Jacquet spent his leisure time in "bull sessions with famous neighbors." When Count Basie wasn't getting his "kicks" playing the organ in his living room, he could be found engaged in "marathon poker games ... famed ... for their high stakes and salty talk."

Though many of its residents were household names in black America, the writer pictured Addisleigh Park as a "typical ... suburban community, with its civic association, women's clubs, Boy Scout troops and Saturday night pinochle games ... lavish lawn parties and hearty cocktail sessions in pine-walled rumpus rooms." Thus, Ebony portrayed a vision of suburban life that many middle-class African Americans could appreciate and to which they might aspire. In its emphasis on comfort and an expressive, consumption-oriented social life, the magazine impressed upon, and no doubt reinforced among, its readers a distinctly middle- or upper-middleclass vision of suburban life. In a suburbanizing nation, Ebony signaled, middle-class African Americans were gaining equality as citizens through equality in their tastes and acquisitions as consumers, not least of which was their consumption of housing.

Advertisements for new tract homes aimed at black home buyers appealed to a cluster of similar values, further suggesting the strength of this vision among the new black middle class, as well as the pressures for conformity that shaped it. A 1947 ad for the Hempstead Park sub-division in West Hempstead, Long Island, was typical. It pictured a modest, saltbox-style home in a background of trees, while the text extolled the virtues of the house and neighborhood. For just $9,900, no cash down, black veterans and their families could own "4½ spacious, sun-filled rooms" with "large picture windows," on a "large landscaped plot" just a "short walk" from schools, shopping, and Hempstead Lake State Park. With the exception of the ad's placement in a black newspaper, there was nothing to distinguish it from hundreds of advertisements aimed at white veterans. Hempstead Park's amenities, emphasizing children, leisure, home ownership, and a picturesque residential setting, fit squarely within the mass suburban ethos of the period.

Ten years later, an advertisement for three subdivisions in the San Fernando Valley, north of Los Angeles, appealed to the same suburban imagery. The ad in the black-owned *Crown City Press* of Pasadena featured a sleek, garage-dominant ranch house framed by tall trees and text that urged, "Give your family the pleasure of living in Pacoima's Quality Circle." A map indicated the "desirable San Fernando Valley location," marking such features as Hansen Dam recreation area, the San Gabriel Mountains, a school, a public park, and a pool, as well as the highway to downtown Los Angeles. In addition to situating these developments in a recreation-filled landscape that had already become synonymous with middle-class suburban living, the ad emphasized the "exquisitely modern" but cozy amenities of the houses themselves, including "sliding-glass walls," "large, cheerful kitchens," and "brick fireplaces," plus a choice of nine "exciting exteriors." Like advertisements for thousands of white subdivisions after World War II, these ads could not have evoked a more distant imagery from that of the chicken coops, "second handed lumber," and upstairs renters that characterized working-class suburban life at the time. They marketed modern, affordable comfort in an environment oriented toward nuclear families and leisure, just a short commute from the central city—a suburban dream firmly anchored in the postwar mainstream.

As these examples indicate, another important feature of postwar black suburbia was an emphasis on the suburbs as a "better place for children" to live. In the early years of the baby boom, children gained prominence in suburban advertising for African Americans, much as they did in ads designed for middle-class whites. "Here is the safety of suburban living for your children," boasted the developer of Ronek Park, a thousand-home subdivision in North Amityville, New York. "Yes, here, the entire family can enjoy the pleasures and advantages of a wonderful new community offering everything you ever dreamed of." Another broker, who specialized in "high class neighborhoods" of Westchester County, New York, encouraged urbanites to "bring up your children in this suburban paradise." The increasing incorporation of children in developers' advertisements also reflected a shift in the class composition of black suburban migration after the war. Though prewar ads often mentioned schools and parks among a list of community facilities, subdividers rarely mentioned children directly—certainly less often than they referred to chickens or vegetable gardens.

Even ads for homes in unplanned suburbs such as Robbins, Illinois, which had attracted working-class blacks since World War I, were not exempt from the national celebration of child-rearing that succeeded the war. A 1946 campaign for "homesites" in the Lincoln Manor subdivision depicted children playing in the front yard of a new home while a woman sat on the front steps watching them, and perhaps waiting for a breadwinning father to return up the front walk. Blending elements of old and new, the ad portrayed a square, brick-faced bungalow typical of Chicago's southwest suburbs, plus a large garden plot—tilled for row crops, no less—at the back of the lot. The image of a stay-at-home mother belied economic reality for millions of African American families, but through such advertisements, suburban developers reinforced a vision of middle-class domesticity even in suburbs that had long been home to the black working class.

Suburbanites themselves were also more likely to mention children as the basis for residential choice, often doing so in class-specific ways. Discussing his search for housing, a black professional from upstate New York reported that "locality would take precedence over price for me because I have a family to bring up and want them to grow up in an area which will aid in their development." Another described his preferred place of residence as "an area where the schools provide opportunities to give my children a good education, and where they could skate, bike ride, and keep pets." The musician Milt Hinton explained that he and his wife moved to the leafy environs of St. Albans from an apartment in Manhattan because they were expecting a baby and "we wanted a nice, clean place to raise a child." In contrast to the emphasis that working-class suburbanites had placed on extended families, children and nuclear families loomed large for the postwar middle class, and suburbs appeared the ideal place to raise them.

The centrality of children in middle-class ideology emerged in discussions of other preferences as well. For African Americans who valued racial integration as the antithesis of segregation, children were an important justification. Celebrity couples such as Jackie and Rachel Robinson and Sidney and Juanita Poitier justified their decisions to look for housing in mostly-white neighborhoods in just such terms. "We feel if our children have an opportunity to know people of all races and creeds at a very early age, their opportunities in life will be greater," Jackie Robinson explained. For the Poitiers, it was the lack of such opportunities in Los Angeles that caused them to rethink their move to that city in 1960. After having difficulty finding a house in West Los Angeles, Sidney Poitier stated, "Our children are established in a multi-racial community in Mount Vernon [New York]. They attend multi-racial schools. The difference in color is no longer a curiosity to our children. We don't want to barter that kind of atmosphere for something that is hostile." Likewise, Winston Richie, a dentist who moved to Shaker Heights, Ohio, in 1956, explained that he wanted his children to learn that they "could compete with all people at all levels if they are prepared themselves. Living in an all- black community," he argued, "makes this lesson a bit harder to learn, or at best, it comes later in life." For parents such as these, the decision to select a suburban neighborhood rested heavily on the opportunity they perceived for their children to grow up as equal citizens.

RACE, CLASS, AND SUBURBANIZATION

If many new suburbanites aspired to goals and amenities that they shared with middle-class whites, they also approached homes and neighborhoods as people with a distinct history and with experiences that distinguished them from whites. "Being middle class," sociologist Mary Pattillo-McCoy notes, "did not annul the fact of being black." Discrimination blocked African Americans' most ordinary aspirations, forging from their individual choices a politics of housing linked to the quest for racial equality. Suburbanization underlined racial cohesion in a practical sense, too, by forcing house hunters to rely on black social and institutional networks, especially if they sought housing beyond established black areas.

Direct confrontations with racism also shaped the experience and understanding of suburban life. For thousands of families, the search for housing was a struggle that left economic as well as emotional scars. Legal activist Loren Miller explained:

> Those who cannot buy in the open market in a free-enterprise economy are subject to obvious disadvantages. The special market to which they are forced to resort tends to become and remain a seller's market. Supply is limited. In the ordinary situation that supply will consist of those items that cannot be sold or will not bring satisfactory prices for one reason or another in the open market. The disadvantaged buyer is in no position to reject shoddy merchandise or haggle over prices. He must take what he can get and pay what he is asked.

The struggle for housing could be emotionally trying as well. Black home seekers described their experiences in the housing market as "difficult," "degrading," "nerve-racking," or "like knocking your head against a wall." After numerous unsuccessful attempts to find a home in upstate New York, a black engineer admitted to researchers that "in all my life I have never felt so completely shut out." A doctor's wife in San Francisco suggested that repeated rejection in the housing market had left her feeling "like a leper and a criminal." A psychologist recalled the search for housing with equal poignancy: "Having worked my way up to a responsible position, I had gained a certain amount of self respect. Then I moved to this town and had to find housing, and once again found myself viewed as something less than human. This problem is more than economic—there's a great deal more involved." A black physician concluded, "Any kind of move for a Negro family today is expensive in terms of dollars and ruinous in terms of mental happiness."

Jim and Ann Braithewaite's experience in suburban Philadelphia illustrates the emotional repercussions that many couples felt in trying to move to the suburbs. Repeated encounters with racism put a strain on their marriage and family, affecting how they viewed themselves and the people around them. When discrimination "happens to you it hurts more," Jim Braithewaite explained. He had difficulty sleeping. His mind wandered at work. Resentments welled up inside. "I just kept thinking about it," he said. "I was tired twenty-four hours of the day." Moreover, he felt bitter, alienated, and prone to "explosion," all of which "made for a very unhappy family life."

In addition, the experience led him to focus his anger outward, questioning his job with a Cold War defense contractor and even his "allegiance to society." He asked himself, "Why am I defending this kind of people—people who have so great a desire for personal satisfaction that they place this above all other convictions they may have—religious, national, and sociological?" A year after their move, the Braithewaites' three children were adapting well to their new schools, and they counted white friends among their circle of playmates; yet the scars remained. "What does it cost me to be a Negro?" Braithewaite asked rhetorically. For upwardly mobile African Americans, such questions perhaps never seemed so real nor the answers so disheartening as during the search for suburban homes.

African American suburbanites were also more likely than whites to express ambivalence about their present home. Many families moved where they did because it was the only place available. More than half of families in Dorothy Jayne's 1960 study "had no choice" in the home they bought, and a number expressed dissatisfaction with their neighborhoods, for reasons ranging from the proximity of taverns or busy thoroughfares to poor transportation and shopping, distance from schools, and subsequent changes in the racial and socioeconomic character of the neighborhood. In several instances, the family's arrival touched off panic selling by whites. "It's like the black plague," said one couple. "Everyone wants to escape." Others felt isolated or intensely scrutinized, like "goldfish in a bowl." One woman reported poignantly, "I don't want to be intimate with my neighbors, but I had hoped they would be friendly." Another lamented that the neighbors "are killing us with silence."

For black pioneers, especially, the desire for equal amenities and opportunities for children often ran at cross-purposes with their desires for safety and a sense of belonging. For those who moved to mostly white areas, moving day was often the prelude to hostility, vandalism, and even violence. The William Myers family, who broke the color bar in Levittown, Pennsylvania, endured two months of organized harassment. Local whites paraded in cars at all hours, the phone rang constantly, and a white group rented an adjoining house from which they blared songs such as "Dixie" and "Old Black Joe" throughout the day. With the help of a group of supportive white neighbors, the Myers family chose to hang on. Nonetheless, they longed for black company. "They used to say about Levittown, 'You never have to live in Levittown and look at a black face,'" William Myers said. "I'd like to look out and see a black face." Even under the best circumstances, many pioneers found it difficult to "feel completely comfortable" or to escape the gnawing awareness that "there are people within a quarter mile who don't want me here."

If suburbanization reflected a fruition of black economic success and civil rights activism, it was an uncertain and often painful harvest.

As these examples suggest, the meaning and experience of suburbanization was bound up in African Americans' experience as racial outsiders in white-dominated space and society. In a world where public places were routinely hostile and whites behaved as though the greater part of metropolitan territory belonged to them, private spaces such as homes and neighborhoods became places of refuge from, and sites of resistance to, the wider white world.

In many suburbs, black pioneers sought to create racial communities that transcended place by maintaining and reinforcing contacts with other African Americans. Suburban pioneers often worshipped, shopped, and purchased services such as hairstyling in black neighborhoods "back in the city" or in black communities nearby. They maintained ties with black peers through active involvement in sororities, fraternities, and other social or civic organizations, and they made special efforts to find black peers for their children. One family in southern New Jersey recounted the miles they and other parents logged in order to maintain a black peer group for their teenage children via "the biggest car pool you ever saw."

In addition to reaching outward for social contacts, African Americans turned inward on their homes to create safe, private places that shielded them from the worst abuses of public space. Though many pioneers were joiners by nature, participating in community activities such as parent-teacher and neighborhood associations, most nurtured what sociologists St. Clair Drake and Horace Cayton described as "home-centered" social lives based on family, relatives, and close friends. A family who designed their own house "planned [the] living room with the idea of entertaining church groups here." One suburbanite remarked archly that he hadn't moved to Westchester County, New York, to "eat and drink" with his white neighbors. Families entertained "professional groups, church groups, wives' clubs, [and] bridge clubs," as well as "children's and international groups."

The largest number of postwar suburbanites avoided the hazards of racial isolation altogether by settling in neighborhoods where a significant number of blacks already lived. Racial discrimination and fears of "having a cross burned on my lawn" acted as weighty constraints on choice. But African Americans also made decisions that magnified racial concentration because, as a respondent told researchers in Philadelphia, they simply felt "more at home" with other black people. The actress Ruby Dee gave voice to this sentiment, recalling why she and her husband, the actor Ossie Davis, selected an "already well integrated" neighborhood of New Rochelle, New York, when they moved from a smaller house in nearby Mount Vernon. Though a white acquaintance urged them to strike a blow for open housing by buying in one of the suburb's all-white areas, they declined. Dee explained:

> I want my children to feel safe. I want to feel safe. I'm away so much, I want to be friends with my neighbors. I don't want to be tolerated, on my best behavior, always seeking my neighbor's approval. I want to be able to knock on a door, assured that my neighbor would more likely welcome any one of the family. Or if I should need help ... I admire the pioneers who risk so much in the process of integration, but I cannot break that ice .... Thanks, but no thanks. We just don't choose to struggle on this front.

Surveys suggest that Dee and Davis were in good company. In the late 1950s, anywhere from 45 to 65 percent of African American home seekers expressed a preference for neighborhoods that were at least one-half black. For the majority of African Americans who indicated preferences for interracial living, racial isolation was apparently something they hoped to avoid. Most upwardly mobile African Americans—black people with the greatest latitude of personal choice—simply preferred areas where an appreciable number of black families already lived.

Suburban racial congregation also reflected the conduits of information and association available to African American families. Like most Americans, blacks trusted their social networks—friends, neighbors, relatives, church members, co-workers, and other associates—for information and assistance in finding places to live. Because of their exclusion from conventional real estate channels, however, the legacy of past segregation reinforced the concentration of home seekers in just a handful of suburban areas. One study of middle-class families in Philadelphia, for example, revealed that 80 percent of respondents had "no Negro friends who lived in predominantly white areas outside the city limits." In such circumstances, media reports of white resistance and stories of racial hostility that passed through the grapevine gained weight in black perceptions of suburban opportunity. Lacking firsthand knowledge or positive experiences with white suburban areas, many families preferred to avoid the unknown, a fact that tended to funnel black suburban migrants to just a handful of already integrated or mostly black suburbs.

Emphasis on homes and neighborhoods as safe space was not unique to African Americans, of course. As historian Elaine Tyler May demonstrates, many postwar parents perceived suburban homes as "a secure private nest removed from the dangers of the outside world," a "warm hearth" in the midst of the Cold War. But for African Americans, who experienced not only the international anxieties of the era but the palpable dangers of domestic racism, the vision of home as a refuge had special resonance. As sociologist Bart Landry points out, because middle-class blacks were "denied ready access to the recreational and cultural facilities in the community," they "developed a lifestyle centered around home and clubs. The home grew in importance not only as a comfortable, secure place that shielded them from the stings of white society but was also the center of their social life."

Black-oriented publications reinforced this connection, celebrating hospitality and conviviality focused on black homes and neighborhoods. *Ebony*'s "home" columns dwelled on such features as "pine-walled rumpus rooms," "informal redwood den[s]," "spacious" patios "fac[ing] a big swimming pool," "expensive oak wood" bars "with matching chairs, phonograph radio combination and two large sofas," "lavish lawn parties," and "expensively equipped kitchen[s]." To be sure, tasteful entertaining was a staple of home-oriented magazines targeted at whites, but this emphasis had special resonance among African Americans, who were excluded from or faced harassment in public spaces frequented by middle-class whites. In the postwar era, *Ebony* portrayed an idealized domestic life, reflecting the exceptional value that middle-class blacks placed on their ability to entertain well at home. Not surprisingly, *Ebony*'s 1951 article on St. Albans evoked an image of the neighborhood as "self contained," a "refuge" and a "happy haven," applauding it as a place where residents found "comfort, relaxation, and breathing space." Early residents had overcome white attempts to restrict the area, the writer pointed out, but by the 1950s the neighborhood was the site of not racial activism but "placid privacy," where celebrities "come home to rest." Just as many working-class African Americans had used their homes as shelter from the insecurities of wage labor under industrial capitalism, members of the rising middle class valued their homes and neighborhoods as places of shelter from the racial hostility they experienced in public life. Whether they created spatially separate black enclaves or dispersed racial communities centered on private homes, they sought safe black spaces in the suburbs.

In these ways, race shaped the process of suburbanization, even as growing numbers of African Americans entered the middle class. These markers were not primarily governmental nor imprints of the state, but were rooted in localized struggles between black families and communities and the white people around them. By the same token, African Americans' attempts to attain and control suburban space contributed to a continuing conversation about class in black communities. Given the pervasiveness of race as an organizing feature of postwar society, however, even the process of class stratification tended to reinforce a sense of racial solidarity among African Americans.

"A BETTER CLASS OF PEOPLE"

Since the nineteenth century, class had been an important feature of African American social life, but within the racialized society of the United States, class strata in black communities rested largely on distinctions that African Americans drew "relative to other blacks." Based in part on objective characteristics such as occupation, income, and wealth, which situate people within the wider political economy, class distinctions also reflect values and behavior related to work, education, leisure, consumption, and place of residence. Just as important, class implies a relationship among differently situated individuals and groups in a given society. For African Americans, who were barred from the achievement of stable occupational and income markers that were essential to class standing among whites, class distinctions had traditionally relied on patterns of behavior—what historian Willard Gatewood describes as "performance"—that people developed as a means of identifying their peers and distinguishing themselves from others. Even as a larger cohort of African Americans attained economic positions comparable to those of middle-class whites in the postwar period, class remained a distinction that African Americans drew largely with reference to other blacks.

Of course, class was a spatial as well as social distinction. For the urban black middle class, in particular, physical separation from poor and working-class blacks was an important emblem of class status. Writing in the 1940s, St. Clair Drake and Horace Cayton argued that socioeconomic divisions within black communities produced a process of "sifting and sorting" by neighborhood. More recently, Mary Pattillo-McCoy concluded that "like other groups, African Americans ... always tried to translate upward class mobility into geographic mobility." In this view, class was not merely a measure of what one did for a living or how one behaved, but also how and where one chose to live. In the postwar period, suburbanization represented a continuation of this process across the city limits.

The comments of middle-class suburbanites reveal that concerns about class and distance from poorer blacks were thoroughly intertwined with other residential preferences. In various contexts, middle-class blacks drew implicit contrasts between the types of neighborhoods to which they aspired and those in which they had been "bottled up" with other African Americans before the war. As the housing activists George and Eunice Grier reported, middle-class blacks sought the "freedom to choose an environment in accord with middle-class standards, instead of housing restricted to the overcrowded, run-down neighborhoods generally available to Negroes." However, the contrasts that families drew focused on the social environment as often as the physical. "I would be very satisfied with an all-Negro neighborhood if it were a decent neighborhood," one black professional told the Griers. "I do not see why I, because I am a Negro, should be forced to live in a neighborhood where I have nothing in common with others around me." A black attorney in San Francisco expressed a similar recognition of class difference when he commented that the "thing that struck me when I moved out of the ghetto was that for the first time I was friendly with my immediate neighbors. They have the same interests that we do." Reinforcing this impression, leading black real estate brokers in Westchester County, New York, reported screening clients on the basis of their "social and cultural qualifications" in order to protect the "character" of suburban neighborhoods and ensure that their customers were a "credit ... to the race." Referring to people he called "Negro trash," one broker exclaimed, "I wouldn't damage a neighborhood with people who don't know how to live in it. I put them in their place."

GENDER ROLES IN SOCIOCULTURAL AND HISTORICAL CONTEXT

By Marjorie M. Schweitzer

T his chapter examines the sociocultural norms and historical context that existed in North America from the 1930s forward and some of the changes that occurred during that time. This summary background provides an essential framework for understanding the lives of the authors as they returned to school, did fieldwork, and became professional anthropologists. There are many excellent volumes that describe these years in greater detail. We focus here on events we feel were particularly relevant to the lives narrated in this volume, as well as for women in general.

HISTORICAL CONTEXT: A BRIEF REVIEW

The decade prior to World War II was marked overwhelmingly by the Great Depression. To help counteract some of the consequences of the Depression, President Franklin D. Roosevelt engineered several work programs to assist the vast numbers of unemployed, mostly men. In 1935 Congress passed the federal Social Security Act, which created insurance funds for survivors, the elderly, and the unemployed. Women were often the first to be let go as businesses failed. They did what they could to provide for their families, cobbling together various ways to make money: they opened beauty parlors in their homes, took in washing, cleaned houses, and boarded lodgers.

With the offcial entry of the United States into World War II in December 1941, everything having to do with work changed. Men from all walks of life joined the military, creating an enormous vacuum in factories, particularly in the defense industry. Women on the home front did what they could to help the war effort: they turned in their scrap metal and kitchen grease to be used for war matériel, and they tried to live as frugally as possible. But women did not stay at home. They responded in great numbers to the need for workers in the factories. The Office of War Information recruited women, and the National War Labor Board announced that they must be paid the same wages as men. They took jobs in munitions factories, they built airplanes, and Rosie the Riveter became the poster woman for the war effiort. Even today she remains the symbol of women's active and essential contribution in the winning of the war. By 1944 one of every three women defense workers had previously been full-time homemakers; many of them were also mothers.

After many arguments against allowing women in the military, Congress passed a bill in 1942, a few months after Pearl Harbor, to establish the Women's Auxiliary Army Corps (WAAC; later Women's Army Corps, WAC), and soon every branch of the military had a women's unit. At the end of the war, records showed that WACs had served in every theater of operation,[6] and along with women in the other divisions of the military, had handled a wide range of jobs, including flying aircraft. Although the armed forces were reluctant to accept women in their ranks, the manpower shortage changed their minds. Women had become essential to the military war effort.

Women may have been essential workers, but they were not yet equal workers. For example, the air force required women to achieve many more hours of flying time than men to qualify as pilots, women had to be high school graduates while men did not, and women were paid less than men with fewer qualifications and less experience. Typically they could not achieve rank, and even after serving with skill and valor, were denied honors given to their male counterparts. For the thirty-eight women pilots killed in the war, there was no pay for the transport of their bodies, no money for burials, no flags to drape on their coffins, no Gold Star given to their parents. In all branches of the military, women faced outright hostility from some officers and enlisted men. Outside the military, certain politicians and religious leaders also decried their participation.

Black women worked in war plants, in white-collar offices, as volunteers, in the USO, as WACs, and ultimately in the Army Nurse Corps. The segregation that black women endured in their communities continued in the military as they served in a segregated unit. Black women fought three concurrent wars: World War II, the war for the participation of women in the military, and the war against racism. Along with black men, they asked, "Are You for Hitler's Way (Race Supremacy), or the American Way (Equality)?"

After the war, attitudes and conditions changed dramatically again. The men who were fortunate enough to come home from the war wanted and needed jobs. They also wanted to go to college. As a result, women were suddenly and unceremoniously told to stay home. Many women who had worked during the war realized that they either wanted to work or needed to work in order to meet the rising cost of goods and the renewed emphasis on consumerism. However, instead of being asked to work in place of the men who had gone to war, they were told to leave the job for the veteran. They were encouraged to focus on being wives, mothers, and homemakers. Suddenly society frowned upon the notion of women working outside the home as a businessperson or as a professional. Social norms dictated that it was acceptable for young brides to become schoolteachers or nurses or secretaries—but just until the first child was born.

The children born after World War II, between 1946 and 1964, are known as the Baby Boomer Generation. They were largely the children of stay-at-home moms. Particularly in middle-class families, "[m]other vest[ed] all of her pent-up energies and needs on her two or three children, dragging them from one organized activity to another, lavishing attention on their 'progress' like a horticulturist in a hothouse."

No longer held back by the Depression and freed from the drain on production of household goods that occurred during the war, Americans now found themselves in a new era: increased wages accompanied a feeling that it was important to build houses and furnish them and to take advantage of the postwar good times. "Although the 'home of consumption' was firmly entrenched in American culture" by the 1930s, there was added emphasis on consumerism after the war. Women were the focus of this consumer society, and the print media supported the "happy housewife" syndrome. It was her "duty" to be an integral part of a society recovering from war. If a housewife and mother found herself with small qualms of dissatisfaction or feelings of self-doubt with the roles she played, she was encouraged by advertisers to go to the store and buy: what better way to raise her spirits than to buy a new hat, new drapes for the dining room, or new clothes for the dinner she was hosting for her husband's boss.

Of course, during and prior to the mid-twentieth century, many women defied the constraints on women's occupations and professions outside of the home and became writers, physicians, pilots, and even senators. Clearly, though, this was the exception rather than the rule.

In the 1960s America witnessed wide-ranging transformations that affected the position of women and ultimately the lives of their male partners and children. This second wave of the women's movement tackled a host of issues, among them the right to fair treatment at work and at school. These changes were part of a larger cultural upheaval in the 1960s that penetrated all levels and facets of society.

Young people coming of age in the 1960s engaged in a wide-ranging social and political rebellion against the consumer culture of their parents. "The very idea of preparing vigorously for a 60-year career in the suit-and-tie world followed by a few years' retirement, then a terminal illness caused by pollutants, did not appeal at all to quite a number of young Americans." This counterculture movement effectively changed the cultural landscape of the United States.

Against the backdrop of the 1960s cultural upheaval, several events directly affected women. Not the least of these was the approval in 1960 of a contraceptive known simply as the Pill. Although some argue that the Pill was (and is) yet another instance of women being forced to take sole responsibility for reproduction, it did allow women the option of timing their pregnancies or opting out of pregnancy entirely. "For women across the country, the contraceptive pill was liberating: it allowed them to pursue careers, fueled the feminist and pro-choice" movements, and encouraged more open attitudes towards sex.

In *The Feminine Mystique* Betty Friedan encouraged women to envision a life beyond the consumer, helpmate, and caregiver roles expected of them in the 1950s. In naming their unspoken and often-unarticulated feelings, Friedan's book awakened in women the possibility that perhaps there was another path they could follow. Women began to think that yes, perhaps they could do something more than worrying about tattletale gray laundry and peanut butter sandwiches. Maybe they could go back to school, get a good job, and still raise a family and be a wife!

There were some feminists in this era of the 1960s who argued, on the other hand, that "the workplace offered women no escape from society's restrictive views," and it was certainly true that women would encounter sexism in professional life. In 1963 President Kennedy's Commission on the Status of Women called attention to discrimination in employment, unequal pay, continuing legal inequality, and a lack of social services for working mothers. The Equal Pay Act of 1963 became the first law prohibiting discrimination based on sex. This law has been effective in improving employment practices and attitudes, but women's earnings today still lag behind those earned by men. Change in these areas was high on the agenda of the powerful National Organization for Women when it was founded in 1966.

During the same period, black women made critical contributions to the civil rights movement. Racial and gender equality were now linked, and the unique experience of black women recognized. In fact, the word *sex* was added to Title VII of the Civil Rights Bill. When it was finally passed, the Civil Rights Act of 1964 prohibited "employment discrimination on the basis of sex."

The 1970s brought further gains, both sweeping and incremental. The legalization of abortion through the ruling of *Roe v. Wade* in 1973 was perhaps the most radical and controversial of these. It was a major turning point in reproductive rights that also had implications for women's professional lives.

Among the many professional gains women saw in this decade, the effort within universities to integrate women's voices and experiences into traditional—and traditionally male-dominated—academic disciplines is particularly relevant in this volume of narratives by women anthropologists. In 1970 the first women's studies program was established, and by the mid-1970s such programs were being offered at nearly forty universities. By the end of the decade, at least thirty thousand women's studies courses were offered annually at colleges and universities across the nation. *Women's Studies: An Interdisciplinary Journal* and *Feminist Studies*, both launched in 1972, and *Signs: Journal of Women in Culture and Society*, begun in 1975, provided much-needed outlets for the publication of research on women's issues. The new teaching styles and methods that emerged in university courses during this period have been recognized as the most revolutionary in educational innovation.

Further gains were represented by Title IX of the Education Amendments of 1972, which prohibited discrimination on the basis of sex in federally funded education. Although we may hear more in the media about Title IX and its far-reaching influence on sports (both women's and men's), it has had a profound effect on women's involvement in the academic side of higher education. The 1997 report *Title IX at 25: Report Card on Gender Equity* gave Title IX its highest marks for increasing women's access to higher education.

Further gains appeared as black women scholars formed the Association of Black Women Historians in 1979 to encourage research on black women's history and push for the integration of that history into the main history texts. The association also provides important opportunities for black women historians to network and mentor other black women.

The 1980s sent women into space, into corporate boardrooms, and into politics. Other legislative advances included the 1986 Supreme Court ruling against sexual harassment, though it is somewhat sobering to note that it was not until 1998, after a flood of sexual harassment cases in the 1990s, that the Supreme Court clarified contradictory case law concerning sexual harassment in the workplace. It was a decade in which women felt that much had been accomplished, but much remained to be done.

While bias was less blatant in the 1980s, it was still widespread in various forms. For example, gender bias was apparent in the way girls were treated in school, how they were portrayed in textbooks, and whether or not they received the kind of encouragement that would have propelled them into science and math courses with confidence. Other analysts argued that the media—ads, movies, and TV—presented many images that were harmful to both sexes.

While we have presented here a brief summary of the events of the twentieth century, there have been new challenges and rewards for young women in the 1990s and 2000s. We consider some of those issues in the final chapter of this volume.

GENDER ROLES: WHAT DO THEY MEAN?

This summary of events that took place in the twentieth century clearly demonstrates how much gender roles can change. In this section we first consider the complexity of culture as we address the nature-nurture debate—the question of biology versus culture in the creation of gender roles; we then describe the gender roles that were prescribed for women and men at mid-twentieth century; and, finally, we evaluate some of the forces that underlaid and supported those gender roles.

People everywhere categorize the many features of their world—material artifacts, ideas, and people. Categorizing is a shorthand that allows us to function in the social world; lumping items into categories makes it possible for us to handle all of the cultural clues that come at us each day in blinding complexity. But lumping also carries with it the danger of reacting to categories of events and/or people in a way that makes individuals invisible. We cannot see the trees for the forest. When we see groups of women or men, we make certain assumptions about them based in part on what we learned while growing up and on our experiences as adults. When we characterize, or stereotype, groups of people and assume that they will behave in a particular way, we are denying them their individuality and often their full potential. Such is the nature of the stereotypes associated with gender roles.

Nature versus Nurture

The age-old question of whether nature or nurture is the determinant of human behavior is still being evaluated and debated today. Some believe that biology (nature) determines role behavior, while others believe that socialization and enculturation (nurture) provide the more important foundation, overriding almost all of the sex-related characteristics of males and females.

From the nurture viewpoint, Ortner and Whitehead argue that "natural features of gender... [and] of sex and reproduction, furnish only a suggestive and ambiguous backdrop to the cultural organization of gender and sexuality." Chafetz agrees that the more or less well-defined roles of men and women are socially prescribed and not inherent in the sex. They are not, in other words, innate.

Those who attacked the feminist movement in the 1970s, as well as those who continue to argue against role changes today, assume that biology is the basis for gender roles and behavior and thus gender roles cannot and should not be changed. Often people are afraid of change: it threatens their current positions, or they find they are faced with rather fundamental assaults on their beliefs, or they do not have the skills or desire to adapt to new understandings of their world.

Why does this question matter? It matters because when we weigh the evidence provided by anthropology, other social sciences, and the biological sciences, we find overwhelming evidence that behaviors are learned and changeable. We recognize that we are not bound by our gender roles and the stereotypes that have grown up around them. They are just that—stereotypes that have been promoted by and shored up by culture, society, and history.

According to Jonathan Marks, "Ultimately, the fallacy is not a genetic but a cultural one—our reduction of the important things in life to genetics." He criticizes sociobiologists who study "the biological roots of human behavior, whether or not they exist" in the pursuit of an impossible goal, the discovery of something called "human nature." Marks argues that "[t]here is no human nature outside of culture. ... Nature and culture act as a synergy. If the human is like a cake, culture is like the eggs, not like the icing—it is an inseparable part, not superficial glaze. Whatever humans do or look like is a product of both." Suffice it to say, the authors in this volume welcome changes towards a more egalitarian society, one that recognizes the full worth and potential of *all* of its members. We come down strongly on the side of enculturation and socialization as the defining factors in the creation of gender roles. As anthropologists we believe that human beings are malleable and cultures are immensely varied in their expectations for their members. Because there are so many different behavioral prescriptions, we argue that gender roles have more to do with the way people are socialized than with their respective sexes.

There are no easy answers. As we learn more about the brain and the differences that do exist between the sexes, we must conclude that we still do not know exactly how biology interacts with social factors and what these differences mean.

Although we cannot provide the final answer on the question of nature versus nurture, we do wish to point out how gender role stereotypes in North America have affected women's lives and to suggest that changes in behavior can be enlightening and rewarding for both females and males. Because of the restrictions inherent in gender role stereotypes, we assert that both men and women can benefit from a broad interpretation of gender roles.

GENDER ROLE STEREOTYPES AND THEIR COSTS

Here we examine gender role stereotypes that existed at mid-twentieth century in order to explore the bases for their existence, the cost of limiting the gender roles of both men and women, and what they bode for present society and future generations.

Chafetz describes the gender role stereotypes for white middle-class and upper-middle-class females and males that were prevalent in the 1960s and 1970s. Adult women were characterized as weak and nonathletic homemakers associated with the domestic, private sphere of life. They were considered sexually inexperienced, but nevertheless were the ones responsible for birth control. They were described as emotional, scatterbrained, and passive followers.

By contrast, adult males were described as virile, strong, and athletic. They were the bread-winners who worked at jobs in the public sphere. They were regarded as sexually aggressive and unemotional and as dominating leaders considered to be intellectual and aggressive in their dealings with others.

Stereotypical expectations and behaviors are learned at an early age, beginning at birth. However, we focus here on the adult role stereotypes prevalent in the socialization of middle-class white men and women at midcentury.

A girl born in the mid-1960s was expected to become a wife eighteen or twenty years later, ensconced in her (hopefully) computerized kitchen, taking care of her children and husband. The socially accepted expectations and restrictions that characterized the late 1940s and the 1950s remained in place: a woman could work as a teacher, secretary, or nurse only until her first baby was born. A boy born in the mid-1960s was expected to become an active participant in the public sphere—building splendid objects, reading significant documents, or lecturing on important topics. They would become the doctors, lawyers, designers, and bosses, while the girls could aspire to being men's helpmates at work as well as at home.

Gender role conformity carries with it costs for both men and women, to say nothing of the dysfunction experienced by members of ethnic and racial groups who may have more important issues than conforming to the dominant stereotypes. Men who conform to gender role stereotypes often have more obligations but fewer proscriptions on what they do. They complain about what they *have* to do. Women, on the other hand, have fewer obligations and more proscriptions. They complain about what they *can't* do. Sanctioning women to be passive and men to be active can create costs that clearly do not enhance the lives of either group. The costs and rewards for both sexes depend in part on whether one abides by the roles that are expected or tries to adopt behavior that is contrary to what the stereotypes dictate.

Midcentury socialization may have prepared girls for the roles of homemaker and caretaker of her husband and children, but it did not prepare her for roles outside of the home. Some women left with an "empty nest" and no alternative role might develop psychological problems. With "no one to take care of" after the last child left home, they lost their primary role and their sense of worth. Women who conformed to the domestic stereotype were handicapped if they were widowed or divorced since they were unprepared for a job or profession.

THE FOUNDATIONS OF MIDCENTURY GENDER ROLE STEREOTYPES

It is not possible to include here all of the factors involved in mid-twentiethcentury role stereo-types, but we want to note four important features of society and culture that have permeated the lives of both women and men: 1) religion and the role of the patriarchal church; 2) the legal system and women's rights; 3) the value assigned to domesticity; and 4) language and communication styles.

Patriarchy in the Church

The dominance of patriarchy in religious institutions in the prescription of gender roles is undeniable. In many expressions of the Christian religion, for example, women have been measured against an unattainable model, that of the Virgin Mary and the Virgin Birth. In contrast, patriarchal interpretations of the Christian Bible have held that womankind is evil and the source of all disaster. Thus there have been only two extreme roles for women: the good woman or the bad woman. Procreation within the bonds of marriage has been the only way a woman could avoid being regarded as "dangerous." The "proper woman" was chaste and unassuming, not reckless or sensual.

The division of labor (and all societies have some sort of division of labor) in the United States and other Western societies is related to the patriarchal foundation of the Judeo-Christian religious heritage, and is sometimes characterized as the "public" sphere for men and the "domestic" or "private" sphere for women. According to patriarchal mores, womanly virtue meant silence or a passive expression (or no expression) of personality and behavior that acquiesced to every demand and desire of the men in her life, beginning with her father, and later her husband. Women had few or no roles in the church and were expected to be stay-at-home mothers and wives. The subordination of women as a basic tenet of the church has been slow to change.

Women's Rights

Since early federal documents did not expressly mention women, laws regulating women's lives were left to the states. The legal system in forty-two U.S. states is based on English common law; that of the remaining eight states is based on community property law that originated in continental Europe. In practice, these two systems operate similarly. Common law held that "the legal existence of the woman is suspended during the marriage, or at least is incorporated into that of her husband." Although the Fourteenth Amendment (1865) defined for the first time the terms citizens and voters as male, both the Fifth and Fourteenth Amendments were supposed to procure "equal protection of the law" to everyone. On more than one occasion, women were excluded. For example, it was not until the second decade of the twentieth century that women, except in isolated cases, gained the right to vote after suffragists protested against the U.S. entry into World War I in 1917, proclaiming that "[d]emocracy should begin at home." Congress finally passed a suffrage bill that went into effect in 1920.

During the first half of the twentieth century, women were denied credit in their own names, and work-related discrimination against women was permissible. Protective legislation regarding how long and when a woman could work was not covered under the due process clause of the Fifth Amendment. It was not until 1971 that gender-preference statutes were struck down by the Supreme Court.

While it is not possible to detail here all of the different levels of law (federal, state, or local) or the different types of law (common law or case law) and their interpretations, it is worthwhile to note that many aspects of the legal system and public policy have reinforced the "separate and unequal" treatment of women over the decades, supporting stereotypical interpretations of gender roles in a patriarchal expression of the law. In fact, income tax laws and Social Security benefits still have unequal effects on women and men. And in many cases, positive changes have been piecemeal, as different states have changed different aspects of the law.

The Value of Domesticity

In the 1970s U.S. homemakers were doing over $250 billion of unpaid work a year, but none of this production was included in calculations of the gross national product, and women were given no economic credit for these labors. Nor was homemaking highly valued in noneconomic ways, despite the fact that it was essential to the "good woman" role. Because women's work is so vital on the one hand—after all, what is more important than raising the next generation to be caring, productive individuals?—and is so devalued on the other hand, women suffer from a conflicted sense of their own worth. We address this issue further in the last chapter, "Lessons for Today," as we assess the conditions for women in the 1990s and early twenty-first century.

Language and Communication Styles

The insights of feminist thought suggest that "concepts of gender structure the perception and the organization of all of social life." This echoes the Sapir-Whorf hypothesis that language shapes and constrains thought. Language, then, is a major factor in interactions between men and women.

Language has a persuasion all its own. It is "the fundamentally symbolic activity that permeates and suffuses all forms of human activity." In essence, it is the thread that binds together the different parts of culture. Language and cultural norms begin to affect an individual's identity from the moment a baby is born. Knowing whether it is a boy or a girl is fundamental in directing the parents' attitudes and reactions to their newborn, which will be modeled after cultural views they learned regarding males and females. The descriptive terms used to talk about the newborn convey subtle but influential images. By using certain descriptive terms for each gender, we automatically characterize individuals as boys and girls and later as men and women.

Changes are being made in how we raise our children today. Many people may choose to give a new baby a nonsexist blanket in green or yellow and toys that are nonsexist in their design. But our cultural heritage is strong and persistent. With the words that we still often use for boys, we have already started persuading a baby boy that he is expected to be strong, active, and even aggressive. And one day we will expect him to be ambitious, dogmatic, practical, logical, experienced, and adventuresome. On the other hand, if we describe a baby girl as dainty and petite, we are encouraging her that she is expected to be "feminine" in her demeanor. It may seem as though there is nothing wrong with this on the surface, but it is what such language implies about expected roles in the future that creates the problem.

The effort to make language gender neutral and more inclusive introduced the use of *she/he* and *him/her*. Although a diffcult and sometimes awkward task, the use of gender-neutral language has been important in lessening gender role bias. After the introduction, for example, of *Ms.* as a term for women comparable to Mr. for men, its use has become standard practice. In the 1970s other changes in language use occurred. Signs for public restrooms changed from "Ladies" to "Women." Advocates for change wanted females to be recognized as normal people, not as a stereotype.

How we communicate with each other is not a trivial matter and often is at the root of misunderstanding. Women's and men's styles of talking tend to be different, including the (sometimes) more subtle nonverbal aspects that are always a part of communication. According to Deborah Tannen, men prefer "report-talk," a public type of speaking through which they attempt to maintain status in a social hierarchy. Women, on the other hand, are more comfortable with "rapport-talk," a more private type of speaking. Women tend to interweave the sentences in their conversation, taking note of what the other person is saying; they express a desire to take turns in talking with others while men tend to center on what they want to say.

Nonverbal aspects of communication also affect the interaction between males and females. While men frequently don't look directly at a person with whom they are conversing, women will usually be tuned into what the other person is saying. As such, she is probably more observant of the nuances of gestures, attitudes, and feelings of the other person. This is often referred to as "a woman's intuition."

Understanding aggressive, passive, and assertive behavior and conversation is fundamental to understanding some of the differences that occur when men and women interact with each other. Aggressive behavior is standing up for your own rights while trying to dominate or ignore the rights of others. Passive or nonassertive behavior means not expressing your own opinions, needs, or ideas and ignoring your own rights. Assertive behavior simply means acknowledging that you have rights and standing up for yourself without violating the rights of others.

Women at midcentury were traditionally raised to be passive. When women acted or talked in an assertive way, they were often perceived as being aggressive. This misunderstanding of the different kinds of behavior and conversation styles still exists and has made it more diffcult for women (and for passive men) to be assertive on their own behalf. Men, on the other hand, were socialized to express independence and achievement with restriction and suppression of emotion; to avoid femininity and homosexuality; and to be socialized toward physical aggressiveness, toughness, and status seeking, often including an aggressive style of speaking.

We can translate these aspects of communication to the business world or—as in the case of the authors in this volume—to the academic world of graduate school and the classroom, PhD committees, and faculty meetings. A man's style of speaking may mean that a woman's more intimate style inhibits her participation in the discussion. When she succeeds in stating her point, she may find herself either not well understood or not credited for an idea for which someone more dynamic and forceful instead is given credit. If she tries to interject her ideas and opinions, she may be seen as aggressive rather than assertive, or she may back down and revert to a passive stance if someone challenges her in an aggressive way.

WOMEN WITH MULTIFACETED LIVES

The women whose narratives compose this volume are women with multifaceted lives who defied the constraints placed on them by the social, cultural, and legal realities of North America in the mid-1900s to achieve their goals. They wanted to become bona fide, full-fledged anthropologists, even though all of them but one had spent several years raising their families. They were well educated and intelligent, and all of them knew that their jobs as mothers and homemakers were important. But they also felt that they were capable of expanding their lives to include more education, fieldwork, a dissertation, and maybe even a job.

The paths they followed to their PhDs were different, as their narratives point out, and not everyone found the job that she might have wanted. But there are many ways to make use of education and experience, and these women provide proof of that. How they achieved success in various guises reflects their persistence and faith in something larger than themselves and their abilities to juggle many roles and to create new ones.

Some women's families gave them unquestioning support; the families of others very little. The women who managed duties at home while also going to school settled on a variety of solutions—making sure the household ran efficiently and someone was there for the children while they attended classes, catching up on the housework on the weekend after several days away at school, planning and preparing meals for the week ahead, juggling kids' activities with the need to study or attend classes, doing laundry, shopping—all of the many and varied household chores that help make a home run efficiently.

Even when spouses were supportive and took over some of the household chores, they usually held down full-time jobs and their time was limited. Some husbands and fathers took charge of household chores, such as the shopping or the cooking. In other cases, husbands and fathers supported their wives' pursuit of an educational dream only if their wives would continue to fulfill all of their wifely and motherly duties. It was a big job to succeed at school without neglecting children and husbands at home.

Almost all of the narrators dealt with some sort of bias on the part of the professors and academic administrators they met. Returning to school to finish an undergraduate degree or take on the more rigorous studies required by graduate degrees meant that they were competing with younger students who were presumably more up to date, and they needed to show that they were up to the task.

Women who stepped outside of the more traditional roles were often greeted with disdain or just plain misunderstanding. They were sometimes looked upon as if something must be wrong with them. Why else would one of the women be rebuffed when trying to enroll in a graduate program? Why else were some looked upon as not serious about their schooling? Both men *and* women were uncomfortable with women who attempted to occupy roles that were not prescribed for them and in many ways were proscribed from their participation.

In general, if a woman wanted to go to college, she needed a higher grade point average than a male applicant. Once there, prejudice against women on the part of faculty and administration was rampant and can be illustrated by one choice comment made at an educational institution in the 1960s: "I know you're competent and your thesis advisor knows you're competent. The question in our minds is are you *really serious* about what you're doing." The authors have their own stories to tell.

Frequently responsible for caring for both their parents and their children, many of the women were bona fide members of the "sandwich" generation. Sometimes these duties coincided with their schedules at school, and they responded in the only way they could—they carried out their family duties and picked up their school duties later. Often untimely events—such as a serious illness or death of a family member—interjected an alarming dimension to their career paths.

For some women in this volume, divorce and the loss of a familiar family setting added other difficult dimensions—either husbands did not grow and change along with their wives, or there were incompatibilities that occurred. Financial issues were important factors for some. For others, however, the support of their husbands and families, both moral and financial, was integral to their success.

This introductory chapter has demonstrated the fact that the ideology behind gender role stereotypes is complex and slow to change. But this chapter has also shown that behavior, events, actions, and laws can gradually effect change for the better. We believe that even while there are strong forces striving to maintain the status quo, society will continue to work for the equality of *all* of its citizens.

THEORIZING GENDER AND THE INTERNET

PAST, PRESENT, AND FUTURE

By Niels van Doorn and Liesbet van Zoonen

The growth of the internet has been accompanied by a profound academic interest in its gendered features and contexts. This chapter first discusses how studies of the relationship between gender and the internet have been articulated through the use of two conceptions of gender common within a feminist theoretical framework: "gender as identity" and "gender as social structure." Yet, as we will demonstrate, studies in these domains often have gender-essentialist and technological-determinist tendencies and ignore the positioned and embodied everyday interactions with internet technologies. We therefore continue with an assessment of approaches that counter essentialism and determinism by focusing on the mutual shaping of gender and technology in situated practices and spaces. We conclude by discussing whether the current prevalence of user-generated content referred to as Web 2.0 raises new questions for research about gender and the internet.

As early as 1993, well before the proliferation of the web, Sandra Herring investigated differences between men and women in their use of language in asynchronous computer-mediated communication (CMC) such as bulletin boards, newsgroups, and discussion lists. Barely 15 years later, research on gender and the internet has burgeoned. The online sphere, with its mixture of information, entertainment, and communication modalities and its convergence of audiovisual technologies requires multidisciplinary theoretical and methodological lines of inquiry. Psychologists, for instance, often examine gender differences in the online behavior of women and men; anthropologists and sociologists regularly investigate how women build communities on the internet; feminist political scientists tend to look at the way women use it to mobilize for social and political causes; cultural studies scholars have a recurring interest in the virtual performance of gendered identities in, for instance, online games; and sociolinguists mostly discuss gendered language patterns in various online contexts. Given this plethora of approaches, any attempt to write about this subject is bound to be incomplete and partial. Nevertheless, we organize our account around what we see as the key conceptual contours of the social science literature in this area.

GENDER AS IDENTITY

Differences

Gender differences online have been a central area of concern in studies of gender as identity. In her pioneering study, Herring (1993) identified two separate discourses online: a feminine discourse encompassing a more "personal" style of communication, characterized by apologetic language use and the prevention of tension; and a masculine discourse, typified as being more "authoritative" and oriented towards action, and characterized by challenging and argumentative language use. When these two discourses met in a "mixed gender" online environment, the masculine discourse dominated: men tended to introduce more subjects and ignored or ridiculed the input of female participants (Herring, 1993). These results led Herring to conclude that the internet perpetuates everyday linguistic inequalities between men and women (Herring, 1995, 1996a, 1996b, 1999; Herring et al., 1995). Similar research, such as a study of newsgroups by Savicki et al. (1996), concluded that newsgroups with predominantly male participants could be characterized as containing a large amount of fact-related exchange and impersonal speech, while female-dominated news-groups featured conflict-avoiding speech and high levels of "self-disclosure." Jaffe et al. (1995) found that women tend to display textual patterns of social interdependence more than men do in both real-name and pseudonymous online conferences, while Kendall (1998) demonstrated that the interactions between "male" and "female" characters in MUDs (Multi User Dungeons—an early type of online fantasy game) were largely predicated on stereotypical gender relations, even though these provided what appeared on the surface to be an anonymous and disembodied environment.

Some research has shown how male dominance is violently reinforced online through the sexual harassment of women in different online contexts (Herring, 2002, 2001, 1999, for an overview see Li, 2005). These studies make clear how gender and sexual identities are mutually constitutive and how, for heterosexual men, the position of the former is strengthened by the oppressive explication of the latter through the use of sexually demeaning language targeted at women.

On the other hand, a detailed analysis by Nancy Baym (2000) of the participants in the online fan community of the U.S. daytime soap All My Children reveals that it is not only the gender of participants that explains particular feminine communicative styles, but also the topic of conversation (in this case a soap) and the offine contexts of the participants. Baym's study suggests that gender cannot be considered the sole explanatory factor for "gender differences" online—a result supported by a small number of others that have found reversed gender patterns. For example, in an experimental study by Jaffe et al. (1999) men abandoned dominant behavior and approached others in a socially aware and helpful way, while Witmer and Katzman (1997) found that women actually uttered more conflictual speech than men. Similarly, Can's (1999) investigation of the language styles in two feminist Usenet newsgroups, alt.feminism and soc. feminism, showed that exclusionary rhetorical techniques can also be found in online environments dominated by women.

Whether these "difference" studies emphasize the reiteration or the reversal of stereotypical gender relations in CMC, they leave the "male/female" dichotomy unchallenged because they focus on generalized types of "male" and "female" communicative behavior. They find evidence for the claim that the internet reconfirms and exaggerates traditional gender relations.

Yet, just as in feminist theory more generally, gender differences are not only a source of women's oppression, but are also seen by some scholars as a source of power. Influenced by Donna Haraway's "cyborg theory," the radical French feminism of Luce Irigaray, and Freudian psychoanalysis, British author Sadie Plant (1995, 1996, 1997) argues that the "digital revolution" marks the decline of masculine hegemonic power structures, as the internet constitutes a non-linear world that cannot be ordered or controlled. Plant's "cyberfeminist" vision conceptualizes the web as a fractured and diffuse structure—one that is uniquely aligned with women's fluid identities and that deconstructs the traditionally patriarchal character of technology. According to Plant, women have a "natural" affinity with new digital technologies because they allow them to explore a multitude of gender identities in a virtual environment where the relation between gender and the body is a contingent construction.

Although Plant's utopian view certainly serves as an encouraging theoretical source for young women who are increasingly immersing themselves in new technologies, it also has a rather peculiar way of combining conceptions of femininity as universally different from masculinity with a view of female identity as fragmented and diffuse. In an awkward effort to merge the two notions, Plant reconciles her version of biological essentialism with the technologically determinist claim that the internet constitutes the key to women's liberation because it allows female multiplicity to flourish. This tension leads Wajcman (2004) to oppose this position, by suggesting that the claim that internet technology is essentially feminine Plant pre-empts the need for feminist political action.

Experimentation

In an effort to break out of this traditional gender binary and further investigate the liberating potential of cyberspace, another strand of research shifts the focus from gender differences to gender experimentation. In early research about "gender bending" the absence of the body in text-based CMC plays a central role. Due to the fact that cyberspace offers an environment in which gender can be disconnected from one's physical body, the possibilities for creating different gender identities become abundant. Studies by Reid (1993) and Danet (1996) examined the construction of gender at the moment in which participants enter "virtual space." For example, Reid (1993) argued that internet relay chat (IRC) users construct their gender identities through the choice of their nickname. "Nicks" may express masculinity, femininity, or even gender ambiguity. "MUDders" are able to choose gendered, gender-neutral, or gender-plural characters when they join. This provides them with an opportunity to actively create their gender (or lack thereof) in virtual space.

Perhaps the most influential examination of gender bending online is Sherry Turkle's *Life on the Screen*. Turkle contends that the internet has become "a significant social laboratory for experimenting with the constructions and reconstructions of self" (Turkle, 1995: 180). In contrast with other studies, Turkle approaches this from a socio-psychological perspective, by investigating the participants' personal reasons for engaging in experimentation with gender and sexual identity, as well as the social context in which these performances take place. This approach places strong emphasis on the relation between online and offline selves. In Turkle's view, online experiments with gender and sexuality are useful tools for the rethinking not only of one's "virtual" gender identity, but also of one's "reallife" gendered and sexualized self (Turkle, 1995). This last point is made especially clear in the book's chapter on "cybersex", in which it is argued that cyberspace offers a risk-free environment where people can engage in the intimate relationships they desire but are afraid to initiate in the real world. The possibilities of online gender bending fit well with poststructuralist theories about identities as non-essential discursive performances that open up space for negotiation (Butler, 1990). In addition, these notions have helped the political struggles of feminists trying to escape the "prison-house of gender."

Yet, notwithstanding its theoretical and political popularity, several empirical studies have suggested that gender bending is uncommon, or is most often conducted for fun or specific game-related advantages rather than to break out of the gender dichotomy (e.g., Wright *et al.*, 2000; Van Doorn *et al.*, 2007). A further problem with these theories is that their focus on escaping the offine confines of gender causes them to ignore the impact of embodied everyday experience on online performances. Turkle herself believes that ultimately the gendered self is rooted in the physical, offline world, even though cyberspace provides us with profound experiences that can lead to "personal transformation" and a reconfiguration of how we perceive ourselves (Turkle, 1995).

This concern about the offline self is shared, for example, by Jodi O'Brien (1999), who also stresses the importance of embodied experience. O'Brien argues that "gender categories evoke a deeply entrenched cognitive-emotive script for who we can be and how we should relate to others," and these make it doubtful whether "cyberspace will be a realm in which physical markers such as sex, race, age, body type and size will eventually lose salience as a basis for the evaluative categorization of self/others" (O'Brien, 1999: 77). Through a reliance on "classification schemes," which cause one to make continual references to the body as connected to the self even though this body is not physically present, the body provides us with a common point of reference that structures our disembodied communication and gives it meaning (O'Brien, 1999). From this perspective, the internet could hardly be considered a site that facilitates the creation of totally fluid gender identities.

Despite their different perspectives, both the "difference" and the "experimentation" approaches focus on gender as identity: a discourse in which individuals engage and through which they assume agency while being simultaneously shaped and disciplined by it. The "difference" studies distinguish between feminine and masculine language patterns and behaviors and conclude that the internet does not change traditional relations of dominance between women and men, femininity and masculinity. In these works gender is perceived as a foundational property, with its internal truth or logic located in the sexed body. It is what makes women and men who they are and it determines human interactions, even in an online context. In contrast, the "experimentation" works implicitly perceive the internet as the determining force, since its facilitation of disembodied communication is said to enable individuals to break out of the traditional confines of socially constructed gender relations. Not only are both perspectives thus rather determinist (favoring either gender or technology as the deciding factor) they also tend to ignore social contexts and structures. One reason for this is that empirical studies on "gender as identity" have mainly focused on the interpersonal online practices of CMC (chat, bulletin boards, online gaming, and so on) while mostly discarding the socio-economic framework in which these practices take place. Although these studies have at times incorporated a notion of embodiment, with the notable exception of Turkle's this is rarely related to a focus on the actual lives of users in everyday social contexts—in other words, gender as a social structure that locates women and men in particular roles in society is usually ignored. We now turn to another field of research that has examined how the internet is engaged in the negotiation of socio-political positions by women and men.

GENDER AS SOCIAL STRUCTURE

Marketing "the feminine" online

A number of feminist researchers have interrogated the internet's commercial spaces. Women online are now routinely addressed in their traditional role as consumers (Van Zoonen, 2002). Market research has produced ever more studies about the online differences between women and men in order to find ways to promote women's online consumption (for example, Parasuraman and Zinkhan, 2002; Rodgers and Harris, 2003; Van Slyke *et al.*, 2002).

Feminist scholars have looked upon these developments with suspicion. Leslie Regan Shade (2002), for instance, warns against the increasing tension "between e-commerce applications directed towards women as consumers and the usage of the internet as a locus for citizen-oriented activities" (Shade, 2002: 10). According to Shade, digital capitalism's rising interest in women as a viable consumer market has decreased the number of online spaces where women can engage in non-profit cultural or political practices, while corporate websites that aim to profit from women's supposed needs and interests have proliferated (Shade, 2002). Similarly, Gustafson (2002) explores the concept of the "feminization" of community online through the interrogation of three popular commercial women's sites (iVillage, Oxygen, and Women.com). Gustafson suggests that "while women are a growing internet population, they are being discursively constructed on the internet as community-seekers and as consumers—traditionally feminine roles" (Gustafson, 2002: 169). Consalvo (2002) also suggests that community and consumption have been coded as "feminine" traits in metaphors used in popular discourse about women and the internet. And while women are now equal to men in their online consumption, they remain far behind when it comes to the production and design of the web and other information technologies (Whitehouse, 2006; Wajcman, 2007).

Internet pornography: from the abject to the everyday?

While women are increasingly targeted as consumers in many of the web's commercial spaces, the single largest commercial enterprise on the internet is still mainly directed at a male audience. The porn industry was one of the first to take its business online and since then has expanded exponentially in size and profit, simultaneously figuring as a further catalyst for the technological innovation that facilitated its growth and pervasiveness (Lane, 2000; Cronin and Davenport, 2001; Lillie, 2004). According to Lillie, there are four general perspectives from which "cyberporn" has been studied. First, behavioral-psychological studies have examined uses and addictions, and have established an agenda for research that describes a range of "healthy" and "unhealthy" online behaviors, while providing possible remedies for "compulsive" uses of online porn. Second, the "effects" tradition of empirical media research has mainly concerned itself with the exposure of children to cyberporn. This has usually recommended policies on increased parental guidance and surveillance or filtering software. The third perspective adopts a political economy approach, studying the many facets of the online porn industry and its development in a broader social context, while the fourth focuses on how different social groups use cyberporn in their everyday lives and is mainly indebted to the traditions of cultural studies and CMC research.

Feminist analyses of online pornography were initially structured around the polarizing debates between radical "anti-porn" feminists and liberal "free speech" or "pro sex" feminists, which took place during the 80s and 90s, mainly in the United States. The most well-known anti-porn feminists of this time, Andrea Dworkin and Catherine MacKinnon, have argued that pornography functions as a system for male domination, where male power is established through the violent degradation of women. Thus, the goal for feminist activists is to dismantle this system of domination. In contrast, next to the rather obvious free speech arguments that have been raised, "pro sex" feminists have applauded pornography for undermining and subverting our culture's repressive attitude to sexuality in general, and female sexuality in particular. What these debates make clear is how discourse about pornography is inextricably linked to conceptions of gender, sexuality, and power (Allen, 2001).

Yet for all the theoretical and ideological discussions concerning pornography in general, there is remarkably little feminist scholarship on online sex. The few studies that do exist generally align themselves with the "established" areas of media research. Feminists working within the "media effects" and "political economy" traditions have tended to center on the hazards of internet pornography for women and children (e.g., Adam, 2002; Burke et al., 2002; Hughes, 1999, 2004), while those with a cultural studies background have focused their attention on online cultures and how they may be redefining the standard gendered codes of porn and sexual practices (Kibby, 2001; Kibby and Costello, 2001; Waskul, 2004).

This last area of feminist scholarship has been gaining currency over the past few years, with studies extending the scope of analysis by paying specific attention to the situated and everyday contexts of internet porn consumption. For instance, Lillie has argued for a need for "porn reception" studies that investigate "the truths of the architecture of knowledge and technologies of sexuality, which pornography as a participant in the construction of the subject's desire and sexual identity works within." An important location for these kinds of studies would be what Lillie terms "the moral economy of the net-worked home" (Lillie, 2004: 53, 58).

New communication technologies have played a crucial role in the production, distribution, and consumption of pornography, both as visually explicit material and in terms of the accompanying discourses of gender, sex, and sexuality (Paasonen, 2006; Paasonen *et al.*, 2007; Attwood, 2002; Cronin and Davenport, 2001; O'Toole, 1999). To a large extent, the internet can be credited for spreading a "diversity of pornographies" in today's media environment, contributing to the omnipotence, normalization, and increased acceptance of sexualized imagery in mainstream cultural products. In fact, this trend is slowly positioning women as another viable consumer market for pornographic content, however unlikely this might seem (Cronin and Davenport, 2001; McNair, 2002; Schauer, 2005). It is in such environments, on-and offline, that sexuality and gender are performed and negotiated, and this makes them a primary target for further feminist research.

Web of empowerment

Despite the previously mentioned efforts to commercialize the concept of "community," it has also played an instrumental role in a variety of feminist activities to empower women in their everyday onand offline lives. Many women's groups and feminist activists have approached the internet as an international platform for such diverse goals as creating support networks, challenging sexual harassment, discussing feminist politics, creating spaces for sexual self-expression, and rallying against social injustices. In this sense, community is strongly attached to a commitment to social change, and resists commercial appropriation by market actors.

Feminist scholars have devoted considerable attention to these social movements, documenting the everyday efforts of women to exercise their rights as citizens in an online environment. Aside from offering a critical look at the efforts by multimedia conglomerates to "feminize" the internet in order to exploit women's consumer potential, Shade (2002) also provides an overview of how women have used the same internet for feminist communication and activism. She describes, for instance, how mailing lists were one of the earliest and most successful tools for building international women's networks, creating hundreds of online discussion groups covering a multitude of topics related to feminism and women's everyday lives. More specifically, Shade illustrates how the internet was used to organize and coordinate the Fourth World Conference on Women, held in Beijing in 1995, and how it enabled Zapatista women to wage a social "net war" against the Mexican government and inform and educate the Western world about their cause. In a similar vein, Kensinger (2003) presents a critical perspective on how the internet was used for promoting social activism and solidarity with women in Afghanistan during the Taliban regime and the subsequent war in the region.

Aside from investigating how the internet can be used for organizing feminist social activism in various "offline" contexts, scholars have also paid attention to women's and girls' online strategies for cultural criticism and self-expression. The so-called "cybergrrls" movement has been the subject of extensive academic enquiry. Of particular interest is how techno-savvy young women negotiate and deconstruct the consumerist messages encoded in their everyday pop cultural environment (Driscoll, 1999; Kroløkke, 2003; Yervasi, 1996). However, according to some critics, a focus on this kind of "postfeminist" cultural renegotiation neglects basic gender inequalities concerning internet access and work-related issues (Wilding, 1998).

As some scholars have pointed out, an important area where women have been working to empower themselves is in the internet sex industry, where they have become increasingly visible as active consumers and producers of pornographic content (Podlas, 2000; Cronin and Davenport, 2001; Attwood, 2002; Smith, 2007). Through this process of emancipation, women are gradually redefining the idea of pornography as an exclusively masculine domain in which women are treated as passive sex objects, in favour of a realm in which they enjoy porn on their own terms and in which they are in control of their sexual practices. This is not only taking place on a symbolic level, for instance through the resignification of "female sexuality" in live webcam shows or in pornographic stories produced and published by women, but also on a material level, with more female entrepreneurs starting their own online business and making profits from pornographic productions (Podlas, 2000; Ray, 2007). Thus, while the porn industry has so far remained a predominantly masculine environment, and sexist representations of women are unlikely to decrease in the future, the internet is for some a tool for women's sexual and economic freedom.

These studies all share a concern with women's agency in relation to the internet, whether it is through the creation of networks for political activism, producing female-friendly pornography, or the feminist reappropriation of digital capitalism's consumer culture. While some see this agency as eroding due to the increasing dominance of male corporate presence online, others emphasize women taking matters into their own hands, effectively using the net to engage in various forms of socio-political action. More generally, internet research that approaches gender as a social structure is effectively concerned with the material-semiotic relation between gender and power at a macro level. Meanwhile, the internet itself functions as an unbiased, ahistorical, and gender-neutral technological instrument that can be used by and against women in the struggle for material and symbolic power. At the same time, gender also appears to be a stable entity in the majority of these studies, principally aligned along the man–woman binary and seemingly untouched by the technology that facilitates these feminist practices. Thus, the biological essentialism and technological determinism witnessed in the "gender as identity" approach tends to resurface here once again in the context of the "gender as social structure" debate (Wacjman, 2004).

Situated practices and spaces

In response to these shortcomings, some feminist research on gender and the internet has started to shift its emphasis from the "identity vs. social structure" dichotomy to the manifold interactions between gender and internet technology, paying special attention to their situated offline/online articulations. Some authors in the field of science and technology studies (STS) have argued that because the experience of ourselves is so thoroughly mediated through our everyday interactions with technological artifacts, we cannot meaningfully study gender without taking into account its intricate relationship with technology (Akrich, 1995). Influenced by this notion, feminist scholars have approached gender as something that is both shaping and shaped by technology. This "mutual shaping" approach generally looks at the intersections of gender and technology on three different, yet interrelated, levels: structural, symbolic, and identity related (Harding, 1986; Cockburn and Ormrod, 1993). Mutual shaping research investigates how these three dimensions of gender are articulated within the web's techno-social spaces, which are themselves gendered in the process. According to this approach, techno-social spaces are not only shaped by their use, but also through the design and production of their technological infrastructure (Wajcman, 2004, 2007). These practices are dependent on many different socio-technical factors, such as the interplay of commercial and institutional interests. Technological change, then, is never the linear result of "techno-*logical*" decision-making, but the outcome of a contingent process.

Research that follows this approach ideally takes into account the whole techno-cultural circuit including the design, development, marketing, consumption, and domestication of specific technologies (e.g., Cockburn, 1992). However, in practice STS scholars mostly conduct detailed case studies that focus on specific elements of this circuit. We will now briefly discuss three such studies, two from a Dutch perspective and one situated in the Norwegian context.

Els Rommes (2002) examines how implicit presumptions about gender roles among the design team worked to exclude and alienate women as users and designers of Amsterdam's *Digital City*—one of the first Dutch experiments with the internet in 1994. Adopting a "gender script" approach, she demonstrates how the desire of the predominantly male design team to experiment with state-ofthe-art technology made it hard for less tech-savvy users to participate in the Digital City. Rommes calls this a typical example of the "I-methodology"found among ICT developers, or taking one's own preferences and capacities as the starting point for designing technology. Since most ICT workers are male, user scenarios implicit in ICT production are severely gendered. The masculine gender scripts that informed the design and development of the Amsterdam Digital City produced a pioneering online space that received international acclaim but it did not attract a diverse group of users. Ultimately, Rommes suggests, the masculine gender scripts implemented in the Digital City's techno-social fabric contained a set of normative assumptions that favored high-tech male users, while alienating other, especially female, users. Only those who already owned a computer with an internet connection, or who had sufficient financial and social capital to purchase one, could get access to the Digital City. Since ownership of a computer and internet access were, and still are, unequally distributed along gender lines in Dutch society, this favored male users (Rommes, 2002). Further, Rommes shows that while women did have access to a computer in their home, they often did not use it because they viewed the device as something that belonged to their male partner.

While Rommes' study centers its attention on the design/development side of the mutual shaping process, other mutual shaping studies focus on how the gendered meanings of the internet arise in the context of usage, and how usage interacts with everyday constructions of gender. Van Zoonen (2002) examines how internet technology is domesticated within everyday practices in Dutch households. Contrary to common claims that the internet constitutes an essentially masculine or feminine environment, gendered meanings of the internet arise, especially at the moment of domestication. Through in-depth interviews with young couples she demonstrates how the "social,""symbolic,"and "individual"dimensions of gender interact with the everyday negotiations of technology use among heterosexual partners living together. Four types of negotiations among the partners emerged from the interviews, constituting "traditional,""deliberative,""reversed," and "individualized"use cultures. While male usage primarily determines these types, the interviews show that this does not automatically result in the construction of a masculine domain in the household, but instead opens up space for shared and feminine appropriations. For instance, a "deliberative" use culture involves explaining the negotiation of domestic computer use in collective terms and is instrumental in constructing a sense of togetherness among the partners: a shared techno-social domain (Van Zoonen, 2002). Technology is effectively gendered through the process of domestication as masculine-and feminine-coded practices mutually add meaning to the artifact. At the same time, the computer and the internet present the members of a household with a techno-social environment in which their gender roles can be renegotiated. This can occur when the computer is identified with work-related tasks, as is shown in some of the study's interviews. In these cases, work or studies are more valued than surfing or gaming and thus get prioritized. In effect, this priority turns out to be male-biased in the context of Dutch households, where men are still the main "provider." As a consequence the domestication of the computer in the household leads, in these cases, to a reiteration of traditional gender roles.

While Van Zoonen's study focuses on the gendered domestication of technology in the home, Lægran (2004) examines internet cafés as "gendered techno-social spaces." Influenced by the actor-network theory of Bruno Latour (2005), she considers technologies, spaces, and gender as mutually constructed in situated processes that involve material and symbolic articulations, as well as both human and non-human actors. Following Latour, technological artifacts are seen as "actants," which are able to acquire agency in the production of space by means of how they are integrated in actor networks. By extending the concept of agency from human to non-human actors, Lægran opens up new possibilities for the analysis of gendered spaces and technologies. Through the inspection of the relation between the two, and by considering both as agents producing meaning alongside human actors, she is able to analyse the material-semiotic processes in which technology and spaces are reciprocally gendered in a physical realm. Instead of creating a space where the masculine connotation of ICT can be deconstructed through the material and symbolic presence of feminine use cultures, internet cafés favor one culture over the other (usually the masculine culture). This leads Lægran to conclude that the internet café, with its female visitors largely invisible, remains "just another boys' room." While mutual shaping research usually takes into account the multiple dimensions in which gender interacts with technology, this study draws our attention to the interrelations of gender, space, and internet culture on a symbolic level. This is effective in showing how offline spaces acquire meaning as a gendered realm, an area that is generally overlooked in traditional research on gender and the internet.

As the three examples above show, mutual shaping theory necessitates a case study approach to examining gender and the internet, in which the manifold dimensions that make up particular gendered practices can be studied in detail. The phenomenon of I-methodology (Akrich, 1995) in the design phase has been taken up as a useful concept in diverse case studies, such as the gendered design of digital games (Kerr, 2002), smart-building projects (Aune et al., 2002), or gendered ICT use in the workplace (Sefyrin, 2005). Also, the concept of gendered domestication has been well developed in theoretical terms (e.g., Cockburn and Dilić, 1994) and has been applied in several studies of old and new media use (Haddon, 2006).

New web, new questions, new outcomes?

Having discussed the main areas of research on gender and the internet, the question for the future is how far the existing approaches can function as adequate theoretical tools for the investigation of new developments—the emerging era of Web 2.0 typified by an increasing number of users producing and sharing their own content.

According to many, Web 2.0, with its non-hierarchical modes of content production and dissemination, has replaced the top–down structure of the so-called Web 1.0. As part of this Web 2.0 buzz, *Time* magazine named "You" their Person of the Year in 2006: a tribute to the "common people who transformed the way we socialize, gather information, and do business on the internet" via rapidly growing web applications and platforms such as MySpace, Facebook, and YouTube. While we should not lose sight of the fact that user-generated content of all kinds has long been a feature of online life, it is worth exploring the implications of Web 2.0 for gender politics.

Given the fact that these new web applications have only recently become the focus of gender-informed research, any attempt to predict outcomes is necessarily precarious. Nevertheless, we can theorize how the previously discussed approaches might be able to provide new and inter-esting insights in the field of gender and internet research. How are the existing approaches able to come to terms with the present internet landscape, dominated by applications that facilitate novel forms of user-generated content?

Dealing first with the "gender as identity" approach, it is most likely that studies investigating gender differences in internet use will continue to find these differences in the way that men and women design their weblogs, provide information on their MySpace profiles, or contribute to a discussion about a video posted on YouTube. These gender differences find their origins in the embodied everyday experiences of internet users and are thus unlikely to be easily altered by any specific ICT application. For this reason, we contend that this kind of "difference" research is continuously reinventing the wheel.

Turning to "experimentation" research, it does not seem plausible that future studies will find much evidence of gender experimentation that transcends or disrupts binary gender discourse. Contemporary internet applications incorporate new and improved visualization technologies, which constitute both a response to and a perpetuation of our preoccupation with the exhibition of everyday "reality." Whereas the "virtual" was once believed to form an alternative to the "real," a space where users could engage in disembodied communication Web 2.0 has definitively collapsed this dichotomy because people upload an increasing number of photographs and home-made videos onto the web, transporting the "real" and "authentic" into cyberspace. One of the realms in which this phenomenon is evident is the "reality porn" niche, which has expanded significantly over the past few years (Barcan, 2002; Ray, 2007). In response to YouTube's policy of not allowing nudity, websites such PornoTube and RedTube are now providing a platform where users can upload pornographic video material (either actually home made or purporting to be) to which other users can respond by leaving comments. Most of these videos focus on the everyday reality of people engaged in sexual practices. Consequently, this dynamic has strongly reaffirmed the "real body" on the screen, which can now be visually tracked to its physicality. It thus seems unlikely that Web 2.0 will cater to much gender bending, with continuous visual scrutiny causing users to be extremely aware of their bodies and those of their peers.

Away from the mainstream, however, the general increase in internet access in the Western world, coupled with considerably lower thresholds for creating personalized content online, do certainly open up possibilities for marginalized gender and sexual identities to be exposed to a larger audience. The visualization technologies that may reaffirm gender and body norms in a mainstream context could also be used by queer and trans-gender people to deconstruct traditional images of gender, embodiment, and sexuality, in addition to simply increasing their visibility. This could cause a grass-roots disruption of what counts as "the real body." Thus, contemporary research on gender as identity should further examine how gender, sexuality, and embodiment are experienced and performed through visualization technologies such as the webcam and internet video software. A relevant question would be how this "body-technology" constellation is affecting our conceptions of embodied gender and the ways it can be mediated online.

When considering the "gender as social structure" approach it is clear that this will remain valuable. As previously noted, multinational corporations have collectively jumped on the Web 2.0 bandwagon and have bought into the current hype around user-generated content. Surely this will have repercussions for how present and future Web 2.0 applications can be experienced and used, with designs now under increasing corporate control, and marketing divisions eager to benefit from the possibilities of new personalized advertisement techniques. This raises the issue of the increased prevalence of pervasive marketing schemes directed at specific groups of female users, in addition to a more general concern about privacy issues. On the other hand, the previously mentioned low thresholds for participation and production that characterize Web 2.0 could have positive effects on the level of women's participation in political activism and opinion formation online. As research in this novel area is still in its infancy, future studies need to investigate the dimensions of women's political efficacy in these new social spaces. However, even if the number of politically active women grows over the next few years, it seems unlikely that the gendered inequalities identified by Herring and others will dissolve solely through an increase in women online.

Further questions in this area revolve around the extent to which users actually have control over the content they are encouraged to produce and how this may be delimited by corporate design teams. To what extent do these new user communities allow for women to engage in politically radical activities, when the -cultural environment of websites like MySpace and YouTube seems to be predominantly concerned with the consumption of entertainment and lifestyles? How "political" can a book discussion on Amazon.com be? Does the type of interaction taking place on the main Web 2.0 sites require a reinterpretation of what it means to be "politically active?" These are by no means new questions, but it is vital to reformulate them in the different contexts of a constantly transforming landscape in which economic, cultural, and political interests will continue to shape the way that people use the internet.

Mutual shaping research on the relation between gender and the various techno-social spaces of Web 2.0 will prove to be an important tool for showing how situated practices of gendered content producers are related to their everyday lives and concerns, with the internet constituting an extension of everyday practices rather than a disruptive alternative to it. Future studies should continue to focus on the occurrence of the I-methodology in the design of current websites featuring user-generated content, as well as examining whether and how traditional gender patterns are reinstated in the domestication of popular Web 2.0 applications. In our own research on the gendered constitution of blogs, for instance, we found that they are on the one hand extensions of the traditionally feminine act of diary writing, and imbue the blogosphere with feminine codes and rituals, while on the other they redefine the act of diary writing as a "technological" practice, enabling men to share in it as "bloggers." This as a clear case of gender and technology shaping each other mutually, with repercussions both for the traditional relations of women with technology, and of men with self-expression. Nevertheless, we also observed male and female bloggers making gender stereotypical choices of blogging content, mode of address, lay out, and hyperlinks in order to create clear masculine and feminine spaces (Van Doorn *et al.*, forthcoming). The mutual shaping of gender and Web 2.0 is, and will continue to be, a fragmented process contingent upon a multitude of situated practices featuring a constant interpellation between particular groups of users and the technologies with which they interact.

CONCLUSION

We started this chapter by acknowledging that the different academic disciplines each have their own perspectives on the articulation of gender in relation to the internet. We identified two initial approaches: "gender as identity" and "gender as a social structure." The internet has been shown to both confirm existing differences between women and men and to enable transgressions of the stereotypical codes of femininity and masculinity. Research has also demonstrated how internet marketing exploits women's social positions by addressing them merely as consumers, while other studies have shown how many women use the net to engage in activism and feminist networking. Whichever of these contradictory possibilities occur depends very much on particular articulations of design, development, use, and users that take place around internet applications. We therefore discussed the mutual shaping approach, which assumes that gender and technology mutually influence each other, with neither gender nor technology as the determining force. Gender and technology are considered "actants" in a network of users and producers whose continuous negotiations and contestations propose specific articulations of gender and technological artifacts. Studies of gender and the internet conducted from such a perspective have identified influential processes such as the I-methodology in the development of internet applications, in which designers and developers (mostly men) adopt their own preferences and capacities as the standard for creating new technological applications, and the domestication process, which refers to the way the internet is integrated in the everyday gendered lives of domestic users.

We concluded by anticipating some research questions that the three approaches could produce when applied to the current social spaces of Web 2.0, and argued that the "gender as identity" studies should focus on the experience of embodied identity as the nexus of gendered techno-social practices; that the "gender as social structure" studies will find an increasingly interesting research field, which demands an emphasis on the tension between user agency and commercial interest; and that the mutual shaping studies will be able to illustrate the situated and diverse articulations of gender and technology in the context of those Web 2.0 applications that facilitate user-generated content. Rather than causing a schism in the established research tradition on gender and the internet, the social and technological features of Web 2.0 are more likely to evoke questions similar to those asked before. Yet these will require a reformulation commensurable with the current socio-technical environment and its foundation in today's political economy.

GUIDE TO FURTHER READING

While this chapter has presented the reader with an overview of the past, present, and possible future of research on gender and the internet, it is by no means an exhaustive account. Shade's (2002) feminist analysis of the opportunities and threats that women face when engaging with the internet serves as a solid introduction to the socio-political aspects of women's internet use. Consalvo and Paasonen (2002) also focus on the politics of women's everyday interactions with the web, but broaden the scope of their book through the additional investigation of more "cultural" issues such as identity construction, embodiment, and discourse. More generally, Poster (2001), Bell (2001), and Trend (2001) all provide insightful analyses on gender identity and the internet from a critical cultural studies perspective, while Schaap (2002) and Campbell (2004) offer two of the most interesting and detailed case studies in this area of research.

For those looking for an elaborate discussion of the relationship between science and technology studies and feminist analysis, Judy Wajcman's (2004) *TechnoFeminism* is an indispensable work, as is the collection of Norwegian case studies edited by Lie (Lægran 2004). Though it might now be considered somewhat dated, Cockburn and Ormrod's (1993) seminal book is sure to remain of interest to anyone curious about the multidimensional relations of gender and technology. Turning to technology's connection to sex and sexuality, O'Toole's (1999) *Pornocopia* offers a vivid account of how porn is consumed and the technological innovations that foster its consumption. Likewise, Waskul (2004) presents a collection of essays, which will prove to be of great use to those with an interest in the political and cultural dimensions of sexual practices in the online environment. These are just a few suggestions for further reading, which will help the reader navigate a path through the growing landscape of gender and internet research.

GENDER PRESENTATION IN BLACK LESBIAN COMMUNITIES

By Mignon Moore

Consider the way that Asa Bambir, Lynn Witherspoon, and Trina Adams explained gender presentation in New York's Black lesbian community to me:

Asa Bambir (Age 34, Executive Assistant):
In New York I saw more of this butch-femme thing and I was a little floored by it, a little shocked, like why do people have to play these roles? ... But at the same time I looked at it in awe, because there was a part of my childhood when I really liked wearing boyish clothes, but I never did. ... So, I was very intrigued by it, and I think over the years I've just been allowing that to surface. I really do like wearing boyish clothes. ... I was definitely drawn to women who were feminine looking, very feminine looking.

Lynn Witherspoon (Age 33, Corporate Attorney):
When I first started to come out ... it was interesting, because I had this type that I was attracted to, and yet when I was going out I was always attracting the more butch-looking women. And I was like, "Oh, I'm carrying this purse," and all of these other things, you know, all of these things you do in the straight community. So I had to change the way I dressed, and I stopped carrying a purse, and I was able to find women who I was more attracted to to go out with. When I first came out I was wearing makeup; I stopped wearing makeup.

Trina Adams (Age 32, Hotel Associate):
In most [Black lesbian] relationships there is one that is more feminine than the other. For some reason that is just the way it is. I've never seen two aggressives together.

I've seen two feminine women living together, but one is always more aggressive. As you talk to them and you are around them more, you realize that one woman is more aggressive. I don't like the labels, but they exist. Because, I mean, we are just gay, and I don't know who started the labels, but it is what it is.

These excerpts show that there are various physical representations of gender in Black lesbian communities, and suggest that portrayals of gender are not arbitrary—rather, in some salient way they structure women's expectations for and within relationships. My respondents' comments imply that in the lesbian social worlds they know, feminine-looking women are attracted to and partner with women who are not as feminine in their physical style and mannerisms, and vice versa. Even when lesbians have a preference for a particular gendered display, they may not like to acknowledge the significance of categories and their meanings for their personal preferences. At least some women exhibit a contradiction between the significance of gender display for their private desires and their wish to downplay or dismiss the categorization of gender presentation among Black lesbians.

Gender presentation among lesbians is a fraught subject that has long been a topic of interest. In the early 1990s, feminist scholars began to document what was framed as a "resurgence of gendered fashion" (Stein 1992, 434), or a revival of butch and femme presentations of self within lesbian communities. Whereas butch and femme styles had been understood prior to the 1970s as expressions of intensely personal experiences around sexual identity, these scholars interpreted gender display as a less serious form of sexual amusement. Categories of gender display were said to be more ambiguous than in past generations, and researchers saw more choice in the types of gender presentation lesbians created. Relative to previous eras, women were now thought to frivolously play on cultural representations of gender: "It's all a game," they found, and gender display was no longer strongly linked to a personal identity or the structure of norms for a community (Faderman 1992; Weston 1993).

Weston's and other's perspectives on contemporary gender display are actually consistent with 1970s lesbian-feminist interpretations of gender presentation that reduced the significance of those aspects of women's experience that related to maleness or masculinity, particularly masculine physical presentations in women. By labeling these presentations of self as "play" or "performance" rather than considering a more serious meaning of their representation and function within lesbian social groups, scholars began to conclude that gender presentation no longer organized lesbian life in any concrete pattern (Eves 2004).

Theoretical challenges to this perspective began to emerge in the late 1990s. Butler (1999) problematized aspects of feminist theory that questioned the legitimacy of gendered behavior within any par ticular gender group. Halberstam's (1998) work on female masculinity began to concretely examine definitions of gender identity and changes in them through an exploration of race and gender in film. Blackman and Perry (1990) called attention to this debate between "lipstick lesbians," who create an edgy femininity to attract women rather than men, bringing greater attention to the sexuality in lesbian identity and "revolutionary lesbian feminists" who continue to eschew feminine presentations of gender. Nevertheless, the field continues to lack empirical analyses of whether and how gender presentation relates to other identities, such as those connected to race, that structure relationships in contemporary lesbian communities.

The existence and meanings of gender presentation for Black lesbians in New York at the start of the twenty-first century are critically examined in this chapter. The terms *physical presentation of gender*, *gender presentation*, and *gender display* are used interchangeably throughout this work following Judith Lorber's definition of "presentation of self" as "a certain kind of gendered norm through dress, cosmetics, adornments, and permanent and reversible body marks" (1994, 31). This gender display may be represented through clothing, physical markers, such as hairstyle, body language (e.g., way of walking or sitting), mannerisms (e.g., way of talking or gesturing), and other expressions of self. The chapter's first section defines three categories of gender display that I have found in Black lesbian communities: femme, gender-blender, and transgressive.

The second section considers the impact—or rather, the lack of impact—of 1970s lesbian-feminism on Black lesbians' presentations of gender. Whereas one influential legacy of 1970s lesbian-feminism has been White middle-class lesbians' rejection of the use of gendered physical presentation, and particularly lesbian butch/femme presentation, as a way of organizing relationships and lesbian community life, I find that many Black gay women are not influenced by this legacy. Instead, they have modified the older butch and femme identities into three fairly distinct categories of gender presentation. Women choose a style for the public and private per for mance of gender which, once formed, tends to remain consistent over time.

Context is essential to the way in which gender presentation is received. A woman walking down 125th Street in Harlem or Flatbush Avenue in Brooklyn wearing an athletic jersey and baggy jeans will not be immediately identified as a gay just because of the way she is dressed, but when she steps into a convention center or nightclub filled with other lesbians, these same clothes will reveal her membership in a distinct gender display category. The categories of femme, gender-blender, and transgressive, in other words, have the most meaning when they are presented in a context in which Black lesbians are present; it is in this context that the subtleties that often accompany a femme or gender-blending presentation of self become clear. Black lesbians' gender presentation choices are influenced, moreover, by cultural norms dictated by race and class, which structure lesbian sexuality and the enactment of gay identity. New York contains many distinct, well-developed sexual communities, and women can become socialized into lesbian communities that are not explicitly based on specific feminist principles, which might be the case if the primary gay public social groups had a political focus. Many of these groups are segregated by race and ethnicity, moreover, facilitating the development of gay identity in racially homogeneous environments. As a result, being gay is not experienced as an identity in and of itself that creates social distance from one's racial group or that is associated with a particular political ideology. In New York, one can be gay and still remain connected to one's own ethnic and cultural groups.

The women who participated in this study are actively engaged in the public social worlds of New York gay life, and the lesbian spaces they frequent are predominantly Black or contain significant numbers of Black people in them. Sixty-one percent of the women I surveyed go to a lesbian or gay bar or dance club at least once a month; 35 percent go less than once a month. Only 4 percent say they never go to lesbian or gay bars or dance clubs. The gay social spaces they frequent are predominantly racially integrated or mostly Black and Latina; just 5 percent spend time at bars and clubs that are predominantly White. The women I studied are entrenched in social networks that are racially diverse but that also have plenty of Black LGBT people in them.

Seventy-two percent said at least half of their friends are Black, while 57 percent said most or all of their friends are Black. The survey also showed that when the Black lesbians in this study spend time with gay people, those people are usually racially similar. Seventy-four percent said at least half of their gay friends are Black, while 64 percent said most or all of their gay friends are Black. Just 7 percent said half or most of their gay friends are White.

As the excerpts that open this chapter suggest, in the Black lesbian communities of New York, physical representations of gender indicated by clothing, hair, physical stance, the presence or absence of makeup, and various other symbols are extremely important markers of identification. An individual's style of clothing broadcasts to the community how she chooses to represent her race and gender, as well as the type of physical representation she is attracted to. The expression of gender presentation attempts to authentically capture other distinctions that characterize larger Black communities: style is used to represent not only gender but social class, ethnicity, culture, and finer group memberships. The modes of gender expression inform and shape social contexts and importantly organize intimate and other social relationships. It takes hard work to represent a particular raced, classed, and gendered sense of self that is deemed authentic by others in the racial and sexual communities that define the social worlds of New York's Black gay women.

In the latter sections of this chapter, I consider how gender pre sentation functions in Black lesbian communities today. First I show how complementarity in gender display grants lesbians the freedom to create a physical presentation of their sexual identity at the same time that it imposes restrictions on whom individuals can partner with. I then look at class differences in attitudes about nonfeminine or "transgressive" gender display. Middle-class lesbians avoid transgressive gender pre sentation because it interferes with their attempts to erect moral and symbolic boundaries that signify their class status and facilitate their assimilation into larger society. Working-class lesbians embrace nonfeminine gender display and use it as an act of resistance to social norms. Asserting a transgressive gender presentation is one way they express feelings of difference from larger society based on the multiple marginalized statuses they occupy. Race has important consequences for the expression of masculinity, and I consider how presentations of masculinity expressed in the Black female body relate to broader notions of hegemonic masculinity and feminist analyses of sexual autonomy. The chapter's conclusion offers four reasons for the persistence of distinct forms of gender presentation among Black lesbians at the start of the twenty-first century.

PHYSICAL PRESENTATIONS OF GENDER

I measured physical presentation of gender in three ways. First, I asked women who responded to the survey to rate their own physical attributes, the physical attributes of their current mates, and the physical attributes of their ideal mates on a scale of one to ten, with one being very feminine and ten being very masculine. These categories represent physical style and mannerisms and are separate from items measuring personality traits and interaction styles (appendix B). I also measured physical presentation of gender by asking a series of open-ended questions in the in-depth interviews about how the respondent perceives her own gender display, whether the type of person she is attracted to influences how she dresses, how she came to decide on a style that was comfortable for her, and how she feels about the labels that exist for different presentations of lesbian gender (see appendix C).

In addition, my fieldwork provided three years of observations of the interview and survey respondents as well as other Black lesbians in a variety of social contexts: restaurants, religious meetings, lesbian and straight bars and dance clubs, house parties and backyard barbecues, book clubs, and black-tie and other formal events. Seeing my respondents repeatedly in a variety of locales allowed me to get a clear sense of how they chose to represent their gender when they were in social settings with other gay people and when they were in predominantly heterosexual spaces. Observing unpartnered women in these settings also allowed me to see the physical presentations of gender of women they were attracted to or chose to date. Observing couples gave me a multidimensional picture of how each dressed relative to the other so I could see, for example, how someone who assigned herself a score of 2 (*very feminine* on the scale) looked next to her partner whom she assigned a score of 4 (*gender-blender*). I examined style in relation to that of a partner and in relation to the styles of other lesbians in the social environment.

I recoded the survey results to create three categories of gender display: "femmes" score between one and three, "gender-blenders" score between four and six, and "transgressives" score between seven and ten. The femme, gender-blender, and transgressive categories of gender presentation are classes of ascription and identification used not just by me as the researcher but by lesbian community members themselves, though the *terms* used by community members to describe these categories vary across age, class, and geographic region.

Femmes

About half of the respondents (48 percent) are femmes, or feminine women. When asked "How do you feel about labels like 'femme' or 'aggressive' or 'butch?'" "Where do you think you would fit in if you had to choose a label?" and "What is it about your style of dress or personality that makes you answer in that way?" the women in this category referred to themselves as "femme," "fem-looking," "femme, sort of" and sometimes "aggressive femme," which indicates a feminine style of dress combined with an assertive or outspoken personality. Women who were attracted to feminine-looking women referred to them as "femme," "feminine," "pretty," and "a real lady." Some middle-class women were reluctant to give themselves a label: they mentioned not liking the labels that exist and not liking the act of labeling someone else's gender presentation. Everyone who turned in a survey, however, assigned herself a score between one and ten on the scale as a way to mea sure her own gender presentation.

In one sense, the style of Black femme women is consistent with what researchers have found for other feminine lesbians: they wear dresses or skirts, form-fitting jeans, tops that are low cut or that show cleavage, makeup, jewelry, and accessories such as purses. When going out socially, they take care to wear clothes that show this gender presentation. But even in more casual settings with other lesbians, they wear clothing that lets others know they want to be seen as feminine, such as makeup and high-heeled shoes. The hairstyles of femme women include long and short relaxed or straightened styles; dreadlocked hair, twists, braids and other "natural"-styles; and head wraps made from African-inspired cloths. Femmes with very short hair or bald heads still exude a feminine image by wearing makeup, large earrings, and other markers of femininity. These styles are consistent with the range of fashions seen on other Black women in New York at the turn of the twenty-first century, and represent a link between lesbian style and Black culture. Blackman and Perry (1990), writing about the strong African-and culturally-inspired looks worn by Black lesbians in the late 1980s, say their presentation of self reflects an effort to bring a particular racial and cultural visibility to their lesbian identities in the White-dominated, public lesbian communities of that time. The styles they portrayed represent the tension of belonging to Black as well as gay cultures and a refusal to give up either one.

A feminine gender presentation is not necessarily connected to any specific personality traits or ideologies about gender or gender display. Women who scored between one and three on the gender presentation scale were no more likely to report a personality or interaction style that was laid-back or assertive than were other women. In this sense, they did not conform to stereo types of feminine women as soft-spoken, submissive, or indirect.

Femmes were the least likely to have entered into a gay sexuality through the pathway I define in Chapter 1 as straight-up gay. They were most likely to be hetero-identified lesbians, having grown up with little or no sense of difference from other Black women; conformists, who experienced same-sex desire in their younger years but did not act on it until much later; or sexually fluid women, who reported ongoing attractions to both men and women. Historically, femme lesbian identity has not been based in strongly internalized feelings of difference, but rather in commitment to a gay life through socializing in the gay world and having intimate and sexual relationships with women. Researchers Kennedy and Davis (1993) and Ponse (1978) found that the gay sexuality of femme women is dictated more by setting and circumstance than by feelings of difference. Harris and Crocker (1997) argued that femme gender presentation is a "sustained gender identity," or a model of critical reshaped femininity and assertive sexuality that is neither biologically assigned nor a mere representation of costumes and play.

Black feminine women have a presentation of self that is consistent with what scholars of the African American experience have identified as the dual character of African American culture. Black lesbians with a femme gender presentation are less affected than are White lesbians by what Harris and Crocker (1997) term "patriarchially imposed femininity" because historically, femininity has been viewed differently by the dominant society and by African Americans themselves when enacted by Black women. Second-wave feminists saw femininity as oppressive, but Black women may not experience it in the same way, because while the social position of Black women has certainly exposed them to gendered oppression, it has left little room for that oppression to be based in characteristics associated with the type of patriarchy experienced by White women, who are depicted as frail, dainty, submissive, dependent, and weak. These stereo types have not been consistent with Black women's self-created, self-imposed femininity.

The femininity achieved by Black women is associated instead with power, in dependence, and leadership. Historian Shirley Carlson (1992), writing about Black community expectations of Black women during the late Victorian era (around the turn of the twentieth century), describes "Black Victoria" as a woman who simultaneously embraced the social expectations of the larger society and emphasized and performed the different expectations for women that emanated from the Black community. This model of Black femininity stressed virtue and modesty alongside intelligence, outspokenness, race consciousness, and work in the public domain. Carlson writes: "The ideal Black woman's domain, then, was both the private and the public spheres. She was wife and mother, but she could also assume other roles, such as schoolteacher, social activist, businesswoman, among others. And she was intelligent" (62). Likewise, Shaw's (1996) historical account of Black womanhood for the middle class during the Jim Crow era (1880s–1950s) persuasively shows that Black femininity encompassed traditional notions of beauty along with intelligence, in dependence, and commitment to the uplift of the racial community. Today, Black gay women who are femme apply this historical understanding of the role of women in African American communities as the model from which they develop and interpret their gender presentation and sexuality.

Gender-Blenders

Gender-blender is a style related to, but distinct from, an androgynous presentation of self. Thirty-four percent of the respondents fit into this category. None of them came into a gay sexuality as hetero-identified lesbians or sexually fluid women. Rather, gender-blenders followed the pathways associated with conformists and straight-up gay women. Rather than de-emphasize femininity or masculinity, gender-blenders combine specific aspects of both to create a unique look. They usually wear certain items of men's clothing, like men's pants or shoes, combined with something less masculine, like a form-fitting shirt or a little makeup. Sometimes their clothes are not specifically men's clothes but are tailored, conservative women's items worn in a less feminine style. Some of the labels used in the community to express this gender presentation style included "soft butch," "futch" (suggesting a combination of "feminine" and "butch"), "sporty," "casual," and "fem-aggressive," which indicates a combination of feminine and masculine gender display. Women attracted to gender-blenders referred to them as "soft butch," "pretty and boyish," "not too hard looking," and as women who are "less feminine ... but who still look like women."

What struck me most about the women in this category was the creativity with which they presented themselves. They almost never wore skirts or dresses, and yet they never looked completely like boys. While androgynous women are often stereo typed as looking very similar to one another—wearing plaid men's shirts, buzz cuts or short hair, no makeup, and comfortable shoes or boots—Black gender-blending women encompassed many different styles. Younger gender-blenders who hung out in the East Village might wear t-shirts underneath button-down men's shirts layered over cargo shorts, with flat 1970s-style Pro-Keds sneakers, in a look similar to that worn by male skateboarders. Gender-blenders from Brooklyn might pair brightly colored dashiki tops with jeans and wear their hair in twists or some other natural style. Or you might see the standard urban uniform of a crisp white t-shirt, baggy blue jeans, fresh white uptown sneakers, and a long ponytail underneath a fitted Yankees baseball cap sported by Puerto Rican gender-blenders from Harlem or the Bronx.

What unites these different fashions as a group is that the style is specifically nonfeminine. The clothes are worn in a loose-fitting masculine presentation, though hips, hair, and breasts signal that the bodies are women's, and the look is softened with lip gloss, eyeliner, or a feminine hairstyle. Because there is so much variation in women's styles of dress, gender-blenders are not necessarily labeled as lesbians in the heterosexual world. In this context, they may appear as straight women who do not dress in an overtly feminine way. It is mainly in lesbian environments that the gendered identity of gender-blenders becomes apparent. Gender-blenders tend to partner with more feminine-looking women.

Transgressives

Eighteen percent of respondents have a non-gender conforming pre sentation of self. They scored themselves between seven and ten on the gender presentation scale and expressed gender in ways that are considered masculine. The majority would be considered straight-up gay according to the categories in Chapter 1, although a few came into the life as conformists. None are hetero-identified lesbians or sexually fluid women.

Transgressive women usually wear men's shirts, pants, and shoes and coordinate these outfits with heavy jewelry, belts with large, masculine buckles, ties, and suspenders (the use of these items varies with age and sense of fashion). Unlike women with a gender-blender style, their clothes are never form-fitting—a clear way to distinguish between a femme and a transgressive who are both dressed casually in jeans and a t-shirt. Their hair might be dreadlocked, braided in a cornrow style that is close to the head, or worn very short and not accompanied by makeup, earrings, or other accessories that would soften the look. In their interviews, transgressive women said they leaned toward being boyish in their clothing and mannerisms. When asked what label they would use to define themselves, many of them readily identified with a specifically nonfeminine or masculine style, calling themselves "boyish" and saying things like "I was always a tomboy from the time I could remember," "I dress aggressive—I don't put on a front for nobody," and "They would call me a butch. I prefer stud, dom, aggressive."

Over and over, transgressive women described themselves as dressing in a way that makes them feel "comfortable." This statement has several meanings. On the one hand, dressing comfortably means wearing casual clothes that allow the body to move freely. On the other hand, dressing comfortably is also associated with feeling good or having a sense of authenticity in their self-expression that is conveyed through their clothing and overall comportment. These women could have chosen larger-sized women's clothes, such as women's jeans that have a loose fit but still complement or help construct a feminine silhouette. They could have worn "sensible" women's shoes. But in seeking out clothes that made them feel comfortable, they specifically and repeatedly chose men's styles and clothes that were structured to portray a more masculine silhouette. Ro Gaul, for example, a licensed electrician born in Jamaica, West Indies in 1963, gave herself a score of seven on the scale. She is tall and thin, with long dreadlocked hair. She says she does not need a label to define herself, but she "could put on a ball gown and [would] still walk like a boy." She dresses fashionably in men's clothes, wearing button-down shirts with a white t-shirt underneath, square-toed men's boots with an animal print, and a large, masculine belt buckle on her jeans. She has to be proactive in creating this look because her slim build makes it difficult to find men's clothes that fit her frame.

Ro says that often when she walks down the street, "guys and girls" look at her like she's "peculiar." Nevertheless, I have seen African American men come over to Ro and to other gender-blending and transgressive women to compliment them on their sense of style in ways that are not hostile but that suggest admiration. They have said things like, "I just wanna tell you I like the way you put that all together; much respect to you," "Excuse me, I like those sneakers and the way you hook them up with those shorts. You have a nice style. Where'd you buy those shorts?" or "I just wanted to tell you I like your look, Ma." The way Black transgressive women present themselves suggests an attempt to incorporate Black social and cultural markers and Black aesthetic style with Black masculinity on their bodies—to display multiple identities while openly acknowledging their gay identity. The responses of some men suggest they have successfully accomplished this goal.

Researchers writing about non-gender conforming lesbians often argue that transgressive identity is based in internal feelings of difference, masculine inclination, and sexual interest in women consistent with my "straight-up gay" pathway into lesbian sexuality. And indeed, the majority of the transgressive women I studied report having the feelings of internal difference consistent with this pathway. I have defined this gender presentation as "transgressive" because women in this group transgress notions of femininity, because many do not like or use the label "butch," and because transgressive is linguistically similar to the term *aggressive*, which many Black lesbians in New York use to denote a woman with a masculine gender display. Transgressive women might have been called studs in a previous generation or butch in the predominantly White women's community, in that they use the female body as the site for signifying masculinity (Halberstam 1998). Most Black lesbians I spoke with were not comfortable calling themselves or the women they desired butch or stud, however. Some did not want to label them at all, while others (mostly working-class women) used "aggressive" to indicate a woman who does not look feminine.

Consider the example of Morgan Banner (born in 1962), a former military officer from Staten Island. When asked, "How do you feel about labels like femme, or aggressive, or butch?" she said: "I hate 'butch,' I hate 'butch.' I don't mind 'aggressive,' and I don't mind 'femme' because I think those categories fit. I mean people at my job, they don't know my lifestyle, but they tell me all the time, 'You're very aggressive,' because it is a standpoint you take. I don't take no shit, I do what I gotta do, and as an aggressive person, I feel like there is nothing I can't do if I put my mind to it." When I asked her how she would label herself if she had to choose a label, Morgan replied, "As being very aggressive." To the question, "What is it about your style of dress or personality that makes you say that?" Morgan responded, "Well, I shop—I wear men's clothes." When asked, "Oh, you only wear men's clothes. Do you shop at men's stores?" she affirmed, "Only men's stores."

While some women identify a masculine style as well as an assertive, dominant personality as components of a transgressive presentation of self, the relationship between physical presentation and interaction style is not at all clear. Many women who report a nonfeminine presentation of self declare they also have an assertive personality, but sheepishly admit that their partners might not agree. Morgan later noted that although she thinks of herself as having an aggressive, dominant personality, her mate calls her "girly" because she has certain emotional responses and other qualities stereo typically associated with femininity: "Sometimes she [partner Shaniqua Banner] teases me and says I'm kind of girly. She says I'm kind of feminine because sometimes I pluck my eyebrows or because of how I used to wear my hair. She says that I'm kindhearted and I'm so soft. ... In the house I'm one person and outside, she says, 'You put on a front outside, you try to act all hard and then you are all soft here.' I mean, I 'water up' [cry], I'm sensitive. My eyes tear when I'm real emotional, so she says 'Oh, that makes you femme. You're femme.'"

Morgan's comments juxtapose two images of the transgressive as assertive and masculine, with an undercover sensitive, emotional, and therefore feminine expression as well. Her partner's comment—"You put on a front outside, you try to act all hard and then you are all soft here"—implies that Morgan's willingness to show a more vulnerable side of herself only takes place in certain physical locations ("here" meaning inside the home) as well as in private emotional spheres ("here" meaning within the relationship). It suggests that there are limited places where Morgan feels comfortable expressing these types of feelings and implies their association with a traditionally feminine demeanor.

The majority of respondents distinguished between having an aggressive style of dress and a dominant or forceful personality, saying the two are separate. Evangelina Tarcel, a feminine woman, for example, said the following: "I have an aggressive nature, but I love my high heels and my lipstick and my eye makeup and my cleavage showing. But if I see something I like, you'd better believe I am going over there to ask her her name [chuckles]." Transgressive women were no more likely than were femme or gender-blending women to report a very assertive or aggressive interaction style, mea sured as a score of seven or higher on the personality scale (Appendix B). Traits traditionally thought of as masculine, such as straightforwardness, asser-tiveness, or being a particularly rational thinker, did not reveal themselves in any consistent way within the three gender display categories. Likewise, gender-blenders and transgressive women often joked about their more feminine partner having the more aggressive sexual appetite, or they admitted wanting not only to give sexual plea sure to their partners but also to receive it. These sexually aggressive behaviors in the more feminine partner contradict the expectations created by studies of butch-femme relationships in previous generations, which suggested that the more masculine-identified partner had to be the more aggressive pursuer sexually.

The three gender display categories contain some overlap. Women who scored a seven out of ten on the physical presentation of gender scale might be considered gender-blenders or transgressives depending on the relationship between their style, the symbols they used to express gender, and their mannerisms. And while in most cases my assessment and my respon-dents' assessments of their gender display category matched, in 20 percent of the cases I as-signed the respondent a category that was different from her self-assignment. This discrepancy was mainly found for middle-class and upper-middle-class lesbians, who, as I explain later in the chapter, were the least likely to report a nonfeminine presentation of self, despite their own responses in the in-depth interviews that suggested otherwise.

My gender display categories are not fixed: women may move further to the left or right on the scale or modify their gender presentation over time as their tastes change. Changes in gender display are not random, however, and gender display does not vary from day to day. When women do shift categories, it is usually for one of four reasons: they have recently come to identify as gay and are negotiating the type of gender display that feels most comfortable, they have moved from one geographic lesbian community to another and adopted new styles or variations consistent with the new locale, they have entered a new relationship and taken on a gender presentation that is oppositional to the new partner's gender display, or they have exited gay communities and taken on a heterosexual (and more feminine) presentation of self.

THINKING STRAIGHT

By Chrys Ingraham

While she may have been a precocious child, Molly, at the ripe old age of 11 had figured it all out. She returned home from school one day and exclaimed to her mother, "I get it now, Mom! It's like a grid! You ask a boy to go with you and if he says yes, you're in. Then you dump him and you become more popular!" Of course, Molly's mom took her daughter very seriously and considering her age asked how she planned to go out with this boy. Molly replied, "Oh mom, you're so old-fashioned. You don't actually go out, it's just a phrase!" What this organic sociologist had discovered by sixth grade was an institution or patterned set of social behaviors and rituals we commonly understand as heterosexuality or in the contemporary vernacular, what it means to "be straight." By sixth grade, this young woman had developed her own heterosexual awareness—she had not only learned to *act straight*, she had also learned to *think straight*.

One of the most significant aspects of this story is that Molly was *learning* heterosexuality. She was discovering how the heterosexual world is constructed and how it operates. More importantly, she was discovering the path to heterosexual privilege or status. Of course, she was also learning that success in this world would mean leaving bodies in her wake but Molly was no shrinking violet when it came to mastering her social world.

In American society, we frequently refer to heterosexuality as something that is naturally occurring, overlooking the myriad ways we have *learned* how to practice heterosexuality, have given meaning to it, and allow it to organize the division of labor and distribution of wealth. To access the "natural" world in any objective way would require that we somehow step outside of meaning systems or cultural bias. In fact, we have developed scientific and social scientific methodologies to enable us to bracket off these effects as best we can. Unfortunately, even with the best research methods, we are still unable to truly attain objectivity or to completely bracket off the ways we give meaning to our world. This is what makes understanding social phenomena as socially produced and as socially created—given meaning by our social world—so critical to understanding. For instance, in many of the debates about sexuality, we pose heterosexuality as the good, normal, and natural form of sexual expression and frame it in opposition to its socially constructed opposite, homosexuality, a term that was not coined until the turn of the twentieth century.[1] We even construct biological sex—whether one is male or female—in terms of opposites—"the opposite sex"—setting up the sexes to be completely different and as potentially in conflict with each other. This is a social priority, NOT something that is naturally occurring. While the sexes may be different they are not, in fact, opposite. The reality is that neither sexuality nor biological sex is made up of opposites; yet, our dominant meaning system imposes that structure. These are both examples of thinking straight—thinking in terms of opposites and polarities when none exist and naturalizing social practices and beliefs rather than seeing them as social, political, and economic creations.

Sexuality is highly variable over the life span. To manage this reality, we have created a set of identity categories and corresponding belief systems to produce the illusion that sexuality is fixed and unchanging and not highly organized and regulated—institutionalized. We use these categories to situate ourselves within a value system that is patterned hierarchically. This means we attach to these categories levels of acceptability and claim social status and legitimacy depending upon which level we occupy. In this heteronormative[2] system where heterosexuality becomes institutionalized[3] and is held up as the standard for legitimate and expected social and sexual relations, bisexuality is less valued and homosexuality the least valued. Additionally, within each of these levels, there are behaviors and identities that are not considered desirable. For example, consider the badly behaved heterosexual—unemployed or dependent husband, sexually or physically violent male partner, cross-dresser, polygamist, promiscuous wife, or marriage resister.

Constructed notions of sexual behavior and sexual identity have become primary organizing categories for many key aspects of social life including but not limited to marriage, family, politics, religion, work, and education. By giving primacy to sexual behavior in these arrangements, we make secondary all other factors in various human relations—intimate, platonic, or formal. In other words, as we socially and culturally create sexual behavior identities as organizing categories, we elevate relations of the body above all other terms for human interaction—mind, heart, soul, values, and so on. Sexuality or sexual behavior becomes the dominant category enabling and disabling a commodity culture that proclaims the primacy of sexuality. Consider, for example, the commonplace market mantra: "Sex sells!" Or, the obsession with Michael Jackson's sexual transgressions, most noticeable when the American media cut away to his arrest at the same moment President Bush and Prime Minister Blair were giving their first live speech in England regarding the war in Iraq. Sexuality or sex issues serve as the currency through which a host of exchange relations and social priorities are established.

Securing this primacy, various descriptive and hierarchical popular culture euphemisms have emerged. The "straight arrow" as the descriptor of a good and moral person who complies with society's rules for appropriate behavior—the "straight and narrow"—has evolved into the commonplace euphemism for heterosexual—someone who is "straight." To "think straight," then, is to comply with the prevailing meanings and ideological messages that organize heterosexuality.

Historically, the phrase "thinking straight" meant thinking clearly or logically. The paradox in the use of this metaphor to describe heterosexuality is that thinking straight rearranges the original meaning by embracing the logical incoherence, in this case, of institutionalized heterosexuality. In other words, to think straight as it is applied to sexuality is to operate inside the ideological contradiction that is the foundation of straightness. Consider the following examples:

- Thinking straight is understanding heterosexuality as naturally occurring and not as an extensively organized social arrangement or means for distributing power and wealth for male to female behavior.
- Thinking straight means believing that the world is only and has always been heterosexual—not historically or regionally variant or as a cultural invention.[4]
- Thinking straight is to confuse *institutionalized* heterosexuality with something that is naturally occurring.
- Thinking straight is using that famous heteronormative and biologically determinist retort that God did not create Adam and Steve, *He* created Adam and Eve. This argument denies the existence of sexual variation in behavior and the role of contradiction, history, and interpretation in *Biblical* references.
- Thinking straight is believing that heterosexuality is universal, the same in all societies as well as the animal world when there is substantial evidence to the contrary.
- One of my favorite examples of thinking straight is the notion that white weddings and diamond rings are heterosexual traditions and not just the effect of very successful marketing campaigns.[5]
- Thinking straight is embracing a sense of entitlement, social and economic, just by virtue of participating in married heterosexual life regardless of the ways that entitlement denies those who do not have access to equal opportunity and citizenship.
- Thinking straight is living in romance or the illusion of well-being that institutionalized heterosexuality promises not in its realities.
- Thinking straight is investing in the power and the promise of heterosexuality without examining and addressing its paradoxes.

This list represents only a sampling of possible manifestations of thinking straight. They can include everything from boy/girl seating at a party to global economic assumptions about the division of labor.

Until recently, even gender and sexuality scholars from across the disciplines studied heterosexuality as either a form of sexual behavior or as embedded within other institutions, such as marriage and family. They overlooked the ways in which ascribed behaviors for women and men—gender—actually organize the institution of heterosexuality. In other words, theory and research on male and female behavior participates in "thinking straight" or what I have defined in earlier writings as the *heterosexual imaginary*:

> [It is] that way of thinking that conceals the operation of heterosexuality in structuring gender and closes off any critical analysis of heterosexuality as an organizing institution. The effect of this depiction of reality is that heterosexuality circulates as

taken for granted, naturally occurring, and unquestioned, while gender is understood as socially constructed and central to the organization of everyday life.[6]

By treating heterosexuality as normative or taken for granted, we participate in establishing heterosexuality—not sexual orientation or sexual behavior, but the way it is organized, secured, and ritualized—as the standard for legitimate and prescriptive socio-sexual behavior, as though it were fixed in time and space and universally occurring.

Beginning with the paradigm shift suggested by Adrienne Rich's landmark essay on compulsory heterosexuality,[7] scholars across the disciplines have worked to make visible the social, historical, and material conditions that institutionalized heterosexuality has preserved. One need only look at the current state of American society and popular culture to determine what interests are at stake in relation to the institution of heterosexuality. The shifting landscape for institutionalized heterosexuality and its organizing institution, marriage, is providing fertile ground for this inquiry.

Historically, marriage as a heterosexual and patriarchal arrangement organizing the economic dependency of women and children relied both on the ideology and reality of the male breadwinner. Following the second wave of feminism, women generally, but especially middle-class women, entered the workforce in record numbers. The result is that women have gained a measure of economic independence from men, earning on average seventy-five cents for every dollar a man makes. The world of possibilities for women had expanded significantly. With these economic gains, women have become economically independent and less dependent upon marriage for their survival. The result of these changes means that the popularity of marriage today increasingly depends upon notions of romance and the marketing of the white wedding as the primary validation ritual. Paradoxically, this effort has resulted in not only securing a desire for weddings among self-identified heterosexuals but among other consumers as well, namely same-sex couples.

As these trends persist, other significant changes are also emerging, primary among them the increasing practice of older women marrying younger men. Frequently, this shift in age relations also indicates a shift in the sex of the breadwinner and with it, a shift in the ideological framing of this relation. Older women are more likely to have established jobs and careers and are more likely to earn more than their male partner. This shift indicates that men are more at ease doing domestic and childcare labor, formerly the exclusive domain of women. Women are entering higher education in greater numbers than men and are also pursuing and occupying more positions of power than ever in history. And, as sociologist Alan Wolfe has found, high divorce rates are increasingly a product of a highly business-oriented culture where issues of trust, loyalty, mobility, and downsizing have a significant effect on marriage.[8]

Perhaps the most powerful influence on the heterosexual imaginary in today's cultural world is the television programming that so contradictorily signals the changing landscape in U.S. heterosexual culture. Throughout 2003 and 2004, so-called "reality TV" shows have proliferated into a smorgasbord of real-life heterosexual romance dramas. Shows such as "The Bachelor," "The Bachelorette," "Joe Millionaire," "Meet My Parents," "Cupid," "For Love or Money," and "Who Wants to Marry My Dad," "Average Joe," "My Big Fat Fiance," have essentially escalated what was once the TV wedding spectacle into heterosexuality-as-spectator-sport or romance-as-reality.

Morning infotainment shows such as NBC's "Today Show" and its counterparts on CBS, ABC, and CNN now regularly provide competitions for on-air weddings. In each of these venues, the public votes for which lucky bride and groom they want to see get married and they vote on all the trappings for the newlyweds' wedding and honeymoon.

This hyper-heterosexual programming, conveying all the traditional rules of heterosexual practice with a few twists such as lie detector tests and million-dollar prize money has powerful competition from some less-thanmainstream (oppositional) programming. From highly acclaimed shows such as HBO's "Sopranos," "Six Feet Under," "Oz," and "Sex and the City" to mainstream offerings such as NBC's "Will & Grace," "Queer Eye for the Straight Guy," "Boy Meets Boy," or "Playing it Straight," each offer weekly fare that includes some version of same-sex sexuality as normative. Even the supporting television commercials and some magazine advertising have been propelled into regularly targeting same-sex couples. They have discovered the gay marketplace.

Add to this that the former "wedding pages" in a variety of local and national newspapers are now called "weddings and celebrations" or "weddings and unions." Most notable of these are the famous *Sunday New York Times* pages that include photographs and announcements of same-sex unions or commitment ceremonies. Even their distinctive narrative offering, "Vows," has included coverage of same-sex celebrations. *Bride's Magazine,* the leading wedding periodical in the world, is also doing a first-ever same-sex feature where a variety of wedding outlets are offering same-sex ceremony planning and products.

As the marketing of romance replaces the economic necessity for marriage, resulting in a $35 billion a year wedding industry, our beliefs about marriage have become increasingly grounded in another instance of thinking straight—the illusion that money buys commitment and longevity. All of these shifts suggest the distinct possibility that the patriarchal institution of heterosexuality and its marriage requirement is rapidly changing and becoming less compulsory.

In addition to internal changes within the institution of heterosexuality, other pressures are changing the way we look at heterosexual entitlement. The gay and lesbian rights movement has made enormous strides toward achieving equal standing under the law with their heterosexual counterparts. Incremental advances in the area of benefits to same-sex and different-sex domestic partners have been made, opening the possibility of litigation that addresses the inequities of entitlements available only to those who participate in state-sanctioned male/female marriage.

Substantial legal advances have also collectively increased the likelihood of gay and lesbian or same-sex equity. A sampling of those changes includes the recent Supreme Court ruling in *Lawrence v. Texas,* overturning sodomy laws in favor of one's right to privacy, long used as a form of discrimination against gays; the passage of a civil unions law in Vermont; the ruling from the Massachusetts Supreme Court that denial of marriage to same-sex couples is unconstitutional; numerous anti-discrimination laws protecting gays and lesbians on local and state levels; hate crimes laws prohibiting violence against gays and lesbians; and the decision on the part of the Canadian courts to allow the legalization of gay and lesbian marriage. The gradual codification of gay and lesbian rights and the growing awareness that benefits and rewards distributed on the basis of heterosexual marriage are inherently undemocratic has led to an erosion of heterosexual supremacist beliefs and practices.

Most recently, this deterioration became evident in the acts of civil disobedience on the part of government officials. The Mayor of San Francisco, arguing that the denial of marriage licenses to same-sex couples violates the state equal protection clause and his oath of office, allowed nearly 3,000 same-sex couples marriage licenses. In New Paltz, NY, the Mayor defied state laws and solemnized same-sex marriages, sanctioning marriage without benefit of state license. His argument was that he did not violate the law, rather the policies of the state health department were illegal. State and local officials from around the nation have joined in these efforts, claiming that denial of equal protection violates both state and national Constitutions.

In response to these activities and claiming the rise of an "activist" judiciary, President Bush proposed a Constitutional amendment that would preserve marriage as a relation between a man and a woman. With this act, the President of the United States and his administration forced the issue onto the national agenda during a Presidential election year, polarizing the American public, and forcing a national debate on the "sanctity" of marriage, claiming that a federal amendment is the only way to stop "activist" officials who "created confusion" by allowing for gay marriage. Thinking straight, Mr. Bush concluded his call for federal activism by reminding Americans that marriage "cannot be severed from its cultural, religious and natural roots" and that it is an "issue that requires clarity."

In the spirit of "straightening up," we must clarify what the boundaries of the real issues are in granting marriage licenses to same-sex couples. First and foremost, marriage is anything *but* "natural." It is a historically variant social arrangement originally established to secure ownership of women and children and thereby guarantee the inheritance of property. Its early history is linked to state control over private property. While governmental practices in relation to marriage vary significantly around the globe, state domestic relations laws in the United States also vary widely and are frequently in conflict with their own constitutions and with the U.S. Constitution.

The 14th amendment clearly states that:

> No state shall make or enforce any law which shall abridge the privileges of citizens of the United States; nor shall any state deprive any person of life, liberty, or property, without due process of law; nor deny to *any person within its jurisdiction the equal protection of the laws.* (U.S. Constitution)

Evident from this amendment is the wording that prohibits states from denying "any person" equal protection. To enact a marriage amendment prohibiting same-sex marriage would not only violate Constitutional law but would place this entire document in crisis by legalizing discrimination on the basis of sex and/or marital status.

Second, the responsibility of the President and the Legislature is to uphold the laws of the land, specifically the Constitution. It is that very document and its requirement that church and state be separate that makes Mr. Bush's position untenable. He cannot provide for laws that attend to "religious" roots no matter how romantic or popular that may seem.

Third, let us be very clear about what is at stake here. This is not a "moral" struggle but a civil challenge. *It is not about bodies.* It is about equality and privilege and how serious American citizens are about preserving those rights, regardless of sex or marital status. To rely on biology as the determinant of civil rights, is to revisit a host of constitutional cases related to race and interracial marriage. Marriage is, in fact, a civil union. To imagine it as otherwise is to confuse the issue with romance, religion, and fantasy. To enact laws guaranteeing civil unions as a remedy for this crisis is to revisit the "separate but equal" decision that brought down segregation.

Finally, make no mistake that religions will insert themselves into this debate. They have a long and dramatic investment in dominating private and familial relations for a variety of ideological reasons. There has been enormous activity on the part of Christian religions in this debate over marriage. The Vatican has launched what they are calling a "global campaign" against same-sex marriage." The lengthy document they issued calls for politicians to resist the momentum being made in the interests of same-sex marriage. Using language that will sound vaguely familiar, their document relies on *Biblical* text and prejudiced assumptions in an attempt to insert themselves into the work of the state. Consider the following quote from the Vatican document:

> [It should not be forgotten that there is always] a danger that legislation which would make homosexuality a basis for entitlements could actually encourage a person with a homosexual orientation to declare his homosexuality or even to seek a partner in order to exploit the provisions of the law.[9]

While this papal document is most notable for its stand against the sanctity of same-sex marriage, it is even more remarkable for its interference in the business of the state and for its glaring omission of the word *love*. Ironically, the language used in this quote mirrors the language used when the U.S. Congress was attempting to eliminate welfare benefits for poor unwed teenagers, claiming that they would get pregnant just so they could access social service benefits. Neither assertion is based in fact.

Pat Robertson and the Christian Broadcasting Network have launched "Operation Supreme Court Freedom," a national prayer campaign to alter the Supreme Court. Claiming that the Court is an example of the "tyranny of an unelected oligarchy," Robertson accuses the Justices of historically distorting the reading of the Constitution by upholding the separation of church and state and an individual's right to privacy. It is these decisions that provided women with protections from state interference in the abortion question and gays protections from state interference in consensual, private sexual behavior. In his campaign against gay rights, Robertson makes a variety of inflammatory and unfounded claims, and asks his followers to pray for the resignation of three justices who have been illness-challenged so that President Bush can appoint more religiously conservative justices. With his own considerable level of distortion Robertson asserts,

> Now, the Supreme Court has declared a constitutional right to consensual sodomy and, by the language in its decision, has opened the door to homosexual marriages, bigamy, legalized prostitution, and even incest. The framers of our Constitution never intended anything like this to take place in our land. Yet we seem to be helpless to do anything about it. Why? Because we are under the tyranny of a nonelected oligarchy. Just think, five unelected men and women who serve for life can change the moral fabric of our nation and take away the protections which our elected legislators have wisely put in place.[10]

Given that this is a democracy not a theocracy and that the law of the land separates church and state, Robertson's concerns echo the fears of many who see the shifts in the historical necessity of marriage as signifying the decreasing importance of religious institutions. This is particularly important in considering whether democracy or religion (which one?) will rule the day when it comes to attending to the challenges of a culturally diverse, advanced capitalist social order.

The Episcopal Church also entered these debates with the highly contested election of the first openly gay priest, Rev. Gene Robinson of New Hampshire, as Bishop. While threatened with the disaffection of a variety of churches throughout the world who oppose the ordination of a gay Bishop, the U.S. Episcopal Church also passed a resolution stating that each diocese can decide on the inclusion of a same-sex blessing in their liturgy. Now as Bishop Robinson has taken his place as a leader in the Episcopal Church, United States, various factions have emerged, threatening to secede from the Church claiming that Robinson's election violates the scriptures and the sanctity of heterosexuality.

The social forces circulating in these debates encourage the public to think straight. In other words, these positions and discussions create illusion and contradiction, not reality and coherence. The matter of same-sex marriage is one of civil, not religious, rights and privileges. The state cannot by law legislate or participate in religious matters—separation of church and state is the law of the land. The primary role of politics in these democratic entities is to provide for the distribution of public resources and opportunities in the context of equal rights for all citizens. Until we establish that health benefits, hospital visitation, rights of inheritance, and access to a partner's social security are a matter of personal choice or citizenship *not* marital status—gay, straight, or single—this will be an issue that will never leave us no matter how much we try to set the record straight.

Considered together, all of these institutions and cultural sites signal that dramatic changes are occurring in institutionalized heterosexuality. The stakes in this cultural shift are high with major institutions such as the state and religion working to re-secure the base they have historically relied upon for their significant power. The substantial amount of activity generated by all these social forces serves as a marker of how important institutionalized heterosexuality has been. These dramatic changes will ripple through our lives for generations to come, making the emerging area of critical heterosexual studies absolutely central to understanding the impact of these changes.

If Molly were in the sixth grade today, she would most likely reflect differently on male–female relations in this hyper-heterosexual historical moment where nearly every mainstream television channel has some version of real-life hetero-sex-in-the-city programming and the very foundation of institutionalized heterosexuality—the exclusive legitimating power of marriage—is in crisis. Thinking straight in this historical moment means responding to growing pressures on the foundation and fabric of institutionalized heterosexuality from a variety of socially significant sites. In essence, the current crisis makes visible the arbitrariness of the identity categories, beliefs, and structures of heterosexuality.

Until the late 1990s, few had pursued a critical examination of institutionalized heterosexuality, one that asks "What interests are served by the way we have organized and given meaning to heterosexuality?" This volume of essays, *Thinking Straight,* contains important and pivotal works in the emerging field of critical heterosexual studies. Written by prominent academics from across the disciplines as well as from international locations, these works interrogate the meanings and practices associated with straightness—the historical, social, political, cultural, and economic dominance of institutionalized heterosexuality. By examining the power, the promise, and the paradox associated with *thinking* straight and straightness, these essays provide insight into the operation of institutionalized heterosexuality: its history, its materiality, its meaning making systems, legitimizing practices, concealed contradictions, and the interests of power it serves.

NOTES

1. Katz, 1995
2. The view that institutionalized heterosexuality constitutes the standard for legitimate and expected social and sexual relations (Ingraham 1999: 17).
3. An established social order that is rule-bound, ritualized, organized, and contains standardized behavior patterns that are also ideologically produced and maintained.
4. Katz, 1995.
5. Ingraham, Chrys. 1999. *White weddings: Romancing heterosexuality in popular culture.* New York: Routledge; Otnes, Celec and Elizabeth Pleck 2003; Cindrella dreams: The allure of the lavish wedding. Berkeley: University of California Press.
6. Ingraham, Chrys. 1994. The heterosexual imaginary: feminist sociology and theories of gender. *Sociological theory* 12(2): 203–219; Jackson, Stevi. 1999. Heterosexuality in question. London: Sage.
7. Rich, Adrienne. 1980. Compulsory heterosexuality and lesbian existence. *Signs* 5: 631–660; Katz, Jonathan. 1995. The invention of heterosexuality. New York: Penguin.
8. Wolfe, Alan. 2002. *Moral freedom: The search for virtue in a world of choice.* New York: Norton; Seidman, Steven. 2002. Beyond the Closet. New York: Routledge; Richardson, Diane. 1996. Theorising heterosexuality: Telling it Straight. Buckingham: Open University Press.
9. "Congregation for the Doctrine of the Faith, Some considerations concerning the response to legislative proposals on the non-discrimination of homosexual persons," July 24, 1992, www.vatican.ca.
10. www.patrobertson.com

CROSSING THE BORDERS OF GENDERED SEXUALITY

QUEER MASCULINITIES OF STRAIGHT MEN

By Robert Heasley

SANCTIONS ON QUEER-STRAIGHT MALES

To act outside the idealized image of the hetero-masculine is to be suspect. And being suspect means being labeled, stigmatized, and ultimately punished. Psychologists have often labeled straight identified males who cross the border in their mannerisms, behaviors, and associations that did not fit the regimen of straightness, as "latent homosexuals." Such a term conjures up an image of "homo in waiting." This leap to label derives from both a rigid adherence to a reductionist approach to viewing all human sexualities as fitting into one of three categories, hetero—bi—homo-sexuality, or landing somewhere on the six-scaled continuum of sexual orientation proposed by Kinsey et al. (1948). It is also a result of the binary perception of gender, with specific qualities associated with the two allowed options of male and female.

Gender-associated qualities are linked closely to perceptions of sexuality. Women are gendered as passive, vulnerable, and nurturing, while males are supposed to be aggressive, emotionally self-contained (meaning nonexpressive), and less nurturing. Gendered sexuality is reinforced by language. For instance, use of the word "luscious" by a male, or a male referring to another male as "pretty" (meaning it as a compliment), are virtually unheard of in the world of straight males; such terms are encoded not only as feminine but also as gay. Everyday sexual experiences of males draw on an inherited vocabulary that reflects the hegemonic masculine. Male discourse about such aspects of sexuality as masturbation reifies the violence inherent within hetero-masculinity, with use of terms such as jacking, choking, jerking, spanking, and beating. Such language, within the context of the interpersonal violence that is part of male culture, limits ways in which males perceive their male-ness, and their heterosexuality.

Males who do not fit comfortably into the hetero-masculinized discourse either by default (a heterosexual male who simply cannot "do" straight masculinity), or conscious effort (males who make a decision not to conform) are neither latent anything, nor are they homosexual. Their way of being is only problematic to those men who occupy the narrow space of hegemonic hetero-masculinity, and women who buy into that limited conceptualization of masculinity. Such problemization is reinforced by mental health professionals who fail to recognize the range of ways of being gendered and sexual.

Kevin, a 25-year-old heterosexual male talked with me about his intentional effort to move into queer identity through conscious nonconforming behaviors, attitudes, and beliefs that associate him with gayness and the feminine, saying,

> I think of myself as less masculine—no, that's not right, I think of myself as more masculine than traditional males. I mean, I can express my masculinity (and hetero-sexuality) in a wider range of ways than maybe most men can.... This sort-of leaves me feeling sorry for how narrowly many straight men experience their masculinity and their sexuality.

Kevin has participated in workshops where being naked with men and sharing massage and intimate touch has been part of the workshop experience, intended to break down the barriers and fears that males have about closeness with other males. This is not your typical 25-year-old hetero-male experience; however, it is one that, for Kevin, provided an opportunity to safely challenge fears and image a changing sense of self, of what it means to be heterosexual and masculine.

His conscious decision to be queer, to disrupt the meaning of heterosexuality and masculinity through embracing what is perceived as gay and feminine, has led him to be open to more sensual relationships with males in his life, as well as to feel closer in his identity with females. If Kevin's story was to appear in the media, or be examined by his parents (who do not understand his pursuit of queerness), his experience would likely be problemitized. Not only would Kevin be seen by the media as strange or different, but his actions may raise fears and anxieties for his family, who, after all, are put in a position of explaining Kevin's choices and behaviors to others. His queerness, although liberating for Kevin, becomes a stigma and a perceived burden to his parents.

At the same time, his pursuit of an intimate relationship with a woman may be second-guessed by the woman, as in the story of Alan at the beginning of this chapter, as though she cannot be certain she can trust him around his heterosexuality. And his male friends, who may not be prepared for relationships with other guys that are intimate and close—and who might be more comfortable with him if he just wanted to talk, but not touch, to do, but not feel—are confronted with whether they can be associated with a border-crossing queer-straight guy.

We conform to gender expectations because they are comfortable, familiar, and reinforced by others (we are rewarded for not breaking the norms), as well as unquestioned (we perceive there really are no desirable alternatives to the normative expectations). We do gender policing and ultimately become self-regulating. For males, such policing has been particularly restrictive.

Boys suffer what can be profound consequences when departing from the norms and crossing the border into what is perceived as feminine as well as gay. The psychological diagnosis of gender dysphoria has been used to label boys who show signs of being "sissies," encouraging parents and teachers to see boys (or girls) acting outside of traditional gendered norms as needing intervention based on the child's presentation of self, not necessarily on any harm or threat the child poses to himself or anyone else. The hegemonic masculine is broadly supported by social institutions, as not only the ideal way to be a boy or man, but ultimately the only way. The typically hetero-masculine male, in contrast, faces no societally imposed intervention based purely on presentation of self.

The heterosexual male who has sex with another male is represented in film or novels as someone who is struggling with sexual identity, who must be at least bisexual (and in a religious context as someone who has sinned). The "sensitive" (translation: "sissy") young boy in films such as "Stand By Me" is portrayed as needing the protection and guidance of an older, heteronormative masculine boy. He needs the older male in the same way girls need a strong male. Likewise, in sociological and psychological literature, straight males-with-queerness may be identified as deviant, or pathologized for being gender inappropriate or sexually confused. On the street and in their schools, family, or workplace, openly queer-straight males may be stigmatized, seen as a curiosity, finding themselves positioned along with gay males in a world that is "other," and thus vulnerable to homophobic oppression.

Consider the male who identifies as a feminist and gay advocate. He is apt to be perceived as gay, and may not feel welcome in the company of stereotypically straight males. This is particularly the case if he also refuses to participate in traditional male culture, for example, if he does not attend sports games, or questions the value of competitive and contact sports, or prefers lesbian/feminist vocalists such as Indigo Girls, Melissa Etheridge, or another girl-band. Consider the fate of the straight male who is sexual or sensually close with another male, and openly acknowledges the relationship, even while defining as straight.

RECOGNIZING QUEER-STRAIGHT WAYS OF BEING

These examples suggest a queering of hetero-masculinity in a variety of ways. However, we have no language or framework for considering the ways in which straight men can disrupt the dominant paradigm of the straight-masculine, a language that could provide legitimacy to the lived experience.

In an earlier article (Heasley, 2004), I proposed a typology of straight-queer males—males who disrupt both heterosexuality and hegemonic masculinity—as a contribution to the expansion of the conceptualization of straightness and of masculinity, in order to represent a truer picture than has been articulated of straight males' experiences and ways of being. Such a typology is needed for several reasons. It provides a way to expand upon the very notion of what is legitimized as being hetero-masculine and it allows us to "trouble" gender and sexuality as suggested by Judith Butler (1990), Michel Foucault (1978), and others. More specifically, it allows us to acknowledge a broader range of what exists, affirming elements of sexualized masculinity that have historically been treated as an exception and, in the kindest rendition, perceived as "nontraditional" male.

"Traditional males" are the ones society understands. Even if there are problems associated with the image, there is acceptance and legitimacy accorded to the typical-ness of his presentation. The "nontraditional" male, however, presents an unknown. Even though there are problems associated with the image of the traditional man, there is acceptance and legitimacy accorded to the typical-ness of his presentation. The "nontraditional" male, however, presents an unfamiliar package, even if the qualities he exhibits are seen as desirable, such as being an attentive, nurturing father. His difference demands justification, explanation. Being "non" means "not having." Applied to gender and sexuality, the implications are profound. The very labeling of a subject as the absence of something (such as labeling women as "non-men") reifies the dominant group while subjugating the subordinate. "Non" erases. And in the process, it problematizes other. For a straight-queer man, there is no place for awareness of self in relation to what is. He becomes the negative deviant, he is isolated, and in the process, is vulnerable to reactions in the form of stigma, labeling, and isolation by the dominant group. "Non" has no history, no literature, has no power, and no community. "Non" requires an invention of self.

By creating a typology of queer masculinities of straight males, we give space and language to lived experience, and set the stage upon which narratives of straight-queer men can find a home. My own experience of being a straight-queer man has contributed to my interest in creating a language through which I could come to know myself, and come to have agency in the knowing.

Recently, a new acquaintance, a straight male, told me that if he did not know I was married with three children, he would have assumed I was gay. Since hearing this is not an uncommon experience for me, I asked him the question I usually ask men (and women) who assume my sexual orientation to be gay—why? His response was typical—I talk with my hands, my voice is not deep, I care nothing about major sports, I am clearly a feminist and talk about gender, rape, violence as well as questioning male socialization (of course, I also teach and write in the areas of gender and sexuality!). He has also seen me greet close male friends by kissing them on the lips, hugging deeply, and at a social gathering, dancing together. "Must be gay... !"

It has always bothered me that I had come to define myself (and be defined by others) as "nontraditional." Yet, unless I were to give up what I feel to be my authentic self, I just could not "do" traditional (meaning, hegemonic-straight-masculinity) without changing: (a) what I find comfortable in terms of my body, (b) the intimacy I desire in my relationships with other men, (c) my sexual/sensual awareness, and (d) my politics that are informed by feminist and queer theory.

Writing in the mid-1970s, Bob Brannon introduced four themes that framed ways of being masculine: No Sissy Stuff, Sturdy Oak, Big Wheel, and Give 'Em Hell. These themes continue to be in evidence today, as institutions from the military to the media emphasize these qualities for becoming "successful" males. Implicit in these categories is the assumption that all males are raised to be heterosexual. Brannon's four themes created a framework for breaking down types of masculine representation, all of which fit nicely into what Connell (1987) would later call hegemonic masculinity. The sexuality of males in Brannon's categories has only one dimension, hetero-masculinity. Given the extensive discourse about gender and sexuality that has taken place over the past thirty years we can now look at male's experience with an eye on straight-queerness and its disruption of the normatively gendered sexual.

Consider the following categories as an attempt to capture the ways this disruption takes place and an emerging legitimization of queerness within the hetero-masculine.

A TYPOLOGY OF STRAIGHT-QUEER MASCULINITIES

1. Straight sissy-boys
2. Social-justice straight-queers
3. Elective straight-queers (or the elective queer)
4. Committed straight-queers
5. Stylistic straight-queers
6. Males living in the shadow of masculinity (including Informed Inactive, Scared Stuck, and Uninformed Inactive)

These categories are nonlinear and nonhierarchical. They are clearly not exclusive; aspects of various males' lives are likely to fit with greater or lesser degree of comfort in one or in all categories depending on such factors as context and life stage. Each category, however, carries with it unique characteristics that queer the meaning of the heteromasculinity.

Straight Sissy-Boys

These are straight males who just cannot "do" straight masculinity. The sissy-boy appears to others as queer, although that is not his intention, nor identity. He often experiences a response from the dominant culture, and perhaps from queers, as if he were queer. These males experience homophobic oppression for their apparent queer-ness, particularly as boys and young males when they are taunted and even attacked. They are likely to be isolated from straight male culture, and/or choose to separate themselves from the dominant male culture. Straight sissy-boy males may associate primarily with girls/women as opposed to actively engaging in gay male friendships and social networks, perhaps in part because of a desire to not be seen as being gay, beyond what is already perceived by others. Such males have varying degrees of homophobia or comfort/discomfort with homosexualities. Being perceived as gay by others is not necessarily a conscious choice and thus they may not have a conscious openness to the effect they have on queering their environment. Yet, just the existence of males who appear as "nonstraight" because they do not fit the image of the normative hetero-masculine serves to disrupt that masculinity and sexuality, simply by the sissy-boy showing up as straight.

Examples

Alan's story, introduced earlier, of running a personal ad with the headline, "Must be gay? Think again sister" suggests elements of the sissy-boy male. He has learned to value his presentation that leads others to perceive him as being gay. He uses it in his ad to find a partner.

My own experience as a young male helps me identify with this category as well, having been perceived as a sissy as a child, within my family and school. My inability to perform masculinity to meet my father's expectations gave impetus to his referring to me as a sissy and discounting my positive attributes, as well as contributing to his verbal threats and physical attacks. In elementary school, I did not participate in competitive sports, although the few times I attempted to do so, I was inevitably a "last pick" by whomever was captain of the recess baseball game. In high school, I avoided the hallways where the guys who harassed the sissy-boys and sexualized the girls hung out (that they were the same hallways is in itself a statement about the status of the sissy male, used by hegemonic males as part of their performance to affirm their heterosexuality).

I found safety in my role as a student volunteer in the library, on the forensics team and debate club, and in taking private acting classes after school (all experiences that have served me well as an adult, but experiences I took on, in part, as a means of avoiding the land mines of straight masculinity). I was also vulnerable to adult males who pursued young boys for sex. As a sissy male walking the streets of my town or hitchhiking (the normal way boys in my family got from town to home in a rural area), older men made sexual advances, at least in part, I suspect, due to my apparent vulnerability. I did not look like the type of young man who would beat them up! The irony of having to struggle with attacks by straight peers for being a sissy, dismissal by a hegemonically masculine father for not being male enough, and being vulnerable to sexual molestation by adult males because of a sissy presentation, suggests that males in this category can, and do, experience challenges from nearly every angle.

It was easy, however, to find girls to date. Like Alan, I was attractive as a friend to girls due to the very qualities that made me vulnerable to male dismissal and abuse; although it was necessary to establish my heterosexual interest in "making out" (which I enjoyed!), I was not likely to pursue sexual interaction beyond what a particular girlfriend initiated.

Social Justice Straight–Queer

Males in this category take action publicly in support of those who identify as gay, lesbian, bisexual, or transgender and at the risk of being marginalized by straight males and/or being responded to as if they were gay. Thus, their actions represent risk-taking, placing themselves in a position of possibly being threatened, stigmatized, or violated as a result of association with gayness. A key element in this category is the deliberate public expression by straight males, verbally or through action, in ways that disrupt both heterosexuality and masculinity.

Examples

Eric is a middle-school age boy who consciously acts as a public advocate when as a new kid on a soccer team, he chooses to be friendly with Thomas, a classmate whose sissy-boy characteristics have left him shunned by the other boys. When I talk with Eric, he is aware that he is challenging homophobia by acting as an ally for Thomas, and taking risks as a new kid at this school. At the same time, Thomas pursues such behaviors as listening to girl bands on his walkman (does not attempt to adapt to normative hetero-masculinity), even though he is threatened. Simply by refusing to adapt, both boys contribute to queering hetero-masculinity because they are a threat to the status quo.

In another example, Jake is a straight male in his mid-twenties, and is very close with his brother who is gay. He attends social events and retreats with primarily gay and bisexual males, and actively participates in public demonstrations in support of gay rights.

Both Eric and Jake disrupt the meaning of masculinity and straightness; they show up in masculine space (competitive sports, for instance) and pursue heterosexual dating relationships, and yet are not comfortable with the often homophobic behaviors associated with the hegemonic straight masculine. Social justice queers can be trusted to not "go along" with male norms in order to gain approval of other straight males. Rather, they use the privilege they have as straight males to interrupt the hegemony of the hetero-masculine at the interpersonal or social system level, and join the queers as an ally.

Elective Straight–Queer

Elective straight–queer identity can be seen as straight men performing queer masculinity. Males in this category elect to move into queer masculinity as a means of liberating themselves from the constrictions of heteronormative masculinity. Such males can move with varying levels of comfort back into "straight masculinity" without necessarily losing power within the dominant culture. They "flirt" with queerness, taking on queer characteristics, kissing, dancing, dressing, and moving the body queer-ly, but within the context (setting) of the queer world where it is safe, for instance, the gay bar. Men in this category move into queer space and may take on queer ways of interacting, not based primarily on a social justice principle, but just for the purpose of personal enjoyment, comfort, and desire. Moving into queer space may permit them to be more fully themselves, providing the opportunity to discover the breadth of their masculinity and their sexuality, exploring ways of being associated with what had previously only been presented as "other."

Example

Andy is a straight 30-year-old male and identifies as somewhat of a gay spirit. He has never found himself sexually aroused by males. In high school and most of college, he was what he called a "typical" straight guy, participating in homophobic put-downs, and hanging out with other guys while sexualizing relationships with women. After becoming friends with and starting to hang out with a gay male co-worker during college, he began to see the fun of being in gay space. For the past five years, Andy's social life has primarily focused on going clubbing (dancing at night-clubs) and partying with gay males. His former workmate became his roommate, and now most of his best male friends are gay. He has attended gay strip shows that included performances of sexual acts and says the experience has allowed him to let go of his own inhibitions when it comes to his body and dancing, and to find comfort in an environment of men. One benefit of having a gay social life, he says, has been accumulating "a great wardrobe" that contributes to the flamboyance he brings with him to his position as a popular art teacher in a progressive high school. Andy was recently married, with his gay friends among others in attendance, to a woman who initially did not pursue dating him because she assumed he was gay.

Committed Straight–Queer

Committed straight-queers practice at being queer with the intention of personally benefiting from moving toward queerness as an integral aspect of their sexuality and their masculinity. While the elective straight-queer may or may not be interested in learning about queer-ness to expand his own sexual and gender boundaries, this is clearly the intent for committed straight-queers who see queerness as a desirable way of being, see benefits for their own life and potentially (at least for some) for society in terms of moving toward changes in institutions such as the family, religion, and the law. Committed straight-queers like queer space and ways of being. They distance themselves from what they see as the constrictions of the hegemonic straight masculine. If they move into the straight-masculine at all, it is more likely to visit, to participate in, for whatever reason, but not to identify with straight-masculinity.

There has been a similar movement by males who "get it" about feminism and have a determination to change the way they experience masculinity to incorporate identity with women, accessing women's culture and integrating ways of being that might be perceived by the larger culture as "feminine." Committed straight-queers look to queers for direction and ways of being.

Examples

Kevin, the young man quoted earlier as describing himself as "more masculine than traditional males" exemplifies this category. Over the last eight years, he has made a conscious decision to not present himself as a "straightmasculine" male. Kevin pursues intimate physical and emotional relationships with other males (straight and gay). He is open to being sexual with another male, although at 28, has not experienced an orgasmically sexual same-sex relationship. When he was 17, he entered a recovery program for recovering addicts where he developed a consciousness about his use of (heterosexual) pornography and his pattern of manipulating females in order to have sex, a pattern encouraged by his male peers. In the program, he heard the stories of women his age who had been sexually abused or raped, and began to understand the violence associated with much of male sexuality. He decided to become celibate, for an extended period of time, which included breaking his addiction to pornography. During this period, he also heard the stories of males in his therapy group who identified as gay. He began attending gay narcotics anonymous meetings, developing close friendships with gay men, both older men who mentored him, and younger males he came to mentor.

His recovery story is powerful in that he came to appreciate the role both hegemonic masculinity and heterosexuality played in his own life through knowing the experiences of others who lived on the margins. While Kevin does not desire that part of gay male culture that sexualizes relationships, he does desire that which he perceives as queer masculinity, the masculinity that is not dominated by or dictated to by men's control of women and other men, where sexuality becomes in both cases the tool of control—the threat of sexual and physical violence toward women who do not respond to male desires, and the threat of physical, and at times sexual, violence toward males who do not conform to heterosexualized masculinity. Kevin admits that he finds strength in stepping outside the cultural image of heterosexual masculinity.

In a second example, Tim and Jon, who met as Freshman year roommates, are college seniors who define as straight. They desire sex with women, talking specifically about their love of cunnilingus, vaginal intercourse, and the feel of women's bodies. They both have girlfriends with whom they are sexually active. Tim and Jon are best friends, and describe themselves publicly as being "nonorgasmic boyfriends." They say they like to queer straight space as a political act, but they also simply love being intimate and exploring the ways to be in relationship with each other. When alone, they have engaged in kissing and sexual play with each other. Jon states that this has allowed him to more fully practice his sexuality. Tim, a former high school football player, says that at some point he would like to have oral sex (both active and passive) with another male, and to experience anal penetration. Tim, a sexuality educator and advocate on his campus, introduced Jon to wearing skirts. Initially, they did this when they were at home and with their girlfriends, or at parties with gay and lesbian friends and other queer-straight males. More recently, they have occasionally worn skirts on campus, and at times, held hands when walking together.

Neither Tim nor Jon see themselves as bi-sexual or gay and they generally are not erotically attracted to other males. They do, however, question whether those categories make any sense for them or anyone. Tim and Jon are intentional in both their public and private exploration of queerness. They disrupt the hetero-normative masculine when alone in order to experience their private sexuality. When in public, their behaviors are political, but also a means to express gendered sexuality in a way that is increasingly comfortable and familiar to them.

Stylistic Straight–Queers

There are a growing number of straight males—film and recording artists, athletes, fashion models, and "metrosexual" males—who intentionally take on a presentation of self that is traditionally associated with gay male culture. These "stylistic straight-queers" allow themselves to develop and display an aesthetic, such as stylish hair cuts and clothes, having facials and pedicures. In so doing, they are attracting the attention of gay men, as well as those straight males who can identify with the border crossing identities. They also get the attention of straight women who find themselves attracted to what is perceived as a "gay" aesthetic or a "gay" sensitivity.

Straight males in this category are taking risks of being rejected by hegemonic hetero-masculine males while at the same time they can gain commercial and sexual capital from the appeal to both straight women and a segment of the queer male population who themselves have been socialized to pursue straightness as the ideal (for themselves and for their sexual partner) in the way African Americans have had "blondness" romanticized and sexualized as the ideal.

While stylistic straight-queers have the benefit of using their straight-male privilege for commercial and relational gain, by moving into gay space in a public way they are also, even if unconsciously, participating in border crossing behaviors (or at least the appearance of such) and thus queering the hegemonic hetero-masculine. They are disrupting the meaning of straight and of masculinity, making it harder for the general public to infer sexual orientation from stylistic cues.

Examples

British soccer player and media celebrity David Beckham identifies as straight while assuming queer-identified characteristics. Known for his polished nails, going to gay bars, and publicly proclaiming his acceptance of gay male culture (as well as declaring his heterosexuality), Beckham currently has perhaps the highest profile in this category. Earlier examples included such performers as Mick Jagger (when he was still androgynous) and basketball player Dennis Rodman (when he was wearing wedding dresses). Straight male actors who play gay characters and perform sex scenes on the cable television series "Queer As Folk" and the actor who plays Will on the television show, "Will and Grace" are among the many males queering up masculine sexuality by their active participation in queer roles.

A recent issue of *OUT* magazine (April, 2003), marketed primarily to gay males with an emphasis on fashion, featured a photo section entitled "The Carlson twins take it off." Kyle and Lane Carlson started their modeling career with Abercrombie and Fitch, a mainstream clothing company that uses homoerotic imagery to sell their products. In dozens of interviews in a variety of media outlets, the Carlson twins make it clear that they are straight. At the same time, they appear in sexualized poses (without women) in magazines that appeal to gay men. In the issue of *OUT*, they are not only featured in sexually suggestive poses, as an exclusive for the magazine, but their family—including father, mother, siblings, and in-laws—is featured as well. The appearance of the Carlson family, from rural Minnesota, serves to queer not only masculinity but also straight families, at least stylistically.

Males Living in the Shadow of Masculinity

Straight males living in the shadow of the hegemonic hetero-masculine are men who avoid displaying difference, but are not completely comfortable with, and somehow do not "fit in" with the heterosexualized masculinity that is all around them. They may (or may not) "get it" in terms of disagreement with the traditional male role, at the intellectual, emotional, or physical level, but are unlikely to do anything to either change or challenge the status quo, or change themselves around how they do heterosexuality and/or masculinity. Often, these males are seen as "quiet."

I see them sitting in my classroom, often in the back, with baseball caps on backward, seldom speaking up, yet obviously engaged in listening. In their class essays on gender and sexuality, they often share personal reflections that are insightful, expressing a desire to see changes in how society constricts both masculine and heterosexual expression. But if there were no written assignments on the topic, I (like others in the class) would never know these males were able and willing to challenge hegemonic heteromasculinity. We can assume that their voices are not raised publicly due to fear of being labeled gay, not masculine, and because they lack role models for and personal experience with such public "outing."

Males living in the shadow of masculinity are unlikely to take risks in interrupting gender and sexual expectations, although they are also less likely to participate in the oppressive aspects of masculinized heterosexuality. In some ways, they may be seen as the "sweet guys" who do not engage at least in the more oppressive aspects of straight masculinity.

Although they do not display any "queer" public behaviors or express attitudes that put them at risk in confronting the dominant system, they still contribute to the queering of masculinity by not actively participating in the dominant system. Since we know that systems of oppression require agreement of members who have qualities identified with the oppressor group to participate in supporting the system, males in this category subvert the dominator group simply through their inaction, while at the same time avoiding any overt appearance of challenging the system.

Often, it seems, it is the women in their lives—their female friends, girlfriends, wives, or mothers—who see the tears, fear, or anger these males feel in response to the constrictive nature of the hetero-masculine. They are also more likely to see the playful male, the spontaneous and emotional male, the excited, gleeful male, who hides from public view for fear of punishment and rejection by those who dominate the system.

There is a wide continuum in terms of the knowledge and awareness about gender, or alternatives to heteronormativity among the men who might fit in this "shadow" category. One way of thinking about the variation among men in the shadows is by looking at the following three subcategories. Like the overall typology presented in this chapter, these subcategories are not exclusive, but rather represent an attempt to organize patterns that appear to have some commonalities among members of this large group. The categories are: Informed Inactive, Scared Stuck, and Unaware Inactive.

Informed Inactive Some men who hide in the shadow of masculinity are "informed inactives." They are informed about sexuality, gender, and masculinity and are likely to understand and support feminism as well as gay rights. They are straight, but not "narrow" in terms of knowledge and even attitudes on the subject of gender and sexuality. Yet they do not act overtly on what they know or how they feel. Males in this category may find ways to display behind-the-scenes support for queer gay men, but are not comfortable being queer-straight men, or putting themselves in positions publicly where they might be perceived as gay.

Thus, they are unlikely to display nonconforming behaviors, or appear in queer space unless accompanied by a girlfriend or female friend. They are also unlikely to take any personal risks, emotionally or sensually, with close male friends, or present themselves through body posture, language, or physical appearance as queer, particularly not while they are with straight male friends in public.

In private space, with close friends or with women, such males may take on a nonhegemonic male appearance or behavior such as talking seriously and respectfully about homosexuality, or they may cross-dress in front of a girlfriend, or talk cute/sweet using nonmasculinized language when in bed with their female partner, or even lying in their female partner's arms, being held and cuddled. Generally, this category represents men who are informed and knowledgeable, but who remain behind the scenes when it comes to changes in their presentation and experience of heterosexual masculinity, or public advocacy and support for changes in the system.

Scared Stuck Some straight men can talk the language of queerness, can quietly have gay friends but cannot "do gay"—cannot transcend into being physically close (not necessarily sexual) with another male. They would not feel comfortable if others perceived them to be gay, although they are comfortable with quietly being an ally to gays. Like the Informed Inactive men, they "get it," but are able to go a little further in terms of their interpersonal relationships. Yet, unlike males who are social justice queers, they are less likely to be public advocates, and unlike committed queer-straights, they are reticent to adopt personal qualities of being queer. Men in this category can accept queer-ness, and even intellectually embrace it, but hold back for whatever reason from doing the personal work that would be needed to allow themselves to become queer-straight identified. They lack the confidence or perception that they can go beyond the intellectual "acceptance" of queer masculinity for "gay men" but not for themselves. They may cheer others on, even have friends who are queer-straights, but do not move into the experiential sphere of queer masculinity. They appear to be stuck in the forms of traditional masculinity, to overtly know better, yet at the personal level, the default for such males is "normal" even if in intellectual and emotional respects, they realize "normal" is not what it is cracked up to be.

Unaware Inactive Another place on the spectrum of "shadow males" are those who are also inactive in any intentional queering. Such males may realize that they do not "fit" within traditional straight masculinity, and are not necessarily comfortable with the status quo, but they do not perceive that change is possible, individually or culturally. These males do not appear gay or connect to a queer world in any way, but they also do not do straight hegemonic masculinity. Having no awareness of what queer masculinity is, their life in the "shadow of masculinity" leads them to do enough straight masculinity to get by, which means wearing appropriate male clothing so that they do not stand out, knowing enough about normative heteromasculine expectations to "pass." If they are on a construction crew or in a board room of men who act out hetero-masculinity in their language and behavior, they might choose to eat alone at lunchtime. If they are sitting with other straight men who are talking in hyper-masculine, sexist or homophobic terms, they will not attempt to change the topic, but neither will they participate. Rather, they fade into the background.

In college, they are the men who stay in their rooms, away from the noise of masculinity that ripples through the hallways (the "hey, look at me!" noise of the masculinized corridor). They do not do hyper-straight male language-do not use "cunt" or "let's go have a few brews" or know the names of NFL players. They avoid the hyper-male scene whenever possible.

Males living in the shadow of masculinity may be what Crane and Crane-Seeber (2003) refer to as sweet guys, but they also can be pretty shut down emotionally. Expressing straight male emotions such as anger does not fit for them, nor do they allow themselves "female emotions" such as crying when they are sad or expressing fear. It is safer to not say anything, not show anything, and attempt to get by. The body of these men is not represented in the image of straight or gay masculinities—there is no appearance or an image of "self," no public voice, only quiet knowing of being "different"—a self-identity of being "non." They may live inside the space of computers, musical instruments, books, or other such places that provide safety from the storm of heteronormative masculinity. Almost by the nature of living in the shadow, they seek each other out and "play" most of their lives with other men who quietly "go along" with the mainstream, but are never fully engaged in the dominant hetero-masculine world.

Jim, a graduate student, noted that this category reminds him of many of the boys he knew in high school, who,

> ... were not queer-acting at all but were simply not good at masculine privileged activities such as sports, hitting on girls, being the class clown, or knowing about cars. These were guys who were "straight" in appearance (and no doubt took time when dressing each morning that they appear straight) but were good at math or playing the trombone, things that were not going to get you a date with the homecoming queen. Some may refer to these boys as "dorks" or "nerds." These men are not forced to hide because of what they do (as young overtly queer acting boys must do). Rather, they are outside of normative masculinity because of what they are unable to do, the privileged activities and interests of boy culture. These boys know they are pretty low in the social hierarchy but would probably just understand themselves as unpopular as opposed to unpopular because they are not good at "boy stuff" (J. Fulton, personal communication, June 27, 2003).

These boys, as Jim suggests, would not be likely to do the analysis to understand their experience; they would not add a "gender component" to thinking about their relatively low status, and the particular form of isolation they experienced from those with the highest status. And they certainly are unlikely to add a sexual component to any thinking about their status, seeing that their position is not only a result of failure to perform hegemonic masculinity but also hegemonic heterosexuality. This is similar to how, given the general absence of consciousness about social class in the United States, those at the bottom socioeconomically are very aware of their relative status, but unlikely to pursue analysis at a level of acting out against the oppressive nature of the system and its institutions. The oppression is instead internalized to the point of hopelessness and lowered expectations.

GIVING LEGITIMACY TO QUEER MASCULINITY

Border crossing can be dangerous, and in the midst of oppressive systems that threaten those who take the risk to cross it seems ominous and even undesirable. The queer-straight male holds a position that, regardless of where one falls in the typology presented here, is not institutionally supported. It is a status that may find support from other marginalized groups including women and gay queers, although even that may be a mixed bag, given that some forms of queer-straight masculinity, such as the elective or stylistic straight-queer, may result in men in these categories gaining social capital beyond what is possible for women or gay queers (who do not have the same options).

At the same time, there is little institutional support for straight-queer males, when compared to the privileges extended to hegemonic heteromasculine males. At least not yet. And there is no clearly defined social movement for males that attempts to raise consciousness and invite the level of change that will queer straight masculinity. Not yet.

The benefit of building a typology of queer masculinities is to extend voice and legitimacy to the queer-ness that already exists within the straight male world. It is an attempt to contribute to the discourse initiated by the first wave of the feminist movement, and the actions of the earlier gay movement dating back to Germany in the nineteenth century that found currency in the United States in the mid-twentieth century. What has been consistent in both the feminist and GLBT movements throughout the past century is that the discourse on sexuality and gender in these communities has provided an appreciation for the diverse ways in which gender and sexuality take form. Naming the diversity within the construct of masculinity–and its relationship with queerness, gives voice and legitimacy to the queer-ness that exists within the straight male world. It will ideally provoke greater discourse on the topic and extend awareness of the influence of the hegemonically straight masculine not only over gay men, but straight males as well.

There are many questions to explore, such as what is the attraction of moving outside the hetero-masculine norm? What is gained? Is this "using" queerness as a cover–to avoid dealing with straight masculine environments where threats are great? Do elective queer-straight males in queer space privilege straightness at the expense of queers? Is this an honoring of queerness or a use? Is there a difference between queer experiences by straight males that takes place in private space vs. public space?

Queer forms of straight masculinity represent something much more than just men who are "nontraditional." Rather, they suggest a masculinity and male heterosexuality that extends the reach of societal perceptions of both, and one that for males in any of these categories, allows potential for evolving a broadened definition, resulting in expanded norms and expectations, for who straight men are and who they can be.

Why are the types of males discussed in this chapter disrupting heteromasculinity? It is because they queer the environment of the hetero-masculine by, for whatever reason, not fully participating in the normative system. And they provide a hiding place for males who are queer and do not feel safe or competent in passing in heterosexualized masculine environments. Queerstraight males' respective refusal to actively participate in the dominant system serves to stall the system itself. Their absence, and, at the very least, their lack of full participation in hetero-masculine culture weakens the system of oppression that is an essential part of normative hetero-masculinity. At the same time, many of the queer-straight males identified with these categories actively challenge the assumptions of the hetero-masculine, the dichotomous thinking that has been a cultural stronghold and the core legitimizing force of gender and sexual oppression.

Creating a language for queer-straight males is in itself a queering of hegemonic hetero-masculinity. It is an attempt to change social attitudes around both male sexuality and masculinity and provide support for both those in the trenches of queerness and those males who are in the shadows. It turns the volume up, giving legitimacy and voice to a way of being for queer-straight males.

By looking closely to see, and validate, the queering that goes on by straight males, it is possible to recognize a range of ways in which males problematize hegemonic masculinity and heterosexuality, and by doing so, disrupt one of the most privileged identities in Western society.

REFERENCES

Bem, S. 1995. Dismantling gender polarization and compulsory heterosexuality: should we turn the volume down or up? *Journal of sex research*, 32(4): 329–334.

Brannon, R. 1976. The male sex role: our culture's blueprint of manhood, and what it's done for us lately, in D. David and R. Brannon (eds.) *The 49th percent majority*, pp. 1–45 Reading, MA: Addison & Wesley.

Butler, J. 1990. *Gender trouble*. New York: Routledge.

Connell, R. 1987. *Gender and power*. Cambridge, MA: Polity.

Crane, B. and J. Crane-Seeber, 2003. The four boxes of gendered sexuality: good girl/bad girl and tough guy/sweet guy, in R. Heasley and B. Crane (eds.) *Sexual lives: A reader on the theories and realities of human sexualities*, pp. 196–217 New York: McGraw-Hill.

Foucault, M. 1978. *The history of sexuality*, Vol. 1. New York: Pantheon Books.

Heasley, R. Queer masculinities of straight men: creating a typology. *Men and masculinities*. Sage. Vol. 7. 3 January 2005.

Ingraham, C. 1999. *White weddings: Romancing heterosexuality in popular culture*. New York: Routledge.

Kinsey, A. C., W. B. Pomeroy and C. E. Martin. 1948. *Sexual behavior in the human male*. Philadelphia: W. B. Saunders.

Kindlon, D. and M. Thompson. 1999. *Raising Cain: Protecting the emotional life of boys.* New York: Ballantine Books.

Pollack, W. 1999. *Real boys: Rescuing our sons from the myths of boyhood.* New York: Random House.

Rich, A. 1980. Compulsory heterosexuality and lesbian existence. *Signs.* 5: 631–660.

Seidman, S. 1992. *Embattled eros.* New York: Routledge

Spring fashion: the Carlson twins take it off, *Out,* April 2003, 72–85.

St. John, W. 2003. Metrosexuals come out, *The New York Times,* June 22, 9–1, 9–5.

MAINTAINING MANLINESS IN LATER LIFE

HEGEMONIC MASCULINITIES AND EMPHASIZED FEMININITIES

By Robert Meadows and Kate Davidson

This chapter seeks to illustrate two of the ways in which age matters to feminisms. Primarily, it demonstrates how centering on the lives of old men can offer insights that can inform, challenge, and change feminist theories, research, and practice. Percolating throughout this analysis is our premise that *age relations* present critical axes of inequality that subordinate old men (particularly in relation to other, younger, men) and that these age relations make the study of old men informative and challenging.

Thompson (1994: 16) identifies a divide within the gerontological literature between those who believe that old men are emasculated by aging and those who suggest that old men may have to adapt to fit into a new, but not substantially different, dominant ideological form of masculinity as they age. The assumption within both schools of thought is that manhood is constructed "through and by reference to 'age'" (Hearn 1995: 97) and that a sense of maleness is defined and redefined throughout the life course.

Offering an explanation as to why men's relationships with masculinities change as they age, Carrigan, Connell, and Lee (1985) and Connell (1995) suggest that there are multiple masculinities that coexist in time and space and that compete for dominance. Of particular note here is hegemonic masculinity or the dominant, most "honoured or desired" form of masculinity (Connell 2000: 10). Hegemonic masculinity refers to those behaviors and practices that embody the "currently accepted answer to the problem of the legitimacy of patriarchy," which make a successful claim to authority and which guarantee the dominant position of men over women (and other men) (Connell 1995: 77; Coates 2003). Within contemporary Western societies, the dominant, hegemonic ideology is said to prioritize such traits as physical strength, virility, wealth, self-control, and aggression (Calasanti 2004). It is also said to prioritize youth (Whitehead 2002). As men age, their withdrawal from the occupational breadwinner role, their possible loss of sexual potency, their diminishing physical strength, and the onset of illness can all weaken their relationship with this dominant ideology (Arber, Davidson, and Ginn 2003).

In a circular and somewhat paradoxical manner, the study of old men can uncover "the young and middle-aged biases that inhere in typical notions of masculinity" (Calasanti and King 2005: 19) precisely because these typical notions are age dependent and so are no longer available to many old men. In essence, old men are *absent* from a masculinized space and, as a result, are often afforded the status of "other." As Renold (2004) suggests, those who occupy this position can express the defining characteristics of both their own situation and the group from which they are excluded. The dialogues offered by old men can allude to the very nature of dominant forms of masculinities and reinforce the suggestion that ideal notions of manliness are based on younger men.

Accounts can be especially revealing when the man is able to approximate the hegemonic ideal earlier in life. Yet the most privileged men lose power as they age, and even those who have achieved or approximated hegemonic forms earlier in life are unlikely to maintain such power in old age. Those whose lives have been shaped by advantage may be the most surprised by a loss of power, and this surprise may enable them to see the precariousness of their position, and their own place within power relations may become more apparent (Calasanti and Slevin 2001).

Developing these arguments further, in the first section of this chapter we discuss "being old and being a man" and illustrate how old men offer a window to hegemonic forms of masculinity through their *absence* from this space. We then move to highlight how the study of old men also gives entrée into strategies men may call on to cope with the tensions between aging and dominant forms of manliness.

Both of these sections share a similar explanatory framework. Within our study, the men presented insights into the nature of hegemonic forms of masculinity, and the strategies employed to remain approximated to them, through narratives that alluded to changes in their *production relations, power relations,* and *emotional attachments*. These are three of the structures that any analysis of gender must consider (Connell 1995, 2000) and the sites where masculinities are configured as either "us" or "them." Reflecting this, our discussions within the initial segments of this chapter are framed around these subdivisions.

Within the third section of this chapter we draw on Renold's suggestion that notions of otherness are reinforced not only through being absent from a masculinized space but also through *inhabiting* spaces associated with "emphasized femininity" (2004: 252). These spaces are defined around compliance with subordination and orientated to supporting the desires and wishes of men (Connell 1987: 183). Providing care, for example, is a labor reserved principally for women (Calasanti 2004) and, as a result, tends to be seen as a feminine space. As men age, they not only become absent from youth-dominated hegemonic forms of masculinity but also increase their chances of inhabiting feminine space. Those who occupy these feminine spaces also invoke strategies in an attempt to remain approximated to hegemonic forms.

In the final section of this chapter, we illustrate instances where these strategies fail. Old men choose between attempting to continue approximating hegemonic forms (and failing) or formulating an "alternative masculinity" that can incorporate behaviors that do not derive from one's sex (Pease 2000). We show that, either way, the men are, at all times, cognizant of the ideal even though they might have difficulty meeting these standards in the past or present.

Throughout these discussions, we draw on empirical data collected from a sample of eighty-five men older than age sixty-five (all names are changed to protect anonymity), representing a variety of marital statuses: thirty were married or cohabiting, thirty-three were widowed, ten were divorced or separated, and twelve never married. Approximately half of the men in the sample were aged sixty-five to seventy-four, and half were older than seventy-five. Interviews lasted between one and two hours and were predominantly conducted by an older male social scientist. The interviews were semistructured and framed around the men's history, their present circumstances, and their perception of family and friendship relationships, social support, and health-related behavior.

Two further aspects of the sample are worth noting here. First, the vast majority of the men served within the British Forces at some point in their lives, either during the hostilities of World War II or during Conscription, which lasted in the United Kingdom until 1960. The military environment was an almost exclusively male domain, and there it was imperative to assert their masculinity to distance themselves from both femininity and homosexuality (Segal 1990). What was considered appropriate masculine behavior was reinforced through traditions and customs within military life. The men also had experienced some degree of discipline, self-discipline, and deprivation of personal freedom and to some extent could call on these reserves in later life when faced with challenges to their autonomy and sense of control. Second, all the men were white and most had enjoyed years of stable or serial-continuous employment, some having achieved well-paid and high status careers, even from quite modest beginnings. The sample therefore comprised relatively privileged men who had benefited from the prosperity resulting from post-World War II social, economic, and welfare state improvements in the United Kingdom.

BEING OLD AND BEING A MAN: THE YOUNG BIAS WITHIN HEGEMONIC MASCULINITIES

Schoolboys are said to define hegemonic heterosexual masculinity through football, fights, toughness, competitiveness, and overt heterosexuality (Renold 2004). Yet these defining features and notions of normal manliness have neither intelligibility nor power without the "contrasting presence of an abnormal gender" (Boldt 1996: 119, quoted in Renold 2004: 251). That is, for a group to be dominant, there is a requirement that at least one other group is subordinate.

Old men play a part in offering normal manliness intelligibility, thereby revealing the characteristics of both the dominant group and the subordinate group. Within the present study, the men's narratives concerning these characteristics were made richer by the fact that, as Suls and Mullen (1983–84) suggest, temporal comparisons are frequently used by old men and women; that is, men and women compare their past and present performance in similar facets of life to gauge improvement and deterioration.

In essence, the "male as breadwinner" paradigm (production relations) was prioritized within discussions of how the men used to live, and its loss was mourned. Similarly, with age the men were forced to reflect on their lack of power and sexual prowess (emotional relations), and through this reflection, they illustrated the importance of these relations to dominant forms of manliness.

Production Relations

Production relations refer to the structuring of production, consumption, and distribution (Connell 1987: 103) and involve the gendered allocation of tasks and the nature and organization of this work. Within our study, some men mourned the changing nature of the gendered divisions of labor. Kevin, who was "pretty senior" in his business, noted that his wife did her part by being "absolutely super at entertaining" and made a "good wife and mother." Kevin continued to explain that since his wife had died, he had missed the "normal" division of labor: "I now have to undertake considerable domesticity, which I hate. I miss the normal marital relationship."

Similarly, Earl said that not being "able to do the things I used to do makes me very sad." For example, Earl, in common with many of the men, had always been responsible for cutting the grass. He lamented having to hand this task over to his daughter but was able to ameliorate the regret by remarking that "she seems to enjoy doing it, so I suppose it's OK." What is interesting is that many of the men described a division of labor in the garden. Derek was responsible for the vegetable garden: "If you can't eat it, I don't grow it. She [his wife] does the pretty things, flowers and all." Derek was proud that he could still cut the grass, although he admitted it took longer "these days."

Professional success and wealth are both tied into production relations and hegemonic masculine ideologies (Calasanti 2003), as men's control of corporations and accumulation of private fortunes and wealth are all part of the construction of masculinity (Connell 1995). Thus, often the men spoke with pride about their financial achievements and the fact that their wives never had to work outside the home, as well as their recognition of the ways this has changed with advanced age. Angus stated that he "had a terrific career, no question about that. I don't suppose there are too many people around who have had a career such as I have. *And I've lost it, it's gone now"* (our emphasis).

The body is intrinsically related to production relations. For old men trying to enact hegemonic forms of masculinity, having a body that cannot perform adequately is perceived as a problem (Calasanti and Slevin 2001: 65). In a compelling autobiographical account, Jackson (1990: 58) describes how his ability to give an obsessive energy to his paid work was dependent on his wife looking after him at home, and in its turn, this energy fueled the patriarchal social order. Jackson strove to achieve hegemonic masculinity through a single-minded concentration on his intellectual work. This intense focus on his mental side left him to neglect his body, leading to a denial of emotions and bodily experiences. In the end his body broke, making him weak, dependent, and passive. The ideal form of manhood is said to concern "doing" (Calasanti and Slevin 2001), and within the present study the men spoke of the conflict between the decaying of the physical body and their need to be able to perform in appropriate, masculine ways.

> For many years I've told myself, in terms of physical ability, that I would still do everything that I did when I was twenty. Now in the last five years I've had to accept that, you know, that's a dream ... and it's tough. (Angus)

Throughout the interviews the loss of bodily performance was expressed in terms synonymous with a loss of manliness. Although aspects of this can be conceptualized around production relations, the men's dialogues also illustrated an interrelationship between changing bodies and a change in power relations.

Power Relations

As Connell (1995, 2000) suggests, the main axis of power within Western worlds and beyond is the subordination of women and the existence of male domination. Within our study the men's stories frequently turned to earlier demonstrations of power over women and children. Clive offered a particularly lengthy discussion of how, despite his adult son's insistence that his financial affairs had nothing to do with him, he took control of his son's bank account and "made him" pay into a savings bond. Similarly, the data are replete with stories of men putting their foot down with their wives and knowing best what would be good for them. For example, within an interview containing stories of women ("wrongfully") accusing him of violence and harassment, Dan recalled how his "putting his foot down" was the start of his marital problems: "My wife said that when the daughter got married we had got enough room and they could live with us here and I said to my wife, 'No, that is not going to happen.'"

The prevalence of these stories was again amplified by the fact that this power was now receding for many of the men. For example, Dan's discussion of putting his foot down with his wife was situated within dialogues of how his daughter manipulates him and shows a lack of respect toward him now. Furthermore, on occasion the men evoked a real sense of vulnerability and a fear of violence. For example, for some men a "lack of respect from the young" manifested itself into fear of walking into certain parts of their towns and fear of encountering intimidation and verbal abuse.

> One very charming, elderly gentleman who lives near there, he's been not physically attacked but verbally abused and had things thrown at him while he's been walking around the streets, so he doesn't go that way any more. They [the young] have no respect for age at all. (Damien)

As well as offering a perspective on hegemonic forms, this loss of power can cause great surprise to some men and, consequently, has epistemological importance. Feminism starts with the assumption that knowledge is socially situated within the hegemonic young, white, heterosexual male paradigm (Arber et al. 2003). However, feminist discourse suggests that women's experience of oppression can offer an alternative view of lived reality. To achieve a feminist standpoint, then, one must engage in the struggles necessary to see social life from the point of view other than that of the "ruling gender" (Harding 1997: 169). Aging, and especially physical breakdown and decay, can connect the old male with weakness, dependency, and passivity; call into question traditional power relationships (Jackson 1990); and engage old men in struggles that may provoke an alternative view of lived reality.

Emotional Relations

Here we are predominantly concerned with what Connell (1995) describes as *cathexis;* that is, desire as emotional energy and the practices that shape this desire. Along these lines, Katz and Marshall (2003) note the increasing importance of the link between continued sexual functioning and resistance to aging. To the extent that aging is associated with a decline in sexual functioning, this nonsexual functioning can play a part in reinforcing feelings of oldness and can prevent old men from occupying hegemonic masculine spaces.

Men's stories often demonstrated the centrality of sex to their masculine identities. Clive discussed how he started going to the movies with girls when he was thirteen and always "fancied the opposite sex," ending with the question, "No harm in that, is there?" Reflecting on his marriage, Darren stated, "We had a proper sex life." Similarly, Harry proclaimed that he and his wife "were both into sex, no worry about that." Yet these dialogues were predominantly in the past tense. In essence, the old men within the present study were harking to their past to hold themselves to the sexual standards of the young and middle aged (Calasanti and King 2005). They knew, and offered dialogues concerning, what they were "supposed" to be.

Clyde, for example, noted that a lack of sexual functioning created a sense of loss in his life, and he, arguably, was aware that this shifted him away from what he was supposed to be. For Clyde, "one of the effects of aging or high blood pressure is the medication you take prevents you from doing certain activities"—an allusion to sexual intercourse. He was now, at least, able to occasionally perform sexually through the use of a pump ("I use it just for my own satisfaction") but lamented the doctor's refusal to prescribe him Viagra. He now had "gaps" in his life, of which sex seemed to be a major component. Such gaps were a major theme throughout the data and represented men's realizations concerning where they stood in relation to hegemonic masculinity. Earl, discussed previously, knew that the division of labor required him to mow the lawn, and Dan was aware that men should sit at the head of the household and that children should respect their fathers.

None of this is meant to suggest, however, that old men necessarily become ungendered. It has become widely stated that as men and women age, gender divisions begin to blur (Gutmann 1987) as men become "kinder and gentler," partly through a reduction of aggression-related hormones (see Davidson 2004 for a discussion) and partly through a change in their status as the breadwinner (Courtenay 2000). Instead, we argue here that the men employ strategies to continue approximating hegemonic masculinity. We illustrate this next, returning again to the overlapping structures of gender relations: production relations, power relations, and emotional relations.

RESISTING OTHERNESS

Production Relations: What I Can Still Do

One of the strategies employed by the men was to associate aging with physical decline, not chronology per se, and to demonstrate, where possible, their youthful manliness by illustrating what they can "still do." For example, Fenton stated that he can do all sorts of work: "You know. I can mow the lawn." Similarly, Clive, discussing the "old peoples walk," told us,

> So we were coming back onto the estate by car, and we are going past the shops, and there is a man who is about two years younger than me coming out of a post office with a stick; and there is a woman coming out of [a shop] with a stick and they are doing this "old peoples walk"—do you know what I mean? [Gets up and demonstrates.] It involves a lot of very careful walking—there is nothing brisk about it at all. So I said

to [son], "Why do they—is that a habit?" So John says—there is a moments pause and he says—"No, I think you have to go on a course for that, Dad." I just collapsed laughing, you know, because some old people are old before their time and actually enjoy being old. I don't want to be old. I'm not old, am I?

Associating aging with physical decline enabled some of the men to express hope that "they never get old": a prima facie illogical statement, made possible by associating aging with a physical state that one could bypass by dying before one becomes infirm. Gilleard and Higgs suggest that aging becomes an identity that is framed through resistance (2000: 60). Echoing this, Minichiello, Browne, and Kendig (2000) describe how old people resist being seen as old by dismissing chronological age as irrelevant and by reserving the label *old* for those in physical or mental decline. Similarly, Fairhurst (2003) illustrates how chronological age does not connect a person to being old-fashioned. Rather, men and women bind cultural knowledge about lifestyles to age. Thus, ways of behaving, whom you mix with, and physical activities can all play a part in perceptions of age (Fairhurst 2003: 40). All in all, the individual struggle to maintain a balance between stereotypes and experiences of the aging self requires tenacity and energy (Featherstone and Hepworth 1991).

Power Relations: Being Better Than Others

A further strategy men in our study employed involved "being better than others." The social comparison literature in aging speaks to this strategy. Social comparison theory assumes that people have a drive to evaluate their abilities and that, in the absence of an objective comparison, this need is satisfied through evaluating oneself in comparison with similar others (Frisby 2004: 326). In her study of black women and idealized images, Frisby (2004) divides the social comparison processes into self-evaluation, self-improvement, self-enhancement, and the concept of similarity. Within the previous quotation, for example, Clive appears to be undertaking self-enhancement comparisons. His discussion of the old people's walk involves downward comparison; that is, comparisons with others who are seen as inferior or less fortunate (Frisby 2004). Similarly Mike states that he has "a chap not much older than me just next door and he never gets outside." Identifying who is "better" than whom is a value-laden exercise that reflects definitions of normalness and appropriate behavior. The process can engender a feeling of power within one group and feelings of powerlessness within others.

Emotional Relations: Proving the Young Ones Wrong

The final strategy the men in our study discussed involves exaggerated notions of heterosexual prowess and expulsion and disassociation of homosexuality (Renold 2004). For example, in relation to a conversation about how he used to form friends with the opposite sex, Angus confirmed his heterosexual nature by stating that he likes "the opposite sex ... who doesn't?" and situated himself as normal by making jokes about homosexuality and those "people who are different." Similarly, throughout the interview, Reg made much innuendo about women generally and the size of his penis and made constant reference to his continued sexual abilities. When asked important areas he thought that had not been fully probed during the interview,

Clive's one-word answer was "sex." He thought that his wife was very lucky because he kept himself fit, which helped his lovemaking. Clive suggested that most young people believed that sex was impossible after the age of forty-five, and he took pride in the fact that he could still make love despite his age, proving young people wrong in the process.

The strategies discussed within this section of the chapter remain similar (although somewhat amplified) when old men are confronted with the additional challenge of being old and occupying a potentially feminized space. Emphasizing power, control, functional ability, and "doing" remain favored strategies here.

CAREGIVING

Aging is fluid (Calasanti and Slevin 2001), affecting everyone, and is a complex, multifaceted phenomenon. A person's social location intersects with aging, adding further dimensions to the tensions that exist between aging and masculinities. On the more macroscale this can involve elements of an individual's race, gender, and class. On a microscale this can involve social situations, such as caregiving, that can locate the male within feminine spaces.

For example, old men within our study attempted to combat the potentially negative image of caring in relation to their gender identity by defining it in functional, instrumental terms. As Kaye and Applegate suggest, the old male caregiving orientation is characterized by displays of "rationality with feeling" (1994: 230). The employment-based identity transfers to the caregiving role (p. 228). Gary, for example, described how it was "his job" to deal with his wife's death certificate, although his children had offered to attend to this, because he was her husband and lover for fifty-two years. Similarly, Darren offered the following story of how he came to be the one to offer his wife personal care:

> We thought we'd get someone in to give it a try to wash her and dress her, but the ones they sent down were tiny little women and of course Peg was rather tall, she was 5'10" or something, you see. And once or twice she used to call me to the bed, and of course they couldn't manage to lift her up, and with different girls each week, I thought, no, this is a waste of time, it's no good. So I said, "No, don't worry, I'll do it myself"—so I did it myself. But we had a nurse come in to bathe her on occasion, weekly or whatever it was. She did a tour of the district and she'd come here on the Friday morning or something like that, but the rest I did myself. Yes, I looked after her all the time. Just like doing another job, except indoors!

Darren decided that he was the best person to offer "proper care" for his wife and took on the task in the spirit of another career, but this time within the domestic environment (indoors) rather than the traditional public sphere. Through a specific definition of caring, Darren is also attempting to construct a particular self-identity. Men have the potential to construct numerous self-identities through different ways of speaking about their actions. Indeed, in their discourse analysis of fifteen stories written by Finnish husbands caring for their demented wives, Kirsi, Hervonen, and Jylha (2000) identify four different ways men spoke about their actions. One of these, agency speech, involves presenting oneself as a person who has control of his own life and environment (Kirsi et al. 2000). Drawing on the work of Russell (2001), Calasanti (2003: 22) suggests that men adopt a managerial style to care work that enables them to separate "caring for" and "caring about." Caring for—that is, functionally ensuring someone is looked after—may approximate the hegemonic space, which prioritizes physical strength and self-control, to a larger degree than caring about, which involves emotions to a far greater extent. This is especially so when "caring for" involves stoically "carrying on" rather than stopping or accepting help. Gus, for example, talked about how his reply to a nurse who stated, "We are worried about you, you know," was to categorically state, "No, I will carry on."

Gus' and Darren's dialogues allude to being better than others, thereby also employing social comparison strategies—a lesser person would have "given in" or "given up." In some respects the previous quotation from Darren, concerning "getting someone in to wash and dry" his wife, could be seen as undertaking self-improvement comparisons. He considered dealing with the professional carers as a "waste of time" and chose to undertake their role himself. Similarly, Earl offered the following quote about the time his daughter and son-in-law offered to take his wheelchair-bound wife on holiday. Here he is undertaking a comparison with younger, fitter, stronger individuals.

> [I don't know] how the hell they managed her, but only four days that was all they could cope and they took her to Austria and she always wanted to go to Austria. They took her, with the wheelchair and everything and my daughter done all what I done and she said, "Dad, I don't know how you ever did it."

Power relations also manifest themselves in the ways in which the old men strive to be more emotionally controlled than those around them. Being able to exercise such power over others is intrinsically related to the fact that men do not perceive caring as a burden, manage to maintain their autonomy, and gain increased self-esteem, admiration, and gratitude (Davidson, Arber, and Ginn 2000: 548).

An example of this power is Forrest's story about how his adult sons were unable to come to terms with their late mother's early onset dementia, creating a barrier between them that was still evident at the time of the interview, ten years after her death. Forrest considered he held the moral high ground over his sons' refusal to accept their mother's condition. He discouraged them from attending her funeral because they could not support him or her when she was alive; he felt they did not deserve to be there with him after she had passed away. Similarly, Fitz explained how one of his daughters slipped into what he described as "self-pity" when his wife (her mother) died, while his other daughter was "far more sensible and well-adjusted," like him. On occasion this went further, and some men emphasized controlling both their own and others' emotions. As Barry stated, discussing his wife who had cancer,

> I always took the attitude "Now come on, come on. We've got to have a strong mind about this, you know. We're going to beat this cancer." But I always wonder whether I should have talked more to her about dying and all the things that you don't know until you do. But I have no guilt; I have no guilt, because whatever I did, I did. I have no guilt.

The strategies discussed within the past two main sections of this chapter can be seen as ways that old men, whether caring or not, cast their activities to be in line with the notions of power, production relations, and cathexis required by hegemonic forms of masculinity. However, such strategies will eventually fail because of the impossibility of approximating youthful character-istics indefinitely as one ages. This leaves old men with the option of continuing to apply these imperfect and, ultimately, ineffective strategies or to adopt alternative masculinities.

ALTERNATIVE MASCULINITIES

Just as some old men do not have the resources to buy youth-inducing products, some old men do not have the resources to employ any of these negotiation strategies as they age or when caring. In such instances, the old men may drop the attempt to approximate hegemonic mas-culinity altogether and, instead, engage with alternative masculinities. For example, Jackson's bodily breakdown caused a conflict between hegemonic ideals and his own available reality, but this conflict, he suggests, helped him "to give up traditional power without losing face" (1990: 69). At the same time, those embracing alternative masculinities can incur "high social and emotional costs" (Renold 2004: 249). For example, poor, black men, excluded from legiti-mate employment and thus part of hegemonic masculine ideals, may compensate by engaging in dangerous behaviors such as drug dealing (Calasanti 2004).

This is not, however, to suggest that an either—or situation occurs. It is not the case that old men will either approximate hegemonic forms or embrace alternative masculinities. As many of the previous quotations illustrate, for some men, their attempts are "enough" for now and enable them to believe that they are still approximating hegemonic forms. It is rather that these strategies cannot continue forever.

Indeed, within our study few men embraced alternative masculinities; instead they main-tained the struggle to approximate hegemonic forms and do "enough" for now. When they did engage with alternative masculinities, it was, as with Jackson (1990), because they were a complete "physical wreck." As the following statement from Sean suggests, some old men understood that they could no longer be as active and, as such, could no longer conform entirely to hegemonic masculinities.

> I don't want fortunes or anything like that, but it would be just lovely to wake up one
> morning and say, "Well I am a little bit fed up, let's have a change of scenery, let's go
> and book something." [My brother] does that and he is never home, and the result of
> that is he is far more active than me and you wouldn't believe he is eighty.

In Sean's case, he had just had a heart-valve replacement operation, and the strategies available to him to compensate for this loss of activity and attempt to stay approximated to hegemonic forms were limited. In essence, Sean's physical ailments were acknowledged as giving him a life very different from his "normal" one and were absolutely "pulling him apart."

In relation to caring, Earl could not control his wife's decaying body as "she always had bowel trouble." In addition, lifting his wife "fourteen times a day" became too much for his aging body to take and, despite having a home care assistant, no one was around to witness his caring during the majority of the day. He considered he had become "invisible," and his physical deterioration went unnoticed by those around him. The "hard labor" of caring had taken a toll on his health, and even though he was only in his late sixties when she died, he felt unable to pursue activities such as playing bowls and joining social clubs, which had been curtailed by his caring responsibilities. It is interesting that—and we don't wish to negate the love Earl obviously had for his wife—he was one of the few men who expressed feeling cheated because he had to care for his wife:

> I feel cheated, I feel cheated out of life. Because I was so lively, I was always full of fun when I was a youngster, always parties and I was always invited everywhere but I honestly, after looking after her for thirty years, I feel as if I have been cheated.

The physical decline described by Earl and Sean provoked critical reflection on their lives in a way that reflects Jackson's (1990) discussion of how his bodily breakdown enabled him to "legitimately" take up an alternative masculinity:

> I have done a lot of silly things because I was very headstrong at that time too. I was very much in control of the family, but I have learned to be—I have allowed myself to be trodden on once a while, and it seems to work better. (Sean)

Here, Sean's insight illustrates an acceptance of alternative ways of dealing with his manliness, and although he associates relinquishing control with being trodden on, he admits that life seems to be easier when you "give in." In much the same way, Earl rationalized his daughter's taking over the responsibility of cutting the grass because she seemed to enjoy the task.

For most of the men, the loss of youth, power, and health was expressed as a source of regret rather than anger or pragmatism. However, their accounts were peppered with alternative explanations, strategies, and justifications in dealing with their changing roles and relationships as a result of growing old.

CONCLUSION

Within this chapter, we describe how age matters in two ways. The first way concerns age relations. Percolating throughout this chapter has been the observation that even the most privileged men lose power as they age. Hegemonic ideals of manliness emphasize physical strength, (hetero-) sexual virility, and professional status. These are facets that are tied to youth, and as such manliness must be negotiated and renegotiated in relation to age. Men struggle to attain or approximate hegemonic masculinities throughout their lives, but in later life it becomes apparent that even those who could achieve such standards earlier cannot in old age.

The second way age matters is that centering on the lives of old persons can challenge and inform feminist thinking and practice. In essence, old men become "other" through their absence from the hegemonic masculinized space and, occasionally, through also occupying a feminine space. As Calasanti and Slevin (2001) argue, those whose lives have been shaped by advantage may be most surprised by the loss of power that comes with aging and the status of "other." This may, in turn, provoke men to see the nature of their dominant position (Calasanti and Slevin 2001).

Focusing on the lives of old men challenges and informs feminisms in three ways. First, the study of the old man can illustrate the very nature of the defining facets of hegemonic masculinities. As old men become removed from hegemonic spaces and become aware of the precariousness of their own position, they become able to reflect on the (numerous) positions they have inhabited throughout the life course. Certainly, the old men's dialogues reinforce the contention that ideal notions of manliness are based on younger men. For example, the men mourned the loss of the division of labor, regretted having to undertake domestic labor, and longed to return to their lost careers. Similarly, physical decay caused the men some difficulties as it prevented them from enacting hegemonic forms of manliness that are expressed through physical strength, virility, and self-control (Calasanti 2004).

Second, the study of old men also gives entrée into strategies called on to cope with the tensions between aging and dominant forms of manliness. Echoing the work of Minichiello et al. (2000), the men in this study resisted the label *old* by disassociating old age from chronology. These strategies seem similar whether the old men are absent from masculinized space only or are both absent from and inhabiting a feminized space. For example, a large majority of the old men within the study, regardless of being caregivers, employed social comparison strategies, comparing themselves favorably to those around them to illustrate how physical strength, virility, wealth, and self-control were not as diminished as they *could* be. This points toward the possibility that the strategies men employ across the life course to approximate hegemonic forms are similar but somewhat amplified within old age as the precariousness of one's position becomes increasingly evident. However, old men cannot approximate hegemonic forms indefinitely; at that point, what is left is the choice between attempting to continue approximating hegemonic forms (and failing) or formulating an alternative.

Finally, the investigation of old men offers emancipatory possibilities. Unlike most other social inequalities, everybody will experience the loss of privilege that comes with aging. This opens up the possibility of each individual critically reflecting on how power operates (Calasanti and Slevin 2001), which in turn hints at the possible creation of a "mens anti-patriarchal standpoint." For Flood (1997), men's anti-patriarchal standpoint is possible, because the ontology of privileged groups is not completely determining. However, this involves more than simply will or moral conviction; a change in "lived reality" is required. Being old creates such an opportunity, and men's own subjection to domination and their resulting experience of otherness provides the potential for them to find points of contact with women (Flood 1997: 3–4).

SOCIETY, SEXUALITY, AND DISABLED/ABLEBODIED ROMANTIC RELATIONSHIPS

By Sally A. Nemeth

"It must make you feel really good to know that I could be with anyone I want, and I am here with you." I have to wonder what Joe, my former lover, would think if he knew I introduced a selection on communication and disabled/ablebodied persons' romantic relationships with the off-hand comment he made to me on a steamy Saturday night some five summers ago. He might be surprised to realize that occasionally I recall his remark with a tinge of enlightened smugness and a smile of amusement at its pomposity and presumption. Yet, there is still a part of me that buys into his assumption, kicking and screaming as my ego might be; this part of myself is trained to believe that as a blind woman I am lucky to find an ablebodied partner. Much as I hate to admit it, it did feel good to have a handsome, ablebodied man who wanted "me."

In this selection I discuss disabled/ablebodied romantic relationships and some of the disability-related factors that influence their development and maintenance. I begin with a look at the socialization of children with disabilities in terms of the ways in which they become identified with and develop identities through their disabilities. Second, I follow this with a brief discussion of societal messages that demonstrate and/or institutionalize negative attitudes about sexuality and disability. Third, I examine a few specific issues relevant to disabled/ablebodied sexual relationships. In the final section, I review what has been said about how people with disabilities negotiate their relationships and provide some tentative guidelines for partners with and without disabilities.

SOCIALIZATION OF CHILDREN WITH DISABILITIES

Children with disabilities enter the world with minority status (Braithwaite, Emry, & Wiseman, 1984). Typically the sole disabled family member, they are socialized at home and in the larger society in accordance with the norms and attitudes displayed in both these environments. Generally, attitudes surrounding disability are rigid, negative, and limiting (Braithwaite, 1985; Farina & Ring, 1965; Fish & Smith, 1983; Kleck, Hiroshi, & Hastorf, 1986; Thompson & Seibold, 1978; Zola, 1982b, 1984). Much attention is often lavished on disabled persons' physical needs while social, emotional, and sexual needs are downplayed, discontinued, or ignored altogether (Zola, 1982a).

According to Olkin (1997), children with disabilities are likely to witness the stigmatization and ostracization of disabled peers and have few adults with disabilities after which to model themselves. They acquire self-concepts amid a variety of mixed familial, peer, societal, and media messages that question their potential for life relationship success as well as their worth as human beings. They become objectified through politically correct labels and medicalization, wherein health professionals equate who children are with the level of function of their bodies. Olkin further noted that children with disabilities may feel they lack control not only over how their bodies feel and respond but also over who touches their bodies, and when, how, and for whom their "defective parts" are placed on display. Children who are disabled may also come to understand genetic testing and disease prevention strategies to mean that people like themselves should not be born and that a life like theirs is not worth living (Olkin, 1997).

These children discover, through attempts at social interaction and play, that being different adversely affects how other children assess their limitations (Thompson, 1982a) as well as their playmate and/or friendship suitabilities. They soon learn that a disability harnesses them with the burden of responsibility for approaching others and making friends (Asch, 1984; Weinberg, 1982). Ablebodied children learn that, although helping people with disabilities is positive, engaging in friendships with them carries significantly greater social risk (Blackman & Dembo, 1984; Weiserbs & Gottlieb, 1995).

During adolescence, when dating and sexuality are usually explored, disabled youth generally come to realize that the standard norms of attraction and romance do not apply to them. Discussions about romance and sex are often avoided by parents, teachers, health care providers, and sometimes also by ablebodied siblings and/or peers, either in a misguided attempt to shelter children with disabilities from emotional pain, or because they perceive these issues to be irrelevant (Hwang, 1997). Correspondingly, children and adolescents with disabilities are frequently encouraged to focus their energies on goals presumed to be more realistic and attainable than dating, marriage, and childbearing—school being a common point of emphasis (Phillips, 1990). The tendency for messages surrounding their sexuality to be mixed, when mentioned at all, is illustrated well by a respondent in Phillips' study. This blind woman reported that during her childhood, her family alternatively advised her to work hard at becoming self-sufficient, because she would be unlikely to marry, and that she should marry a kind, ablebodied boy to take care of her.

The traditional gender role, taught to virtually all females, holds that girls should be "sugar and spice and everything nice." The song, *At Seventeen*, written and so eloquently sung by Janis Ian, also informs us that it is the pretty girls who get to go on dates. Often, girls with disabilities are not considered marriageable (Simon, 1988; Welner, 1997), which can be devastating to their feelings of self-worth (Hwang, 1997). In fact, girls who are disabled before adolescence rate their parents' expectations for their potential to marry and have children lower than daughters who become disabled during or after adolescence (Rousso, 1988). Emphasis placed on the female as caregiver, learned by both sexes in childhood, has been noted as a primary contributor to divorce when a wife becomes disabled and dependent on her husband (Greengross, 1976; Mairs, 1996).

For disabled boys, the process is similar. Boys learn that, above all, they should not be weak or emotional, like girls (Bem, 1993). They absorb the male myths of sexuality—that sex must always lead to orgasm; men should always be ready .and anxious for sex; the penis is the primary instrument of sexuality; that males must be able to always perform and satisfy their partners; and that those who cannot perform are inadequate and unworthy of lovers (Tepper, 1997; Zilbergeld, 1992). Men who are disabled are commonly judged as sexual noncontenders because they may appear limited when observed through the lens of the traditional male gender role, which mandates self-sufficiency, competitiveness (especially in athletics), and physical strength. Phillips (1990) described one young man with a disability who arrived at the front door of his date's home, only to be promptly dismissed by her father with the remark that no daughter of his would be permitted to date someone who was not a whole man.

Disabled children, having formed their identities amid a continual flurry of mixed, often discontinuing messages about their worth as human beings, their physical and/or mental capabilities, and their relationship potentialities, tend to acquire lower self-esteem than ablebodied children (Thompson, 1982a, 1987), They reach adulthood only to face similar types of stigmatization and attitudinal barriers. In the next section, these societal influences that affect disabled/ablebodied persons' communication and relationships are discussed.

SOCIETAL ATTITUDES TOWARD SEXUALITY AND DISABILITY

It is well established that communication between the disabled and ablebodied is characterized, at least initially, by rigidity, stereotyped perceptions, uncertainty, and discomfort and that having a disability negatively impacts relationships between these groups (Belgrave & Mills, 1981; Braithwaite et al., 1984; Kleck, 1968; Thompson, 1982b). Where possible, ablebodied persons are likely to avoid communication with people with disabilities altogether (Thompson, 1982b).

The vast array of media messages reflect and/or reinforce a presumed dual dimensionality of people with disabilities (Zola, 1984). Messages depicting an outstanding–helpless dichotomy dominate, portraying them either as heroic super crips or as tragic, usually embittered and angry, unfortunates worthy only of pity and charity. They are seldom seen as whole and complex, leading the same kinds of everyday lives as ablebodied people (Kroll & Klein, 1992). As illustration of the helplessness message, Hwang (1997) noted:

> Women with disabilities in soap operas generally tend to languish pathetically at home clad in robes until they have the decency to die poignantly or, they remove themselves from the plot so their husbands can find real women; that is, unless they become miraculously cured and then go on to resume normal lives, (p. 121)

Zola (1983) took issue with the opposite pole of the dichotomy—the super-crip image of people who "overcome" their disabilities, stating that this message is misleading and detrimental. It sets up the presumption that the only admirable or even acceptable way of adapting to disability is to refuse to be limited by it. The life-long work of disability maintenance, and the mundane successes and disappointments of daily living are misconstrued by the super-crip image as giving in and failing to try (Zola, 1983).

Societal messages about sexuality and disability seem to indicate that the American public fails to perceive people with disabilities as sexual beings. Society's narrow definitions of what constitutes sex; for whom romantic relationships are acceptable and natural; and the monumental value it places on health, youth, beauty, and physical perfection keep sexuality and disability taboo (Zola, 1982a). "Sick people" are not expected to have desires or be desired (particularly not by ablebodied people), despite evidence that people with disabilities do engage in and enjoy romantic/sexual relationships (Kroll & Klein, 1992; Mairs1996; White, Rintala, Hart, & Fuhrer, 1993; Zola, 1982a, 1982b).,

This message, so deeply ingrained, is incorporated into societal structures. Many institutions for people with disabilities are architecturally designed and monitored to prevent "unacceptable" relational behaviors such as romance and sex from occurring (Hwang, 1997). The fact that women with disabilities may need gynecological and/or obstetric care is overlooked by the failure to make office and examination procedures/equipment accessible (Welner, 1997). Additionally, the social security system incorporates major financial penalties for marriage into the rules for its disabled recipients of federal support (Waxman, 1994).

Stigmatization and attitudinal barriers surrounding disability affect the development and maintenance of romantic relationships. In the next section, I explore four issues: passing, equity, emotion, and autonomy as they relate to disability and disabled/ablebodied romantic relationships.

ADULT ROMANTIC RELATIONSHIPS AND DISABILITY

I remember clearly the first time I went to a restaurant with a romantic partner and was asked, "Would you like a Braille menu?" I was horrified. I had been found out, and I cried over the loss of my ability to "pass:"—to pass myself off as ablebodied. For those of us with disabilities, passing is a way to avoid stigmatization (Goffman, 1963). Socially, passing may be perceived as a way of appearing more approachable and, for some people with disabilities, a way to improve chances of attracting an ablebodied romantic partner (Phillips, 1990). Some disabled persons restrict the number of possible relational partners by refusing to befriend and/or date other disabled persons, viewing their decision as an issue of perceived social marketability. That is, "settling" for a disabled partner is tantamount to admitting an inability to compete for the choice goods of the sexual market (Phillips, 1990). Ironically, this attitude may extend to a generalized suspicion of ablebodied people who choose to initiate a relationship, particularly a romantic relationship, with someone who has a disability (Mairs, 1996; Phillips, 1990). Sometimes, ablebodied partners attempt to cloak disability to avoid undue attention, stigma by association, or being judged as strange and/or suspect for dating someone with a disability (Phillips, 1990). Too often, discrimination occurs because of the belief that to associate with a person who has a disability, whether as friend, lover, or acquaintance, must mean there is also something wrong with the ablebodied person (Fisher & Galler, 1988).

At times, people fall into more than one minority group and may attempt to choose in which way they most hope to pass. For example, gays and lesbians with disabilities are doubly stigmatized; some choose to accentuate their sexuality and hide their disability because they view the latter as being more denigrating (Appleby, 1994). This can be especially isolating (Saad, 1997). According to Hillyer (1993), a person who is both homosexual and disabled is usually the only member of a family who is characterized by both of these stigmatizing identities. Unlike the pride instilled by family members and communities surrounding race or ethnicity, families typically train gay disabled members to feel ashamed and to hide these identities. For gays who have AIDS and are asymptomatic, passing is relatively easy because society holds the general presumption that all people are heterosexual and ablebodied unless proven otherwise (Anderson & Wolf, 1986).

Fisher and Galler (1988) interviewed women involved in disabled/ablebodied friendships; because friendship is often a component of romance, perhaps some of their data may also have implications for romantic relationships. Fisher and Galler found reciprocity to be a friendship theme valued by both partners. Respondents discovered through their own friendships that reciprocity is a key element in maintaining a shared sense of relational equity. Years ago, I became extremely offended when people referred to my ablebodied romantic partner as "special" for dating a disabled woman. To me, this attitude implied that my partner was "special" for choosing to be with someone who could not contribute equally to the relationship. Considering the beliefs that society holds about relationship roles and the limitations of people with disabilities to fulfill those roles, the attitude that disabled/ablebodied relationships are inevitably unbalanced is not very surprising; this may be a barrier through which relational partners need to work.

People with disabilities sometimes feel they have to be especially "good" relational partners to make up for what their lovers are giving up by staying with them—the potential for a "normal" relationship. They sometimes believe they have to compensate for their disability-caused relational limitations by being overly giving, supportive partners (Fisher & Galler, 1988). One way this gets translated into behavior is denial or suppression of any negative or unpleasant emotions. There is the sense that expression of discontent, including anger, implies that they are ungrateful for their kind treatment (Zola, 1982a). If they internalize the anger, it can lead to self-loathing and/or resentment; if they vent the anger, they run the risk of being perceived as the stereotypical bitter cripple with the expectation that the world owes them. There is often a thin line between martyrdom and self-pity, and there is a fear of a rejection that will not only be emotionally damaging but will also leave them with limited assistance. My current partner summed this up by telling a friend, "She thinks that if she pisses me off, she won't get any help."

Emotional strength exhibited by suppression of negative emotions can be part of the air of independence. According to Phillips (1990), most of us have deeply internalized the folk ideas: "stand on your own two feet," "it is better to give than to receive," and "we must help those who cannot help themselves." Thus, the conditions under which one should ask for and/or provide assistance (especially in initial interactions) typically have been clouded by uncertainty (Emry & Wiseman, 1987; Emry, Wiseman, & Morgan, 1986). Over the years, I have heard many ablebodied people say that people with disabilities do not want help, they want to be independent. Thus, to attempt to help a disabled person, they believe, may be interpreted as insulting or paternalistic and lead to negative feelings or interactions. Sometimes this does occur. Likewise, people with disabilities, especially in the era of the Americans with Disabilities Act, are expected to desire independence. For myself, and my friends with disabilities, there is anxiety surrounding the notion of allowing ourselves to become "too" dependent on our romantic partners for fear of greater vulnerability should those relationships end.

Concerns over equity and autonomy are not one-sided. According to Fisher and Galler (1988), ablebodied women feel a sense of responsibility for their disabled friends. They also experience uncertainty about what their own rights are within the relationship. In other words, even though, they tend to understand and confirm their disabled friends' rights to emotional and physical support, they seem to be less certain of their own entitlements within the relationship.

In my experience, ablebodied partners sometimes feel they are maneuvering through a relational mine field, moving carefully and waiting for a wrong word or action to blow up in their faces, unsure of the exact amount of empathy or assistance that will prevent accusations of paternalism or indifference. I have been told that they struggle, too, over when to insist on helping and when to let go and believe that if we say we can do something or that we do not want help, we mean it. My partner has found this to be especially difficult when I am angry at him because he knows my instinct is to blast the message "I'll show you that I don't need you around!" This situation has been nicely illustrated on occasions of my insistence on paying $25 to take a taxi home from his house and his insistence on driving me home after we have had a fight; it has always been for me, on some level, a struggle over power and control.

Despite barriers to relationship development and struggles with the issues discussed above, people do come together as romantic couples. Understanding that we come to these disabled/ablebodied relationships with societally imposed disability baggage is perhaps the first step in negotiating relationships that work. The next section is focused on the reported ways in which people who are satisfied with their disabled/ablebodied romantic relationships have negotiated issues and/or roles within them.

NEGOTIATING DISABLED/ABLEBODIED ROMANTIC RELATIONSHIPS

People who have satisfying disabled/ablebodied romantic relationships seem to have successfully stepped beyond their socialization to redefine relational roles and expectations. According to Tepper (1997), part of this negotiation can include the redefinition or complete rejection of traditional gender roles (i.e., who works outside the home and who cares for the house and children). It may also involve attitudinal shifts in definitions of acceptable and fulfilling sex. Because for some disabling conditions, sex can be problematic—in terms of privacy (Heslinga, Schellen, & Verkuyl, 1974), mechanics and positioning (Hwang, 1997; Tepper, 1997), as well as physiological responses to illness (Nichols, 1995) and/or side effects of medications (Schover, 1989)—experimentation and discussion become essential Many people attribute new value and fulfillment to touch, communication and pleasuring that may or may not lead to intercourse and/or orgasm (Zola, 1982a).

Relational partners need both autonomy and connection (Baxter, 1993). Therefore, disabled/ablebodied couples need to negotiate satisfying levels and types of reciprocal support. This negotiation could involve agreeing to attribute equal value to physical, emotional, and mental forms of support, deciding to obtain volunteers and/or hire outside help for certain tasks, and may also entail what Baxter referred to as reframing: "transformation of meaning in which the contrasting elements of a given contradiction cease to be regarded as antithetical to one another" (Baxter, 1993, p. 101). For example, a couple might reframe "assistance with bathing" as "bathing together," or they may reframe assistance with transportation to work from "dependency" to "car pooling."

Over time, they may discover circumstances where passing is desirable, and become coconspirators. They may agree that the ablebodied partner should serve as a mediator in certain contexts (i.e., securing appropriate accommodations in a restaurant) or speak for the disabled partner (i.e., defending against stigmatization or discrimination). These actions tend to occur once partners have become comfortable with each other and the disability's place in the relationship, but caution is needed to avoid discontinuing the partner with the disability or crossing boundaries of independence or a disabled person's desire to educate the general public (Fisher & Galler, 1988).

Disabled/ablebodied couples may need to establish boundaries that maintain comfortable levels of dialectical tension not only between autonomy and connection, but also between openness and closedness in their relational communication. The ultimate value of complete openness and honesty in relationships is an interpersonal myth. For married couples, Bienvenu (1970) noted: "Regulating the disclosure of private information has been identified by some as a more productive route to a successful marriage than practicing complete openness" (p. 222). Partners must recognize that disclosure of private information including expression of anger, resentment, and other negative emotions, although important for each, must be balanced within the long-term goals of the relationship. Together, couples can work toward a sense of trust in each other's abilities to both express and receive unpleasant messages (Zola, 1982a). Confirmation and mutual respect are key.

CONCLUSION

Children with disabilities are typically socialized within families and cultures that hold negative attitudes toward and perceptions of disability. Through media representations, family communications, and social interaction, disabled girls and boys are bombarded with messages that they are less desirable or outright unfit as romantic partners. In adulthood, these internalizations can result in struggles over issues of passing, autonomy, reciprocity, and validity in establishing and maintaining romantic relationships. Disabled/ablebodied couples satisfied with their relationships are likely to redefine roles and expectations, reframe dialectical tensions, and develop trust in their abilities to communicate effectively.

DISCUSSION QUESTIONS

1. How does the socialization of children with disabilities affect how they view their relationship potentialities? How might it affect their communication with potential romantic partners?

2. Think of societal messages you have received about people with disabilities over your lifetime. Choose three and discuss how these have helped and hindered you in communicating with others who have disabilities.

3. Discuss the potential advantages and disadvantages of passing for both disabled and able-bodied partners in a relationship. What might be some circumstances when couples would agree to try and pass? How could this be negotiated?

SECTION IV

Social Institutions: Family, Work, Education, Religion, and Health

T he next set of readings covers social institutions. Social institutions are "a collection of patterned social practices that are repeated continuously and regularly over time and supported by social norms" (Ferris & Stein, 2013). We come into contact with these institutions daily, and they shape and constrain our lives. Social institutions are also agents of socialization that shape how we think about the world, conforming our norms and values to that of the dominant culture. In this section, we first begin with the most influential social institution and agent of socialization—the family.

Beginning with family life, the nature of families is that they are ever evolving. There has been a variety of movements to save or preserve the "traditional" family in our society. The idea is that a specific "traditional" familial configuration is under attack and things must be done; laws must be passed to ensure that this specific—again, "traditional"—familial configuration remains intact. Families, like other social phenomena we have discussed, are culturally specific. Their meaning, function, and configuration have changed over the course of time. The meaning of family is not static, but changes as society changes.

When we think of a traditional family in our society, we think of a nuclear family—mother, father, and children. The idea of a "traditional" family marginalizes those familial configurations that fall outside of the "normative" model. The (in)famous Moynihan Report (1965), conducted by former U.S. senator and sociologist Daniel Patrick Moynihan, saw pathology and disintegration in black families headed by single mothers. He saw families headed by these women as the foundational reason for black poverty. This explanation, however, stigmatized and blamed nontraditional black familial configurations for black poverty, while neglecting structural mechanisms codified by the government such as segregation, job discrimination, and other aspects of institutionalized racism for its role in constructing these conditions. While it is true that rates of marriage among African Americans are much lower than that of Whites, focusing on one definition of family ignores the strength of alternative familial configurations that are present among nonwhites.

In "The Color of Family Ties: Race, Class, Gender, and Extended Family Involvement," Naomi Gerstel and Natalia Sarkisian discuss the different familial configurations of people of color. This reading examines the prevalence and importance of extended family ties of nonwhites. These familial configurations are just as important in providing resources, both tangible and intangible, to nonwhite families. A monolithic definition of family renders these non-nuclear families invisible, problematizing and devaluing their existence.

When it comes to marriage, it is assumed that everyone—especially women—wants or should want to get married. To not be married (again, especially for women) has been seen as deviant in our society. If a woman is not married, it is because she cannot get married due to some fault of her own. Society has used some pretty demeaning words for unmarried women such as "spinster" or "old maid" to characterize the flaws causing the unmarried woman's fate. The reading "Out of Wedlock: Why Some Poor Women Reject Marriage" by Margaret Walsh chronicles the narratives of poor and working-class unmarried mothers about their status as unmarried women and mothers. Their voices and experiences challenge heteronormative assumptions about the institution of marriage and the assumed benefits they confer to women especially, as well as situating these women as active agents in the direction of their own lives.

There was a time when marriage for women was seen as more of a necessity, less of an option than it is today. Because women were shut out of many economic opportunities granted to men, they were forced to depend on men economically. The need for marriage served not only to elevate a woman's social status, but to even validate her existence; her survival was oftentimes dependent on her attachment to a man. Even during this time in our society, not all women wanted to be married and argued that only men benefit from marriage. A woman's wants, needs, and dreams were expected to take a backseat to those of her husband's and family's. For women, marriage was a form of enslavement and a barrier to realizing their full potential as a human being. The next reading is about a woman living during the late 19th and early 20th centuries who was quite vocal about her disdain for marriage. "A Feminist Search for Love: Emma Goldman on the Politics of Marriage, Love, Sexuality, and the Feminine" by Lori J. Marso introduces students, and perhaps sociologists, to the writings of the anarchist Emma Goldman on the sociopolitical institution of marriage, gender relations, family, and the emancipation of women.

Similar to marriage, having children is something that has been seen as a "natural" desire by women to realize their full potential. If nothing else, childbearing has been seen as the primary purpose for women in our world. Having children in and of itself has evolved in meaning as society has evolved. Where having multiple children was once a necessity in order to help generate economic resources, children went from being small workers to this entirely new social category in the 20th century, where they were seen not as small adults, but larger babies to be cared for by their parents or guardians up until the age of 18—sometimes longer! No longer are children seen as economic resources; now, they take up resources.

The advent of birth control had a dramatic impact on women's ability to plan their families and have greater control over planning their own lives. However, even today, a woman choosing to not have children, though acceptable, is not considered "normal." It produces an identity that is suspect to many and subject to questioning. In "Marginal and Misunderstood: The Myths and Realities of Living Childfree," Laura Scott discusses the marginal status conferred to childless adults, especially couples and the assumptions that contribute to their stigmatization.

The next couple of readings discuss different aspects of work. In this country, the saying is that if you work hard you can attain the American Dream. However, there is a variety of constraining mechanisms that do not guarantee this outcome; this has become increasingly difficult in recent decades, given major shifts in our economy. Many low-skilled jobs have been moved overseas, credentialization is more important in the job market than ever before, and wages have remained stagnant while inflation has increased. In "The Job Market," Daniel Dohan continues his research of barrio life in Southern California, focusing here on the work life of barrio residents. Many of these residents are what is referred to as the working poor—they work, sometimes two or three jobs, but are still barely able to make ends meet. These jobs lack a living wage, meaning that the wages earned from their job(s) are not enough to live off of.

One barrier to equal access to the American Dream has been employment discrimination. It was not until the Civil Rights Act of 1964 that it became illegal to discriminate based on race, sex, religion, and creed. It was also during this time that affirmative action became a tool to help ensure that employers would abide by the Civil Rights Act. This tool has been hotly contested and racialized in the discourse on American employment and higher education. In the reading "White Identity and Affirmative Action," Beverly Daniel Tatum investigates how Whites perceive, interpret, and react to affirmative action. While doing so, she also breaks down what affirmative action is and its purpose and goals, as well as explaining how it works to combat the enormous effects of subtle racism.

Education is another agent of socialization that socializes us from childhood to learn to become functioning members of society. All children by law must participate in education, but as *Brown v. Board of Education* revealed to the public, not all American education is equal, and there are great disparities between black and White segregated schools. Even after school segregation was deemed illegal by the Supreme Court, there are vast differences between resource-rich schools and those with poor resources. The differences can even be seen in how the students of these schools see themselves and others in the world. "Learning Privilege: Lessons of Power and Identity in Affluent Schooling" by Adam Howard gives us insight into the less-often-studied "elite schools," their educational framework, and overall worldview from which they operate and transmit knowledge to their students.

Religion, like many other social institutions is a dynamic structure that morphs and changes, much like a cell in one's body throughout the course of time. Religious denominations are always forced to respond to the social issues of their time, using their interpretation of their religious text and understanding to guide them on their path. Whether it be issues regarding race, gender, or sexuality, religion shapes society just as much as society shapes religion. In "Religious Coalitions for and Against Gay Marriage: The Culture War Rages On," David C. Campbell and Carin Robinson study the coalitions formed across religious faiths, as well as the rupture within Judeo-Christian denominations regarding the issue of gay rights and gay marriage, in particular during the height of the same-sex marriage controversy.

As a social institution, the health care field teaches us what is healthy and what is not. We all know what the four food groups are because of the institutionalization of health and medicine and its partnership with education and the media. Through a similar synergizing of institutions, we know to wash our hands regularly because it has been shown to prevent virus and disease transmission. However, like any social institution, health care is a reflection of social norms, and at the same time helps shape our norms. It is socially constructed and not purely based in objective scientific reasoning.

Some people argue that our society has become increasingly medicalized. Medicalization is referred to as the labeling of certain behaviors and conditions as medical—given meaning as a medical problem. It is a social enterprise which uses the medical field to control and construct illnesses out of behavior that is problematized. For example, alcoholics and addicts were once thought of as bad people. Now, they are sick people in need of medical intervention. Conversely, homosexuality was once thought of as an illness in need of medical intervention; now, it is no longer seen as problematic by the medical community. The same goes for home births. Women have been giving birth to children in hospitals only in recent history. I can refer to my own grandmother as a classic example of this new trend. She had seven children, and only the last one, my mother, was born in a hospital. Now, home birth is seen as deviant, meaning not the norm and something people react negatively to. Similarly, breast-feeding had to actually make a comeback because at some point in the 20th century, formula was promoted by the government, the corporations who make it, and the medical industry as "normal" and less problematic than mother's milk! Home birth today is seen as either "woo woo" or just downright irresponsible and dangerous. In "Introduction: A Lifetime's Labor: Women and Power in the Birthplace," the introductory chapter to the book *Laboring On* by Barbara Katz Rothman, the author reflects on how her personal choice to have a home birth spurred a lifetime career of investigating the medicalization of childbearing and its subsequent marginalization.

Another reading on health, "Race, Social Contexts, and Health: Examining Geographic Spaces and Places" by Takeuchi, Walton, and Leung, looks at the effect residential segregation has on health outcomes on racial minorities. The health disparities between Whites, Hispanics, and blacks are well documented. However, researchers are finding that inequality plays a larger role in the production of illness than anyone ever imagined. Even something as seemingly biologically deterministic like our health is shaped and constrained by social factors and geography.

REFERENCES

Ferris, Kerry, and Jill Stein. *The Real World: An Introduction to Sociology*. 4th ed. New York, London: Norton, 2014.

DISCUSSION QUESTIONS

1. How have social changes affected the idea of "traditional" roles for women in the family and society? How are these roles affected by race and class?
2. In what ways have broader societal changes impacted the idea of "traditional" roles for women within the family? How are these roles affected by race and class?
3. How are some lessons that students learn unintentional? Why are these unintentional lessons the most consequential for what students are learning in school?
4. In what ways are health and illness socially constructed? Offer examples.

THE COLOR OF FAMILY TIES

RACE, CLASS, GENDER, AND EXTENDED FAMILY INVOLVEMENT

By Naomi Gerstel and Natalia Sarkisian

When talking about family obligations and solidarities, politicians and social commentators typically focus on the ties between married couples and their children. We often hear that Black and Latino/a, especially Puerto Rican, families are more disorganized than White families, and that their family ties are weaker, because rates of non-marriage and single parenthood are higher among these minority groups. But this focus on the nuclear family ignores extended family solidarities and caregiving activities. Here we examine these often overlooked extended kinship ties.

Taking this broader perspective on family relations refutes the myth that Blacks and Latinos/as lack strong families. Minority individuals are more likely to live in extended family homes than Whites and in many ways more likely to help out their aging parents, grandparents, adult children, brothers, sisters, cousins, aunts, uncles, and other kin.

According to our research using the second wave of the National Survey of Families and Households, as Figures 21.1 and 21.2 show, Blacks and Latinos/as, both women and men, are much more likely than Whites to share a home with extended kin: 42 percent of Blacks and 37 percent of Latinos/as, but only 20 percent of Whites, live with relatives. Similar patterns exist for living near relatives: 54 percent of Blacks and 51 percent of Latinos/as, but only 37 percent of Whites, live within two miles of kin. Blacks and Latinos/as are also more likely than Whites to frequently visit kin. For example, 76 percent of Blacks, 71 percent of Latinos/as, but just 63 percent of Whites see their relatives once a week or more.

Even if they don't live together, Blacks and Latinos/as are as likely as Whites—and in some ways more likely—to be supportive family members. But there are important racial and ethnic differences in the type of support family members give each other. Whites are more likely than ethnic minorities to give and receive large sums of money, and White women are more likely

Naomi Gerstel and Natalia Sarkisian, "The Color of Family Ties: Race, Class, Gender, and Extended Family Involvement," *American Families, A Multicultural Reader*, 2nd edition; ed. Stephanie Coontz . Copyright © 2008 by Taylor & Francis Group. Reprinted with permission.

247

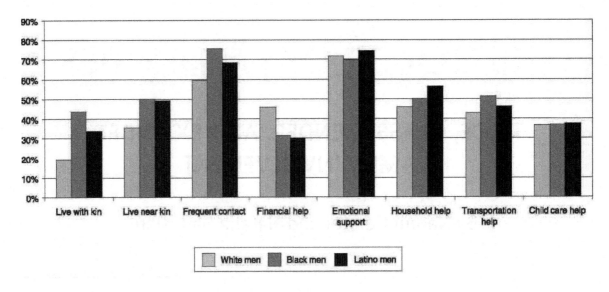

FIGURE 21.1: ETHNICITY AND EXTENDED KIN INVOLVEMENT AMONG MEN

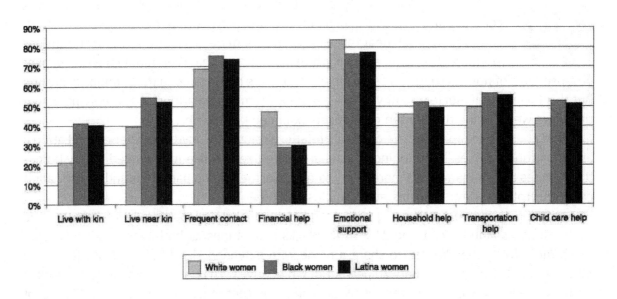

FIGURE 21.2: ETHNICITY AND EXTENDED KIN INVOLVEMENT AMONG WOMEN

than minority women to give and receive emotional support, such as discussing personal problems and giving each other advice. When it comes to help with practical tasks, however, we find that Black and Latino/a relatives are more likely than Whites to be supportive: they are more likely to give each other help with household work and childcare, as well as with providing rides and running errands. These differences are especially pronounced among women.

This is not to say that Black and Latino men are not involved with kin, as is implied in popular images of minority men hanging out on street corners rather than attending to family ties. In fact, Black and Latino men are more likely than White men to live near relatives and to stay in touch with them. White men, however, are more likely to give and receive large-scale financial help. Moreover, the three groups of men are very similar when it comes to giving and getting practical help and emotional support.

These data suggest that if we only consider married couples or parents and their young children, we are missing much of what families in general and families of color in particular do for each other. A focus on nuclear families in discussions of race differences in family life creates a biased portrait of families of color.

EXPLAINING RACE DIFFERENCES: IS IT CULTURE OR CLASS?

When discussing differences in family experiences of various racial and ethnic groups, commentators often assume that these differences can be traced to cultural differences or competing "family values." Sometimes these are expressed in a positive way, as in the stereotype that Latino families have more extended ties because of their historical traditions and religious values. Other times these are expressed in a negative way, as when Blacks are said to lack family values because of the cultural legacy of slavery and subsequent years of oppression. Either way, differences in family behaviors are often explained by differences in cultural heritage.

In contrast, in our research, we find that social class rather than culture is the key to understanding the differences in extended family ties and behaviors between Whites and ethnic minorities. To be sure, differences in cultural values do exist. Blacks and Latinos/as are more likely than Whites to say they believe that extended family is important; both groups are also more likely to attend religious services. Blacks tend to hold more egalitarian beliefs about gender than Whites, while Latinos/as, especially Mexican Americans, tend to hold more "traditional" views. But these differences in values do not explain racial differences in actual involvement with relatives. It is, instead, social class that matters most in explaining these differences.

It is widely known (and confirmed by U.S. Census data presented in Table 21.1) that Blacks and Latinos/as tend to have far less income and education than Whites. Families of color are also are much more likely than White families to be below the official poverty line. In our research, we find that the differences in extended family ties and behaviors between Whites and ethnic minorities are primarily the result of these social class disparities.

TABLE 21.1: EDUCATION, INCOME, AND POVERTY RATES BY RACE

	WHITES	BLACKS	LATINOS/AS
Median household income	$50,784	$30,858	$35,967
Percentage below poverty line	8.4%	24.7%	22.0%
Education:			
Less than high school	14.5%	27.6%	47.6%
High school graduate	58.5%	58.1%	42.0%
Bachelor's degree or higher	27.0%	14.3%	10.4%

Source: U.S. Census Bureau, 2005.

Simply put, White, Black, and Latino/a individuals with the same amount of income and education have similar patterns of involvement with their extended families. Just like poor minorities, impoverished Whites are more likely to exchange practical aid and visit with extended kin than are their wealthier counterparts. Just like middle-class Whites, middle-class Blacks and Latinos/as are more likely to talk about their personal concerns or share money with relatives than are their poorer counterparts.

More specifically, it is because Whites tend to have more income than Blacks and Latinos/as that they are more likely to give money to their relatives or get it from them. And the higher levels of emotional support among White women can be at least in part traced to their higher levels of education, perhaps because schooling encourages women to talk out their problems and makes them more likely to give (and get) advice.

Conversely, we find that the relative economic deprivation of racial/ethnic minorities leads in many ways to higher levels of extended family involvement. Individuals' lack of economic resources increases their need for help from kin and boosts their willingness to give help in return. Because Blacks and Latinos/as typically have less income and education than Whites, they come to rely more on their relatives for daily needs such as child care, household tasks, or rides. The tendency of Blacks and Latinos/as to live with or near kin may also reflect their greater need for kin cooperation, as well as their decreased opportunities and pressures to move away, including moving for college.

SOCIAL CLASS AND FAMILIAL TRADE OFFs

How do our findings on race, social class, and familial involvement challenge common understandings of minority families? They show that poor minority families do not necessarily lead lives of social isolation or lack strong family solidarities. The lower rates of marriage among impoverished groups may reflect not a rejection of family values but a realistic assessment of how little a woman (and her children) may be able to depend upon marriage. Sociologists Kathryn Edin and Maria Kefalas (2007) recently found that because disadvantaged men are often unable to offer women the kind of economic security that advantaged men provide, poor women are less likely to marry. Instead, these women create support networks beyond the nuclear family, regularly turning to extended kin for practical support.

Reliance on extended kin and lack of marital ties are linked. In another analysis of the National Survey of Families and Households, we found that, contrary to much rhetoric about marriage as a key source of adult social ties, marriage actually diminishes ties to kin. Married people—women as well as men—are less involved with their parents and siblings than those never married or previously married. These findings indicate a trade off between commitments to nuclear and extended family ties. Marriage, we have found, is a "greedy" institution: it has a tendency to consume the bulk of people's energies and emotions and to dilute their commitments beyond the nuclear family.

On the one hand, then, support given to spouses and intimate partners sometimes comes at the expense of broader kin and community ties. Indeed, married adult children take care of elderly parents less often than their unmarried siblings. Marriage can also cut people odd from networks of mutual aid. Married mothers, for example, whether Black, Latina, or White, are often unable to obtain help from kin in the way that their single counterparts can. Although the "greedy" nature of marriage may pose a problem across social class, it is especially problematic for those less well off economically, as these individuals most need to cultivate wider circles of obligation, mutual aid, and reciprocity.

On the other hand, support to relatives sometimes comes at the expense of care for partners, and can interfere with nuclear family formation or stability. Indeed, individuals who are deeply immersed in relationships with extended families may be less likely to get married or, if they marry, may be less likely to put the marital ties first in their loyalties. Several decades ago in her observations of a poor Black community, anthropologist Carol Stack (1974) found that the reciprocal patterns of sharing with kin and "fictive kin" forged in order to survive hardship often made it difficult for poor Blacks either to move up economically or to marry. To prevent the dilution of their social support networks, some extended families may even discourage their members from getting married, or unconsciously sabotage relationships that threaten to pull someone out of the family orbit. As sociologists Domínguez and Watkins (2003) argue, the ties of mutual aid that help impoverished individuals survive on a day-to-day basis may also prevent them from saying "no" to requests that sap their ability to get ahead or pursue individual opportunities.

Overall, we should avoid either denigrating or glorifying the survival strategies of the poor. Although social class disparities are key to understanding racial and ethnic variation in familial involvement, it is too simple to say that class differences create "more" involvement with relatives in one group and "less" in another. In some ways economic deprivation increases ties to kin (e.g., in terms of living nearby or exchanging practical help) and in other ways it reduces them (e.g., in terms of financial help or emotional support). These findings remind us that love and family connections are expressed both through talk and action. Equally important, focusing solely on the positive or on the negative aspects of either minority or White families is problematic. Instead, we need to think in terms of trade offs—among different kinds of care and between the bonds of kinship and the bonds of marriage. Both trade offs are linked to social class.

WHY DO THESE DIFFERENCES IN FAMILY LIFE MATTER?

Commentators often emphasize the disorganization and dysfunction of Black and Latino/a family life. They suggest that if we could "fix" family values in minority communities and get them to form married-couple households, all their problems would be solved. This argument misunderstands causal connections by focusing on the family as the source of problems. Specifically, it ignores the link between race and class and attributes racial or ethnic differences to cultural values. Instead, we argue, it is important to understand that family strategies and behaviors often emerge in response to the challenges of living in economic deprivation or constant economic insecurity. Therefore, social policies should not focus on changing family behaviors, but rather aim to support a range of existing family arrangements and improve economic conditions for the poor.

Social policies that overlook extended family obligations may introduce, reproduce, or even increase ethnic inequalities. For example, the relatives of Blacks and Latinos/ as are more likely than those of Whites to provide various kinds of support that policymakers tend to assume is only provided by husbands and wives. Such relatives may need the rights and support systems that we usually reserve for spouses. For instance, the Family and Medical Leave Act is an important social policy, but it only guarantees unpaid leave from jobs to provide care to spouses, children or elderly parents requiring medical attention. Our findings suggest that, if we really want to support families, such policies must be broadened to include adult children, needy grown-up brothers and sisters, cousins, aunts and uncles. Similarly, Medicaid regulations that only pay for non-familial care of ill, injured, or disabled individuals implicitly discriminate against Blacks and Latinos/as who provide significant amounts of care to extended kin. "Pro-marriage" policies that give special incentives to impoverished women for getting married may penalize other women who turn down marriage to a risky mate and rely instead on grandparents or other relatives to help raise their children.

Extended family obligations should be recognized and accommodated where possible. But they should not be counted on as a substitute for anti-poverty measures, nor should marriage promotion be used in this way. Policymakers must recognize that support from family—whether extended or nuclear—cannot fully compensate for the disadvantages of being poor, or minority, or both. Neither marital ties nor extended family ties can substitute for educational opportunities, jobs with decent wages, health insurance, and affordable child care. Instead of hoping that poor families pull themselves out of poverty by their own bootstraps, social policy should explicitly aim to rectify economic disadvantages. In turn, improvements in economic opportunities and resources will likely shape families.

DISCUSSION QUESTIONS

1. Why, according to the authors, is the traditional definition of "family values" problematic in sociological study?
2. Why do the authors consider marriage to be a "greedy" institution?
3. How might the Family and Medical Leave Act be amended to benefit lower-class families?

MARGINAL AND MISUNDERSTOOD

THE MYTHS AND REALITIES OF LIVING CHILDFREE

By Laura Scott

"That's selfish." I was in a friend's kitchen, discussing the common motives for remaining childfree, including my own, when she made this rebuke. I was stung. Here was a person who knew me and liked me, so I thought. But apparently she saw a serious flaw. I didn't want to be a parent, so I had pursued other interests, like work, travel, and volunteering with youth. My childless status freed me to make these alternate choices, but in her judgment they were motivated primarily by selfishness. In that moment, I wondered what, short of working with lepers in the slums of Calcutta, could redeem my intentionally childless soul.

Later, I invited attendees of the 2005 No Kidding! Convention in Philadelphia to share with me "the dumbest question you have ever been asked as a childfree person." One woman recalled the time a coworker, informed of her childfree status, asked incredulously, "You and your husband don't have kids?! *So what do you do?*"

There are five definitions, or senses, of the word "marginal" in my *Webster's New Collegiate Dictionary*, two of which seem to accurately describe my experience being childless by choice in North America:

1. Located at the fringe of consciousness.
2. Close to the lower limit of qualification, acceptability, or function.[1]

If you can't imagine a life without kids or you believe parenthood is the only responsible pathway to maturity and fulfillment, or that all married couples should have children in order to propagate the species, preserve our way of life, or serve God's will, how might you respond to the intentionally childless couple?

Judgmentally or supportively? Or perhaps you'd rather not think about it at all, because doing so might open up this prickly question: Why *do* we have kids?

Perhaps it's just easier to cling to the idea that the childless by choice are a minority of nutcases who are in a hopeless state of arrested development, crippled by infantile needs and selfish desires.

THE SELFISH ASSUMPTION AND OTHER MYTHICAL MONSTERS

After that evening with my friend, I felt compelled to define "selfish" for myself. What did it mean to me? I understood it to represent people who pursue their own needs or wants without regard for others. I certainly identified with the first part of the definition—I was focused on my own needs and desires. I was an entrepreneur who lived by the credo "Do what you love, and success will follow." I believed firmly in the win-win principle—that looking after your own best interests and the interests of others are not mutually exclusive pursuits. I happily gave to charities, volunteered my time mentoring teens, and paid taxes. So I felt that the second part of the definition—"without regard for others"—didn't apply to my situation. The negative connotations of selfishness involve the selfish person victimizing someone. Whom was I hurting? Other than depriving my parents of a grandchild, I felt fairly certain that my "selfish" path had been free of roadkill.

Call me self-determining, not selfish.

The "selfish" label should not have bothered me. If I know I'm not selfish, why should I care what other people think? But I did. And I do—for myself and the other childfree by choice. If we allow these stereotypes to persist or go unchallenged, we invite discrimination and marginalization. If others believe we have chosen the childfree path based purely on selfish motives, then they can assume selfishness trumps all the other, more compelling reasons to remain childless.

When I started my research, I quickly found that I was not the only childfree person disturbed by the "selfish" label. When I asked my participants, "What myth or assumption about people who are childfree/childless by choice do you feel is the most unfair or misleading?" the response I received most often was: "that we are selfish."

One of my participants, Kathryn, said, "I think that thinking it through and deciding not to bring a child into this world—knowing the type of person you are—is one of the most unselfish acts you can do."

Kathryn knew women who had remarried who already had children from a previous marriage, and yet had felt pressured by their new husband to have another child, due to what Kathryn characterized as ego. "He wants to have his own child, to carry on his name; the stepchildren are not enough. And I just think if people really loved children and just wanted a family unit, then there are orphanages around the world packed with children who need homes. But it's not about that. Kids are an extension of themselves, so that plays in my head when people throw out the 'selfish' thing."

Theresa's response typified that of my other respondents: "Selfishness is by far the most unfair and tiresome assumption people make. They assume we are rolling in cash and live in a mansion and take lavish holidays every year. Ha! I wish." Theresa called it the "default assumption," and although this annoyed her to no end, she realized people had no basis to believe otherwise: "They don't know me. They don't know the dollars I give to charity. They don't know the time I devote to women's issues. They don't know that I will drop everything to come to the aid of my friends and family."

As my survey revealed, there are many reasons why someone might choose childlessness. Yet selfishness remains the assumed motive, despite a lack of evidence to support that claim.

A 1998 British study of childless men and women, conducted by Fiona McAllister and Lynda Clarke at the Family Policy Studies Center, concluded that "childfree people were not self-centered individuals. The absence of children did not necessarily mean the absence of other caring responsibilities." This was true in my own sample of interview subjects as well. I encountered many voluntarily childless people who, like Nick and Diane (profiled in Chapter 5), had taken responsibility for the care of elderly parents and other relatives, or had harbored young relatives for long periods, or had adopted at-risk animals or mentored at-risk children.

McAllister and Clarke's study also found that "a rejection of parenthood was not matched by a rejection of children's place in society. Most childless people were in favour of supporting children through taxes." So why, in the face of studies proving otherwise, do these stereotypes persist?

Blame it on our culture. Despite the fact that we see little evidence of child-centric government policies or funding, our culture remains pronatalist, and our perception of intentional childlessness is filtered through that lens.

In her paper titled "Choosing Childlessness," sociologist Kristin Park wrote, "The general influence of pronatalist beliefs can be seen in the negative evaluations of the intentionally childless that are documented in many studies. Compared to the involuntarily childless and to parents, the voluntarily childless are seen as less socially desirable, less well-adjusted, less nurturant, and less mature, as well as more materialistic, more selfish, and more individualistic."

Perception is everything, and the childfree will continue to be characterized this way until we confront these notions. Below are some of the most common assumptions about the childfree (outside of selfishness) that can—and should—be challenged.

ASSUMPTION 1: THE CHILDLESS BY CHOICE DON'T LIKE KIDS

Let me start by saying that yes, there is a minority of the childless by choice who do admit to having an aversion to children. And some would even go so far as to confess that they'd be happy if a child never entered their orbit. Some have chosen not to have kids because they can't tolerate the noise and the chaos small children typically bring to an environment, or because, frankly, they simply don't like them. And aren't we glad they made that decision?

Personally, I happen to think that not wanting to be around kids is an excellent reason for not having them. We all know people who can't stand kids but had them anyway—perhaps not intentionally, but the result is the same. I had a boyfriend in high school whose mother passed away when he was a child, leaving him alone with a remote and neglectful father who really didn't like children—any children, not even his only son. While we were dating, I rarely saw his father outside of his favorite chair and never heard him speak more than two sentences to his son or to me.

I suspected this man had more serious and pressing problems than simply disliking children, but I did feel sorry for his son. So I applaud those people who have the level of self-awareness and honesty to admit that they just plain don't like kids and take the necessary steps to ensure they don't have them. As the Aussies say, "Good on ya, mate!"

If parents need proof that the childfree hate kids, they don't have to look far. Many of the childfree websites offer forums or safe places in which the childfree can rant about injustices in the tax code, "family-friendly" workplace benefits that exclude childfree families, and unruly children and their "breeder" parents. Some of the vitriolic comments I see on these sites make me squirm, but I have learned these opinions are just that: one person's opinion. Personally, I don't like the word "breed" or "breeder." I don't use it in reference to humans, because it reduces to a mindless biological imperative something that many parents feel is a very profound event.

If you looked solely to the Internet to gauge how the childfree regard children, you might very well come away with the impression that we all hate kids. Yet a dislike of children is not typical of the majority of the childless by choice I have interviewed and surveyed. Actually, I was surprised by how many of the voluntarily childless I met during the course of my research who had actively sought jobs or volunteer work that involved them in regular interactions with children. I met daycare workers, teachers, child advocates, social workers, tutors, mentors, and, yes, even a professional clown.

"Being childless by choice doesn't mean you hate kids," wrote Jodi. "In fact, my friends' children are smart, funny, loving, interesting people who just happen to be kids."

What I have come to understand after many years of studying the childless by choice is that the decision to remain childless is typically not a rejection of children so much as it is a rejection of cultural norms, assumptions, and ideals that support parenthood as the normative life course over all other options.

So please, don't assume all childfree people hate kids. Invite them to your child's birthday party or ask them if they would like to coach or mentor or—yikes!—even baby-sit once in a while. They may politely decline your invitation, or they may surprise you and become the best coach or baby sitter you could ever hope for.

ASSUMPTION 2: THE CHILDLESS BY CHOICE ARE IMMATURE

One of the reasons why many of us actually enjoy children's company is that we are reluctant to let go of the pursuits of our youth that continue to give us pleasure. Perhaps this is why the childfree are often labeled immature, but I like to call it being young at heart.

Anthony, an army officer and pilot, met his wife, Sara, through their college skydiving club, and they have been jumping into, and out of, planes ever since. Trond and Roz still love getting down and dirty and being silly, and look forward to weekends with their friends who have kids, saying, "We teach them how to play." Even though I was a reluctant baby sitter, kids always loved it when I came to baby-sit because I never tired of playing dress-up.

Okay, so maybe we *are* immature, but not in the way we are often perceived as and criticized for being—as slackers who are afraid to grow up and take on adult responsibilities. The assumption that the only path to responsible adulthood is parenthood is another tired remnant of a pronatalist culture that clearly does not hold a stitch. For the past five minutes, I have been sitting in front of my computer, mining my gray matter for a memory of one childfree person who might be described as a slacker. As I flip through my mental Rolodex, I recall CEOs, financial analysts, military careerists, nurses, professors, teachers, farmers, filmmakers, pharmacists, IT professionals, and engineers, but no one who was still living in their parents' home, unwilling to step up and be a self-sustaining and productive adult in the world.

ASSUMPTION 3: THE CHILDLESS BY CHOICE ARE UNFULFILLED

There is this image, perpetuated in films and in literature, of the tragically lonely and unfulfilled person being redeemed, or given new life, by the introduction of a child into their world. The crone of our fairy tales is always a childless woman, portrayed as cranky, isolated, and feared. The childless man on the big screen is successful on the surface but unhappy, self-centered, and blissfully unaware of how bereft of soulful purpose his life is until he becomes a father or takes on the father role for a needy child. The primary staple of celebrity magazines is the story of the sex-or substance-addicted rock star who finally agrees to check into rehab because of the transformative effects of fathering a child. If I didn't know better, I would think that the twelve-step program now has a thirteenth step: Have a kid.

It plays well. The cute kid as a transformative tool is a lot more fun than a cancer diagnosis, though both are useful if you want to motivate a character to reassess his priorities. So maybe that's why the path to fulfillment is clogged with strollers—because our cultural stories make it so. In contrast, most of the stories about childless people are predictably tragic: They die alone, unloved or unlovable, or they commit suicide.

This characterization of the childless contrasts starkly with what I heard and saw as I traveled through North America. One thing that struck me as I reviewed the transcripts and video of my interviews was how generally content people professed to be. There was very little evidence of dissatisfaction, or hoping and wanting. Mark, age forty-six, expressed it this way: "I'm married. I don't have kids. I don't see a void, I just see my life." Sara, age twenty-nine, said, "I feel very fulfilled as a person, and as part of a couple, just the way we are."

Theresa felt she needed to debunk this common myth. "Our lives are not empty because we lack children. On the contrary, we have more time and energy for other things to enhance our lives."

ASSUMPTION 4: THE CHILDLESS BY CHOICE WILL REGRET THEIR DECISION NOT TO HAVE CHILDREN

Every time I had the chance to interview a childless by choice couple, I asked the question "Have you ever regretted your decision not to have kids?" No one admitted feeling regretful, though Debb did confess one small thing: She thought her husband would have been a great adult for a little kid to grow up around. He disagreed.

Every other voluntarily childless person I spoke with either said, "No, I've never regretted not having kids" or acknowledged fleeting twinges, or the possibility, of regret. "Call me in thirty/forty/fifty/sixty years and I'll tell you," they would say. The people I interviewed were all under the age of seventy, and the prospect of remorse seemed far off for them.

The concerns most people had about their childlessness were not the threat of regret, but rather things like "What do I do when I am alone and I can't take care of myself?" or "Who's going to get all my stuff?" Loneliness was not a major concern. Many of the people I spoke with had an extensive social or family network in place to assist them when they needed help or companionship. Some were already funding long-term care and imagined they would end up being cared for by private nurses or in a residential facility of some sort at the end of their life.

These people thought it was crazy—not to mention just plain wrong—for people to have kids just so they would have someone to take care of them when they got old. As Kathy pointed out, elder care in the United States is provided increasingly by people who aren't blood relatives. I did a bit of investigating and, sure enough, I found that adult children represent only 37 percent of elder-care providers in the United States.

Jennifer was in a childfree marriage for five years before she lost her husband to a heart attack. "When Dan died, people would say, 'I bet you regret not having kids, now that he's gone'— not even phrasing it like a question. Sometimes I would respond and say, 'No, actually, I am so grateful that I do not find myself a single mom now.' Dan's death really did help validate my decision. I had to spend a lot of time during the grief process learning about myself and what I want the rest of my life to look like—and kids were nowhere in there." Biological kids, that is, since Jennifer ultimately ended up embracing a stepmom role when she later married a man with grown children.

Jennifer was in her mid-thirties when we corresponded. Does regret come only with advanced age? I wondered. Again, I turned to the studies.

A Canadian study conducted by Sherryl Jeffries and Candace Konnert compared the regret and psychological wellbeing of seventy-two women over the age of forty-five who were voluntarily childless, involuntarily childless, or mothers. When it came to evaluating psychological well-being, Jeffries and Konnert found that "the voluntarily childless women had the highest total scores (indicating greater well-being), mothers scored slightly lower, and the involuntarily childless women had the lowest scores." When it came to regret, they reported, "Among the voluntarily childless women, all but one reported either no current child-related regrets, or regret that was 'minor,' 'fleeting,' or 'more of a curiosity than a regret.' Almost all reported no change or less regret with age, or that they were even more convinced that their decision to remain childless was the right decision."

This was also true for Sue, an early articulator, who told me that the thing that most validated her choice to have a tubal ligation at age twenty-six was the fact that "I am completely at peace with my decision thirty-one years later. I can honestly say at age fifty-seven that not having children was one of the best decisions I've ever made in my life. I have absolutely no regrets, and don't anticipate any."

Sylvia was also fifty-seven when I interviewed her, and was concerned about aging issues, as she was currently without a partner and was an only child. "The only regret I have is that there will be no one to look out for me in my old age, or pass my belongings down to. I have the fear of lying in my home, dead for days, before someone realizes it." But then she countered, "When I hear about all the problems people have with their children, I do not miss having children in the least."

The specter of regret seems to be a cultural assumption more than a real fear harbored by the childfree. I heard many stories of couples being warned by their families and peers that they'd rue their decision, but observed very little evidence of this sentiment among the childless by choice themselves.

ASSUMPTION 5: THE DECISION NOT TO HAVE KIDS IS AN EASY ONE

The suggestion that not a lot of thought goes into the decision to remain childless ranks right up there with selfishness as a common but unfounded assessment of childfree motives and processes.

The myth that we made the decision lightly really annoys the hell out of me," said Debb. "We spent hours and hours talking about whether we wanted kids—the costs and the benefits. We researched the issue. I wrote an honors thesis on the topic." Her husband, Mark, agreed: "When people make the decision not to have children, it is very thought out, probably more so than the decision to have kids."

Misty described her process: "I have thought more about having children than anyone else I know. I knew I never had the desire in the first place, and I had to examine what I would gain, or miss out on, based on my decision." However, the word "decision" didn't feel right to Misty, either. "I don't know if it was so much a decision as a realization of something that was already there." Either way, it was something she had thought long and hard about because she had realized, as she put it, "how little I had in common with people who wanted kids."

Tamara understood that every choice a person makes has consequences, and that making a choice moves other options off the table. This is true if you choose to have kids or if you choose not to. "One problem with mainstream American culture is that we take these words 'freedom' and 'choice' to mean we should have choices about everything all of the time, but that's not the case. When you choose something, it locks you into a path. The freedom was once there, but when you've chosen, you have to accept the consequences. It's not like, 'Wait a minute, I don't like these consequences; where's my choice?' You've already made it."

ASSUMPTION 6: THE CHILDLESS BY CHOICE ARE MATERIALISTIC

I blame this assumption on the unknown person who coined the acronym DINK—double income, no kids. This term is used to describe a relatively affluent, childless demographic, but more often is used, like "yuppie," to describe a lifestyle associated with conspicuous consumption and materialism.

This is how the DINK demographic was characterized in an article featured on Time.com:

"The members of this newly defined species can best be spotted after 9 PM in gourmet groceries, their Burberry-clothed arms reaching for the arugula or a Le Menu frozen flounder dinner. In the parking lot, they slide into their BMWs and lift cellular phones to their ears before zooming off to their architect-designed houses in the exurbs. After warmly greeting Rover (often an akita or golden retriever), they check to be sure the pooch service has delivered his nutrition-ally correct dog food. Then they consult the phone-answering machine, pop dinner into the microwave, and finally sink into their Italian leather sofa to watch a videocassette of, say, last week's *L.A. Law* or *Cheers* on their high-definition, large-screen stereo television."

A tad over the top, don't you think? However, this is the vision people conjure up when the term "DINK" is invoked. Last I checked, double incomes were the norm for most families of two, or four, in North America. Gone are the days when one person's income can support the average household living above the poverty line. We can no longer assume (if we ever could) that the two-income childless or childfree household has the discretionary dollars, or the inclination, to fund the kind of lifestyle described above.

The reason why you might find more DINKs in the gourmet-grocery store after 9:00 PM is that they likely work full-time and can't shop during business hours. They might work longer hours than their coworkers who have children, sometimes because parents have to go to a recital or catch a soccer game. To the consternation of millions of single, childless, and childfree persons, the people who are expected to stay behind are them.

I've lost count of the complaints I've heard from the child-free that their coworkers take advantage of their parent status to get off early or work fewer hours. This type of discrimination is well documented on childfree websites and in books like Elinor Burkett's *The Baby Boon: How Family-Friendly America Cheats the Childless*. Claudia, an executive with a Fortune 500 company, wrote to me and said it was unfair to assume "that since we don't have children we can work 24/7! Life is more than work ... even for the childless." Yet parents don't appear to sympathize. They are struggling and in a time crunch, and many imagine you have no life outside of work. You don't have kids?! *What do you do?*

The childfree, on average, do have more free time and discretionary income than their par-enting counterparts, but what they do with that time and money is likely quite different from what the *Time* magazine article described. In my survey and interviews, I did not ask what income bracket my respondents fell into. However, I did interview most couples in their homes, so I can say, truthfully, that I saw zero architect-designed mansions or purebred dogs with concierge services. What I saw most often were modest homes or apartments, and pets rescued from shelters.

Most of the people described as DINKs will become parents one day, and will willingly give up a good chunk of their discretionary income to their children. They won't stop buying, they'll just buy differently: They'll get tickets to Disneyland instead of Dubrovnik; they'll choose the SUV over the sporty hybrid; they'll invest in college funds rather than Roth IRAs. Some go into serious debt to fund their expanding family, which is one reason why mar-ried couples with children are more than twice as likely to go bankrupt than are childfree couples (according to a survey of 2,200 U.S. families conducted by Elizabeth Warren and Amelia Warren Tyagi).

So what do the childfree spend their extra dollars on—that is, those who actually have something left after paying the bills? Based entirely on my observation, it's travel, hobbies, housing, relatives, pets, and charitable donations.

Angie and her husband, Mike, saw their disposable income not as another reason to remain childless, but as a side benefit, and they were strategic about how they spent their money. Mike thought he would make a good father, but, like Angie, he was ambivalent about parenthood. When they ultimately encountered fertility issues, they decided to accept their fate. "While we had options and so much new medical technology available to us, we did not opt to use it," said Angie. "We'd known other couples who were in panic mode, trying every possible, expensive method to conceive, without success. We also opted out of adoption. I guess we sort of felt that this was 'meant to be' for us and got on with other aspects of our lives."

Angie and Mike had given many hours and dollars to their favorite causes. "My husband and I agree that you do not have to be a parent to be a positive influence on a child's life. Volunteering with organizations like Big Brothers Big Sisters, family shelters, and charitable organizations are some examples of how we contribute. Also, our position as a childless couple allows us to donate more to charitable organizations—likely much more than the average family would even consider contributing."

ASSUMPTION 7: PETS ARE CHILD SUBSTITUTES FOR THE CHILDFREE

The one part of this stereotype I cannot challenge is the fact that the majority of the childless by choice I encountered had at least one pet.

But really, are these animals standing in for children? I don't think so. People see actress Betty White with her "babies" on those 1-800-PetMeds advertisements and presume these pampered animals are child substitutes for the childless. They are not. Jerry made the distinction, suggesting pets may be *better* than kids. "Having a pet is almost like having children," he said. "But unlike human children, your pet will likely never experiment with dangerous drugs, and as long as a pet is spayed or neutered, you need never fear that it will come home pregnant or make other animals pregnant."

Rob did acknowledge that "our pets are our kids," but he rejected the notion that they are child "substitutes."

I wouldn't use that word," he told me. "When I say that our pets are our kids, I'm saying they are important and loved and part of the family. It's frustrating when a pet dies and someone says, 'It's only a pet' or, 'You can get another one next week.' Try saying that to a parent."

Although the childless by choice couples I interviewed clearly cherished their pets, I did not see any diamond-studded collars or shrines to Fluffy. I did see a lot of found or rescued animals of questionable pedigree. Wayne and Gina had even adopted a family of feral cats that they went to feed daily in an abandoned lot next to their local Wal-Mart. They were afraid that if they didn't feed them, Wal-Mart management would call Animal Control and they'd be euthanized.

Many people did point to their pets and say, "This is my nurturing outlet." They enjoyed the give-and-take of the pet-human relationship, and some even referred to each other as Daddy or Mommy to their pets. This sometimes perplexed the people's parents, who had observed how well their sons and daughters cared for their pets and, unsatisfied with the furry grandchild, requested the "real" grandchild. But these pet owners were all acutely aware that caring for a pet and raising a child were completely different tours of duty.

ASSUMPTION 8: EVERYONE IS CAPABLE OF BEING A "GOOD" PARENT

While I was writing this chapter, the Nebraska state legislature was about to amend its new "safe haven" law, which allowed parents to abandon their children at hospitals without suffering legal consequences for abandonment. In the five months after the original law took effect, thirty-five kids were left at Nebraska hospitals, most of them adolescents. The state legislature held a special session to change the language of the law to limit the age of the abandoned child to thirty days in order to reflect the law's original intent.

Despite the weekly news reports and media portraits of overwhelmed or abusive parents, horrific custody battles, desperate housewives, and deadbeat dads, there is a lingering assumption that all people are capable of parenting and should be encouraged to do so.

Yet many of the people I interviewed didn't feel they would make good parents for any number of reasons, or they felt they were unable, or unwilling, to make the sacrifices or the changes to their lifestyle that would be necessary to be responsible parents. Others felt strongly that the desire for a child is a prerequisite for parenthood; without desire, many of the people I surveyed felt there was no choice, believing that it is morally wrong to risk getting pregnant if you are not going to happily welcome a child into your life.

Kristin summed it up perfectly. "It bothers me when people assume the worst motives for the decision. Like childfree people just can't be bothered with the sacrifices or hassles of parenting, or that we want to do lots of material consumption instead, or take long vacations. Few people seem to be able to give credit that the decision might have been thoughtfully made based on an honest appraisal of one's priorities, personality type, skills, or goals. If parenthood is a role that everyone is supposed to adopt, that doesn't allow for people to be inclined toward it—or not—at the outset. Rather, it's claimed that you learn the skills and adopt, or are transformed toward, the necessary temperament on the job."

The childless by choice I interviewed believed it was risky to assume effective parenting is something you learn on the job. What happens if you are wrong and turn out not to be a good parent? And really, isn't it a bit naive to assume that the well-being of your child is entirely under your control?

Angie had an older sister whose marriage ended in divorce, leaving her with three children. "I think the risk factor of knowing that so many marriages end in divorce, and the odds that women are most often the parent who ends up raising children alone, had a big influence on me. Another factor in this decision-making process was working with troubled children and teens after college." Angie had spent much of her career in public health. "To me, it was frightening and sad to see what the kids, as well as the parents, were going through. Despite the fact that some parents worked so hard to do everything right, in the end it was peer pressure and society that became the major influence. It was quite eye-opening. While I'm not sure that this experience was a primary factor in remaining childless, it certainly had some impact on my view of parenthood."

The childless by choice could not ignore that fact that even those parents who want children and try to be good parents sometimes fail to raise healthy and happy children or are severely overwhelmed by the task. Neither was a desirable outcome, and many of my participants recognized that their lack of enthusiasm for parenthood, coupled with a perceived lack of skills or aptitude, increased their risk of failure.

CHALLENGING THE DEFAULT

In the absence of information on the real motives for voluntary childlessness, the "default" assumptions hold sway. If you've never had a serious conversation with a childfree person about their reasons for or the consequences of childlessness, how would you know what was fact and what was fiction? And what would you think if the answer were simply "I never wanted to be a parent"?

If the fear-based myths and preconceived notions about a childfree life—regret, arrested development, lack of fulfillment—don't apply to the majority of the voluntarily childless, what does?

After years of research and interviews, I am tempted to say contentment does, but that state of being is sometimes marred by others' perception that it can't be authentic. How can you be a happy, fully realized adult without kids?

In a pronatalist society, anyone who rejects the default of parenthood or admits to being less than thrilled about the prospect of being a parent is often perceived as a "child hater" or "selfish." These assumptions, and our minority status, put the childfree squarely in the category of "outsider" and are likely why the childless by choice still experience stigmatization in North America.

Compared with other, more visible minorities, the child-free do not experience as much overt discrimination or exclusion on a daily basis. Like our gay and lesbian peers, we have found that we can assimilate fairly well, provided we hide our status from those who might take issue with what some people call a deviant lifestyle. This is not the ideal solution, of course. The childfree, like all minority groups, hope for a time when we can be accepted for who we are and how we live, but that time will come only as a result of empathy and some level of understanding. In the meantime, we find ways to adapt as we live on the margins. We find like-minded peers and communities who embrace or validate us. However, there remains the challenge of finding acceptance for the childfree life in the culture of the majority, in a society that idealizes parenthood for all its citizens. And as long as the rationales for choosing this life appear defective or are misunderstood or simply imagined, the entire decision-making process (along with those who make the unsanctioned choice) is going to be perceived as flawed by some.

This is why I feel it is important to challenge the myths and tell the truth about life without kids. In the following chapters, we'll explore the culture in which we live, how the childless and childfree adapt—or not—within its confines, and the disadvantages of a childfree life.

OUT OF WEDLOCK

WHY SOME POOR WOMEN REJECT MARRIAGE

By Margaret Walsh[1]

The latest U.S. Census Bureau survey reports that 4 million American households are made up of unmarried couples, a major increase over the last generation. About half of single women under 30 have lived with a man outside marriage at some time during their young adulthood. More than half of the couples who marry today will divorce, and women spend more years of their lives unmarried than married. About one in three births are to single women. Women raising children alone are far more likely to know poverty compared to any other group. What do these widely reported trends in marriage, cohabitation, and child-bearing tell us?

In the 1990s, I explored the changing pattern of heterosexual relationships by interviewing working-class and poor women in their twenties and thirties on the topic of marriage and childbearing. These 50 young mothers lived in rural communities in the northeastern United States. Although not a statistically representative group, I selected them to illustrate the variet-ies of ways in which single women with children are coping outside of traditional marriage. The welfare reforms of 1996 overtly encouraged marriage as a solution to poverty, but these women knew better. They had no illusions about the connection between marriage and money in their own lives. Some of them had been married for a time. These women's experiences show that marriage does not bring them the security, stability, and respectability touted by conservative politicians. Poor women who marry the poor men in their neighborhoods do not benefit from the economic privileges that middle- and upper-class marriages promise: steady income, health care benefits, child support. Those benefits are reserved for women and children connected to men with a steady income who share their resources. The decisions that poor women in my sample made to marry and divorce (or to avoid marriage altogether and look for other sources of help as they raise their families) offer insights about economics and gender relations, about the growing independence of women, and their shrinking expectations of men.

MARSHA'S STORY

Twenty-nine-year-old Marsha was born in New Hampshire, but she and her siblings rarely stayed in the same school for more than a year or two. Her father's work in the military transported the family to Texas, Arkansas, Missouri, Arizona, and California before he retired in the late 1980s to northern New England. Her mother used to say Marsha had "an adventurous soul" because she would hunt, fish, and explore whatever her new surroundings had to offer.

> I didn't stay long enough to make those kind of close friends but we were very lucky, you know, because some of the things we've seen, other people don't get to see in a whole lifetime.

Surprising her family and friends, Marsha settled down early. At 19, she was impressed by a burly 26-year-old man she met at the state fair and they dated for four months. At the time he worked at a construction job in another state, but he drove home on weekends so they could spend time together. The relationship progressed quickly. "One day he just flat-out asked me to marry him, and I don't know if it was because I was so young or if I was stupid or I was just love-blind or whatever they call it. I said yes." Marsha became pregnant with their first child within two months, and stopped working. Even before their baby was born, she worried that the marriage was a mistake. Most of their early problems were financial.

> I never knew where the money was going. He made eight dollars an hour at the time, which wasn't bad. I got $30.00 a week for grocery money and to pay whatever other bills that need to be paid. We had our water, gas, electricity, turned off quite often and there were times where I had to beg them to leave it on for maybe a day or two, until I could pay it, and sometimes they would because I had a small child.

They fought over money and never seemed to have enough. Her husband's view was that he should be able to support them without her working. Yet, he could not earn enough to pay the bills. So he blamed her for their troubles, and insisted that she do more with less. Marsha decided to work to supplement their income but it was a struggle: "Every job I had was sabotaged. He didn't want me doing what I wanted to do. He wanted me to do what he wanted me to do." Despite her own early wanderings, she planned to raise her family in one place, and she refused to give up on the relationship.

> My ex-husband couldn't pay bills and I couldn't figure out why we were always moving and then, when I figured it out, I took the checkbook away from him, but that still didn't work, so we ended up moving quite a bit while we were married.

The couple had two more children over a period of six years, but both Marsha and her husband were miserable:

> I got to the point when I didn't care anymore. I didn't care about the house. I didn't care about nothing. I lived in a house which had a hole in the floor, you know, almost two foot wide in all directions. I had to put a piece of plywood over it, so I wouldn't fall through. I would ask him, 'Fix this.' The sink was falling in. You'd sit on the toilet, and you'd have to hold on for dear life. I lived in an absolute shack and a lot of people thought it was all my fault.

The final break in the marriage came when he moved out of their house and in with a new girlfriend. Marsha recalls that when she filed for divorce she realized it was the first time she ever actively stood up for herself in the marriage. She won full custody of the children with the support of her ex-mother-in-law who testified on her behalf in divorce court, and then helped Marsha find a decent job. "She pointed me in the right direction and it was something I really needed and still, to this day, she says I'm her daughter."

After the divorce, Marsha worked 75 hours a week as a deli manager, trying to make ends meet. She was proud to have stayed off welfare at first. But "it got to the point where my babysitter finally told me one day that my son just walked alone for the first time. Now I had seen my older two kids walk so that really upset me." Coincidentally, Marsha was fired from her job the very next day because she told a supervisor that her manager was stealing money from the store. The date was December 24.

> I felt like the weight of the world had lifted off my shoulders and I went home, cooked Christmas dinner and, after the kids were asleep, I sat down and decided what I was going to do. I didn't want to go on welfare, but I knew, if I didn't, I would not get the education I needed to provide for my kids, because my ex-husband was not doing a great job. I got eighty dollars a week, child support, for all three of them and not apiece either.

In the three years since her divorce, Marsha has achieved many of the things she thought she would have accomplished during her eight-year marriage.

> Just sitting at the table every night, eating supper together, talking about the day, we didn't have that until I got a divorce. There was no structure. I was always wondering what was going on with him and I was trying to get everything settled at home and it was one thing after another. Now we have a decent house to live in, clothes for my kids, and food. And once we get home, from about three o'clock until 8 o'clock at night is time for my kids. You know, I didn't have that until I got divorced.

Marsha wants to graduate from college and find a decent job in the computer field.

I want to be able to pay for everything, without having welfare nosing around in my business. I just want to be stable in my own life. I don't want somebody else providing for me, so if they leave, I'm not depending on their money to take care of me and my kids.

Marsha does have a new boyfriend who she describes as mainly a friend. "We've been close. But, it's not where he is living with me or anything. I don't want that. I've got my own place. I pay my own bills and that's the way I want it. And it's the same with him."

WHY MARRIAGE? WHY NOT?

Although the details differ, the theme of Marsha's story was repeated again and again in the interviews I conducted with young women about their relationships with men and their views of marriage. These were women I met at community colleges, childcare centers, and family health clinics. Like Marsha, some of the women who are now divorced had married young, often in their teens, to gain independence from parents or to fill the space after leaving high school. They married their first sexual partner, sometimes only after discovering an unplanned pregnancy. Without the resources to invest in a marriage—good jobs with benefits, money for a house, a rainy day fund—their hopes and expectations for the relationship plummeted. Their experience of failure reflected their gendered understanding of the marital roles of wife and husband, which neither was able to fulfill. As teenagers, they embraced idealized versions of the domestic and work spheres. Their men had not won enough bread, and they, as women, had not adequately made a home.

MARRYING THE FIRST GUY WHO COMES ALONG

Television soap operas feature romanticized images of married couples with leisure time, material possessions, and few responsibilities. The availability of contraception, the expansion of higher education, and the extension of "youth" from the teens to the mid-twenties in the United States have increased the age at which people make many life decisions. However, research studies suggest that most pregnancies (regardless of the race, age, or class of the mother) are "unplanned" in the sense that they are unexpected or ill timed. For some women marriage is the only answer to a pregnancy when it occurs unexpectedly. No other alternatives are considered because no other options exist at the moment. As one woman facing pregnancy at age 17 described it,

> I got married because I got pregnant and I wasn't doing it by myself. I wasn't going to have a child by myself. And also because the father of the child was not sexually abusive, physically abusive, emotionally abusive. I figured, 'I made the bed, I'll lie in it?'

In this example, the problem of single motherhood was "solved" by marriage. One of the main factors women considered when deciding about marriage was how a future husband would behave based on evidence from their courtship. Finding a man who was not abusive was "good enough" and she married him. However, this man did not have a steady job, and he was not involved with baby care. The mother was punishing herself for being irresponsible, and she was afraid of living alone. Eventually the couple divorced, however, and she did raise her child on her own.

MONEY CHANGES EVERYTHING

Poverty strains relationships; yet, sometimes women "try out" marriage believing the popular notion that it is the one solution to their problem. Just as many couples are programmed to believe that having children requires marriage, couples also come to think of the marriage as a means to prosperity. In the interviews I conducted, this myth dissolved as soon as poor couples crossed the marital threshold. In the scenario described above, the wife described coming home from her winter wedding to a trailer that had snow literally coming inside from the leaking roof and piling blanket on top of blanket for warmth. "I remember thinking, 'Is this what love is?' 'Cause this sure isn't what marriage is supposed to be. I didn't have a clue." Trying to keep warm in an unheated trailer was less than romantic and posed serious danger to their health and to the baby. Before long, they moved in with her parents, and the fighting began as they lost privacy and struggled under their new responsibilities as new parents themselves. Their increased dependence on family for financial help after the first child came ran contrary to everything they expected from marriage. The relationship never recovered and they split five years later. Another important factor in women's orientation toward marriage is their assessment of their parents' relationship and economic standing.

CHANGING ATTITUDES ABOUT MARRIAGE

The women I interviewed talked at length about their parents and siblings, often comparing their families of origin to the households they formed when they had their own boyfriends, husbands, and/or children. In the 1960s and 1970s, their own parents married to bring security to their relationships and worked in steady manufacturing jobs to provide resources for their children. They wanted to earn enough to be able to purchase a home, a trailer, or a camp for their families. They wanted their children to have a better life than they had themselves. Not all families achieved this goal, however. Some parents went through periods of unemployment and hard times, hoping that things would eventually get easier. Some mothers tried to hide family problems and "make it okay." Even when their marriages were in trouble, most of the couples decided to stay together at least until their children grew up, especially those from religious backgrounds.

In early adolescence, these young women began to form their own ideas about the kind of adult they hoped to be. They saw their options for the future by looking at their older siblings and friends, and they received messages from important people in their lives—parents, relatives, and teachers. The quality of these interactions strengthened or diminished their aspirations, opened or closed their opportunities for the future. As teenagers, these women's friendships and their romantic relationships with men also began to shape their future.

The single women in my study who viewed marriage favorably shared similar family histories. The majority were raised by two adults with steady incomes, putting them in the solid working-class or lower middle-class categories. They grew up in large families with relatives living nearby. Most women reported seeing their grandparents on a regular basis. Often, they remembered visiting with cousins and other members of their extended families on Sunday afternoons after Church to share dinner before beginning another week. The parents of the women in my study had four or more children spaced close together. The community institutions surrounding these couples as well as their friends and families supported and encouraged the success of their marriages.

Only a few of the women had college-educated parents, but some of the women's fathers had spent time in the military, learned new skills, and "saw the world" for a couple of years. They married in their twenties, and saved for a house. Some lived at home with their parents for a few years to save money or to help out with younger brothers and sisters. Some ran small family businesses; or, fathers worked in manufacturing jobs with benefits and earned enough so that mothers could take breaks from work when their children were young. After graduating from high school, mothers worked as secretaries in a local business or sometimes in one of the many factories. The wives and husbands had different responsibilities, but they talked over and agreed on aims and goals for their family. They had high expectations for educating their children, and they earned enough money to pay their bills and make ends meet. These couples had the financial resources to care for their children, and with two parents, they had the luxury of spending time together, talking and listening to one another, and enjoying each other's company. In some sense, then, they resembled those idealized images of prosperity displayed by married couples on television and movies at the time. These marriages held their economic value and their emotional worth for the family and community.

By contrast, the women in my study who held unfavorable views toward marriage also shared some characteristics. As a group, they had parents with unsteady work histories and long periods of unemployment. Most of their parents did not finish high school, and they married young with few other options. Because neither parent had valuable work skills, the families had no choice but to move when a job opportunity arose. Few families owned any property at all, and some of their marriages broke up from economic pressures that led to constant arguments. As children, these women were more likely to spend time in single parent families or in "blended" families—with stepparents and stepsiblings. When one of their parents remarried, they often moved again to another home, where they had to adjust to a different school environment and make new friends.

Many of these women recalled that they felt uncomfortable at school, and they had too many burdens at home to care about doing well in school. They did not play sports or receive any special recognition, and they did not receive "the right kind" of attention from teachers in the classroom. Their parents may have been supportive but stressed themselves, and the girls heard all of the family fights and knew exactly how tight money was for the month. They felt they were "not like the other kids" who had new clothes and spending money while their mothers shopped at the Salvation Army and used food stamps at the grocery store. These households were overwhelmingly poor and struggling. While the marital relationships they described may have begun with love, romance, and emotional connections, they did not (could not?) hold their economic value to the couple, the family, and community. These families were poorer.

LIFE AS A WIFE: THE DREAM AND THE REALITY

When I asked women about their family plans when they were younger, almost everyone recalled stories of playing with dolls and acting out the roles of Bride and Mommy with their school friends. But the dream and the reality were in conflict. As one woman put it, "I thought I'd have the house with the garden, the husband and kids, the white picket fence. You know. It didn't work out that way, but the next best thing is what I have now. I still have a family."

After becoming pregnant, the women did not know what to expect from motherhood but compared to their male partners, they felt ready for the responsibility. Some of the women worked as nursing assistants and preschool teachers, making enough for themselves but not able to easily support families alone. Most often, they described their former boyfriends and husbands as immature, unfaithful, and unemployed. Before entering marriage, these women looked for any alternatives that would help them stay single and set up independent households. For those with resources, this meant relying on their parents and extended families. For others, this meant settling for the men or relying on welfare, since their own families were usually too burdened to help them and their new child out.

Some women compared their own relationships to their parents' marriages, and they wondered if they could do better. For others, their relationships reminded them of their parents failed marriages, and they worried that their attempts at marriage would be doomed from the beginning. Because my study consists only of divorced, separated, or never married women, I am not able to compare these single women's histories to other couples who remained married. I also do not know how the male partners would describe their own feelings about these failed relationships. However, it is fascinating to consider how these young women's attitudes about future relationships have changed since their dreamy childhood. With the hindsight of divorce or the present struggle of raising young children outside of marriage, many women firmly rejected the possibility of marriage (or re-marriage) for themselves. They felt ambivalent about starting new relationships, and others were saddened that the "institution of marriage" had failed them.

> I am not in a hurry to get married. I'm still young. If this one works, fine. If it doesn't, I'll move on.

> It's a piece of paper. I feel if you love somebody, you don't need a piece of paper. You don't need to change your name. You don't need to go through all of that. It's good for your income tax—when you make your annual claim.

> I don't know about marriage … it's a total commitment and we need to be ready. That's your life partner from the wedding until you die, and I just think people say that without thinking about what it actually means.

One could argue that children require a larger (more demanding) commitment than marriage; yet, none of these women expressed regrets about motherhood. One woman said that if she were not a mother, "I probably wouldn't even be here. I'd probably be in a different state living a whole different life." Instead, they found that having children kept them "grounded" and helped them to aspire to higher standards for themselves and the men in their lives. They quickly moved beyond their early romantic visions of marriage and made a more realistic assessment of whether the benefits of marriage outweighed its limitations. When deciding about marriage, the women weighed their options—sized up the relationship with the child's father, consulted with their own parents and friends—and most did not marry. Others divorced within a few years. The ability to choose a life that was different from their own mothers' experience depended on how much assistance family members could offer, their own work opportunities, and educational prospects. Women who chose to head families alone over marriage were more likely to have support systems in place at the time they became pregnant.

Policies that advise poor young mothers to marry only reinforce inequalities that exist in the social structure. In these types of discussions, marriage is wrongly used as a proxy for economic stability. Women need good jobs of their own, not merely an available man, so they can make good family decisions for themselves. Poor young mothers, regardless of marital status, need better paying work, help with caring for children, and greater financial assistance so that they can pursue their own education. Marriage may—or may not—come later.

NOTES

1. This essay draws on Walsh's *Mothers' Helpers: The Resources of Female Headed Households in a Working Class Community,* Ph.D. Dissertation, University of New Hampshire, 1997.

A FEMINIST SEARCH FOR LOVE

EMMA GOLDMAN ON THE POLITICS OF MARRIAGE, LOVE, SEXUALITY, AND THE FEMININE

By Lori J. Marso

Goldman (1969a, 62) defined anarchism in the following way:

> [Anarchism] stands for the liberation of the human mind from the dominion of religion; the liberation of the human body from the dominion of property; liberation from the shackles and restraint of government. Anarchism stands for a social order based on the free grouping of individuals for the purpose of producing real social wealth; an order that will guarantee to every human being free access to the earth and full enjoyment of the necessities of life, according to individual desires, tastes, and inclinations.

Goldman's "beautiful ideal" necessitated the emancipation of women. Though many anarchist writers acknowledged the importance of women in the movement, none of the principal male theoreticians gave sustained attention to questions of feminism (Ackelsberg 1991, 17). Like socialist feminist Alexandra Kollantai, Goldman had to fight her political colleagues on the question of which issues were to be labeled "digressions" and which were central to the revolutionary movement. Goldman (1970b, 253) recalled a conversation with Peter Kropotkin, for example, in which he complained that the anarchist paper, *Free Society*, would do better were it not to "waste so much space discussing sex." And even when there was agreement on the political importance of sexuality, there was, as Ackelsberg (1991, 26) put it, "more than one way to apply an anti-authoritarian analysis to sexual and familial relations." Could free sexual expression exist between equals, and how would women's reproductive role influence her social and political contributions? Goldman was certain about at least one thing. Her life experience had made it clear that no true freedom for women could exist without a fundamental revolution at the intimate level between human beings in their relationships of love and sexuality. She insisted on bringing to light the inequality manifested in our most intimate relationships such as marriage and the nuclear family. Debating the role of women in the 1935 Spanish anarchist movement, Goldman (1975) berated a colleague for claiming it is the "innermost wish" of Spanish women to have "broods of children." Goldman retorted:

> All your assurance not withstanding, I wish to say that I have yet to meet the woman who wants to have many children. That doesn't mean that I ever for a moment denied the fact that most women want to have a *child*, though that, too, has been exaggerated by the male ... . I have seen too many tragedies in the relations between the sexes; I have seen too many broken bodies and maimed spirits from the sex slavery of woman not to feel the matter deeply or to express my indignation against the attitude of most of you gentlemen. (p. 186)

Goldman recognized sexual and reproductive freedoms as the cornerstone to basic human rights, seeing the curtailment of these freedoms in the most common and accepted practices mandated and promulgated by and through the state. Marriage, for example, condemns women to "life-long dependency, to parasitism, to complete uselessness, individual as well as social" (Goldman 1969c, 228). It compounds the degrading effects of capitalism, annihilating woman's "social consciousness, paralyz[ing] her imagination, and then impos[ing] its gracious protection, which is in reality a snare, a travesty on human character" (p. 235). The home, "though not so large a prison as the factory, has more solid doors and bars" (p. 233).

Ironically and tragically, these prison bars of marriage rarely fail to tantalize young women. The bars appear "golden," their shininess "blind[ing] woman to the price she would have to pay as wife, mother, and housekeeper" (Goldman 1969e, 224). In spite of her oppression, "woman clings tenaciously to the home, to the power that holds her in bondage" (Goldman 1969f, 197). Goldman seized on the heart of the problem: What women are taught to desire also denies them their freedom. The very substance of what makes a woman feminine is what holds her in bondage. Being a mother, a wife, and a lover, as defined by Goldman's historical moment, was to be financially, emotionally, socially, and politically dependent. Studying sexuality in nineteenth-century feminist thought, feminist historians Ellen DuBois and Linda Gordon (1983, 12) noted the contradictions women lived: "What was conceived as women's greatest virtue, their passionate and self-sacrificing commitment to their children, their capacity for love itself, was a leading factor in their victimization."

But the options for women were very limited. A woman might even be aware of her potential slavery within marriage yet walk into it open-eyed having surveyed other, even less desirable alternatives. "We find many emancipated women who prefer marriage, with all its deficiencies, to the narrowness of an unmarried life, narrow and unendurable because of the chains of moral and social prejudice that cramp and bind her nature" (Goldman 1969e, 221).

What were the alternatives beyond marriage? If a woman were to remain unmarried, she might be labeled a spinster, a loose woman, or a whore. Partially in response to these limited alternatives, the late nineteenth century witnessed the rise of the feminist movement. Women activists of many political persuasions advanced new visions of gender relations, women's social role, and even, of course, women's potential role in politics. Some feminist historians have called the late nineteenth century a "golden age for single women," noting opportunities for gainful employment, and even new fashions—out with confining corsets and hoopskirts, replaced by dark skirts and simple blouses (Ware 2002, 3). Yet even the more progressive options had their drawbacks. Goldman claimed (1969e) at the time that taking on the role of the new woman was to accept the notion that women must make themselves professional—even male—to be taken seriously. She found that the American suffragists, for example, bought into the idea that if woman is to be emancipated, she must give up on her femininity, her sexuality, and everything that makes her a woman. Echoing conservative antisuffragists but from a profoundly different political perspective, Goldman argued that the suffrage model taught women they needed to relinquish any claims to femininity to be free.

Susan B. Anthony, as the most famous example, seemed to embody this sacrifice of femininity for the cause by being openly critical of the time and effort that "baby-making" stole from the women's rights movement (Wheeler 1995, 49). Goldman argued that the suffrage model made it appear that gaining freedom as a woman could only be purchased at the price of losing one's femininity. And as suffrage became married to the Progressive movement, the emphasis on female morality repulsed Goldman.

Yet though Goldman ridiculed the claim that women were morally superior to men and especially the suffrage claim that "women's nature suited them to the new social responsibilities of the state" (Evans 1997, 154), she also emphasized that women should be allowed and encouraged to freely express what she called their true femininity. Goldman (1969e, 214, 215) clamed that what she identified as partial or external emancipation makes modern woman an "artificial being"—a woman who must be confronted "with the necessity of emancipating herself from emancipation." This woman is a "compulsory vestal, before whom life, with its great clarifying sorrows and its deep, entrancing joys, rolls on without touching or gripping her soul" (p. 217). This woman is not "brave enough to acknowledge that the voice of love is calling, wildly beating against [her] breast, demanding to be heard, to be satisfied" (p. 222). "Emancipation, as understood by the majority of its adherents and exponents, is of too narrow a scope to permit the boundless love and ecstasy contained in the deep emotion of the true woman, sweetheart, mother in freedom" (p. 217).

In short, Goldman disagreed with her suffragist sisters on almost everything. She argued especially vehemently that the fight for, and even the winning of, the vote was bound to ensnare women in new chains.[1] The kind of freedom gained through the law would only constitute a partial freedom, an empty promise. Goldman (1969e, 224) repeatedly insisted that the vote would never and could never fundamentally transform women's lives: A woman might consider herself free but, in reality, she would only be trapped within new confines.

The alternatives, then, as Goldman assessed them, were severely limited. Why would any woman willingly choose to live an unconventional life? Were there even any models women could choose to follow if they desired something more than a conventional life or partial emancipation? Seeking to articulate a vision of true freedom, Goldman offered her own life as an example to others. It is in her life as example that she attempts to most clearly distinguish her politics from the suffragists as well as the moralists inside and outside the suffrage movement. In her two-volume autobiography, *Living My Life*, Goldman spoke candidly about her early and varied sexual experiences, her longings and desires, and her many passionate love affairs, often with younger men.

Throughout her essays on sexuality, love, and marriage, Goldman (1969c) maintained a distinction between marriage and "real love," forced motherhood and the "mother instinct," false/partial and "true" emancipation. "Marriage and love have nothing in common," she wrote (p. 227). A "healthy, grown woman, full of life and passion" must be "free and big enough to learn the mystery of sex without the sanction of State or Church" rather than "subdue her most intense craving, undermine her health, and break her spirit" in the battle to abstain from "the sex experience until a 'good' man comes along to take her unto himself as a wife" (p. 231). Marriage sanctions a motherhood "conceived in hatred, in compulsion" (p. 236): "Yet, if motherhood be of free choice, of love, of ecstasy, of defiant passion," it would be a "free motherhood" (pp. 236, 237).

Real or true freedom, in Goldman's (1969f) definition, does not spring from externally granted laws or rights but rather from woman's soul. If woman is to be truly free, not only in law but in terms of personal liberation, "her development, her freedom, her independence, must come from and through herself" (p. 211). By refusing to be a "sex commodity," refusing to "bear children, unless she wants them," refusing to be "a servant to God, the State, society, the husband, the family," woman will make herself a force for "real love, for peace, for harmony" (ibid.).

But the choice for true freedom involves difficult sacrifices and brings on complicated dilemmas. Can sexual varietism satisfy a person's emotional desires, especially if one has a desire for an intimate confidante and committed lover? Does one have to completely give up on emotional commitment or mutual dependency to be truly free? Goldman's wish was to live her life as a free woman while simultaneously living within community and within mutually supportive bonds. She hoped to live in accordance with her philosophical and political ideals demonstrating that women's lives could be free as well as emotionally satisfying. Goldman (1969e, 224) proclaimed, "If partial emancipation is to become a complete and true emancipation of woman, it will have to do away with the ridiculous notion that to be loved, to be sweetheart and mother, is synonymous with being slave and subordinate."

In an effort to realize the goal of free motherhood and to work toward true emancipation for women, Goldman employed various political methods. She worked tirelessly on the birth control campaign for over ten years. Advocating knowledge of and access to birth control for all women fruitfully combined Goldman's philosophy of anarchist freedom with concrete measures toward political and social change. At the same time, however, the philosophical problem that the reality of children and lovers posed remained a thorny one for anarchist feminists like Goldman. Even if motherhood and mutual reciprocity were freely chosen, could a woman be fully free as an individual when her life was emotionally intertwined with another or, as in motherhood, if she were completely or even partially responsible for another human life? Questions of mutual dependency and reciprocity remained nagging ones for Goldman in her philosophy and in her life.

LIVING WITHIN THE CONFINES OF FEMININITY

Goldman's reading of Mary Wollstonecraft's life points to how she thought about the dilemmas within her own life and the feminist politics of her time. Building her case against the suffragists, Goldman (1981, 116) looked to Wollstonecraft's life to prove the "inadequacy of mere external gain as a means of freeing their [our] sex." Goldman noted,

> Mary's own tragic life proves that economic and social rights for women alone are
> not enough to fill her life, nor yet enough to fill any deep life, man or woman. It is not

true that the deep and fine man—I do not mean the mere male—differs very largely from the deep and fine woman. He too seeks for beauty and love, for harmony and understanding. Mary realized that, because she did not limit herself to her own sex, she demanded freedom for the whole human race. (ibid.)

Referring repeatedly to beauty, love, deep emotion, and affection in this essay on Wollstonecraft, Goldman emphasized the importance of the transformation needed in intimate relations for the revolutionary movement. Goldman identified Wollstonecraft as a kindred spirit, a woman with deep and unwavering commitment to intellectual life and the revolutionary movement. She also identified with her as a woman who longed for true love. As Goldman put it, "Life without love for a character like Mary is inconceivable, and it was her search and yearning for love which hurled her against the rock of inconsistency and despair" (p. 119).

The dilemma of the political and feminist woman in love, the relationship between feminine desire and anarchist feminist authority increasingly occupied Goldman's thoughts as she ended one failing or unsatisfying relationship after another. Goldman's autobiography made clear her frustration in trying to live in intimacy with someone while maintaining her political activities and identity. Her constant desire was to find a partner with whom she could combine politics with intimacy. Ed Brady, for example, an anarchist colleague with whom Goldman shared her life, work, and bed for almost five years, initially was someone on whom Goldman pinned her "dream of love and true companionship" (Goldman 1970b, 151). "Surely it must be possible," she hoped, "for a man and a woman to have a beautiful love life and yet be devoted to a great cause" (p. 154). The tug of war between the emotional and the political was a constant dynamic in Goldman's life: "To the end of my days I should be torn between the yearning for a personal life and the need to giving all to my ideal" (p. 153). Though Goldman claimed that her "giving to humanity" only increased her own need, making her "love and want Ed more" (p. 193), Brady felt, in contrast, that Goldman's "interest in the movement" was nothing but "vanity, nothing but craving for applause and glory and the limelight" (p. 183).

Examining her work in conjunction with her life, it is clear that Goldman was trying to reconcile sexual and individual freedom with the demands of love and mutual reciprocity. Candace Falk (1990), one of Goldman's feminist biographers, argued that the tension between a desire for love and the commitment to anarchist principles remained a primary one throughout Goldman's life. In reading Goldman's enormous volume of correspondence, Falk identified a "tone of desperation, even of resignation" (p. xii) that is unassociated with Emma, the freedom fighter. When Goldman "was vulnerable to political repression, she responded with daring and defiance, but when she was vulnerable in a love relationship it triggered feelings of abandonment and desperation" (p. xiv).

Goldman's dream of ongoing political partnership and intimacy was only realized for moments at a time. When she met another of her lovers, Ben Reitman, Goldman (1970b, 425) hoped it might signal the start of a "new chapter in [her] life" with someone "who was lover, companion, and manager." Reitman was Goldman's lover during her most tumultuous years on the birth control campaign. Goldman wrote of the "great hunger for someone who would love the woman in me and yet who would also be able to share my work" (p. 433). In *Living My Life*, Goldman intentionally denied her intense passion for Reitman and the ways she was beholden to her desire to make the relationship work.[2] In a 1909 letter to Reitman, she expressed the contradictions she felt in her life. Goldman (2001, 98) desperately feared losing Reitman's love and companionship while still desiring to be a model of freedom and independence for others:

> Meetings, free speech, are nothing to me now, if my love, my life, my peace, my very soul is to be mutilated. Work with you, so long as I had faith in your love, meant the greatest, sweetest joy in life. That may account for my utter abandonment, my utter dissolution to my love for you. That may also account, why I the woman who has been treated with respect by friend and foe, could crouch on her knees and beg and plead with you … I have no right to bring a message to people when there is no message in my soul. I have no right to speak of freedom when I myself have become abject slave in my love.

Goldman despised her dependency—on Brady, on Reitman, and on her own longing for intimacy and affection from another human being. Living outside the boundaries of conventional society and defying all expectations for women made it nearly insurmountable for Goldman to achieve the kind of emotional fulfillment for which she so desperately hoped. This was certainly not an unusual situation for feminists of the period, particularly for anarchist feminists as they chose to so radically reject social norms. Feminist theorist Ann Ferguson (1995, 373) reminds us that "our fragmented subjectivities require support by a number of oppositional communities that provide alternative meanings and material support." Though Goldman was the center of multiple anarchist communities and alternative forms of family, she continued to long for a special intimacy with one individual. Redefining models of family and ways of intimacy was a particularly difficult challenge for women of Goldman's historical moment. Others, too, were struggling with these same questions, yet lacking the material and psychological resources it would take to so radically redefine ways of loving, each individual felt they were struggling alone. Documenting "modern love" in Greenwich Village in the early twentieth century, Ellen Kay Trimberger (1983, 143) argued, "Women might give each other private support, but there was not at this time a women's movement that publicly discussed changes in personal life, marriage, and sex, nor one that helped women articulate what changes were in their interests."

Goldman's contemporary, feminist Voltairine de Cleyre, also struggled alone with questions of self-definition. In a study of anarchist women, Margaret Marsh (1981, 135) argued that de Cleyre's correspondence reveals "that grinding poverty drove her to contemplate marriage for economic security, that she suffered periods of acute despondency because she considered her life a failure, and that on one occasion her depression nearly resulted in suicide." Goldman (1975, 128), remarking to Berkman in one letter that she longed to express "love and affection for some human being of [her] own," suggested a break with the philosophy of anarchist feminists who argue that sexual freedom necessarily implies a rejection of emotional possession. Putting sexual freedom and the critique of domesticity at the center of her analyses, de Cleyre felt that to conquer jealousy and to reject any claims or hold over any other individual was central to a revolutionary strategy. To be jealous or possessive was to make a claim to private property.[3] Though Goldman (1998, 215) made similar claims against jealousy, seeing it as the "most prevalent evil of our mutilated love life," she tempered her condemnation by acknowledging that the "two worlds" of "two human beings, of different temperament, feelings, and emotions" must meet in "freedom and equality" if they are to conquer the "green-eyed monster" (pp. 221, 216, respectively).

As Goldman fluctuated between desires for political and personal fulfillment, times of political disappointment became for her the moments when she felt most powerfully that something was lacking in her life as a woman. Writing to Berkman in 1925 of an anarchist friend and colleague, Goldman (1975) described the "tragedy of all us modern women":

> It is a fact that we are removed only by a very short period from our traditions, the traditions of being loved, cared for, protected, secured, and above all, the time when women could look forward to an old age of children, a home and someone to brighten their lives. Being away from all that by a mere fraction of time, most modern women, especially when they see age growing upon them, and if they have given out of themselves so abundantly, begin to feel the utter emptiness of their existence, the lack of the *man*, whom they love and who loves them, the comradeship and companionship that grows out of such a relation, the home, a child. And above all the economic security either through the man or their own definite independent efforts. Nearly every modern woman I have known and have read about has come to [this] condition. (p. 131)

This is a condition Goldman knows well. Despite the fact that she struggled to free herself from the confines of traditional marriage and motherhood, despite the fact that she lived a life of sexual freedom and political activity, in private correspondence Goldman said that she suffered from having failed to achieve a long-term relationship that would satisfy her feminine desire.

GOLDMAN'S "BEAUTIFUL IDEAL"

How might we understand the meanings and contradictions of what Goldman refers to as feminine desire? When Goldman made reference to *femininity*, the *mother instinct*, and *woman's soul*, she articulated a very basic difference between men and women, but she intentionally did not specify whether that difference is based in biology, psychology, social–political hierarchies, psycholinguistic–symbolic organization, or some combination of these factors. Goldman's appeals to difference were often used rhetorically but reflect her own observations about her life and the lives of other women she knew. Goldman's radical life and practical activities put her in contact and solidarity with huge numbers of women of all classes and types. In her lectures and campaigns for birth control and women's sexual freedom, she reached out to women of the middle classes; at the same time, working for the rights of prostitutes and gays, Goldman appealed to both lower and middle classes and radical and liberal audiences. In addition, her years working as a midwife for impoverished women who could not afford doctors, health care, or a back-alley abortion put Goldman in intimate contact with the destitution of the poorest and most desperate women.

Yet in spite of Goldman's knowledge of the ways women are divided, she still often grouped women together in a category without any subtle or even obvious distinctions. As a propagandist, Goldman tended to exaggerate many of her claims, speaking of women in an uncomplicated, even essentialist, way. While fully aware of the differences between and among women,

Goldman still found it appropriate to speak of women as differentiated as a group within a structure of gender inequity. And she continued to speak of feminine desire.

In challenging the notion of a rational and unitary subject, psychoanalytic theory has been helpful in attempting to explain some of the more seemingly irrational and contradictory aspects of our personalities, especially sexual desire. In labeling her desire as feminine and in valuing romantic love, Goldman was at odds with her more rational or political self that would choose to remake these aspects of conventional femininity. In Goldman's life we witness a philosophical and political commitment to a complete break with traditional norms of femininity combined with what appears as personal sadness over the failure to achieve and maintain what might be considered conventional kinds of feminine-gendered bonds (i.e., within a monogamous love affair or with a child). Here, a psychoanalytic explanation of desire as yearning for unattainable fulfillment—as in the Lacanian analysis—might offer a way of understanding Goldman's lament for an unattainable intimacy she called feminine.

Yet Goldman herself questions the way the feminine has been shaped by social, historical, and economic constraints and never accepted the idea of the feminine as an unshaped or unchanging essence. Goldman never even specified what women might do with a newfound freedom or with the possibility of expressing an authentic feminine desire. She found it more important for her audiences to understand that gender inequity structures the world to severely limit women's freedom than to specify what women might do or what women might want once they have the opportunities. Goldman consistently emphasized the importance of the theatrical and the performative in appealing to audiences, sparking their untapped radicalism and jolting their political consciousness. In her work to move people to action, Goldman (1969b) stressed the importance of the utopian dimension of her thought. She was certain that to rouse social discontent with current conditions, an appeal must be launched to "both mind and heart" (p. 17). Goldman counted herself among the "real revolutionist[s], the dreamer[s], the creative artist[s], the iconoclast[s] in whatever line" (Goldman 1987, 51–52). Her searing critique of current political–economic–social conditions promised a new vision, what she called a "beautiful ideal" of a new society where the human spirit would be free of oppression and restored to dignity and worth. Her vision was that of a feminist anarchist future where all would be free in love and work to develop themselves as fully human and creative beings.

Given this focus on the performative, Goldman would agree with feminist theorists such as Stevi Jackson (2001, 260), who reminds us "our subjectivities, including that aspect of them we call emotions, are shaped by the social and cultural milieu we inhabit, through processes which involve our active engagement with sets of meaning available in our culture." Lauren Berlant (2000, 2), too, emphasizes the material, cultural, and historical context which structures how our most intimate relationships get played out. She notes the mix of fantasy and materiality in stressing the importance of understanding "how to articulate the ways the utopian, optimism-sustaining versions of intimacy meet the normative practices, fantasies, institutions, and ideologies that organize people's worlds." Goldman's life and theory serves as a case study of the ways her desire for a new kind of intimacy and longing for the beautiful dream of her anarchist vision were to butt up against the harsh reality of the lack of community, material, and psychological support needed for her vision to transpire. At the same time that Goldman delivered an anarchist dream of woman's desire to be free from oppressive social conditions and expectations, she could only hint at how this revolution might create a space for new forms of intimacy and specifically how a newly liberated feminine desire might be articulated within these changes.

Central to this though, as I argue throughout this chapter, was Goldman's commitment to the free expression of sexuality. She was as disillusioned with normative conceptions of desire and femininity as she was with the elusive quest for equality. Though Goldman portrayed her own sexuality as heterosexual and longing for commitment and constancy, her ideal makes space for people to express themselves sexually in whatever way they might desire. Once freed from the grip of normative heterosexuality with its accompanying claims about the conventional family, traditional motherhood, the duties of men and women, and so on, Goldman was convinced that people would invent new and freer ways of expressing themselves in their most intimate relations. Goldman flirted with the idea of having a lesbian love affair—and she may have even done so—with anarchist colleague Almeda Sperry, who clearly adored her (Katz 1992, 523–29). Reframing the struggle for women's, and indeed human, emancipation in terms that speak to our needs for freedom, Goldman was able to put forward the absolute necessity of freeing women on their own terms without having to sacrifice love or varieties of sexual expression and without reference to male-defined and state-centered notions of equality as the measure by which to judge progress.

Familiarity with Goldman's experience, however, reminds us of the constraints patriarchy imposes on the lives of even the freest-thinking women. Having witnessed the failure to achieve her political ideal in the United States, and completely disillusioned by the revolution in the Soviet Union, nearing the end of her life Goldman was particularly bereft of ideals on which to pin her hopes. In a letter to Berkman written in early 1929, Goldman (1975, 145) related the difficulty of writing her autobiography, having to relive and remember her passions in light of their demise:

> It is not only the writing, it is living through what now lies in ashes and being made aware that I have nothing left in the way of personal relations from all who have been in my life and have torn my heart …. I should have known that it would be torture to revive the past. I am now paying for it.

Must the inspirational be accompanied by the terrifying, as Goldman witnessed in Wollstonecraft's life and was fulfilled almost as prophecy in Goldman's? Surely the fact that these two women were able to talk so frankly in letters about dilemmas they experienced as women trying to recreate models of love and sexuality speaks to the necessity of studying the personal alongside the philosophical–political. Goldman (1981, 121) remarked, "Had Mary Wollstonecraft not written a line, her life would have furnished food for thought ... but she has given us both, she therefore stands among the world's greatest, a life so deep, so rich, so exquisitely beautiful in her complete humanity."

From studying Goldman's life as it intersects with her philosophy of love, freedom, and sexual expression, we are reminded of the contradictions of feminine desire under conditions of patriarchy as well as the necessity of changing consciousness to embrace new forms of intimacy in our most personal relationships. One important contribution Goldman made is her theorization of feminine desire as distinct from male models of femininity. Important, too, is the fact that Goldman's theory of individual freedom and the centrality of sexual expression and desire for this freedom does not exist as an abstract concept untethered by social–political change. Her utopian vision of a feminist future, though unrealized in her own historical moment, might inspire us to move forward. Engaging in the work of feminist genealogy is to learn from the experience, disappointments, and theoretical inspiration of women who have come before us. This represents one step toward breaking the cycle of endless repetition of the same battles. Goldman's life represents the difficulty, as well as the necessity, of believing in a feminist future that can inspire new visions of freedom.

THE JOB MARKET

By Daniel Dohan

O ften, the jobs in Guadalupe and Chávez resembled the "prizes" awarded to "lucky" contest winners in the classic joke: first prize was one job; second prize was two jobs. In the barrios, working was better than idleness. Jobs *were* prized. But given the monetary rewards and conditions on the job, the prize was one that few residents embraced without ambivalence.

Nearly everyone I knew in Guadalupe and Chávez worked in jobs that paid low wages, provided unsteady working hours, and provided few possibilities for upward mobility. Even though these jobs fell within a small slice at the bottom of the labor market, they were the most important source of income for residents in both Guadalupe and Chávez barrios.[1] Guadalupe residents worked as janitors, home health care workers, gardeners, construction laborers, table bussers, dishwashers, store clerks, and fast-food cooks. Some Guadalupe residents worked in the light industry of the Silicon Valley, including assembly of computer chips, food packaging, and warehousing. In Chávez, residents worked in the same jobs as in Guadalupe: fast-food cook, janitor, construction laborer, table busser, dishwasher, and warehouse laborer. Workers in Chávez also found positions in small manufacturing shops working as chromers, sheet metal workers, or painters; a few worked in larger unionized establishments, but most did not. Some Chávez residents had jobs in government or human services, such as community outreach worker, youth counselor, secretary, or intake nurse. No matter what the specific title, tasks, or employer, for most residents I knew in the barrios, jobs hadunpleasant drawbacks: low wages, unreliable hours, negligible security, or some combination of all of these problems.

The job market thus represented a conundrum for residents in both barrios. Good jobs—jobs that might turn into a career and lift a family out of poverty—were hard to come by. The wages from more readily available work often failed to gain residents and their families much economic security. This chapter explores this conundrum through an analysis of residents experiences and understandings of local work opportunities. I show how a variety of challenges made job markets in Guadalupe and Cháez more a source of ongoing difficulty than a source of manifest opportunity. These challenges included employers who appeared to have little interest or incentive to invest in their workforce or to provide a safe and pleasant work environment; residents relatively low levels of human capital—English-language skills and educational attainment in particular—that closed off better-quality jobs; and the difficulty of addressing these problems through organized and individual appeals for change. The challenges of the job market provide the context for understanding the experience of unemployment, and I conclude this chapter by describing the experience of unemployment for several barrio residents.

WORKERS AND EMPLOYERS

Most residents I knew in Guadalupe and Chávez worked in jobs that paid poorly, provided part-time or irregular hours, and provided unsteady tenure over the long term. Many residents in the barrios saw these qualities of jobs as a reflection of employers' power and desires. In the view of residents, employers were solely interested in making money and cared little whether a job was competently completed, under what conditions, or with what implications for their employees' quality of life.

The on-the-job experiences of a group of men in Guadalupe exemplified these views. The men were all janitors in large office buildings in and around San Jose, and they regularly had lunch together at Rita's restaurant in the late afternoon before starting their swing shifts. I joined them occasionally and over the course of several months developed a sense of their frustration with their work.

During my first lunches with the group, I discovered that much of the men's frustration stemmed from their feeling that they were not able to do their work properly. The men all had a substantial knowledge about cleaning techniques. One afternoon before lunch, for example, I watched as Victor, who was running his own janitorial business at the time, instructed a young man about how to properly clean the linoleum floor in his office. He outlined the steps to be followed and explained why certain cleaners had to be used in a particular order. Victor warned the young man against taking shortcuts such as one-coat solutions that, he warned, clean the floor fine but over time corrode the linoleum. He pointed out bare spots on the floor that reflected this kind of shoddy technique.

At Rita's, many complaints concerned how employers did not let the men do their jobs properly. All of the men worked for *contratistas,* contractors who supplied the large firms of the Silicon Valley with an outsourced labor force. These firms had made it possible to replace the higher-paid in-house janitors that the firms used to hire directly. As the *contratista* system became established in the South Bay, the various contractors bid against each other for cleaning jobs. Wages declined and workload increased as the costs of the competition were passed on to the workers. Scholars have documented these changes in the Silicon Valley and in other cities in California.[2] The janitors knew about it from personal experience. At Rita's the men talked about how the *contratistas* were paying less or hiring poorly trained workers. Frequently, according to the men, the *contratistas* hired the most recently arrived immigrants who were least able to defend themselves. One day Luis complained about how his boss had suddenly expanded the number of offices in his assignment; now there were only four workers per floor in his bank building downtown.

In the midst of these changes in contracting, Victor started his own cleaning service with a few contracts at local churches. His business was meant as an alternative to the *contratistas*, he told me. He emphasized that his workers were properly trained, even if he himself had to retrain them in unlearning improper techniques they had picked up in other jobs. His service cost a bit more than others, he knew, but he also believed that by properly cleaning his workers saved money on wear and tear. In addition, Victor's service offered social benefits. It was a Catholic business that sought to promote social justice. He paid his workers a living wage, and he hoped to eventually turn the business over to his workers and move on to new entrepreneurial pursuits himself. But the business ran out of steam after only a few months and long before Victor had achieved his social justice goals. Like the other businesses in San Jose, Victor concluded, the churches ultimately just wanted the lower price. He had to let his workers go, and like them he returned to the employ of *contratistas*.

The treatment that workers received at the hands of the janitorial *contratistas* exemplified more general patterns. The employers of Guadalupe and Chávez residents did not invest in their employees. Intense competition among employers and the availability of workers led to the degradation of conditions at work, the deterioration of hourly wages, and an increase in work duties. Rather than moving up into positions of greater pay, autonomy, or power over time, workers in Guadalupe and Chávez often found that low-wage jobs in San Jose and Los Angeles seemed to become progressively less rewarding.

A small number of residents in each barrio proved the exception to this rule, however. They worked in positions where tenure was rewarded. Oscar, a Guadalupe resident, ran the presses at a local printing company, and after several years he was promoted to the job of plant supervisor. His on-the-job familiarity with the machinery was the key element that gained him a promotion. In his new job, he earned overtime pay, supervised the younger press operators, and had substantial autonomy given that his boss, the plant manager, relied on him to communicate with the Spanish-speaking workforce. In Chávez, Cynthia recalled how her mechanic's skills had allowed her to rise to a position of autonomy and responsibility in a small transportation company. She had been hired as a van driver, but her supervisor noticed that she was able to repair her own van whenever it broke down. This led to a promotion where she operated almost as a freelance driver/mechanic within the company. She managed her own schedule, repaired her van and those of other drivers as needed, and recalled it as the best job she had ever held.

Occasionally, as Oscar and Cynthia could attest, barrio residents worked in jobs that provided positive experiences of engagement, autonomy, and advancement, but experiences such as those of Luis, Victor, and the other janitors in Guadalupe were more often the rule. Residents' experiences told them that most barrio employers preferred paying a low wage to supporting conscientious workers.

THE ROLE OF HUMAN CAPITAL

Residents in Guadalupe and Chávez found working in low-wage jobs unrewarding in many ways, so it was not surprising that many sought to move into better positions. Moving out of low-wage jobs could be difficult, however, because the residents I knew often found that the better jobs toward which they aspired appeared to require credentials, skills, or experience—in short, human capital—that they did not possess. In Guadalupe, residents frequently felt they did not speak English well enough to get better jobs, and residents in both barrios often felt that better jobs demanded better credentials and substantive skills than they had been able to acquire in local schools.

In Guadalupe generally, residents took it as an article of faith that speaking English was necessary to get a better job. This faith was born of repeated experiences such as occurred one day in a local hiring hall where many Guadalupe residents sought work. Mary was a bilingual volunteer who worked in the center, screening incoming calls from potential employers and attempting to match job seekers to jobs. I saw the following events in July 1994:

Mary has several jobs she is trying to fill and stands in front of the room of fifteen men and women who are seeking positions. Most of the jobs she has are for two- or three-day stints as gardeners or domestics, but one is for a full-time position behind the counter at a soon-to-open deli. Many are interested in the position, but Mary quickly eliminates them all from consideration. "You need to speak *English* to do this job," she tells the group. "I speak English," replies René, who has his hand up. Mary says to him, in a pretty good imitation of a fast-paced New Yorker, "I'll take a turkey on rye with pickle and mustard, hold the lettuce and mayo." And then slower and with more careful diction, "What did I ask for?" René confesses that he did not understand. "A-ha!" she exclaims, and she snaps her fingers a few times. "You need to be quick *quick* to do this job." René ends up settling for a short-term gardening job that does not require English. Over the next hour, several others who express keen interest in the deli job also fail the language test, and later Mary turns over the job to an Anglo-American woman.

The events at the hiring hall that summer afternoon provided an unusually stark illustration of how language barriers restricted residents' attempts to get better-paying and more stable jobs. In other cases, residents found that knowing English was not necessary to get a job but was crucial for mobility within the work site. The experiences of Oscar illustrated this dynamic. His English-language skill, rudimentary to be sure, coupled with his long tenure was enough to move him into a supervisor's position at the print shop. The many workers at the site who spoke no English whatsoever never got the chance to impress the owner with their own qualifications to move up in the organization.

In Chávez, where facility with English was rarely an obstacle, many residents found that their educational attainment and credentials frustrated their attempts to attain better-paying and more stable jobs. The experiences of Lisa, a twenty-four-year-old Chávez resident who was a clerk at a health care clinic, provide an example. A mother of two, Lisa had left high school when her first child was born and had not received her diploma. I recorded the following field note at work soon after Lisa and her friend and co-worker Rosa had been briefed about the future of the clinic by a senior administrator. The administrator headed the East Los Angeles health care consortium that operated the small Chávez clinic with funds from a special grant, and the grant had not been renewed. Rosa was directly employed by the consortium; the end of the special grant did not threaten her position. Lisa's salary came from the grant, however, so her position was vulnerable.

Lisa and Rosa begin to talk about going back to school. Lisa wants to return for her Graduate Equivalency Degree (GED), and Rosa says that the clinic would support her if she wanted to go back. Rosa says that she herself went back for her GED but it took her about five tries before she finally got it. She kept signing up and going and then quitting and then going back and so on. Lisa says that she went back to school, too, but after a while in the continuation school [where students work toward the GED] they switched her into a job-training program. That program was good because she learned all these skills and got the job at the clinic, but they said she would also finish her GED and she never did. She was going to one of the local high schools, but it got to be too much. She was going to work and then to school. She'd leave the house before her kids were up and get home after they'd go to bed so she would never see them. It was too hard never seeing her kids, she says, so she dropped out. Now she wants to return to the continuation school in order to get her high school diploma. The class meets nine to eleven in the morning and she thinks that maybe the clinic will let her get away from work for that time in order to attend. If she gets that diploma, she thinks she'll be able to keep her job with the clinic, because with the GED the clinic will be able to hire her to its full-time staff.

For several years, before returning to school and joining the clinic, Lisa had relied on public assistance. Her enrollment in the job-training program, where she learned medical-clerical skills, helped her overcome the barriers to employment that she had faced as a single mother without educational credentials or employment experience. My impression was that Lisa was a well-prepared and competent worker. Being from Chávez and bilingual allowed her to adeptly handle the clinic's patient population, all of whom were residents of Chávez and other nearby low-income neighborhoods. Staff and clients sang her praises. Nevertheless, with only a few months at her first full-time position, Lisa still felt tenuously attached to the job market. She believed that the lack of a GED made her more likely to be laid off than clerks who had the credential. It seemed that neither practical skills as a clerk nor practical knowledge as a longtime resident of the low-income barrios offered the same employment security as a GED.

As it turned out, when the special grant that paid Lisa expired, the clinic kept her on staff by moving her into a new position. The administrator spent a few hours training her to handle the financial screening and paperwork that would be crucial for the small clinic's continued existence. In her new position, Lisa's rapport with community members was particularly valuable. She knew whether incoming clients were Chávez residents or not, and in many cases she knew what kind of access they had to health insurance. Lisa used the threat of charging for services to turn away some clients from the clinic, and for some whom she believed really needed care she forged paperwork to get them through the initial screening process.[3]

The experiences of René and Lisa highlight how human capital shaped residents' experiences on the job market. On the one hand, lack of human capital—Ren's lack of English and Lisa's lack of credentials—could hamper workers. Once they were working, as the experiences of Oscar and Lisa illustrate, workers in both communities often turned out to be competent and valued workers. Even for the most competent workers, however, lack of credentials remained a source of insecurity and vulnerability.

ADDRESSING LABOR MARKET PROBLEMS

Residents of Guadalupe and Chávez were aware of the problems posed by low-quality jobs and their own limited human capital, and they attempted to address them directly. Some workers tried to organize. In Guadalupe, attempts by resident and nonresident activists to organize janitors were hotly contested by employers, who assumed they would have more difficulty keeping wage rates low if workers of Guadalupe and other barrios were represented by a union. In a general sense, Guadalupe residents knew about and supported the union's efforts and goals, but when it came down to particulars many residents wanted concrete evidence that the fledgling union was turning money and support into better working conditions and higher wages for workers. The following field notes, which capture a conversation among three middle-aged Mexican immigrants, convey how union promises to improve wages and work conditions played out in Guadalupe.

Martín and Macario are discussing the corruption of unions when Héctor joins the conversation. Héctor was an official in one of the big unions in Mexico City before coming to San Jose, and he begins to defend the union. He says that it is the only way janitors will get ahead with the *contratistas,* if they all organize together and get better working conditions. But Martín is skeptical. "No, I'm not going to pay them [the unions] any more money," he says. "I already paid them so much money, but they don't do anything with it. They just take it. They opened the new union headquarters—that nice new building—but at the opening celebration, how many people there were workers in the union? Only ten people of that big crowd. Hétor pleads with Martí that the union needs to stay strong because contract negotiations are coming up soon, but Martínis not moved by this argument. They have just nearly doubled his workload at his job at one of the large Silicon Valley computer companies. How am I going to do the job right now? he asked. How I have 250 offices, five conference rooms, and five large bathrooms to clean between 6:00 p.m. and 2:00 a.m. The union just makes noise, but they should stop that [the increasing workload]. There's no way to clean that much in one shift. So now I'm going to have to rush through and not clean things right, and the job will not be done right.

Unions represented a compelling argument about how to address the problems of low wages and poor working conditions. By negotiating collectively with employers, unions could improve the conditions at work by pressuring employers into raising wages and establishing and enforcing work rules. Residents in Guadalupe supported these ideas, but their everyday experiences told them that support of these ideas did not quickly translate into practice. Most of the Guadalupe residents I knew did not attend organizing meetings, and union activists and community leaders—not rank-and-file workers—dominated the meetings I observed. The union's presence in the city and signs of its increasing power in local affairs, signs including the opening of the new union headquarters, failed to inspire much interest or commitment in Guadalupe residents.

Residents in the low-income barrios also addressed problems of low-wage labor markets through direct appeal to local help-providing organizations. Government and nonprofit agencies often provided assistance to residents of both barrios as a matter of course, but they rarely addressed employment problems directly. Nevertheless, residents believed that these agencies had tremendous resources at their disposal, and they appealed to them for help on the labor market, as Chávez residents Paul and Elena did in the spring of 1995. The two went to see a housing authority official to appeal the case of a tenant who faced a heavy fine and possible eviction for failing to pay rent. The tenant had fallen behind in her rent payments when her husband became unemployed following an accident on the job.

Paul and Elena went down to the central office for public housing for the city for a meeting with one of the midlevel managers there. This official was a Chicano who had grown up in one of the working-class suburbs of the San Gabriel Valley, and on previous occasions Paul had had cordial and friendly relations with him. Elena said that today the official had been rigid and unhelpful when it came to dealing with the problem of the tenant, and Paul lost his temper. Paul blamed the problem on the housing authority official. "They forget where they came from," he said. "Just sit on their ass, pushing paper around and collecting thirty or forty thousand dollars a year. Their job is to help people out in the projects, but they don't care about them at all."

When it came to the daily problems that inevitably though unpredictably arose for residents dependent on low-wage labor markets, residents of both barrios regularly turned for assistance to public and nonprofit agencies—the housing authority, job-training centers, non-profits dedicated to helping immigrants adjust their legal status. Like Paul and Elena, however, residents often came away from these experiences frustrated. Government and nonprofits addressed the difficulties of low-wage work through official programs: job training, summer employment, legal outreach, parenting classes, and the like. But agency staff often appeared unresponsive and occasionally appeared hostile to direct appeals by residents for concrete assistance or even simple understanding. Many residents saw this unresponsiveness as a function of staff persons distance and insulation from residents everyday concerns and dilemmas. Thus, Paul blamed the housing authority official's unresponsiveness on the fact that he held a secure, well-paid job. The distance between those who helped from those they helped made it difficult for residents to bring leverage to bear on staffers during times of need. In everyday life, though regularly appealed to, the helping agencies of local government and nonprofits failed to provide reliable and timely assistance for low-wage workers.

Residents of both barrios also made direct appeals to another powerful local influence, the employers themselves. In Chávez, many residents believed they had some leverage over local employers. In the past, direct pressure on local merchants had led to the hiring of public housing residents. When a shuttered store in Chávez prepared to reopen under a new owner, Ron, a former gang member and active member of the Chávez community, explained, "They're opening up that store again …. They closed it down last year, and then these Chinos [Asians] are opening it up again. But we have to make sure that they do something for the community. They would just hire their own people to work that store, but we're going to make sure they hire some homeboys. I already talked to people about it. If they don't hire homeboys to work there—and not just one but a bunch of guys—then were going to boycott. The owners of the new store seemed likely to respond to pressure from the community because they needed to capture the business of Chávez residents if they were to succeed. In addition, Ron hinted that their property was at risk if they did not maintain good relations with the community. He was not surprised that the new owners made a point of hiring some Chávez residents when the store opened some weeks later.

Employers also occasionally responded to more personal appeals. When Guadalupe resident Oscar and his wife Natalia had their first child in San Jose, they were shocked by the expense. But Oscar had already established a good working relationship with the head of the printing company, and he was able to secure a loan to cover the hospital bills. Paying the loan back through paycheck deductions pushed Oscar, Natalia, and their children into reliance on public assistance for a period of time, but without the cash from Oscar's boss, the family had no idea how they were going to pay the thousands of dollars of medical expenses incurred during the routine delivery.

UNEMPLOYMENT

Guadalupe and Chávez residents saw the job market as a place of opportunity for highly skilled and credentialed workers or for workers with union protection, government employment, or a decent boss. But most of the people I knew in the barrios did not work in this job market. They lacked skills or credentials required for more desirable positions, their employers seemed interested only in maximizing profits, and they worked without union or government protections. These qualities of local job markets provide the context for understanding unemployment among barrio residents.

Unemployment has distressing or even devastating consequences for low-income workers and their communities, and the unemployment rate is an widely understood and easily grasped indicator of the quality of life in a low-income community. Scholars and policy makers measure unemployment by using a survey to determine how many workers in a community or the nation are actively looking for work. A 5 percent unemployment rate, for example, indicates that for every hundred workers interviewed, five said that they were out of a job and looking for work. The 5 percent figure counts only "workers," so it specifically excludes children (people younger than eighteen), retired people (those older than sixty-four), and anyone of "working age" (eighteen to sixty-four) who is not actively looking for work, such as homemakers. The picture of unemployment conveyed by this survey measure is that unemployed people are a group of people who spend their days searching in vain for an employer willing to take them on.

I did not use a survey to measure unemployment in Guadalupe and Chávez, but I tried to directly assess which workers in these communities were actively looking for work. This turned out to be a difficult task. For every resident who was clearly spending his or her days in a frustrated search for employment, there were many more who were having trouble finding a job they wanted to take. I met men and women struggling with unemployment in both barrios, but, for reasons I discuss in detail in Chapter 5, these problems were especially pressing for young men in Chávez barrio.4 The experiences of Benji, a Chávez resident in his early twenties, were fairly typical of residents who spent considerable time in a frustrated search for work, while for Christian, another Chávez resident, unemployment played a complex role in a complex work history.

After Benji had graduated from high school in the early 1990s, he had looked for work near Chávez but had been unable to find anything satisfying. Believing that some more years of education and some concrete job skills would ease his way into steady work, Benji enrolled in a course to learn cable television maintenance and repair. He held some temporary positions while training, and the school had implied that they would find him a job once he graduated. As graduation neared in the early summer of 1995, he optimistically predicted he would find a job, earn more money, and establish an independent household. However, several months after the completion of the training course, Benji had still not found secure employment, and he continued to live in his mother's apartment in the projects. Still, he remained optimistic. He took it as a positive sign that he had found temporary jobs. Given the popularity of cable television, Benji was sure it was just a matter of time until he found a steady job that would allow him to get together the money for the security deposit on his own apartment.

Unemployment seemed to sneak up on Christian. He was a twentyfour-year-old lifetime resident of Chávez, and he had not graduated from high school. He began grappling with unemployment after completing jail time for his role in an attempted armed robbery of a local *tienda*. For four months after getting out of jail and re-entering his mother's home in Chávez, Christian stayed away from criminal enterprises, dividing his time between caring for his baby daughter, working occasionally at construction or car repair, and performing as part of a local rap group. He was essentially idle during these months. Initially, Christian believed that the period of idleness was a time during which he and the band members were working on new material and preparing to go into the studio to record their first full-length CD. If he had been responding to a survey, I am not sure whether he would have said he was idle and looking for work during these months. But after performing at several events, the lead singer of the band split off from the group to pursue a solo career. "When we did that gig over in Las Vegas, this agent saw Pedro and really liked him. But this guy said that he wanted Pedro but not the rest of the band, and Pedro left us. That was fucked up," explained Christian.

Christian had not seemed troubled that he was unemployed while the band was working gigs and preparing for studio sessions. Now, with the band ruined by the leader's defection, Christian became more discouraged about the long period of time he had gone without a regular job. He began to spend more time hanging out on the streets, and he complained that he was depressed and bored. He knew that his background made him an unattractive prospect for most employers, and he figured his best chance of finding employment was in construction, where he had some experience and contacts and where he could take advantage of special programs to employ public housing residents, high school dropouts, and ex-felons. A steady construction job did not come quickly or easily, but after an additional two months Christian found a position at a nearby site and entered a one-month period of reduced hours and wages while he underwent training. Finally, after seven months of more or less complete idleness—some partially self-imposed and some at the mercy of the labor market—Christian began working full time. He was guaranteed only a few months of work. When the specific project he was working on ended, the firm probably would let him go and he would again be on the job market.

Christian believed that lacking a high school diploma and carrying a criminal record extended his period of unemployment. At the same time, much of his unemployment reflected his own hopes for success with the band. For Christian, the meaning and role of unemployment changed over time, with a period of voluntary loose connection with the labor market gradually becoming a time of frustrated exclusion from work. Significantly, Christian's experience on the job market was similar to that of Chávez residents who, on the face of it, seemed more employable and more focused on finding regular employment.

The experiences of Benji and Christian illustrate the role of unemployment in the lives of many barrio residents. Most people could find some kind of work, as Benji did after graduating from high school, but often these easily found jobs offered few financial rewards or career possibilities. Searching for a better position could consume many months, and, as Christian found, the reward at the end of this long search often would be a position that promised only a few months of pay before the job search would have to be resumed. Better qualifications, such as

Benji's technical training, might increase the wages earned in a particular job, but this training by no means guaranteed residents an easier job search or shorter periods of unemployment while job searching.

When we measure the unemployment rate with a survey, we attach a clear meaning to the notion of "high unemployment"—frustrated workers, economic struggle, and negative consequences for the community. Sometimes barrio unemployment carried these connotations. But unemployment had a variety of other meanings as well. Benji's original experience with unemployment came when he left the labor market to go to cable school, while Christian stayed off the job market to pursue band life and take care of his daughter. Technically, while Benji was in school or Christian was in the band, neither was unemployed. In the barrios, choices such as these were often understood as choices or opportunities. At the same time, one wonders: If Benji had landed a good job straight out of high school, would he have gone to cable school? And would Christian have stayed in the band so long or been as willing to be a full-time parent if he had been able to find a job coming out of jail?

The unemployment rate is a measure of frustration—of the number of people who want to work but cannot find a job—that is easily and reliably measured with just a few survey questions. In everyday barrio life, however, unemployment includes a variety of complex relationships between residents and jobs. What kinds of jobs do residents believe are available to them? What constitutes the volition to work? Would a resident take any job? Or did it make more sense to be picky and search for an attractive opportunity? Residents frequently transitioned into and out of jobs. Understanding these dynamics requires an appreciation for what residents expected to gain from working, what workers had to offer employers, and how workers sought to improve their collective position on the labor market.

Contrary to my expectations, during fieldwork I saw residents in both Guadalupe and Chávez confronting a similar catalog of job market difficulties: employer exploitation, difficulty competing for better-quality jobs, limited power to effect positive change, and regular unemployment. I was not surprised that barrio residents found the labor market frustrating, but I did not expect to find residents in *both* barrios frustrated by the same sorts of problems. I had expected residents in Chávez, with its higher unemployment rate, to be manifestly less connected to local jobs than the people I knew in Guadalupe. I had expected that the residents of persistently poor Chávez would have much more difficulty finding *any* sort of job than the people I knew in Guadalupe. To be sure, unemployment was more frequently a problem for people I knew in Chávez than it was in Guadalupe, but both communities had strong connections to the labor market. Neither barrio appeared to be experiencing a job market collapse.

This is good news for the barrios, but it is also puzzling news for researchers. Often researchers interpret high unemployment rates as a reflection of job market collapse. With a poverty rate above 50 percent and unemployment at 20 percent, the statistics paint Chávez as a community where work has disappeared. The theme of this chapter, however, is that residents in both Chávez and Guadalupe found opportunities for income earning on the job market even though pursuing these opportunities meant confronting substantial challenges and frustrations. Thus, I see the job market in the barrios as a source of prickly prizes that residents pursued despite practical challenges and personal ambivalence. In the next chapter, I delve further into the nature of barrio jobs by examining how residents held on to the prizes they garnered in local job markets.

WHITE IDENTITY AND AFFIRMATIVE ACTION

"I'M IN FAVOR OF AFFIRMATIVE ACTION EXCEPT WHEN IT COMES TO MY JOBS."

By Beverly Daniel Tatum

Because of the persistence of residential segregation and the school segregation that often accompanies it, the workplace is one of the few places that the lives of people of color and Whites regularly intersect. Those intersections can sometimes lead to close friendships and serve as a catalyst for Whites to begin to examine their own racial identities. But even when the workplace is only a site of superficial exchanges across color lines, the presence of an affirmative action policy can be enough to draw an individual's attention to his own Whiteness. What will affirmative action mean in my life? Will I get the job I want, or will it go to some "minority"? Will the opportunities I expected still be there for me, or will I be the victim of "reverse racism"?

Even those Whites who have not given much thought to their racial identity have thought about affirmative action. As sociologist Howard Winant writes, assaults on affirmative action policies are "currently at hysterical levels .... These attacks are clearly designed to effect ideological shifts, rather than to shift resources in any meaningful way. They represent whiteness as *disadvantage*, something which has few precedents in U.S. racial history." Though there is almost no empirical evidence for this "imaginary white disadvantage," the idea has achieved "widespread popular credence."[1]

In my classes and workshops, the concern about White disadvantage takes the form of questions about affirmative action and "reverse discrimination." Inevitably someone has a story to tell about a friend or relative who was not admitted to the school of her choice, or a parent who lost a coveted promotion because a "less-qualified" person of color took that spot. It is interesting to note that the "less-qualified" person in the story is always a person of color, usually Black, never a White woman.[2] (When these stories are told, I often wonder how the speaker knows so much about the person of color's résumé.)

Whenever possible, I defer the discussion of affirmative action, at least until a basic understanding of racism as a system of advantage has been established. I do this because it is very difficult to have a useful discussion about affirmative action with a person who does not understand the concept of White privilege. If someone uses the phrases "affirmative action"and "reverse racism"in the same sentence, it is usually a sign that a lesson on White privilege is needed. This is not to say that everyone who understands White privilege supports affirmative action policies, but at least that basic understanding assures that all parties in the conversation recognize that there are systematic social inequities operating in our society, and that the playing field is not level. We may have different opinions about how to fix those inequities, but an acknowledgment of the inequities is essential to a productive conversation.

After assigning several readings on the topic of affirmative action, I ask my students to write essays about whether they think it is a good idea and why. If they are opposed to affirmative action, I ask them to propose an alternative approach to dismantling the system of advantage in the arenas of educational and employment opportunity. Several years ago, one young White woman wrote the following sentence in her essay:"I am in favor of affirmative action except when it comes to my jobs."I wrote in response, "Which jobs have your name on them?"

The sense of entitlement conveyed in the statement was striking. Of course, she wanted to get the jobs she applied for, and did not want to lose out to anyone, especially on the basis of race,a factor over which she had no control. Yet she seemed to assume that because she wanted them,they belonged to her. She assumed that she would, of course, be qualified for the job, and would therefore be entitled to it. What was she assuming about the candidates of color? She did not seem to take into account the possibility that one of them might be as qualified, or more qualified, than she was. The idea that she as a White woman might herself be the recipient of affirmative action was apparently not part of her thinking. While she expressed a desire for equity and justice,she also wanted to maintain her own advantage. She was still sifting through some confused thinking on this issue. She is not alone.

WHAT IS AFFIRMATIVE ACTION?

There has been much public debate about affirmative action since its inception, with little attempt to clarify concepts. Politicians' interchangeable use of the terms *affirmative action* and *quotas* have contributed to the confusion,perhaps intentionally. The term *quota* has a repugnant history of discrimination and exclusion. For example, earlier in the twentieth century, quotas were used to limit how many Jews would be admitted to prestigious institutions of higher learning.

But despite common public perceptions, most affirmative action programs do not involve quotas, though they may involve goals. The difference between a goal and a quota is an important one. Quotas, defined here as fixed numerical allocations, are illegal, unless court-ordered as a temporary remedy for a well-documented, proven pattern of racially-motivated discrimination. Unlike a quota, goals are voluntary, legal, and may even be exceeded. Goals are not a ceiling meant to limit (as quotas did in the past). Instead, goals provide a necessary target toward which to aim. As any long-range planner knows, goals are necessary in order to chart one's course of action, and to evaluate one's progress. Goals are an essential component of effective affirmative action programs.

The term *affirmative action* was introduced into our language and legal system by Executive Order 11246, signed by President Lyndon Johnson in 1965. This order obligated federal contractors to take affirmative action to ensure that applicants are employed, and that employees are treated during employment without regard to their race, color, religion, sex, or national origin. As set forth by this order, contractors were to commit themselves to apply every good faith effort to use procedures that would result in equal employment opportunity for historically disadvantaged groups. The groups targeted for this affirmative action were White women, and men and women of color (specifically defined by the federal government as American Indian/Alaska Natives, Asian or Pacific Islanders, Blacks, and Hispanics). In the 1970s, legislation broadened the protected groups to include persons with disabilities and Vietnam veterans. Though Executive Order 11246 required affirmative action, it did not specify exactly what affirmative action programs should look like.[3]

Given this lack of specificity, it is not surprising that there is great variety in the way affirmative action programs have been developed and implemented around the country.[4] The executive order had as its goal equal employment opportunity. But in practice, because of continuing patterns of discrimination, that goal cannot be reached without positive steps—affirmative actions—to create that equality of opportunity. Consequently, affirmative action can be defined as attempts to make progress toward actual, rather than hypothetical, equality of opportunity for those groups which are currently underrepresented in significant positions in society by explicitly taking into account the defining characteristics—sex or race, for example—that have been the basis for discrimination.[5] These attempts can be categorized as either *process-oriented or goal-oriented.*

Process—oriented programs focus on creating a fair application process, assuming that a fair process will result in a fair outcome. If a job opening has been advertised widely, and anyone who is interested has a chance to apply, and all applicants receive similar treatment (i.e., standard interview questions, same evaluation criteria and procedures), the process is presumed to be fair. The search committee can freely choose the "best" candidate knowing that no discrimination has taken place. Under such circumstances, the "best" candidate will sometimes be a person of color, "too good to ignore."[6] In theory, such would seem to be the case, and because process-oriented programs seem consistent with the American ideal of the meritocracy, most people support this kind of affirmative action.[7] At the very least, it is an improvement over the "old boy network" that filled positions before outsiders even had a chance to apply.

Goal—oriented affirmative action also provides an open process. However, when the qualified pool of applicants has been identified, those among the pool who move the organization closer to its diversity hiring goals are favored. If the finalist hired was qualified but not the "best" choice in the eyes of those who don't share the goal, the decision is often criticized as "reverse discrimination."

Though the process-oriented emphasis is more palatable to some than the goal—oriented emphasis, in practice the process—oriented approach is often quite ineffective. Despite the attempts to insure a fair process, search committee after search committee finds the "best" person is yet another member of the dominant group. What goes wrong? Some answers may be found in the research of social psychologist John Dovidio and his colleagues.

AVERSIVE RACISM AND AFFIRMATIVE ACTION

In "Resistance to Affirmative Action: The Implications of Aversive Racism," John Dovidio, Jeffrey Mann, and Samuel Gaertner argue that White opposition to affirmative action programs is largely rooted in a subtle but pervasive form of racism they call "aversive racism." Aversive racism is defined as "an attitudinal adaptation resulting from an assimilation of an egalitarian value system with prejudice and with racist beliefs." In other words, most Americans have internalized the espoused cultural values of fairness and justice for all at the same time that they have been breathing the "smog" of racial biases and stereotypes pervading the popular culture. "The existence, both of almost unavoidable racial biases and of the desire to be egalitarian and racially tolerant, forms the basis of the ambivalence that aversive racists experience."[8]

Pointing to the findings of several impressive research studies, these social psychologists argue that because aversive racists see themselves as nonprejudiced and racially tolerant, they generally do not behave in overtly racist ways. When the norms for appropriate, non-discriminatory behavior are clear and unambiguous, they "do the right thing," because to behave otherwise would threaten the non-prejudiced self-image they hold. However, Dovidio and his colleagues assert that in situations when it is not clear what the "right thing" is, or if an action can be justified on the basis of some factor other than race, negative feelings toward Blacks will surface. In these ambiguous situations, an aversive racist can discriminate against Blacks without threatening his racially tolerant self-image.

For example, in a study in which White college students were asked to evaluate Black and White people on a simple "good-bad" basis, where choosing *bad* rather than *good* to describe Blacks might clearly indicate bias, the students consistently rated both Blacks and Whites positively. However, when the task was changed slightly to rating Blacks and Whites on a more subtle continuum of goodness, Whites were consistently rated better than Blacks. For instance, when the rating choice was ambitious–not lazy, Blacks were not rated as more lazy than Whites, but Whites were evaluated as more ambitious than Blacks. Repeated findings of this nature led these researchers to conclude that a subtle but important bias was operating. In the eyes of the aversive racists, Blacks are not worse, but Whites are better.

How might such a bias affect hiring decisions? Would this kind of bias affect how the competence of Black and White candidates might be evaluated? To explore this question, a study was conducted in which White college students were asked to rate college applicants who on the basis of transcript information were strongly qualified, moderately qualified, or weakly qualified. In some cases the applicant was identified as Black, in other cases as White. When the applicant was weakly qualified, there was no discrimination between Black and White applicants. Both were rejected. When the applicant had moderate qualifications, Whites were evaluated slightly better than Blacks, but not significantly so. However, when the applicant had strong qualifications, there was a significant difference between how strong White candidates and strong Black candidates were rated. Though the information that had been provided about the candidates was identical, the Black applicants were evaluated significantly less positively than the White applicants. The subtle bias that Dovidio and his colleagues have identified does not occur at all levels, but it occurs when you might least expect it, when the Black candidate is highly qualified. In this and other similar studies, Blacks could be seen as good, but Whites with the same credentials were consistently rated as better.[9]

The bias was even more apparent when the Black person being rated was in a position superior to the White evaluator. While high-ability White supervisors were accepted by subordinate White raters as being somewhat more intelligent than themselves, White evaluators consistently described high-ability Black supervisors as significantly less intelligent than themselves. So even when the Black supervisor is more competent than the White subordinate, the White again sees the situation as though a Black person less qualified than themselves is being given preferential treatment. The researchers speculate that the bias is accentuated in this scenario because the possibility of being subordinated to a Black person threatens deeply held (though perhaps unconscious) notions of White superiority.[10]

Social psychologists Susan Clayton and Sandra Tangri also discuss the illusory nature of "objective" evaluation, and offer another reason that the pattern of underestimating the abilities of competent Black candidates is so widespread. They suggest that when an evaluator expects a weak performance and sees a strong one, the strong performance is attributed to unstable causes such as luck or effort. Unlike "innate" ability, luck or effort can change and are therefore unreliable. However, strong performances based on ability will probably be repeated. Strong performances attributed to ability (the explanation likely used for White male candidates) are viewed more positively and more often rewarded than performances assumed to be based on luck or an unusual effort.[11]

Dovidio and colleagues conclude:

> The aversive racism framework has important and direct implication for the implementation of affirmative action–type policies. Affirmative action has often been interpreted as "when all things are equal, take the minority person." Our research suggests that even when things are equal, they may not be perceived as equal—particularly when the minority person is well-qualified and the situation has personal relevance to the non-minority person. Because Whites tend to misperceive the competence of Blacks relative to themselves, resistance to affirmative action may appear quite legitimate to the protesters. Insufficient competence, not race, becomes the rationale justifying resistance.[12]

The particular irony is that the more competent the Black person is, the more likely this bias is to occur.

The research that has been discussed here has been framed in terms of Black-White relationships.[13] Of course, affirmative action programs may also involve other people of color as well as White women.[14] Yet the Black-White emphasis in the aversive racism framework seems well placed when we consider that researchers have found that negative attitudes toward affirmative action are expressed most strongly when Blacks are identified as the target beneficiaries. As Audrey Murrell and her colleagues point out, "whereas giving preference based on nonmerit factors is perceived as unfair, giving such preference to Blacks is perceived as more unfair."[15]

Now we can see why affirmative action efforts focusing on the process rather than the outcome are likely to be ineffective. There are too many opportunities for evaluator bias to manifest itself—in the initial recruitment and screening of applicants, in the interview process, and ultimately in the final selection. Competent candidates of color are likely to be weeded out all along the way. Those that make it to the final selection process may in fact be "too good to ignore," but as the research suggests and as I have seen in some of my own search committee experiences, for Black candidates "too good to ignore" can mean too good to hire.

"NOT A PREJUDICED BONE IN THEIR BODIES": A CASE EXAMPLE

During the first nine years of my teaching career, I taught on two different campuses. In each case, I was the only Black female faculty member throughout my tenure. Though both institutions identified themselves as "equal employment opportunity/affirmative action employers," my experience on search committees in those settings taught me a lot about why there weren't more Black women or many Black men on campus. Black applicants "too good to be ignored" regularly were ignored, sometimes because they were too good. "Can't hire him, he's too good, he won't stay." "She's good, but not exactly what we had in mind." "He gave a brilliant talk, but there's just something about him, I can't quite put my finger on it."

In at least one instance, I thought I could put my finger on it, and did. When I raised questions about racial bias, I was told by the chair of the search committee, "I've known all of these [White] people for years. There's not a prejudiced bone in their bodies." If you've read chapter 1, you know how I feel about that comment. In this particular instance, I replied, "You know, I don't think anyone on the committee would intentionally discriminate, but I know that people feel most comfortable with people like themselves, with the kind of people they've grown up around, that they play golf with. When interacting with someone who doesn't fit that description, there may be a kind of uneasiness that is hard to articulate. So when I sit in a committee meeting, and White people all agree that a Black candidate is well qualified for the position, better than the competing White candidates in fact, but then they say things like, 'I'm not sure if he's the right person for the job,' 'I'm not sure what kind of colleague he'd be, I just didn't feel comfortable with him,' I think we have a problem."

We did have a problem. In this case, rather than offer the Black candidate the position, it was declared a failed search and the position was advertised again the following year. I was not asked to serve on the next search committee, and perhaps not surprisingly, there were no Black candidates in the pool of finalists the second time around. Did the Black candidate recognize the discrimination that I believe occurred, or was it seen as just another rejected application? I don't know. But this case highlighted for me one of the reasons that affirmative action is still needed. As social psychologist Faye Crosby writes,

> Affirmative action is needed to lessen bias in the paid labor force because affirmative action is the only legal remedy in the United States for discrimination that does not require the victims (or someone with a stake in their welfare) to notice their condition and come forward with a grievance on their own behalf .... In affirmative action, designated individuals monitor the operations of institutions and so can notice (and correct) injustices in the absence of any complaint. This monitoring role is crucial because an accumulation of studies have shown that it is very difficult to detect discrimination on a case-by-case basis, even when the case involves the self.[16]

When we examine the aggregate data, case after case, hiring decision after hiring decision, the idiosyncracies of particular cases recede and the discriminatory pattern can emerge. Then we can make a change.

KEEPING OUR EYES ON THE PRIZE: GOAL-ORIENTED AFFIRMATIVE ACTION

Though the research on evaluator bias is dismaying, it also points us in the direction of an effective response. Remember that when expectations for appropriate behavior are clearly defined and a biased response can be recognized, Whites are consistently as positive in their behavior toward Blacks as toward Whites. If administrators clearly articulate the organization's diversity goals and the reasons that such goals are in the organization's best interests, the appropriate behavior in the search process should be clear. If we keep our eyes on the prize, we can get past the bias.

Some might say, "Doesn't such an outcome-based focus lead to instances of 'reverse discrimination,' when well-qualified majority-group candidates are rejected in favor of a less qualified candidate from an underrepresented group simply because that candidate meets the diversity goal?" Certainly that could happen, but only in a poorly administered program. When affirmative action programs are functioning appropriately, no one is ever hired who is not qualified for the job. To do so undermines the program and is patently unfair to the newly hired person who has in effect been set up to fail.

In a well-conceived and implemented affirmative action program, the first thing that should be done is to establish clear and meaningful selection criteria. What skills does the person need to function effectively in this environment? How will we assess whether the candidates have these required skills? Will it be on the basis of demonstrated past performance, scores on an appropriate test,[17] the completion of certain educational requirements? Once the criteria have been established, anyone who meets the criteria is considered qualified.

Now we can consider who among these qualified candidates will best help us achieve our organizational goals for diversifying our institution. If one candidate meets the criteria but also has some additional education or experience, it may be tempting to say this candidate is the "best," but this one may not be the one who moves us toward our diversity goal. Because of the systematic advantages that members of the dominant group receive, it is often the case that the person with the extra experience or educational attainment is a person from the majority group. If our eyes are on our organizational goal, we are not distracted by these unasked-for extras. If we need someone who has toured Europe or had a special internship, it should already be part of our criteria. If it is not part of the criteria, it shouldn't be considered.

And if making our organization a more inclusive environment is a goal, then perhaps we should have that goal reflected in our criteria so that whoever is selected can support the organization's goals. Fletcher Blanchard, author of "Effective Affirmative Action Programs," suggests what some of these new criteria might be: the extent and favorability of one's experience working in multicultural settings, the experience of being supervised by managers of color, experience of collaborating in multicultural workgroups, or living in racially-mixed communities, fluency in a second language, or substantial college coursework in the study of multicultural perspectives.[18]

In my own consultation with school systems interested in increasing their faculty of color, we have discussed the need for such new criteria. The number of young people of color entering the teaching profession is still too small to meet the demand. While effective recruiting strategies can increase a school system's likelihood of being able to attract new teachers of color, many White teachers will still be needed to replace retiring teachers in the coming years. Schools concerned about meeting the needs of an increasingly diverse student population should be looking specifically for teachers of all backgrounds with demonstrated experience in working with multiracial populations, with courses on their transcripts like Psychology of Racism; Race, Class, Culture, and Gender in the Classroom; and Foundations of Multicultural Education, to name a few.

Criteria like these are important for all candidates, but they are also criteria which are more likely to be met by candidates of color, because people of color often have more life experience in multiracial settings than many White people do. However, because such criteria are not explicitly race-based, they are also criteria which should withstand the legal assaults that many affirmative action programs have experienced.[19] Should these legal challenges move us into a post–affirmative action age, such criteria will be increasingly important in the search and selection process. Under any circumstance, clarity about organizational goals and qualification criteria will lead to better and more equitable selection decisions.

WHITE DISADVANTAGE REVISITED

When the dominant identity of Whiteness goes unexamined, racial privilege also goes unacknowledged. Instead, the achievements that unearned privilege make more attainable are seen as just reward for one's own efforts. The sense of entitlement that comes as the result of privileges given and received without notice goes unchallenged. When that sense of entitlement is threatened, it is most often experienced as an unfair personal penalty rather than as a necessary and impersonal leveling of an uneven field. An understanding of what affirmative action is and is not often changes the perception of White disadvantage, especially when coupled with an understanding of White privilege. For example, Stanley Fish, a White man who understands both privilege and past and present patterns of employment discrimination, explains clearly why he believes affirmative action policies are justified even when such policies cost him a job he wanted.

> Although I was disappointed, I did not conclude that the situation was "unfair," because the policy was obviously not directed at me ... the policy was not intended to disenfranchise white males. Rather the policy was driven by other considerations, and it was only as a by-product of those considerations—not as the main goal—that white males like me were rejected. Given that the institution in question has a high percentage of minority students, a very low percentage of minority faculty, and an even lower percentage of minority administrators, it made perfect sense to focus on women and minority candidates, and within that sense, not as the result of prejudice, my whiteness and maleness became disqualifications. I can hear the objection in advance: "What's the difference? Unfair is unfair: you didn't get the job." ... It is the difference between

an unfairness that befalls one as the unintended effect of a policy rationally conceived and an unfairness that is pursued as an end in itself.[20]

Are there reasons to resist such an understanding? Absolutely. Describing interviews with "angry White men" from working-class communities, Michele Fine reveals how these men, displaced from jobs by the flight of capital from their cities, blame their misfortune not on corporate greed but on African Americans. Explains Fine, Black people are psychologically "imported to buffer the pain, protest the loss, and still secure the artificial privilege of whiteness."[21] In a societal context where historically the scapegoating of the "other" has been standard operating procedure, it is easier to do that than critically examine the large structural conditions that have created this situation.

Speaking from her vantage point as a White female psychologist who has studied affirmative action for many years, Faye Crosby comments on this anger: "For those who study affirmative action, the attitudes of angry and frightened White males can provoke some impatience. But to end the impatience and become sympathetic with aspects of the resistance to affirmative action, I need only remember how privilege has blinded me, too."[22] Rather than dismissing with disdain those who suffer the illusion of "imaginary white disadvantage," she urges engagement in dialogue. For those who are fatigued by the effort, she offers a good reason to continue. "[M]y fervent support of affirmative action comes ultimately from being the mother of White boy-men. It is because I want a better world for my children that I bother to fight for affirmative action."[23]

All of us want a better, more peaceful world for our children. If we want peace, we must work for justice. How do we achieve a more just society in the present context of institutional and cultural racism? Goal-oriented affirmative action is but one potentially effective strategy. Serious dialogue about other strategies is needed, and that dialogue needs to be expanded beyond the Black-White paradigm that has shaped discussions of affirmative action. The voices of other disenfranchised groups need to be acknowledged in the process, because as my students continually remind me, "Racism is not just a Black-White thing."

LEARNING PRIVILEGE

LESSONS OF POWER AND IDENTITY IN AFFLUENT SCHOOLING

By Adam Howard

"**W**hy are we learning about those people?" Jonas, one of my seventhgrade students, asked me during a discussion about homelessness. "This isn't about social issues. Those people are just bad business people," he insisted.

"We're discussing it because homelessness is a big problem in our country and even in our city. It's an important issue for us to be aware of instead of just ignoring it," I responded.

Jonas replied, "Yeah, but it's because they don't spend their money right and don't get jobs to get them out of their situation."

Another boy sitting across from Jonas added, "It's a problem because they just don't want to work so they can live in a house. They're too lazy to get a job."

"I think it's because they don't make the good decisions in life and it's gotten them where they're at," another boy told us.

"Why do you think they don't make the right decisions?" I asked. "What makes people not make good decisions?"

"I think Jonas said it. They're bad business people," one of the boys replied. Fortunately, the bell rang, because I did not know how to respond to their comments at the time. It was one of those moments as a teacher when I couldn't come up with the right response or the perfect question to challenge students' thinking. I was speechless.

During my first year of teaching at an elite private school, I met with ten seventh-grade boys for forty-five minutes two days a week to cover a broad range of issues—everything from puberty to larger societal concerns. It was a designated time for them to feel safe (no girls around) to discuss personal and societal issues openly. On this particular day, I started our discussion by asking them if they had ever seen a homeless person in our city. At first, all of them declared that they had not. Although our city did not have a large homeless population, a visible number of people lived on our downtown streets. To probe further, I asked them if they had attended sporting or other events downtown. Finally, one advisee said that he had seen two homeless men sitting outside the entrance of a sporting event asking for money. "I wasn't about to give them money and nobody else was going to either, because they were drinking and would have just spent it on getting drunk," he reported. After he gave this example, most of the boys said that they also had seen a homeless person at some point in their lives. I discovered that the reason they hadn't remembered coming across a homeless person at the beginning of our conversation was because they ignored them. We continued to talk about homelessness in a very general sense until Jonas questioned the value of "learning about those people."

Later that same year, with another group of students, a discussion of the welfare system emerged from an assigned reading in my sophomore English class. The majority of the students in the class argued that the system did not work, that their parents should not be forced to "support" the poor through their taxes, and that those who were receiving government assistance should just get a job. For the sake of exploring the issue further and sharing my own beliefs, I proposed an opposing argument to them that supported the welfare system: "Some people are forced to rely on government support to survive. They are put in situations where they don't see alternative options for providing for their families. Their circumstances in life are very different than what we take for granted," I argued. My response provoked a debate that eventually spread to the various issues relating to poverty.

The importance of this class discussion for me was in learning my students' perceptions of poor people. One of my students commented, "Our parents have worked hard for what we have. We shouldn't be forced to give it to people who don't do anything." Another student intensely argued, "Those people just want a free ride and want everything handed to them without working for it." The central point of their argument was that since their parents had worked hard, they deserved their wealth and were not obligated to share it with the poor. In their perspectives, wealth meant working hard and poverty meant laziness. The discussion concluded with a student pointing out, "Besides, we don't have to worry about them. Don't you know that's the reason why we have woods around our neighborhood? It blocks the view so we don't have to see them." Again, the students posed the question, "Why are we discussing those people?"

While teaching at this school I frequently found myself lost for words when trying to respond to my students' assumptions of others and the world around them. Their beliefs often represented a view in opposition to what I held to be true. My beliefs and thinking had been powerfully influenced by my upbringing in poverty. I was too unfamiliar with this world of privilege and abundance to teach my students lessons about others and themselves different from the ones they had been taught by most of the adults in their lives. Frustrated, I began to explore my burning questions about this unfamiliar world I had entered.

A CRITICAL INTERPRETATIVE STUDY OF PRIVILEGE

These questions eventually led me to begin a six-year research project at four elite high schools. I began this project by conducting a small-scale ethnographic study at McLean Academy, a private high school located in a suburb of a large Northeastern city. My research at McLean explored questions I'd had before I began teaching affluent students. What were the everyday experiences of students? What were their prevailing ways of knowing and doing? What were the different styles and substances of classes? What were the qualities of school life? These were some of the questions that guided my inquiry. During this study, I made half-day visits to the school every week for two months. During my visits, I observed classes, assemblies, sporting events, and all-school gatherings; conducted interviews with three teachers and the headmaster; and gathered classroom documents (e.g., assignments, examinations) and school publications (e.g., brochures, catalogues, school newspapers). This study gave me a better sense of the social and cultural particularities of school life at a privileged private school.

My experiences teaching the affluent led me to additional and more specific questions about privilege and the advantages of elite schooling. By this point, I was familiar enough with affluent schooling both as a teacher and as a researcher to form critical questions about privilege itself and the processes and structures that reinforced and regenerated it. I extended the scope of the research that I began at McLean to explore questions about the structures, routines, understandings, and practices that influenced the educational experiences of affluent students and what students learned about their place in the world, their relationships with others, and who they were from these experiences. My interest in understanding the processes involved in reinforcing and regenerating privilege as an identity led me to a critical interpretative approach (Brantlinger, 1993, 2003), which drew from the interpretative (e.g., Gilligan, Brown, & Rogers, 1989; Mehan, 1992) and critical ethnography (Anderson & Irvine, 1993; Carspecken & Apple, 1992) traditions. Mehan (1992) claims that interpretative studies can take a closer examination of the processes by which social stratification is generated and, therefore, as Brantlinger (2003) explains, "offers a means to understand the complexities[,] ... conflicted views" (p. 29), and, I would add, experiences of a dominant class. Interpretative studies do not always follow a critical perspective; however, in my approach, I applied critical theoretical positions (e.g., Apple, 1996, 1999; Arnowitz, 1980, 1992; Giroux, 1981, 1992; McLaren, 1989) to interpret participants' understandings and actions. Similar to Brantlinger (2003), I used a critical genre to situate affluent schooling and privilege in the larger context of "unequal power relationships among people" and "the nature of power differentials" (p. 29) in American schooling.

From 1997 to 2001, I conducted studies at two private high schools located in a midsize Midwestern city, Parker Day School and Bredvik School, and at a public school located in a small, affluent town in the Midwest, Oakley High School. During these studies, I observed primarily one teacher's class at each of the three schools. I observed each class approximately thirty times during a school year. I also observed other classes, assemblies, sporting events, and faculty meetings. Additionally, I conducted three interviews with the teacher whom I primarily observed and two students in the teacher's class (one male and one female), who were selected from the students who agreed to participate in the study. I also conducted an interview with the senior administrator at each school. In total, I conducted approximately forty hours of interviews with administrators, teachers, and students at each of the three schools. Finally, as I did in my research at McLean, I collected classroom and school artifacts to gather additional facts about school policies and classroom practices.

THE EVERYDAY NATURE OF PRIVILEGE

Contradictions often arise in what schools *say* they want their students to learn and what they actually *teach* them. Students learn both intended and (purportedly) unintended lessons that are often in conflict. In part, this conflict results from the myriad factors that influence student learning such as social contexts, organizational structures, institutional rules, curriculum, community influences, norms, values, and educational and occupational aspirations. These factors often give shape and life to the unintentional lessons, even when educators and parents *say* and *claim* they want their children/students to learn other lessons. Frequently, these unintentional lessons end up being the ones that are the most consequential for students' lives. Because these lessons often reflect and are parallel with the norms of society, they are experienced as the way things are or perhaps should be even when these norms support oppressive conditions (Kumashiro, 2002). The everyday nature of these lessons allows them to remain hidden as they pervade students' educational experiences and reinforce powerful messages to students about who they are, how they should live and relate to others, what is important in life, and what the future holds for them. The impact on students' lives is far reaching, influencing how they think about others and how they view and feel about themselves.

Just as the term *hidden agenda* conjures up something covert, deceitful, and undisclosed, the hidden nature of unintentional lessons "suggests intentional acts to obscure or conceal—a conscious duplicity that may not always be present" (Gair & Mullins, 2001, p. 23). However, because these lessons often are framed as "normal" and everyday, they are not usually hard to detect. In most cases, they are taught in plain sight and repetitively. The contradiction of something open being hidden not only legitimizes these lessons but masks the cultural processes behind them. By way of analogy, this allows the "white elephant in the room" to remain unrecognized, disguised, and not talked about. The commonsense nature of these lessons functions as a barrier to exposing the meanings and purposes embedded in them, which often reinforce domination. As Apple (1995) explains, what gets defined as common sense may appear to be just the way things are, but they are actually social constructs that function to "confirm and reinforce … structurally generated relations of domination" (p. 12). Their commonsense appearance, as Kumashiro (2002) elaborates, "not only socializes us to accept oppressive conditions [and I would add, cultural processes of domination] as 'normal' and the way things are, but also to make these conditions [and processes] normative and the ways things ought to be" (p. 82). These norms function to suppress alternative versions of what ought to be.

Within the context of affluent schooling, these "unintentional" lessons play an important role in normalizing and hiding in plain view the cultural processes that reinforce and regenerate privilege. They have an everyday presence that keeps them both known and unknown to insiders of these school communities, which validates and supports the cultural processes that they reinforce and regenerate. The unknown, even when it is partially known, cannot be combated. Protected by lessons that make these cultural processes seem how things ought to be, privilege is perpetuated, regenerated, and re-created (Wildman, 1996). These hidden lessons of privilege, therefore, must be brought to an overt level and made less unknown in order to expose the concealed and sophisticated processes involved in the cultural production of privilege. In the next section, I summarize the findings of the research project to surface these lessons that reinforce and regenerate privilege.

LESSONS OF PRIVILEGE

All four schools of this research project are as different as they are similar. Their communities hold different political orientations (conservative/liberal), different forms of social status (old money/nouveau riche), and different types of relationships with their local communities (detached/connected). Oakley is a public institution, while the other three are independent schools. Each school has its own distinctive mission statement, customs, set of rules, requirements and policies, and ideals. Most teachers, students, and parents at these four schools would argue that my list of differences is just a starting point. The four school communities take great pride in their distinctive qualities. Even though there are differences, these communities take similar norms for granted as natural and legitimate. These norms reflect core values—academic excellence, ambition, trust, service, and tradition—that are expressed in a variety of ways and contexts (e.g., in their ideals, missions, and standards; in and outside classrooms; in their school culture; in curriculum) and guide ways of knowing and doing that both create high standards for their educational programs and reinforce privilege.

On one hand, these values reveal their excellence. They promote student success, trust within the community, choices, the importance of service, and the value of connecting the past to the present to give certainty of the future. The schools are places where excellence is the order of the day and students and educators are really good at being good. Of course, their abundance of resources also contributes to their excellent qualities, but all that is good at these four schools does not entirely result from their affluence. The confluence of motivated, dedicated, and hardworking educators and students significantly contributes to the "goodness" (Lawrence-Lightfoot, 1983) found at these schools. However, on the other hand, and often not as apparent to outsiders, the values by which the schools define their excellence also encourage win-at-all-costs attitudes, unhealthy levels of stress, deception, materialism, competition, white ways of knowing and doing, selfishness, and greed. Their values validate "unintentional" lessons that teach students that:

- There's only one right way of knowing and doing.
- Success comes from being superior to others.
- Do whatever it takes to win.
- Fulfillment is gained by accumulating.
- Others are too different from us to relate to.

These lessons and the values behind them embrace particular norms, perspectives, dispositions, ways of knowing and doing, and ideologies that reinforce and regenerate privilege.

There's only one right way of knowing and doing. In pursuing academic success, students at these schools describe what they do at school and what it takes for them to gain academic success as playing a game. Attempting to win the favor of their teachers, participating in the right amount of service and academic and athletic activities, and playing to win are some of the rules of this game. Most students at the four schools abide by these rules and are really good players at the school game. They are hardworking and talented, get good grades and top scores on college entrance exams, and are involved in numerous athletic, service, and other extracurricular activities. They have spent most of their years of schooling learning how to play this game the right way to achieve academic success. This right way is mutually constituted, whereby students both shape and are shaped by the rules of this game (Grenfell & James, 1998). It is within and through the dialectic between the game and the players that hierarchies of power are played out and students' relative positionings are determined.

Like most other African American students at the four schools, Janora, a Bredvik student, believes that she is on the "losing team" in the school game. As she explains, "It sure is a game all right, but we're the underdogs .... [The whites] are on the team that wins all the time." She goes on to explain that the "right way" of playing the school game reflects a "white way" of knowing and doing. She explains, "Everything runs the way that white people do things," and African American students must "act white" in order to be successful (or even "survive") in the school game. An African-American parent at Bredvik similarly points out that white values and ideals dominate the culture of her son's school. Another parent at Parker adds that these values and ideals are often in conflict with those of African Americans. Most of the African American parents who participated in this study believe that their children's schools respect only white ways of knowing and doing and, by so doing, place their children at a disadvantage. African American students remain at a decided disadvantage in a game where the rules are controlled by whites.

Not only are the rules of the game not as fair for students of color as for white students, but they also send powerful messages to all students that white cultural understandings are superior to other cultural groups' ways of knowing and doing. White notions determine the standard for academic success, and this standard encourages narrow-mindedness by providing little room for respecting and learning other ways of knowing and doing. Students keep too occupied with following the "right way" to build the capacity to imagine other ways. The power of this certain way regulates identities, knowledge, and practices. It is through this "right way" of identifying, knowing, and doing that the social transmission of privilege is itself legitimized (Lamont & Lareau, 1988). This version of how things ought to be establishes a set of class-based dispositions, perceptions, and appreciations that reinforce and regenerate privilege.

Success comes from being superior to others. A McLean teacher's statement, "Competition is not a dirty word," represents the general attitude at the four schools in this study. To varying degrees, the schools promote a competitive culture within and outside the classroom context to prepare their students for the "harsh realties and demands of the world outside school" and "to give them the skills necessary to have a competitive edge in life." Outside the classroom, all the schools except for Oakley require students to participate in their athletic programs in order to hone their competitive attitudes and skills. Instead of a requirement, Oakley strongly encourages participation in sports "to give students a more appropriate venue to be competitive than the classroom." Similar to the other schools, Oakley's athletic program is a site for students to strengthen their competitive character.

Students carry their competitive attitudes that are valued and reinforced on playing fields with them into the classroom context. In fact, all but Oakley have designed their overall educational program in ways that encourage students to use skills and attitudes in the classroom that they have learned and developed on playing fields in order to gain higher levels of academic success. Most of the students in this study do act in similar ways in the classroom as they do on playing fi elds. They are playing to win and do what it takes to achieve academic success. Although Oakley students are less competitive in the classroom than students at the other three schools, the increased focus in recent years on gaining admission to selective colleges has spurred competitive attitudes in order to stand out among others. At all four schools, the college-oriented desires and expectations of students and their families provide further encouragement for competition. Students and their families are competing for the college prize.

The competitive environments at these four schools promote individual student achievement over the value of cooperation and group success. Students are taught that academic success is gained by being better than others, or as I heard numerous times over the course of my research, "standing out above the rest." Although all four schools claim to promote a strong sense of community and emphasize the value of community in their mission statements and school publications, their competitive environments disrupt connection, making closeness among students and educators impossible (hooks, 2003). Their emphasis on competition precludes collaboration, which limits the opportunities for students to learn what it means to build and sustain meaningful relationships with others. In an environment where competition is the order of the day, there is little room for arousing collective concern for anything other than self-interests.

Do whatever it takes to win. Most students in this study explain that they are playing the game of school to win and will do what it takes to gain academic success. In their pursuits of academic success, they regularly act in ways to prove that they are "the fi t-test," such as putting other students down to make themselves look better, dominating class discussions to get the attention of their teachers, getting on the good side of the adults in their lives, and, at times, cheating on assignments. Often these strategies successfully give them the advantage in the game. Although I observed students cheating only a few times over the course of my research, several students in these studies, except those at Oakley, claim that cheating is a common practice at their schools. Even at Oakley, Kevin, a student, explains that cheating is acceptable "when teachers put too much or unfair amount of pressure on [students]." Similar to what I heard from several students at the four schools, Kevin believes that cheating is "a survival thing" and "something that you're forced to do." Students believe that cheating is justifi ed in a competitive environment.

Similar to what Pope (2001) found in her study of five students "doing school," behaviors such as cheating, however, contradict "the very traits and values many parents, students, and community members expect schools to instill" (p. 150). By encouraging (and, more importantly, rewarding) success over others, the four schools involved in this research project, some more than others, promote win-at-all-costs behaviors and attitudes. Students learn to value winning above all else, even if this means acting in ways that go against other values that the adults in their lives have attempted to instill in them. Instead of fostering traits such as cooperation and honesty, the schools' competitive environments promote the opposite and provide little room to uphold more important and meaningful values than winning.

Fulfillment is gained by accumulating. Parents in these studies place a tremendous amount of pressure on their children to achieve the level of academic success necessary to gain admission to highly selective colleges. They claim that the reason for this pressure is to make sure their children have fulfilling lives. They describe fulfillment as a sense of happiness and accomplishment, and believe that "going to a good college will make this [fulfillment] more possible. It sets them on the right path," as a Parker parent explains. Parents are acutely aware that a degree from a highly selective college often leads to careers providing wealth and power, which allows their children to maintain their class advantages. Parents believe that their children will feel fulfilled in life if they achieve a level of success that allows them to keep "the comforts of life that they're accustomed to," as a Bredvik mother explains.

Only a few parents mention the cachet associated with their children attending highly selective colleges. A mother at Parker admits, "Every parent wants to be able to tell others that their child goes to Harvard or Yale or colleges like those .... If your child goes to a top-notch college, then you know you're a good parent. You've done your job as a parent." Consistent with what Brantlinger (2003) found in her study of affluent mothers, most of the parents' "self-definitions extended to and incorporated their offsprings' success," and a source of parents' "positive identity was attributing their children's achievement to their child rearing" (p. 40). Some teachers at the four schools, however, argue that the primary source of parents' college-oriented desires and expectations for their children is associated more with status than their feelings about themselves as parents. A Bredvik teacher claims that "[parents] want the status that comes along with their kids going to good schools like they want other things that represent status. I'm not saying it's completely the same as a fancy car, but it's close. If your kid gets into Harvard, then it's like everything else in their lives that shows how successful they are." Symbolic markers of both parents' sense of self and class privilege are figured prominently in parents' ambitious aspirations for their children. Their understandings of what it means to be fulfilled in life are constructed around these markers.

Students feel an intense pressure to achieve the goals that their parents have set for them. The majority of students at these schools believe that their "parents are the biggest factor in what [they] do to get into a good college," as a student at Bredvik explains. A student at Oakley elaborates, "It's never been really an option not to go to college. My parents have been talking about going to college since I was in kindergarten. I've always been told that's what I have to do after high school to be successful later on." Th ese two students' sentiments reverberated throughout my conversations with other students. In striving to meet the expectations of their parents, they do what they have to do to get good grades and high test scores, and they participate in the right number of activities to secure admission to selective colleges. Their schools mediate their parents' expectations by making their "primary responsibility ... to get their students into top colleges," as a teacher at Parker explains. The four schools provide the institutional culture, the college counseling, and the college preparatory programs necessary for students to gain entrance into high-status colleges. Everything about all four schools conveys that all students will continue on to college, and most likely to "good" colleges.

The interaction of family and institutional influences places students at these schools on the ambitious track toward gaining admission to high-status colleges and acquiring the educational credentials necessary to secure and maintain their class privilege. They keep jam-packed schedules that often begin early in the morning (earlier than most adults begin their workdays) and end late at night. After school hours, they are involved in sports, service projects, committee meetings, homework, and for a very few, paid job responsibilities. They study, read, and complete what their teachers assign to get high grades and select courses based on college requirements. They spend most of their time inside and outside school doing what they have to do, or what they think they have to do, to win the college prize, not because they find what they do necessarily engaging. Although not all of what students do is entirely motivated by "transcript packing" (Peshkin, 2001), they are "always thinking about how [what they do] will benefi t [them] in getting into college," as Nicole, a Parker student, explains. The ever-present reality in their choices, activities, and schoolwork is how what they do helps them fulfill their and their parents' college-oriented desires and expectations. Being engaged in what they do takes a back seat to their drive to accumulate the credentials necessary to keep them on the "right path" to a selective college and, as their parents claim, to fulfillment in their lives. They have learned to associate fulfillment with accumulation.

Others are too different from us to relate. One of the striking qualities that all four schools share is their exclusive nature. They promote and emphasize their distinctive, exclusive, and superior qualities to set them apart from others. They are closed off from others and, in various forms, are gated communities. The incredible beauty and abundance of the campuses of McLean and Parker, for example, are a far cry from their surrounding communities. Both schools sit on top of hills detached from their neighbors. Quite the opposite, Oakley and Bredvik share a close relationship with their local communities, but these communities are themselves exclusive. Like McLean and Parker, they are isolated from communities different from themselves.

Oakley is the only school in this study for which this isolation goes against the school's ideals and values. In fact, school offcials at the three private schools work hard at promoting their elite status; they want others to know that they are above the rest. They promote their exclusivity, in part, because they are private and have to "sell their school to families. We have the job of convincing them that they're getting their money's worth," as Parker's admission counselor explains. As a public school, Oakley has a similar form of pressure that comes from the need to demonstrate educational excellence to local citizens for financial support; they have to "sell their school" to their community. Similar to the private schools, Oakley's offcials work hard at making sure that people, both within and outside their community, know that they stand above other schools, even though this attitude runs counter to the school's liberal character. The pressure to secure financial support overrides their liberal ideals. In various ways, all four schools promote their differences from, and pit themselves against, others in expressing their excellence. They regulate "others" to a lesser status to justify and legitimate and thus protect their interests. The class segregation of their school communities is a deliberate choice to maintain their superiority over those perceived as other.

All four schools do emphasize, however, the importance of their students going outside the "bubble" of their privileged environments to be involved in service. Even though the schools place a value on service (and all but Bredvik even require their students to do service), their service projects and activities operate by the "charity model," which allows their students to "give back"—that is, help those who are less fortunate—without promoting social transformation. In fact, the goals of the charitable model of service reinforce privileged ways of knowing and doing by embracing certain unpleasant assumptions about people, especially those different from the service providers. One basic assumption is that any community would function better if only it would act like the service provider. Another assumption is that there are no connections between those who provide service and those who receive service, that they are more different than they are similar. This assumes that their lived experiences, hopes, dreams, and aspirations are so profoundly different that diffculties can be resolved only by finding the one right answer. In this context, service is mainly about the nature of the activity and the work of the service provider. Students are not provided the necessary conditions to step outside their privileged positions to learn from others in the population at large in order to understand and appreciate different ways of knowing and doing. The charity model of service provides little room for students to develop meaningful, mutual, and respectful relationships with individuals outside their closed communities. Even though they are physically stepping outside their "bubble" and crossing lines in social interactions through these service activities, they are not provided the types of experience that allow them to become sensitive to the nature and needs of other social classes and other cultural groups (Brantlinger, 2003). Students continue to be isolated from "others."

INSTRUCTIONAL SETTINGS THAT INTERRUPT PRIVILEGE

For the most part, these five lessons are not "officially" taught as part of the formal curriculum at the four schools. Instead, they are part of the hidden curriculum; that is, "the norms, values, and belief systems embedded in the curriculum, the school, and classroom life, imparted to students through daily routine, curricular content, and social relationships" (Margolis, Soldatenko, Acker, & Gair, 2001, p. 6). There is an extensive body of literature on the hidden curriculum. Phillip Jackson (1968) is generally recognized as the originator of the term *hidden curriculum*. In his observations of public elementary classrooms, Jackson identified aspects of classroom life that were inherent in the social relations of schoolings. He found that particular values, dispositions, and behavioral expectations led to rewards for students and shaped their learning experiences. Furthermore, he found that these features of school life had little to do with the stated educational goals but were essential for success in school.

Since then, several scholars (e.g., Anyon, 1980; Apple, 1982, 1993; Giroux, 1983) have explored the complex ways that the hidden curriculum powerfully influences the educational experiences of students and transmits important lessons to them about particular ways of knowing and doing that correspond to their social class. For example, Jean Aynon's (1980) study of five elementary schools in contrasting social class settings documented how the hidden curriculum works in ways to perpetuate social class stratification of the larger society. School experience of the students at the five schools differed qualitatively by social class. Anyon found class distinctions not only in the physical, cultural, and interpersonal characteristics of each school, but also in the nature of instruction and schoolwork. These differences, as she explained, "not only may contribute to the development in the children in each social class of certain types of economically significant relationships and not others, but would thereby help to *reproduce* this system of relations in society" (p. 90). Anyon argued that classroom practices have theoretical meaning and social consequences that contribute to the reproduction of unequal social relations.

Consistent with this body of research, the lessons that are a part of the hidden curriculum of the four schools hide in plain view the cultural processes that reinforce and regenerate privilege. These lessons send powerful messages to students about their place in the world, who they are and should be, and their relations with those outside of their world. Unacknowledged, these lessons often teach students unintended knowledge, values, dispositions, and beliefs. In fact, most of these lessons are in direct contradiction to the schools' stated goals, which aim to teach students high moral character, integrity, respect for others, and responsible participation in the world. These lessons instead prepare students to lead their lives guided by distinctive ways of knowing and doing that overshadow these more positive, productive goals. They contribute to establishing the taken-for-granted sets of ideas for how things ought to be and the frame of reference for what is considered common sense that function to reinforce and regenerate the cultural meanings students use to construct their identities. As conduits for learning privilege and power, these lessons assist students in constructing privilege as a central component of their identities.

Identities, however, are neither constant nor stable. They are constantly shaped and reshaped by the complex interactions of everyday realities and lived experiences. As students mediate their sense of self-understanding, they can be offered the necessary cultural tools and resources that can interrupt privilege. Students can be taught alternative lessons about themselves, their place in the world, and their relations with others; lessons not only that are more aligned with (purportedly) intended goals for student learning, but that also offer alternatives to privileged ways of knowing and doing. Over the course of my research, I observed only a few moments when instructional settings offered students the necessary tools and resources to interrupt privilege. These moments challenged the everyday, commonsense nature of the lessons that reinforce and regenerate privilege. These instructional settings, often created by the adults in students' lives but sometimes facilitated by the students themselves, shared particular qualities in imagining beyond the taken-for-grantedness of privilege.

One of these qualities was honesty. Students were provided opportunities in their pursuits of academic success to learn ways to deal with, and work through, failure in healthy ways. Students were provided safe spaces to make mistakes and then learn from them. During these moments, the adults in students' lives served as important models by being honest about what they knew and didn't know, honest about moments in their lives when they wished they had made different decisions, and honest about moments when they "messed up." These role models were upholding natural human qualities in their work with students or in their roles as parents. They provided their students/ children opportunities to learn from these qualities—even the imperfect ones. By so doing, these adults taught students important lessons about dealing with failure.

These instructional settings also encouraged openness by expanding the scope of what was considered "the real fudge," to use the words of Ms. Perry at Parker, or in other words, what knowledge was acknowledged as legitimate (Apple, 1999). Curricula, however, are not simply a collection of facts; they tell a story, from which students learn some important (often unintended) lessons. These lessons emerge from what is and what is not included in curricula. As Kumashiro (2002) points out, "What educators do *not* do is as instructive as what they do" (p. 82). When instructional settings encouraged openness, teachers included different, conflicting stories in their curricular choices. They offered their students opportunities to learn from others outside their own cultural group and to learn that there was not just one way of seeing things, or even two or three—there were multiple perspectives on every issue and every story. During these moments, teachers encouraged students to open their minds to others' points of view and to the complexity of the world and the many perspectives involved (Nieto, 2002).

These instructional settings also engaged students in what they were doing and learning. When a student at Parker spent her free time during the school day painting, a group of aspiring writers at Bredvik published a zine of their creative work once a month, another Bredvik student shared her poetry regularly on open mike nights at a local coffee shop, and an Oakley student devoted hours a day on his computer designing a virtual reality game, they were not thinking about how these activities would help them get into a good college. They also were not focused on accumulating. Instead, they were doing what they loved and were passionately committed to doing their best. In these moments, students stepped outside materialistic ways of knowing and doing to find a more meaningful purpose for their activities and pursuits. Even though these moments of engaged learning and doing occurred mostly outside the classroom context, there were a few occasions when students during class discussions and activities struggled for understanding, wanted to learn and work with others, and found fulfillment in what they were doing. These moments allowed students to establish a more intimate connection with their learning (hooks, 1994).

These instructional settings encouraged collaboration and emphasized the value of community. Over the course of my research, I witnessed moments when students worked together on their train ride to school, in the hallways, at lunchtime while grabbing a bite to eat, and on campus during their breaks. In these moments students were going against the competitive nature of their schools in order to learn from each other. Rather than trying to outdo each other, they were engaging with each other in meaningful ways that recognized the value of cooperative learning. Students in these instructional settings learned how to work with others. While doing so, they were building their capacity to imagine someone else's point of view, what Kohn (1992) calls "perspective taking," and learning what it took to establish and maintain supportive, healthy, and positive relationships with others.

Finally, these instructional settings encouraged students to develop the habits of heart and mind necessary for working toward critical awareness. In these settings, a few teachers at Parker and Oakley, for example, used such practices as journal writing, reading, writing, reflection, research, analysis, and observation to develop their students' awareness of the world around them and to urge students to live more meaningfully and justly. These teachers taught students to see through versions of truth that teach people to accept unfairness so that their students were able to envision, define, and identity ways they could work toward a more humane society. In this process, an encounter was created between students and their capacity to imagine beyond privileged ways of knowing and doing. Students were encouraged to make decisions to live their lives as if the lives of others truly mattered. Students were provided opportunities to develop an awareness of the world around them and to learn what it meant to live more meaningfully and justly.

These characteristics do not translate into easy prescriptions for interrupting privilege. They do not serve as easy, quick, or certain alternatives to the ways that privilege is perpetuated, re-created, and regenerated in schools. Moreover, there are other characteristics that could be added. My purpose has been not to be exhaustive but to illuminate the primary ways that educators, students, and parents at the four schools worked toward interrupting privilege. Their efforts serve as examples of the possibilities for redefining, reenvisioning, and reimagining how things ought to be.

A BROADER AGENDA

Interrupting the cultural production of privilege requires intentional efforts on the part of educators to confront and transform lessons students learn about their place in the world and their relations with others. By creating instructional settings—in and outside of the classroom context—that interrupt privilege, we can be more certain about what lessons we are actually teaching students about themselves and others. We can begin imagining ways to work toward "the process through which students learn to critically appropriate knowledge existing outside their immediate experience in order to broaden their understanding of themselves, the world, and the possibilities for transforming the taken-for-granted assumptions about the way we live" (McLaren, 1989, p. 186). By working toward this transformation, we can imagine the possibilities for changing the everyday practices and routines that miscommunicate the ways we want (or, at least, what we say and claim we want) our students to live their lives (Howard & EnglandKennedy, 2006).

We can, however, only imagine and work toward interrupting the cultural processes that reinforce and regenerate stratified structures in schooling. The effects of macroeconomic policies (see Anyon, 2005) and the social class divisions of the larger society overshadow efforts toward *disrupting*, rather than *interrupting*, these cultural processes in schools that perpetuate unequal relations. The United States not only is the most highly stratified society in the industrialized world but does less to limit the extent of inequality than any other industrialized democratic country. Class distinctions operate in virtually all aspects of American life. In the United States, democracy has become more of an economic metaphor than a political concept/ideal (Darder, 2002). It should not be surprising, therefore, that stratified schooling remains durable even with all the efforts over the years toward making American schooling more equal. Replete with uneven access and outcomes, schools continue to reflect the divisions of the larger society (Nieto, 2005). The efforts toward transforming stratified school structures will remain uncertain until democratic ideals are reflected and realized in the larger society. Working toward transforming stratified school structures and outcomes requires us to extend our efforts and attention beyond educational institutions. We must, in the end, develop a larger scope for our equality-seeking work.

However, comprehensive analyses of the reproductive nature of affluent schooling can elaborate and extend our understandings of the ways privileging systems are produced and reproduced. We can develop the necessary cultural script to extend beyond commodified notions that divert attention from, and protect, the concealed and sophisticated processes involved in the cultural production of privilege. By mapping out and exposing the contours of privilege, we can engage in the type of complicated conversation that is needed for understanding how the success of some relates to the failure of many. If social justice is at least one of the aims of scholarship and inquiry (Purpel, 1999), then we must work to unravel the cultural processes that reinforce and regenerate privilege. We must cast our scholarly gaze upward even when this means looking critically at ourselves and unmasking our own complicity with oppression and privilege. We can then hopefully develop a vision for American schooling that has yet to be imagined from the perspectives of our current theoretical frameworks.

RELIGIOUS COALITIONS FOR AND AGAINST GAY MARRIAGE

THE CULTURE WAR RAGES ON

By David C. Campbell and Carin Robinson

THE CULTURE WAR IN THE TRENCHES

Although we would expect to see the greatest evidence of the culture war among the generals, the attitudes of the infantry are relevant also. Leaders must have someone to lead, and so political and religious elitescannot fall out of step with their constituencies. Is there evidence thatthe interfaith coalitions that characterize "culture war" politics describeattitudes about gay marriage? The strongest statement of the culture war hypothesis is that it predicts that divisions concerning gay marriageshould be greater *within* than *between* religious traditions. Within religious traditions, we should see that adherents with divergent degrees of traditionalism differ in their attitudes regarding gay marriage to a greater extent than do people of different religious traditions. For example, a traditionalist Catholic should have more in common with a traditionalist evangelical Protestant than with a progressive Catholic.

To test whether this is the case, we turned to the 2004 National Election Study (NES), whose respondents were asked, "Should same-sex couples be allowed to marry, or do you think they should not be allowed to marry?" They were given the explicit option of indicating that gay marriage shouldor should not be allowed, and they could volunteer other responses, for example, expressing support for civil unions. For simplicity of presentation, we report the percentage of respondents who explicitly opposed any form of legal recognition for homosexual relationships. We divided NES espondents into four religious traditions based on a standard denominational classification system: White Evangelical Protestants, Mainline Protestants, Catholics, and Black Protestants (Steensland 2000; Kellstedt et al. 1996). Note that the category "Black Protestants" consists of allProtestants, either evangelical or mainline, who are African American, while

Catholics can be of any race. Obviously, this is not an exhaustive list of religious traditions in America, but other groups such as Jews, Mormons, and Muslims, are too small to be adequately represented in a survey the size of the 2004 NES (roughly twelve hundred people).

To distinguish between progressives and traditionalists within each religious tradition we relied on an index of four questions, each of which taps into moral traditionalism. Respondents were asked the extent to which they agree with each of the following four statements:

1. The world is always changing and we should adjust our view of moral behavior to those changes.
2. The newer lifestyles are contributing to the breakdown of our society.
3. We should be more tolerant of people who choose to live according to their own moral standards, even if they are very different from our own.
4. This country would have many fewer problems if there were more emphasis on traditional family ties.

We used factor analysis, a statistical technique that compresses the four questions into a single index, and then divided the resulting scores into four quartiles.

Figure 28.1 displays the percentage of those within each religious tradition who oppose gay marriage,[1] dividing people within each tradition between those in the lowest and the highest quartiles of the moral traditionalism index. If the strongest version of the culture war hypothesis were to hold, we should see no difference in attitudes regarding gay marriage across religious traditions—people with the same score on the traditionalism index should share the same level of opposition to gay marriage, regardless of their religious tradition.

The strong version of the culture war hypothesis finds considerable support in figure 28.1. Among people in the lowest quartile of the moral traditionalism index, opposition to gay marriage is very similar regardless of religious tradition. Only 21 percent of Catholics and mainline Protestants, for example, oppose gay marriage. The figure for evangelicals is only slightly higher at 27 percent. The one group with noticeably stronger opposition to gay marriage is black Protestants, at 44 percent. At the high end of the traditionalism index, the similarities are even more apparent. The levels of opposition to gay marriage among evangelicals, mainline

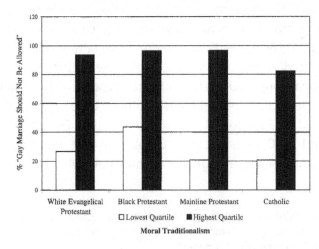

FIGURE 28.1: OPPOSITION TO GAY MARRIAGE BY RELIGIOUS TRADITION.

Protestants, and black Protestants are 94, 97, and 97 percent, respectively. In this case, Catholics are slightly less likely to oppose gay marriage, because "only" 82 percent are against it. A quick glance at figure 28.1 makes clear that, consistent with the culture war hypothesis, moral traditionalism is a far better way to predict opposition to gay marriage than religious tradition.

These data about general public opinion are suggestive, but they can only reveal the *potential* for interfaith coalitions to form to address the subject of gay marriage. The coalitions themselves are actually forged or not, as the case may be, among political and religious leaders. It is thus among the generals that culture war politics should be most evident, and so that is where we turn our attention.

WHO WORKS WITH WHOM, AND WHY DO THEY WORK TOGETHER?

As we trace the coalitions that have formed concerning the subject of gay marriage, the key test of the culture war hypothesis is whether they fulfill two conditions. First, as with the public opinion data, we should see divisions defined more by tensions within religious traditions than between them. Second, we should observe leaders of different religious traditions actually working together in the common cause of opposing gay marriage.

The story of the coalitions working against gay marriage begins long before this particular issue rose on the public agenda. The groups that are now mobilized against gay marriage have their roots in the New Christian Right movement, which began in the mid-1970s as white conservative Christians entered the political scene to speak out against feminism, the legalization of abortion, and the general decay of what they considered to be "family values." Originally the movement was ostensibly ecumenical, as evidenced by the names of two early members: the Religious Roundtable and the Moral Majority. These were groups with aspirations of assembling a broad, ecumenical membership as their leaders sought to attract religious conservatives from Protestantism, Catholicism, and Judaism alike. Notwithstanding a few notable Jewish and Catholic members, however, the awakening of religious conservatives in the 1970s and 1980s was largely an evangelical Protestant affair. In the early 1990s the Christian Coalition arose from the ashes of Pat Robertson's run for the presidency and inherited the institutional legacy of the Christian Right movement. Like its predecessors, it, too, sought to broaden its appeal to groups other than white evangelical Christians. And, also like its predecessors, the Christian Coalition was largely unsuccessful in trying to enlarge its tent (Robinson 2006).

Today, the religious coalitions that have formed to oppose gay marriage are far more ecumenical in their composition. Though having a narrow political focus, the range of participants has greater breadth than the original Christian Right, which was concerned with multiple issues. As was showcased at the Mayday for Marriage rally, participants come from a wider array of religions and races than was the case for the Christian Right movement in the 1980s and 1990s. Indeed, the presence of rabbis at the rally underscored that concern about gay marriage is not confined to Christianity. The old Christian Right laid the foundation, but the structure has taken a different shape.

Given the way the story is covered in the news media, it is easy to miss the interracial, transdenominational nature of the coalition against gay marriage. Because much of it is built on the preceding movement, it is tempting to assume that this is the Christian Coalition all over again. As a case in point, consider how coverage of the Mayday for Marriage rally fed that impression. Speakers at the rally included James Dobson, Gary Bauer, and Chuck Colson, all seminal figures in Christian Right circles. These are well-known, media-savvy figures, and so the news media gravitated toward them in their coverage. Consequently, the media portrayed the rally, and thus opposition to gay marriage generally, as dominated by white evangelicals. Scratch the surface of the movement, however, and you will find evangelical and mainline Protestants, conservative Catholics, orthodox Jews, and even Muslims. Because many of the spokes people for these groups are relatively new to the political stage, they do not get the airtime afforded the familiar faces. Notwithstanding the way the movement is portrayed in the news, however, the denominational diversity that characterizes it is evidence favoring one criterion for culture war politics—a coalition that transcends denominational boundaries.

We have thus far focused on the rally as an exemplar of the anti–gay marriage coalition. But is it truly representative of the groups working against marriage for homosexuals? Far from being an isolated example, the rally fully reflects the cooperation across multiple denominations and religious traditions among gay marriage opponents. Other examples abound. Consider one of the earliest ballot initiatives against gay marriage, Proposition 22 in California, which was on the ballot in 2000. The campaign in favor of Proposition 22 featured cooperation among Catholics, evangelical Protestants, and Mormons, groups that had worked together previously, notably in opposition to pornography. Given the sharp theological disputes between these groups, especially the tensions between evangelicals and Mormons, this ecumenical partnership is remarkable (Campbell and Monson 2002).

Another case in point is the Arlington Group, a coalition of socially conservative supporters of the Marriage Amendment Project (MAP), an organization that serves as the nexus for groups working to pass an amendment to the federal Constitution that would define marriage as the union of one man and one woman. The Arlington Group is committed to defending traditional marriage in addition to addressing other issues of moral concern such as abortion and judicial activism. During the 2004 election cycle, the Arlington Group created another entity, MAP, to spearhead the work on the marriage issue specifically.[2] Although the Arlington Group is housed in the Family Research Council's facility in Washington, DC, and is associated with Christian Right groups such as Focus on the Family and the American Family Association, more than fifty religious or political organizations are members, and the list is anything but homogeneous. From denominational groups such as the Southern Baptist Convention and the Missouri Synod of the Lutheran Church to interest groups such as the Catholic Citizenship, Family, and Human Rights Institute and the Coalition of African American Pastors to state organizations such as Family First of Nebraska and the Center for Arizona Policy, the Arlington Group represents the breadth of the movement.

The number of groups that are under the Arlington Group's umbrella is actually a conservative estimate of the number of religious groups that oppose gay marriage because some gay marriage opponents do not favor a constitutional amendment and thus choose not to affiliate with the Arlington Group. Moreover, the Islam Society for North America, once part of the MAP, voluntarily left the project because of concern that any direct association with Muslims might tarnish the group's public image, owing to anti-Muslim sentiment following the terrorist attacks of September 11, 2001. Also, according to the coalition's staff, the Union of Orthodox Jewish

Congregations of America has worked with MAP to pass the amendment but was never listed as a participating organization (Slatter 2004). Therefore, although the Arlington Group's supporters do not make up an exhaustive list of the organizations opposed to gay marriage, they are nonetheless evidence of the cooperation taking place across denominations, and the Arlington Group is on the front line of the culture war.

A similarly broad coalition characterizes the Alliance for Marriage, another group that opposes gay marriage but also seeks to defend traditional marriage more broadly by addressing issues such as divorce and social welfare policies that discourage marriage. Although it calls foran amendment to the Constitution to ban gay marriage, the Alliance for Marriage has worked less with interest groups associated with the Christian Right than with individual leaders within denominations. For example, the alliance's board of directors includes a rabbi, a Muslim, a minister from the African Methodist Episcopal church, a Hispanicpastor, and a Chinese minister, as well as a number of professors from Catholic universities.

Both the Arlington Group and the Alliance for Marriage provide evidence that opposition to gay marriage has brought together religious conservatives of varied backgrounds, fulfilling one criterion for culture war politics. The second criterion is evidence of tension within a given religious tradition between opponents and supporters of gay marriage. Nowhere has such tension been more apparent than within the black church. Most scholars of religion believe that predominantly African American denominations constitute a separate religious tradition within America because of their unique evolutionary path through the slavery,Jim Crow, and civil rights eras (Harris 1999; Lincoln and Mamiya 1990; Steensland 2000). And within this tradition, there has been a pitched battle about gay marriage. Many African American clergy are theologically conservative and therefore oppose the practice. A number of conservative black ministers have aligned with white evangelicals to fight it. For example, the Traditional Values Coalition, a nondenominational grassroots church lobby that represents more than forty-three thousand congregations, has hosted a number of events specifically targeting the black churches within their constituency. "We're looking for African-American clergy members who have local authority, and we're getting them to hold a summit on marriage, just one issue," the chairman of the Traditional Values Coalition, Reverend Louis Sheldon, said in one media report (quoted in Banerjee 2005). A number of black leaders spoke at the Mayday for Marriage rally, including Bishop Harry R. Jackson Jr., the pastor of the Hope Christian Church in College Park, Maryland, who said the opening prayer. Jackson has said that blacks are especially attuned to the hardship of broken marriages, single parenting, and babiesbeing born out of wedlock. Jackson said, "The bottom line is not about being anti-homosexual—it is about family reconstruction" (quoted in Chang 2005). Jackson and other African American clergy have joined with the Arlington Group, the Alliance for Marriage, or the Traditional Values Coalition to work against gay marriage.

Not all black clergy oppose gay marriage, however. Within the black church we observe the now-familiar split between traditionalists and progressives. In contrast to clergy members such as Harry Jackson, a number of the most prominent African American religious leaders have defined gay marriage as a civil rights issue and thus support the notion of granting marriage benefits to homosexuals. A common line of reasoning among this group is to draw a parallel with the bans on interracial marriage, which the civil rights movement worked successfully to end (Williams 2004). Former Democratic presidential candidate Al Sharpton shares these sentiments and has publicly endorsed same-sexmarriage, going to great lengths to criticize the

Republican Party for using the issue to target the religious black community (Finnegan 2004). After giving a sermon to Atlanta's Butler Street African Methodist Episcopal Church, Sharpton said, "George Bush manipulated a lot of religious feelings about marriage" and used gay marriage to draw attention away from Iraq and other policy positions that might not be aspopular with the African American community (quoted in Plummer 2005). Perhaps the divide within the black church over gay marriage is best exemplified by the public split within the family of Martin Luther King Jr. King's widow, Coretta Scott King, favored same-sex marriage, and King's daughter, Bernice King, opposes it. Coretta Scott King repeatedly compared homophobia with racism and was convinced that her husband would support granting rights to homosexuals if he were alive today. In contrast, King's daughter, who says homosexuality is a sin, is an elder at an Atlanta church that organized a march in opposition to gay marriage in December 2004. She led the march, which began at her father's grave (Barry 2004).

The divide between traditionalists and progressives is also apparent within Judaism. In 1996, when gay marriage had only begun to emergeon the nation's political agenda, the Reform movement within Judaism took a liberal position with respect to this issue. The Central Conference of American Rabbis (CCAR) within the movement passed a resolution opposing any government action that would prohibit same-sex couples from marrying. The congregational arm of Reform Judaism echoed this resolution a year later, saying that they would support legislation allowing same-sex marriage. Within the Conservative Rabbinical Assembly there is an endorsement of gay rights coupled with an intentional silence on the issue of gay marriage. In fact, a small number of Conservative rabbis have performed same-sex Jewish weddings. These groups stand in contrast to the Orthodox Jews who participated in the Mayday for Marriage rally and support the Arlington Group's agenda.

Many Catholic groups—but, pointedly, not all—have also joined with Jews and evangelical Protestants to oppose gay marriage. As a telling example of the fracture within Catholicism over the issue, we point to the divide between the two dioceses in the state of Virginia:[3] the Diocese of Arlington and the Diocese of Richmond. In 2004 the two dioceses jointly adopted a legislative agenda but then individually chose to give priority to various aspects of that agenda. The Arlington Diocese tends to focus on abortion and the traditional family structure, whereas the Richmond group focuses on issues relating to poverty and socialjustice. The Richmond Diocese has not come out in favor of same-sex marriage, but to our knowledge, it has not taken great strides in speaking out against the issue, either. Moreover, the diocese has taken more liberal positions when the issue of homosexuality has been addressed by the Virginia State Legislature. For instance, it supported amending the state's hate crimes law to include homosexuals. In contrast, the Arlington Diocese opposed the measure. The bishop of Arlington has been vocal about his opposition to same-sex marriage, addressing the subject in a homily to his congregants prior to the 2004 election. The differing orientation of the two dioceses is reflected in the religious coalitions in which they participate at the state level. The Richmond Diocese tends to cooperate with more progressive groups such as the Virginia Interfaith Center for Public Policy. The Arlington Diocese has worked closely with Focus on the Family and the Family Research Council's state affiliates to defend traditional marriage and other social conservative policies.

The tension over homosexuality within a number of mainline Protestant denominations echoes and amplifies the debate within Catholicism, the black church, and Judaism. For example, the United Methodist Church has been driven by an internal debate about gay marriage—as a matter not only of public policy but also church policy. In 1999, sixty-eight Methodist ministers presided over a lesbian couple's wedding as an act of protest of church law, which prohibits such ceremonies. The case brought against them was eventually dismissed, suggesting that there is substantial support for same-sex marriage within the church body. This support, though, was not enough to rescind the policy prohibiting same-sex marriage at the 2004 General Conference, where a spirited debate about the subject was conducted. The intensity of the debate is unsurprising; in a case that drew national attention, in March 2004 a jury of Methodist clergy members in Washington State acquitted a fellow minister of violating church law by being in a lesbian relationship. But then a few months later, a similar trial in Pennsylvania resulted in a guilty verdict issued against another lesbian minister, and as a result she was defrocked but was allowed to serve as a layperson in the church (Banerjee 2004). The lesbian minister appealed the ruling, and in May 2005 a committee reversed the decision made by the lower clergy court, citing technical grounds. (The church had never defined the term *practicing homosexual*, which was the basis of the charges brought against the minister.) In October 2005, however, the Judicial Council, the highest court in the Methodist Church, agreed with the original jury's verdict opposing "self-avowed practicing" homosexuals in ordained ministry (Cooperman 2005). The council also said that homosexuals have no immediate right to church membership and reinstated a Virginia minister who had been suspended by a bishop for not allowing a gay man to become a member of his congregation.

The Episcopal Church has been similarly divided about homosexuality, with the ordination of an openly gay bishop leading some Episcopal conservatives to threaten a schism within the church. Although there is obvious sympathy for gay marriage among some of the Episcopal hierarchy (Newman 2005), the Episcopal Church does not offcially perform same-sex marriage ceremonies.

Although there are numerous examples of organizations that have united traditionalist denominations in opposition to gay marriage, examples of religious progressives who have banded together to support homosexual unions are few. The religious progressives who are in favor of allowing same-sex marriage are not mobilized to the degree that religious traditionalists are. They are smaller in number than the traditionalists, and either as a cause or as a consequence, they do not have an infrastructure comparable to the Christian Right's to bring their convictions into the political realm.

The group Clergy for Fairness is the exception that proves the rule. The interfaith group of religious leaders came together in 2006 to oppose a federal amendment to the Constitution that would ban same-sex marriage. In the summer of that year, the group maintained a regular presence in Washington, DC, as both houses of Congress debated the amendment. Representatives of Clergy for Fairness from numerous states visited congressional offices and hosted press conferences. The organization's Web site is perhaps the most sophisticated of its kind, providing links to sample sermons from various religious traditions and talking points about religious liberty and discrimination. Although united in their opposition to a federal amendment, the clergy do not necessarily agree on all issues related to homosexuality and same-sex marriage. Nor does the group take a position with respect to state constitutional amendments regarding same-sex marriage or civil unions.

Other religious groups that support civil marriage rights for same-sex couples are regionally based. The Religious Coalition for the Freedom to Marry, a small interfaith group of clergy, is limited to the New England states and thus a bit player at best in the national drama that is playing out. Similarly, the Colorado Clergy for Equality in Marriage (CCEM)is a group of 104 clergy members from across denominations, working in support of gay unions in the state. Again, there appears to be little coordination between CCEM and any groups on the national stage. The mobilization among religious progressives in support of same-sex marriage rights is hardly an analog to the interfaith organizations which oppose gay marriage.

It seems that the liberal mainline denominations, such as the Episcopal Church and the Methodist Church, are too consumed with the issue of homosexuality within the church to expend much energy on the issue beyond the church. And though there are individual denominations that support same-sex marriages, they represent a minuscule portion of the overall religious landscape. The Unitarian Universalist Association (UUA), a representative body of UU churches, has showed support forsame-sex marriage since 1970. Similarly, the United Church of Christ (UCC) officially came out in favor of gay marriage in a 1975 resolution and reasserted its commitment in 2005.[4] In an attempt to show its inclusiveness, in 2004 the UCC ran a television ad showing a same-sex couple being turned away by an unidentified church, only to be welcomed by aUCC church.[5]

Yet the UCC, one of America's most liberal denominations, is not immune from the traditionalist-progressive divide. Because the UCC is composed of autonomous local churches, the General Synod has little authority over individual church practices. So, for example, when the Western North Carolina Association of local UCC churches banned the ordination of openly gay clergy members in 2003, the General Synod had no authority to overrule the act. Other UCC churches have been critical of the governing body's support of same-sex marriage. The First Church of Christ in Wethers field, Connecticut, the largest UCC church in New England, voted to become independent of the UCC denomination in 2004, explaining that its decision was largely due to the denomination's position regarding gay marriage and other social issues ("Largest UCC church in New England votes to become independent" 2004).

In reviewing the evidence given above, can we say that the religious coalitions surrounding gay marriage support the culture war thesis? Recall the two criteria for observing a culture war among elites: (1) cooperation among leaders of different religious traditions and (2) greater divisions within than between religious traditions. We have seen that both criteriaare met, although perhaps the first to a greater extent than the second. Among gay marriage opponents we find a historically remarkable degree of ecumenism, exceeding the breadth of coalitions formed concerning other cultural issues such as abortion and the Equal Rights Amendment. Traditionalist Protestants, Catholics, and Jews alike have united in their opposition to gay marriage. On the other hand, although religious progressives are more naturally inclined toward interfaith cooperation, there are few examples of ecumenical action among gay marriage proponents. In this conflict, one side significantly outnumbers the other.

We also see some evidence for the other criterion, namely, divisions within religious traditions. Within Catholicism and various strains of Protestantism, religious leaders are split with regard to the question of gay marriage. One should not exaggerate the transdenominational nature of opinions about the issue, however. Certainly, the traditionalist-progressive split is salient, but this does not mean that denominations have ceased to matter. A Southern Baptist, regardless of her traditionalism, is more likely to oppose gay marriage than an Episcopalian, notwithstanding the Episcopalian's degree of orthodoxy. It would appearthat when we look within denominations, the biggest fights over gay marriage occur inside liberal churches—whose congregants appear less unified in their progressivism than conservative church members are cohesively committed to traditionalism.

WHAT STRATEGIES HAVE THEY EMPLOYED?

The breadth of the coalition against gay marriage is interesting as an example of the fault lines that have formed with regard to cultural issues in American politics. Its significance is more than merely academic, however, because the transdenominational nature of the movement is an important element in its political success. The efforts to build a diverse coalition—in terms of race and religion—underscore the political sophistication of the religious activists who oppose gay marriage. They understand the fundamental rule in a participatory political system: numbers matter. Elected offcials are more likely to listen to a large group representing more voters than a smaller group representing fewer voters; all else being equal, a broad coalition beats a narrow one every time. And for the battle over gay marriage, the coalition of opponents has been broad indeed.

Why is there such a broad coalition opposing gay marriage? Given the widespread opposition to the practice, as illustrated in figure 28.1, it may seem inevitable that the opposition to it would have a wide base. But there is nothing inevitable about the institutions that have been developed to lead the charge against gay marriage.

Although the widespread opposition to gay marriage is a necessary condition for a broad coalition, it is not sufficient. The breadth of the coalition is also the result of political experience gained over the previous generation of cultural battles and the political infrastructure that has been built to fight those battles. The coalition is in large part the result of a deliberate strategy employed by evangelical conservatives since the issue first gained national prominence in the mid-1990s, when the Defense of Marriage Act was passed in Congress and signed by Bill Clinton. The specific strategy in play consists of diversifying the coalition opposed to gay marriage, amending state constitutions to ban gay marriage, and, finally, creating the "perfect storm" so that the conditions will be right to pass an amendment to the U.S. Constitution defining marriage as the union of a man and a woman.

A good example of a Christian Right activist who has recognized the political advantage of a diverse coalition working against gay marriage is Matt Daniels of the Alliance for Marriage. Recognizing the limits of the prolife movement, which largely consists of white evangelicalsand Catholics,[6] Daniels sought to create a multiracial movement in defense of heterosexual marriage. A Chinese pastor serving on the advisory board of the alliance notes that Daniels selected advisors and board members with the idea of bringing together people of diverse faiths and races (Wong 2004). As noted above, the Arlington Group is another example of Christian Right leaders' organizing an infrastructure composed of diverse religions and denominations to respond to gay marriage. After the groups were linked at the national level, the local and state affiliates came to coordinate with one another, an important development because the battle over traditional marriage has primarily been waged at the state and local levels.[7]

Examining one state in particular illustrates the political strategy of gay marriage opponents. On November 2, 2004, Ohioans voted to ban the recognition of same-sex marriage by amending the state constitution. The success of this ballot initiative was largely a result of coordination between Ohio affiliates of socially conservative advocacy groups and their national parent organizations. The leading figure in Ohio, Phil Burress, was a familiar face in local Christian Right circles, having run an antipornography group since the early 1990s.[8] When Hawaii's state supreme court issued a ruling in favor of allowing same-sex marriage in 1993, Burress began committing most of his time to fighting gay marriage in his own state. He started the Ohio Campaign to Protect Marriage, now a state affiliate of Focus on the Family and the Family Research Council. To assist Burress and his supporters, these and other national groups contacted their members in Ohio to mobilize them in response to the issue. The American Family Association, for example, sent out mass emails to sixty thousand supporters who live in Ohio to encourage them to sign the petition needed to get the issue on the ballot and then turn out to vote in November. Representatives from the Ohio group met with national leaders regularly. Part of the strategy involved discussing how to conduct outreach to leaders within other religious traditions in the state. As a result, staffers from the Ohio Campaign to Protect Marriage visited a large mosque in the greater Cincinnati area to encourage its members to support the state's ban on gay marriage (Miller 2005). The Ohio group also worked closely with African American churches to gather signatures for the petition. Further broadening the coalition, all twelve Catholic bishops in Ohio made a public statement in support of the state's marriage amendment. With these interfaith relationships in place, the Ohio Campaign to Protect Marriage was able to gather 575,000 signatures in fewer than ninety days to put a measure on the Ohio ballot. Sixty-two percent voted in favor, and thus a ban on same-sex marriage was written into the state constitution.[9]

The example of Ohio, like that of California, mentioned earlier, demonstrates that the religious diversity among groups opposed to gay marriage is not restricted to the national level. Although evangelical groups appear to be spearheading the cause, they depend on a larger community of religious believers to achieve political success. And we expect to see further interreligious cooperation because the success of the Ohio campaign now serves as a template for anti–gay marriage campaigns in other states. Soon after the 2004 election season, which resulted in bans on same-sex marriage added to the constitutions of twelve states,[10] Burress and other religious leaders met in Washington, DC, to discuss the following year's constitutional amendment battles in other states. By igniting support for traditional marriage at the grass roots, leaders at the national level hope to spur constituents to pressure their representatives and senators to support the amendment to the U.S. Constitution. To that end, they remain focused on the states.

As evidenced by the decision to build support for a gay marriage ban state by state, leaders in the movement against the practice have displayed a considerable degree of political sophistication (not to mention patience). This is nowhere more apparent than in their negotiations concerning the federal marriage amendment. Although it is certain to fail in the short term, it will be repeatedly introduced in the years to come. Conservative religious leaders do not expect success immediately. Years ago, prior to the first introduction of the amendment, leaders of the Christian Right met with members of Congress to determine a realistic strategy for enacting a constitutional amendment. They realized the limitations they faced in a contentious Congress and chose to work within those constraints, as illustrated by the wording selected for the amendment. A ban on civil unions, they were told, would never happen. And so instead of an amendment that would explicitly ban civil unions and gay marriage, they opted for one that would prohibit homosexual marriages only. The majority of groups represented by the movement to defend traditional marriage also oppose civil unions, but many of them were willing to focus their efforts on marriage as a political compromise. According to Allison Slatter of the Arlington Group's Marriage Amendment Project, trying to outlaw civil unions would have been political suicide. Using a metaphor that resonates with our discussion of the culture war, she said, "Civil unions require a nuke and nuking is not popular. Restricting marriage to man and woman would require circular strikes, and those are acceptable. We pinpoint the area most troublesome and we stop that" (Slatter 2004). Focus on the Family, equally opposed to civil unions, agreed that pushing for an amendment to address civil unions would not be politically expedient. Instead, Focus on the Family believes that it must defend traditional marriage before attempting tooutlaw civil unions as well. "Being an incrementalist is not an unprincipled approach," said Peter Brandt, the group's vice president of public policy (Brandt 2004). Brandt thinks it wiser to turn to the states to adopt the language necessary to ban civil unions.[11]

Contrast this flexibility with earlier incarnations of the Christian Right movement, which was characterized by absolutism with regard to moral issues. As it has become a more politically sophisticated movement, it has recognized the value of getting half a loaf when the whole loaf is out of reach. The evolving strategy of abortion opponents illustrates this change. When the Christian Right first appeared on the national political landscape, its leaders and organizations took a hard-line stand against abortion, supporting nothing less than an absolute ban on all abortions. In more recent years, however abortion opponents have adopted an incremental strategy by working to enact a prohibition on"partial-birth abortion" (known to abortion rights advocates as "intact dilation and extraction"), supporting parental notification laws, and the like (Saletan 2003). As applied to abortion, the incremental strategy appears to be working. Not only have numerous limitations and restrictions on abortion been successfully enacted, but recent years have seen a small shift toward prolife attitudes among the general public—two developments that are clearly related, although the direction of causality is unclear (Wilcox and Norrander 2002). Incrementalism with respect to abortion has served as a template for the strategy to oppose gay marriage. The half loaf of a gay marriage ban that permits civil unions is better than trying and failing to obtain the whole loaf of banning both.

CONCLUSION

We have seen that the religious coalitions that have formed around the issue of gay marriage—especially in opposition to it—are evidence of what James Davison Hunter memorably labeled "culture war politics." The term is incendiary and perhaps misleading, but the interfaith cooperation it is meant to describe nonetheless includes the groups working to thwart gay marriage in the United States. In its current configuration, the debate about the practice pits opponents comprised largely of traditionalists spanning the religious spectrum against advocates who are predominantly secular but are joined by a small number of religious progressives. We stress that we are not saying that religious traditions are irrelevant in shaping opinions regarding gay marriage. To the contrary, members of different religious traditions vary systematically in their opposition to gay marriage. But the differences among religious traditions are surpassed by the differences within them. Your level of traditionalism within your church matters more than which church you go to.

At the moment, the opponents of gay marriage have the upper hand. Supporters of marriage among homosexuals are in the minority, as evidenced by public opinion polls and the overwhelming margins of victory for ballot initiatives to ban marriage between homosexual couples. As we look toward the future, however, should we expect to see the "culture war" continue? There are two ways to read the tea leaves. On one hand, attitudes toward homosexuality are becoming increasingly liberal, largely because young people are more accepting of homosexuals and gay marriage than their elders. Young people are also less likely than their elders to endorse morally traditionalist opinions. For example, 36 percent of Americans over the age of fifty-five are in the bottom half of the moral traditionalism index introduced above, compared to 72 percent of people under the age of thirty. As time marches on, those young people will come to occupy an ever-larger share of the population. It is thus tempting to say that we should expect to see a cessation of hostilities in the culture war—at least along the front line of gay marriage—in much the same way that racial attitudes changed dramatically over the course of a generation. It is also portentous, however, that the gap in attitudes toward gay marriage between young people at the bottom and at the top of the moral traditionalism index mirrors what we see among their elders. The former gap in is 28 percentage points. Among people over fifty-five, the gap is 32 points. In other words, we see that young people, taken as a whole, have more liberal attitudes about gay marriage than do their elders. Yet among young people, there remains a clear distinction between traditionalists and progressives. This sharp divide suggests that the most apt analogy for attitudes about gay marriage may be not public opinion regarding civil rights. Rather, perhaps a better comparison is with attitudes about abortion, which have remained sharply polarized for decades. If so, we can expect the battle over gay marriage to be with us for a long time.

NOTES

1. Tony Perkins, president of the Family Research Council, in remarks made to attendees at the Mayday for Marriage rally in Washington, DC, on October 15, 2004, and printed in the event's program.
2. Ken Hutcherson, senior pastor at Antioch Bible Church in Kirkland, Washington, organized the first Mayday for Marriage Rally, in Seattle. It drew approximately twenty thousand people.
3. Terms such as *traditional* and *progressive* are contested. Since these are the terms Hunter uses in *Culture Wars*, we have adopted them. We prefer them to *conservative* and *liberal*, since these terms confuse theology with political ideology.
4. For an overview of the composition of the Christian Right, see Wilcox and Larson (2006), chap. 2.
5. This includes any other type of legal recognition for homosexual relationships. To keep things simple, we simply refer to "opposing gay marriage," which should be understood as including opposition to civil unions.
6. After 2005, MAP no longer existed as a separate entity, though the goal of barring same-sex marriage remains a prominent interest of the Arlington Group.
7. For a discussion of religious lobbying activity in Virginia, including a summary of its two Catholic dioceses, see Larson, Madland, and Wilcox (2006).

8. On July 4, 2005, at the Twenty-fifth General Synod of the United Church of Christ, delegates voted to adopt the resolution "In Support of Equal Rights for All." http://www.ucc.org/synod/resolutions/gsrev25-7.pdf (accessed October 17, 2006).

9. Both NBC and CBS refused to air the advertisement, deeming it too controversial.

10. For an overview of the composition of the prolife movement, see Luker (1985) and Maxwell (2002).

11. To understand the strategy one must have some understanding of the structural organization of Christian Right groups. Many national-level groups, such as the Family Research Council, Focus on the Family, and the Christian Coalition, have state affiliates that share the policy platform of the national body. When cooperation is taking place on the national scale, cooperation between state affiliates is likely to follow.

12. For a profile of Phil Burress and his work in defense of traditional marriage, see Dao (2004).

13. In 2004 the wording of state amendments went largely uncontested among the religious groups opposed to gay marriage. Burress, a staunch social conservative, was the original architect of the Ohio amendment, and he put forth a conservative text that banned same-sex contracts in addition to same-sex marriage. Activists from other states chose to pursue a ban on same-sex marriage that did not include a ban on civil unions, possibly thinking that this additional stipulation might decrease the chances of the amendment's passage. In Oregon, for example, an amendment banning same-sex civil unions would have been asking too much from a liberal-leaning state. Oregon voters did pass an amendment banning gay marriage but by only 58 percent, the smallest margin of any marriage amendment proposed in 2004. To date, the text of state amendments has been left up to the discretion or conviction of local evangelical activists and evangelical groups.

14. Two states voted to amend their constitutions prior to Election Day. Missouri citizens voted to amend the state constitution in August 2004 to define marriage as a union of a man and woman. Louisiana voted in September to amend its constitution, outlawing gay marriage as well as civil unions. In November, however, a Louisiana lower court judge overturned the state amendment, saying it was flawed because it included two purposes, banning gay marriage and civil unions, within one amendment. At this point, it seems likely that the ban will eventually be reinstated, however, if only because Louisiana's supreme court is an elected body, and Louisianans voted overwhelmingly in favor of the ban (78 percent).

15. Not all socially conservative advocacy groups have been happy with this compromise. Concerned Women for America, for example, was so displeased with the failure of the amendment to address civil unions that it decided not to directly partner with the coalitions opposing gay marriage in April 2005.

LABORING ON

BIRTH IN TRANSITION IN THE UNITED STATES

By Wendy Simonds and Barbara Katz Rothman

WHAT HAPPENS AT HOME?

Midwifery focuses on pregnancy and birth as processes. Labor is *labor*, difficult *work*, but it is beautiful, normal, "natural" as midwives see it. They work to help women have birth experiences that are spiritual, beautiful, and worthwhile. Pain may be part of labor, risk may be part of giving birth, but they are not the central elements around which midwifery practice is built. When discussing what they're all about, the dominant theme for midwives is facilitating one of life's most meaningful events. Doctors, in contrast, with their risk-orientation, focus much more on the outcome: healthy baby, healthy mom.

To illustrate the differences in their philosophies, we will focus here on participants' views about the topic of home birth. (For an extended discussion of many more aspects of maternity care and birth attendants' discussions of their motivations and practice ideals, see Simonds, Rothman, and Norman 2007.) Home birth is, according to most studies, safer than hospital birth, but doctors in this country have continuously raised opposition to—and political leverage against—home birth.

The smear campaigns against home birth midwifery that U.S. doctors have orchestrated at various times in U.S. history have not, and do not, rely on data that show hospital birth to be safer than home birth, because such data are lacking. One study out of dozens recently showed a higher infant death rate in home births than in other settings (Pang et al. 2002), but critics of that study refute the claim because the authors did not clearly distinguish between intentional (planned) and unintentional home births (see, e.g., MANA press release 2003 and Vedam 2003). All other studies show superior outcomes in terms of maternal and infant morbidity for home births, and equivalent outcomes in terms of mortality (see, e.g., Goer 1999; Johnson and Daviss 2005; and Olsen 1997).

DIRECT-ENTRY MIDWIVES ON HOME BIRTH

Regardless of whether they first attend births at home or in hospitals, direct-entry midwives and midwifery students find that their experiences of home birth make them reconceptualize hospital birth negatively. Many do rotations in hospitals as part of their training, or have experience as labor and delivery nurses or as doulas. In one of the student focus group interviews, they sought to articulate the differences:

ALLIE CORNELL: I've found that the difference between the home and hospital birth is much more profound in the States than in other places. And I've seen hospital births, like I was at [a public hospital in Atlanta] actually. It was my first birth. And it was pretty—I mean, the midwives were wonderful, and I cried. It was a wonderful experience. ... And then in Holland, I saw my first home birth, and was, of course, completely blown away with the difference that it was just a completely different world in terms of it being the woman's environment. The woman's in charge. The woman's the most comfortable she can possibly be. The midwife is the guest. But if you have a woman give birth in the hospital there [Holland], it's almost the same. It's not like you become a prisoner of the hospital who's completely given over all power. You're just—you're now in a slightly different setting. Your midwife is still your primary attendant. And you're still calling the shots. And you go home an hour or two after the birth. I mean, it wasn't this wholly different thing. ... I still felt a difference, but I wondered how much of it was our way of doing hospital birth, rather than *just* the location.

PAULA DANIELS: Hmm. I've only seen two different births in two different hospitals. And I guess major things I noticed that disturbed me ... [were] just watching how the focus was on the [EFM] machine ... the nurses come in, look at the strip, and since I was a student nurse for one of them, she's like, "get the blood pressure"! So I'd get her vital signs and then I'd write 'em down, and the nurse left the room. I was like, this is really disturbing. First of all, she never even really looked at the woman. She looked at the machine. ... I feel like, at least in this country, the hospital tends to take your power away. And your—any sense of self-confidence and any sense of—I mean, you're just completely vulnerable. ... If it's a teaching hospital—there's people in and out you've never seen before, never will see again. Medical students catching your baby. It's just total craziness. And at home, in a home birth setting ... it's your house and you've invited these people in to help you with your process, and it's *your* process.

RUTH RUSSELL: I want to say one other thing, which is about the actual birth of the baby and after that. That there is a *tremendous* difference in my experience. That at home, the baby's born, there's a respect for this sacred moment and time afterwards. And the family is seen as the—*the* unit—that's the whole focus, is the baby and those parents having their time. And that the midwife is monitoring quietly, but you know, doing what she needs to do to make sure that everything's okay, but that isn't the focus. Whereas in the hospital that I worked in, the baby was taken *right away* to the warmer, and the mother could only look from across the room at her baby. And that's the difference of night and day! That moment is taken away from her that she has worked so hard for.

These students contrasted hospital staff's professional indifference with the reverence and unobtrusiveness of midwifery. They depict hospital routines as routinizing, dehumanizing, and mundane—and as ultimately depriving women of real, true, wonderful birth experiences. The group agreed that hospital births don't have to be this way (as in Cornell's example of the hospital births she observed in the Netherlands), but that hospitals in the U.S. were unlikely ever to offer women the control over their births they could have at home.

Most obstetric and nurse-midwifery group practices (and most practices today are group practices) at best offer women the opportunity to meet all the providers who work together in the group. Meeting someone once or twice is not the same as knowing them. Knowing someone, midwives repeatedly say, means one is more likely to trust them and to feel safe with them. Home birth best exemplifies this ethic of "continuity of care." Home birth midwives describe presence through unobtrustiveness: there is something so forceful about *not* taking charge, and simply representing the values that can make someone else who believes in them too feel safe and protected. This is so different from medical paternalism. It is, truly about feeling connected with others while you feel most vulnerable, during what could be a potentially very isolating event.

Many home birth midwives (and advocates of home birth) feel that moving birth into an alien environment staffed primarily (or exclusively) by strangers exacerbates the very slow-downs and pathologies in labor that medicine seeks to "correct." We heard repeatedly how, especially for home birth midwives, taking part in hospital births means adapting to an institutionalized setting organized in ways they find philosophically alien. As Serena Davis said:

Whether these protocols are always necessary or not—you have to fit into them. And sometimes when we see that some of the protocols are just absolutely ridiculous—I'm not going to—you know, I'm not going to say you have to *fight*. But, you know, because a lot of the people that are in the hospital are very territorial and they—sometimes they build up an attitude or a shield around themselves. ... You don't have to do [that] at home, you know! One of the nice things about ... having your baby at home is that you can labor how you want to, you can give birth how you want to. And what I mean by "how you want to" is basically what's the most effective for the mother. ... Sometimes, when you're in the hospital, they don't want you to walk around, they don't want you to walk outside the bedroom. It's just a lot more rules, more regimens there. ... In the hospital, they don't want you to deliver in any position: they want to be able to see, so they can manage. And that's what happens in hospitals: births are managed by machines, by people, by drugs; whereas at home, it's not being managed by anybody, you know, just the ... the natural flow of the body.

Davis starts out by talking about how it's diffcult for *her* in the hospital, but when she moves into discussing home birth, she shifts from talking about how she feels different at a home birth to talking about how the birthing woman ("you") experiences the birth. Home birth midwives are especially identified with the women they work with, both in a personal idiosyncratic way (via the friendships that are formed) and in a kind of womanly solidarity based upon a shared view of birth. In hospitals, women may feel a connection with staff and staff may seek to connect with them, but everyone is subject to obeying institutional protocols. Even though most births follow the same general course of events, from contractions to pushing a baby out, home births are deroutinized. They are deroutinized mainly because they take place one at a time, but also because the overriding philosophy, the general sensibility of everyone involved, is that births should *not* be routinized.

Home birth midwives emphasize that home birth is not "for everyone." They are careful not to speak in universals. They want every woman to at least have access to midwifery, but realize that deinstitutionalizing birth would be impossible given the entrenchment of obstetrics and the prevalence of medicalization.

Several home birth midwives we interviewed raised the humorous analogy of ordering a man to get an erection in a public setting to point out the absurdities of the ways in which birthing women are often bossed around and typically exposed in hospitals. Similarly, Ina May Gaskin (2003) describes an example used by midwife Lisa Goldstein in childbirth education classes to illustrate how difficult it can be to get one's body to perform under impersonal surveillance: "First she shows them a fifty-dollar bill. Then she places a medium-sized stainless-steel bowl on the floor. ... She then offers that bill to the first man who comes forward and pees in the bowl in front of everyone. In all the years she has repeated this routine, she has never handed over that fifty dollars to anyone" (174). Most midwives agree that hospitals can produce inhibitions in a way that one's own environment will not.

NURSE-MIDWIVES ON HOME BIRTH

Unlike the direct entry midwives, nurse-midwives begin their careers as nurses, and then have further education, based in hospitals, in midwifery and obstetrical care. Most nurse-midwives rarely receive training outside of hospitals, so home birth is something they first (and often only) imagine against a backdrop of hospital birth. Except for one group of nurse-midwives doing home birth we interviewed in New York, most of the nurse-midwives and nurse-midwifery students we interviewed intended, expected, or did practice in hospital settings. Most of them felt they couldn't imagine doing home births themselves (as midwives), because the level of responsibility they would have for the well-being of women and babies would be too daunting. They couldn't imagine birth as a situation for which they would not be responsible as *managers* for producing good outcomes. And they showed their fear of birth, which home birth midwives accept and view as integral but not central to, their work. Betsy Ettinger, for instance, recognized her uneasiness about home birth as a product of her training:

> I think I have too much medicine and medical background in me to be comfortable in a home birth. Now, I was comfortable in a birthing center, but I had the safety

net of a medical center across the street. And, I had some wonderful experiences in birthing centers—so beautiful—but I've had beautiful experiences in the hospital. And I guess—and maybe this is my rationale—but I think the birth experience can be a good experience anyplace.

Many nurse-midwives portray birth centers as an ideal compromise between the unknown perils that could happen and the level of constraint of the medical model. Birth centers are more convenient for midwives, too, because they tend to employ larger groups of midwives who can be on call less than they would be in a home birth practice. (However, because of malpractice insurance costs in the U.S., birth centers are risky business ventures.)

We also interviewed several nurse-midwives who were practicing, or had practiced, home birth midwifery. In their discussions of home birth they sounded no different from the direct-entry midwives. Nurse-midwives interviewed (by Rothman) in the 1970s talked about how doing home birth required a reconceptualization of birth; outside the medical context, the meaning of "progress" and the timetables used to assess it, would gradually relax until a paradigm shift had occurred, and risk was no longer the central structuring element of attending a woman in labor (see Rothman 1991).

OBSTETRICIANS ON HOME BIRTH

Most of the ten obstetricians we interviewed expressed an antipathy to home birth because they viewed birth as a potentially pathological series of obstacles, at best a "natural" process that could go wrong at any time and require correction via medical interventions that were not available outside of hospitals. Consider these responses to the questions:

"Have you ever seen a home birth?" and "What do you think about home birth?"

Harriet Murphy: I would have a heart attack if I had to observe a home birth. I would absolutely probably just wet my pants. I *never* would do a home birth. I would think that [only] an idiot would have a home delivery. ... I just can't understand why any reasonable person who loved their child would take a chance with having their child be born dead, which is what they're doing—even if it's a small chance. I have seen too many people go down the tubes in five minutes, and if you weren't in a hospital either the mother could be dead or the baby could be dead.

Lois Silverman: I think that nobody today should be laboring far from a room where they can have a c-section. The American College of OB-GYN recommendation is that you need—in an emergency, you need to have a c-section *done* in thirty minutes. And I think that anyone in labor ... *deserves* that level of care. ... I mean, you can be having a perfectly nat—normal labor at home, and you think you're just in hard labor, and your placenta abrupts from the strength of your contractions; it separates and you start hemorrhaging. Where are you? You're, like, not in the hospital! You don't have an IV. ... Your baby is most likely going to die, and you may not do so well afterwards yourself. I mean, I just don't think it's worth the risk.

Julie Elkmont: I don't believe in home births …. It's risky. I know midwives do that. I don't particularly like that. I mean, what do you do when you are in trouble, and you're home, and things happen? There are patients that get in trouble at the very end, and now you're stuck at home and you're not in a hospital situation. I mean there's a lot of—there's a reason why moms aren't dying anymore. There's a reason why babies aren't dying anymore …. We just don't have that anymore, because we have made a lot of changes …. Why do you have to suffer when you are in labor? I guess if you get some kick out of it, or if you feel that you are a stronger woman. I think there are some patients, they feel that they are a better woman for it. It's like, okay, fi ne, if that's what makes you happy ….

What do you do when somebody's bleeding, and you have no drugs to give that patient to help her stop bleeding and she is having a postpartum hemorrhage? What do you do? You're at home. You call an ambulance. You're wasting time …. I have seen too many things happen. That's why I don't think it is necessarily good. But these stars, Hollywood stars, have their births at home, and have all these midwives, nothing bad—it's good that nothing bad has happened to them. Then everyone reads about it in the paper, and is like "oh, I want to be like so and so"!

Corrinne Wood-Daniels: Well, I do not support home deliveries. I think if a woman should choose not to have the benefit of medical intervention even when it clearly could save her life and the life of her baby, and if she makes that decision, then that is her choice. But she has to understand many of the life-threatening complications of obstetrics come with no warning.

These doctors equate home birth with the direst of consequences—life-threatening situations for babies and mothers, and they equate hospital birth with safety for babies and mothers. They see midwives and women who attempt home birth as misguided (even "idiots," as Murphy said or Elkmont implied when she talked about women imitating movie stars), irrationally choosing pain (Elkmont) or irresponsibly risking trouble that could spiral into irreparable emergency (all of them). Even when doctors say that women have the "right" to make this decision, closer attention reveals their frustration with what they see as poor decision-making (Elkmont and Wood-Daniels). Doctors may even frame the ideology of home birth as masochistic (Elkmont), or as a touchy-feely ruse, cheating women of care they *deserve* (Silverman).

Among the midwives and midwifery students we interviewed who worked outside of hospitals, few spoke about deaths or near-deaths they'd encountered as part of their work. None told of a death that would have been avoided had the mother been in a hospital. This could mean that midwives are reluctant to speak of such matters, but such situations are exceedingly rare, or presumably word would get out. Midwives are well aware of the attitude of the medical profession toward home birth and know that if something does go wrong; doctors and family members may well hold midwives and/or the women who choose them responsible.

Doctors' notion of risk inflates as a result of their interventive training and interventive experience as practitioners. They come to see their interventions as producing (good) results; they never imagine what situations might be like without viewing their (medical, interventive) actions as central. Midwives doing—and women having—home births know that risks exist; the difference is that they view these risks as acceptable, and ultimately preferable to the risks incurred by birthing in hospitals, which doctors do not acknowledge in the first place. Most of the doctors we interviewed did not seem aware that there was any other point of view on home birth but theirs—the story medicine tells about itself that it made birth safer for women and babies, and that home birth is a throwback to a dangerous past practice. This story simply is not true.

Doctors talked about how nice hospitals have become nowadays. Home, they think, can be approximated through cosmetic changes: nice furniture, fancy wood floors. Perhaps if environments are homelike enough, people feel more at home. But redecorating will not alter conventional power dynamics, as long as the precepts of obstetrical monitoring remain in place and the operating room is right down the hall from the LDR "suites." We don't mean to suggest that aesthetic improvements cannot improve people's experiences—they can—but they do not necessarily affect power differentials. They may, in fact, mask them.

Only three doctors we interviewed did not condemn home birth. Here are excerpts from two of their interviews:

> *Laurie Leland:* I do feel strongly that we need to ... have access to things like an operating room if something went wrong ... . You probably wouldn't find me completely on the side of some lay midwives, or whatever. I don't want to jeopardize at all the health of the baby, and I realize that the health of the baby is more important than any—so the issue of trying to make it as natural a process as we can, but still having the benefits of—you know my experience in dealing—when the shit hits the fan on labor and delivery, it really hits the fan and you can't always predict who ... it's going to happen to ....
> *Simonds:* Do you feel like home births are not safe?
> *Leland:* I don't know—that's—I feel sort of conflicted about that.
>
> *Fried:* I'm a little uncomfortable with home birthing. You know, if someone's very low risk and has easy access to a hospital, I think it can be okay. ... I think it must be really *nice* to *not* be in a hospitalized medicalized setting. I think that that could be a real plus. *But*, having practiced high-risk obstetrics for so many years and seen such horrible disasters .... It creates fear in me to think about it.

The differences between what Leland and Fried said about home birth and what the other doctors said was that these two recognized that home birth could be very appealing and different from hospital birth; they acknowledged ambivalence rather than taking a firm position on the issue; and they recognized that their ambivalence was empirically grounded and institutionally produced. Phyllis Fraser was the only doctor we interviewed who had observed a home birth. She said, "It was quite beautiful .... It's not for everyone. But for those who want it, I think they should have the right to do it."

CONCLUSION

Inside the ideology of the medical model, undamaged babies are the end product of the birth process; to ensure a good product, ideally, one must be able to take total control over it should anything go awry. Medicalized thinkers (like Harper and many of the doctors) see access to and use of interventive techniques as providing them with the greatest amount of control they could possibly have, and they can only imagine the lack of such access and usage as inappropriate and dangerous. To reject the hospital, to question the medicalized formulation of the control issue, to them means inviting what they see as *unwarranted* risk. They simply cannot see outside the hospital box.

When we listened to many of the doctors talk about practicing obstetrics, we were reminded of other institutions that enjoy taken-for-granted supremacy and that can systematically produce negative, even violent effects that occur in such a way that they appear uninitiated by actors, because the institutions have ideological lives of its own. Routines and protocols become taken for granted and appear to need no justification or analysis. Militarism, for instance, comes to seem unauthored and inevitable (see, e.g., Enloe 1990, 2000), as do various forms of inequality (class-based, race-based, gender-based, sexual-identity-based, etc.) under capitalism. Milgram's (1974) experiments in which men and women thought they were administering electric shocks to others, Zimbardo's (1992) simulated prison, and actual "total institutions" like real prisons and mental hospitals (see Goffman 1961) show how easily, seemingly automatically, covert sado-masochistic dynamics are produced when hierarchical power structures become commonplace and taken for granted (see also Chancer 1992, and of course, Foucault 1973, 1977). Within such structures, people rarely question what's happening, and those who do tend to have the least power to effect change. Obstetrics is very much an example of this sort of sadomasochistic in-stitution, even when the actual doctors are nice people with positive intentions. It has taken on a life of its own, as all institutions do. Its ideology and practices evidently do damage to people, but it cloaks itself in a scientific white coat and holds fast to its conceptions and methods. But obstetrics has changed in ways that mask its deleterious effects. Just as subtle or covert racism (or any "ism") may be more difficult to see and to combat, so it is with the sadomasochistic hegemony underlying medicalization.

A few doctors we interviewed could see outside the parameters in which they functioned, but they could only occasionally or murkily imagine a better way. And, for the most part, they felt that the changes that had occurred—wallpaper, hardwood floors, conscious women, the presence of significant others—showed that humanitarianism held sway and progress occurred progressively. So they inadvertently (rather than intentionally) tended to promote the reign of medical authority over women's bodies and pregnancy and birth experiences.

Midwives struggled continuously in their work to make compromises, to resist, or to avoid medicalizing women's pregnancies and birth experiences. Working in and outside of the system, they strove to honor the notion that birth is about facilitating women's growth, change, and self-realization, rather than managing risk, avoiding pain, and objectifying bodies.

DISCUSSION QUESTIONS

1. What are the ideologies that shape the medical model?
2. What are some of the very different meanings a pregnancy might have?
3. How is a nurse midwife's training different than that of a direct entry midwife?
4. What are the changes in hospital practice that women obstetricians recommend?
5. List some of the ways that obstetrical practice has increased risk and danger to mothers and babies in birth.

REFERENCES

Brack, Datha Clapper (1976). "Displaced: The Midwife by the Male Physician." *Women and Health* 1: 18–24.

Brendsel, Carol, Gail Peterson, and Lewis Mehl (1979). "Episiotomy: Facts, Fiction, Figures and Alternatives." In *Compulsory Hospitalization Or Freedom in Childbirth?* Leww Steward and David Stewart, eds. Marble Hill, MO: NAPSAC.

Bullough, Vern (1966). *The Development of Medicine as a Profession: The Contribution of the Medieval University to Modern Medicine.* New York: Karger.

Chancer, Lynn (1992). *Sadomasochism in Everyday Life: The Dynamics of Power and Powerlessness.* New Brunswick, NJ: Rutgers University Press.

Curtin, Sally C., and Lola Jean Kozak (1998). "Decline in U.S. Cesarean Delivery Rate Appears to Stall." *Birth* 25 (December): 259–262.

DeClercq, Eugene R., Ray Menacker, and Marian MacDorman et al. (2006). "Maternal Risk Profiles and the Primary Cesarean Rate on the United States, 1991–2002." *American Journal of Public Health* 96 (May): 867–72.

DeLee, Joseph B. (1920). "The Prophylactic Forceps Operation." *Journal of Obstetrics and Gynecology* 1: 34–44.

Donegan, Jane B. (1978). *Women and Men Midwives: Medicine, Morality and Misogyny in Early America.* Westport Conn: Greenwood Press.

Donnison, Jean (1977). *Midwives and Medical Men: A History of Inter-Professional Rivalries and Women's Rights.* New York: Schocken.

Dubos, Rene (1968). *Man, Medicine and Environment.* New York: New American Library.

Ehrenreich, Barbara, and Deirdre English (1973). *Witches, Midwives and Nurses: A History of Women Healers.* Old Westbury NY: Feminist Press.

Enloe, Cynthia (2000). *Maneuvers: The International Politics of Militarizing Women's Lives.* Berkeley, CA: University of California Press.

— (1990). *Bananas, Beaches and Bases: Making Feminist Sense of International Politics.* Berkeley, CA: University of California Press.

Foucault, Michel (1977). *Discipline and Punish: The Birth of the Prison.* Alan Sheridan, tr. New York: Pantheon.

— (1973). *The Birth of the Clinic: An Archaeology of Medical Perception.* A.M. Sheridan Smith, tr. New York: Vintage.

Gaskin, Ina May (2003). *Ina May's Guide to Childbirth.* New York: Bantam.

Goer, Henci (1999). *The Thinking Woman's Guide to a Better Birth*. New York: Berkley Publishing Group.

Goffman, Erving (1961). *Asylums: Essays on the Social Situation of Mental Patients and Other Inmates*. Garden City NY: Doubleday.

Guttmacher, Alan (1962). *Pregnancy and Birth: A Book for Expectant Parents*. New York: New American Library.

Haire, Doris (1972). *The Cultural Warping of Childbirth*. Seattle: International Childbirth Education Association.

Hamilton, Brady E., Joyce A. Martin, and Stephanie J. Ventura (2007). "Births: Preliminary Data for 2006." *National Vital Statistics Report* 56 (December 5). Hyattsville, MD: National Center for Health Statistics.

Hartmann K., M. Viswanathan, R. Palmieri, G. Gertlehner, J. Thorp, and K.N. Lohr (2005). "Outcomes of Routine Episiotomy: A Systematic Review." *Journal of the American Medical Association* 293: 2141–8.

Johnson, K.C., and B.A. Daviss (2005). "Outcomes of Planned Home Births with Certified Professional Midwives: Large Prospective Study in North America," *British Medical Journal* 330(June 18): 1416–23.

Kobrin, Frances (1966). "The American Midwife Controversy: A Crisis in Professionalization." *Bulletin on the History of Medicine* 40:350–363.

MANA press release (2003). "Obstetricians Use Dubious Method in Attempt to Discredit Home Birth." http://www.mana.org/WAHomeBirthStudy.html. (Feb. 11).

Martin, Joyce A., Brady E. Hamilton, Fay Menacker, Paul D. Sutton, and T.J. Mathews (2005). "Preliminary Births for 2004: Infant and Maternal Health." Hyattsville, MD: National Center for Health Statistics.

Martin, Joyce A., Brady E. Hamilton, Paul D. Sutton, Stephanie J. Ventura, Fay Menacker, and Martha L. Munson (2003). *National Vital Statistics Report, Births: Final Data 2002*. Hyattsville, MD: National Center for Health Statistics.

Milgram, Stanley (1974). *Obedience to Authority: An Experimental View*. New York: Harper & Row. Olsen, O. (1997). "Meta-analysis of the Safety of Home Birth," *Birth* 24: 4–13.

Pang, J.W., J.D. Heffelfinger, G.J. Huang, T.J. Benedetti, and N.S. Weiss (2002). "Outcomes of Planned Home Birth in Washington State." *Obstetrics & Gynecology* 200 (August): 253–259.

Rothman, Barbara Katz 1(991 [1982]). *In Labor: Women and Power in the Birthplace*, revised edition. New York: WW Norton.

Simonds, Wendy, Barbara Katz Rothman, and Bari Meltzer Norman (2007). *Laboring On: Birth in Transition in the United States*. New York: Routledge.

Vedam, S. (2003). "Homebirth v. Hospital Birth: Questioning the Quality of Evidence for Safety." *Birth* 30 (1) (March): 57–63.

Zimbardo, Philip (1992). *Quiet Rage: The Stanford Prison Experiment*. Stanford, CA: Stanford University.

RACE, SOCIAL CONTEXTS, AND HEALTH

EXAMINING GEOGRAPHIC SPACES AND PLACES

By David T. Takeuchi, Emily Walton and ManChui Leung

R ace continues to have a strong association with health outcomes. African Americans, for example, have a higher incidence, greater prevalence, and longer duration of hypertension than do whites. These higher rates are a major risk factor for heart disease, kidney disease, and stroke (CDC 2007; Morenoff et al. 2007). The age-adjusted death rates for African Americans exceed those of whites by 46 percent for stroke, 32 percent for heart disease, 23 percent for cancer, and 787 percent for HIV disease (CDC 2007). Among Latinos, Puerto Rican Americans have the highest rate of lifetime asthma prevalence (196 per 1,000) making them almost 80 percent more likely to be diagnosed with asthma. Mexican American adults are 100 percent more likely than white adults to have been diagnosed with diabetes by a physician. Cancer incidence and death rates are higher for Native Hawaiians and Pacific Islanders (549 per 100,000) than for whites (448.5 per 100,000) due to higher rates for cancers of the prostate, lung, liver, stomach, and colorectum among men, and cancers of the breast and lung among women (CDC 2007; Miller et al. 2008). Native Americans, especially males ages fifteen to twenty-four, have substantially higher death rates (232 percent) for motor vehicle-related injuries and for suicide (194 percent) than other racial and ethnic groups (CDC 2007). Asian Americans are 20 percent more likely to have hepatitis B than whites and comprise almost 50 percent of chronic hepatitis B infections; these rates are related to a higher incidence and mortality of liver cancer among Asians (CDC 2006; Miller et al. 2008).

While racial variations in diseases are observed, the meaning and measurement of race is frequently contested. An early explanation for racial differences, which continues into the present but with less scientific support, attributes these variations to genetic differences. Essentialism, or biological determinism, sees racial categories as fixed, distinct, and constant over time. Essentialism suggests that some racial groups are less healthy and more apt to become ill and to die prematurely because they have physical, moral, or mental deficiencies based on their genetic or biological makeup. Genetic theories for explaining racial differences in health status are not widely supported in the contemporary scientific literature. Few genetic differences exist across racial groups, and social scientists challenge essentialist notions of race by arguing that people make attributions about groups based on stereotypes and prejudices that are tied to some physical traits (Omi and Winant 1994; Rosenberg et al. 2002).

Despite the ambiguities and complexities of racial categories, race still matters in many quality-of-life indicators (Smelser, Wilson, and Mitchell 2001). Sociologists consider race categories to be socially created boundaries that change in meaning and importance depending on the social and political climate of the time. Racial categories carry with them implicit and explicit images and beliefs about racial groups that provide rationales for treatment of group members (Takeuchi and Gage 2003). Race is particularly critical and meaningful when individuals have difficulty obtaining desired goods and resources because of their group membership (Williams and Williams-Morris 2000).

While the social science debate about the relative merits of different conceptualizations and measurements of race continues, it is clear by most measures that the population of the United States has become increasingly diverse and complex. Demographers predict that there will be significantly more changes over the next fifty years. Through the 1950s, African Americans comprised the primary racial minority group, with about 10 percent of the adult and 12 percent of the children's population (U.S. Bureau of the Census 2002). In the 2000 census, Latinos were identified as the largest minority group (U.S. Bureau of the Census 2001a); the 281,421,906 people living in the United States reflected the following racial representation: white (75 percent), Latino (13 percent), black or African American (12 percent), American Indian and Alaska Native (1 percent), Asian (4 percent), Native Hawaiian and Pacific Islander (0.1 percent), and other racial groups (6 percent). The complexity of race is magnified when mixed-race individuals are included in the picture. In 2000, when the U.S. census gave respondents the opportunity to check more than one racial group, 6.8 million people (2 percent of the population) identified themselves with two or more races.

Given the increased racial diversity in society and the move away from biological and genetic explanations, how is race linked to health? Scholars have provided a discussion of the possible social, cultural, and psychological factors that help answer this question, such as socioeconomic status, discrimination, coping styles, social support, and stress (Reskin 2003; Williams and Collins 1995). Rather than cover similar ground, this chapter focuses on some of the social and geographic spaces that help frame empirical examinations of race and health. In the United States, race and space are historically intertwined. Racial and ethnic segregation sorts individuals and groups of comparable socioeconomic status into different neighborhood environments and have been primary mechanisms by which discrimination has operated (Massey and Denton 1993). The organization of racially and ethnically segregated neighborhoods reinforces inequality, concentrates poverty, and limits the socioeconomic mobility of residents. These neighborhoods are characterized by inferior schools, lack of employment opportunities, poor housing, smaller returns on real estate investments, unequal access to a broad range of public and private services, and neglect of the physical environment (e.g., landfills, deserted factories, vacant lots). These socioeconomic factors produced by residential segregation have been found to have a significant impact on health outcomes and mortality (Acevedo-Garcia and Lochner 2003; Collins and Williams 1999; Robert 1998).

GEOGRAPHIC DISTRIBUTION OF RACIAL AND ETHNIC GROUPS

The most recent U.S. census estimates show that racial and ethnic diversity is geographically expanding into metropolitan central cities, suburbs, and rural areas (U.S. Bureau of the Census 2008). The United States continues to be a predominately urbanized country, with 81 percent of the population residing in metropolitan central cities and suburbs and with racial and ethnic minorities accounting for 50 percent of residents in some of the largest cities such as Los Angeles and New York City. The urban decline among whites and the increase in racial and ethnic minorities is mirrored in the suburbs, where the white population has decreased from 76 to 72 percent over the past decade (U.S. Bureau of the Census 2008). Reversing trends, nonmetropolitan or rural areas received a substantial net-migration gain from metropolitan areas between 1995 and 2000 as a result of racial and ethnic minority migration from abroad and from other regions. In rural areas, white and African American populations remained stable but the migration of Latinos, Asians, Native Hawaiians, and Pacific Islanders increased the racial minority population to almost 20 percent, with a growth rate eight times faster than that of whites (U.S. Bureau of the Census 2003b).

Racial and ethnic minorities have significant populations in all four regions of the country but are unevenly distributed across these areas. Table 30.1 shows the regional distribution of racial and ethnic groups and their percentage change in the U.S. census from 1990 to 2000. The South experienced the most growth among Asians, Africans Americans, Latinos, and whites, while the Northeast increased for American Indians and Alaskan Natives, and Native Hawaiians and Pacific Islanders. Table 30.2 further shows the five states with the highest proportion of each racial/ethnic group. While California and Texas are in the top five states for all groups and New York is in the top five states for four groups, these three states represent larger or smaller proportions depending on the group being examined. An overall trend, especially among Asians,

TABLE 30.1: POPULATION DISTRIBUTION AND PERCENTAGE CHANGE BY RACIAL/ETHNIC GROUP AND REGION

	NORTHEAST		MIDWEST		SOUTH		WEST	
	% IN 2000*	% CHANGE 1990–2000	% IN 2000	% CHANGE 1990–2000	% IN 2000	% CHANGE 1990–2000	% IN 2000	% CHANGE 1990–2000
American Indians and Alaska Natives	9.08	2.69	17.35	0.11	30.57	1.85	43.00	−4.65
Asians	19.90	0.73	11.71	0.77	19.05	3.22	49.34	−4.71
Blacks or African Americans	18.00	−2.43	18.78	−5.21	53.62	19.26	9.60	−11.63
Hispanics or Latinos	14.88	−1.91	8.85	1.13	32.82	2.55	43.45	−1.76
Native Hawaiians and Pacific Islanders	7.31	4.43	6.33	2.86	13.49	5.80	72.87	−13.09
Whites	19.54	−1.52	25.22	−0.83	34.25	1.41	20.98	0.94

Source: U.S. Bureau of the Census 2000

* Number based on Racial/Ethnic Group Alone or In Combination Population Count

TABLE 30.2: PERCENTAGES OF RACIAL/ETHNIC GROUPS IN STATES WITH HIGHEST RACIAL/ETHNIC PROPORTIONS

AMERICAN INDIANS AND ALASKA NATIVES		ASIANS		BLACKS OR AFRICAN AMERICANS		HISPANICS OR LATINOS		NATIVE HAWAIIANS AND PACIFIC ISLANDERS		WHITES	
California	15.23	California	34.93	New York	8.88	California	31.06	Hawaii	32.33	California	9.91
Oklahoma	9.51	New York	4.41	California	6.90	Texas	18.89	California	25.33	Oklahoma	7.03
Arizona	7.10	Hawaii	5.91	Texas	6.85	New York	8.12	Washington	4.89	Arizona	6.12
Texas	5.23	Texas	5.41	Florida	6.79	Florida	7.60	Texas	3.33	Texas	5.87
New Mexico	4.65	New Jersey	4.41	Georgia	6.57	Illinois	4.33	New York	3.27	New Mexico	4.88
Total	41.73	Total	55.06	Total	35.98	Total	70.01	Total	69.14	Total	33.81

Source: U.S. Bureau of the Census 2000

Latinos, Native Hawaiians, and Pacific Islanders, is migration to states not in the top five as well as to suburban and rural counties, with Latinos the most geographically dispersed. Of note, the 2000 census recorded a very high state-level net-migration rate (563.1 percent) of Native Hawaiians and Pacific Islanders to Nevada, which points to a steeper trend of high population growth outside the top five states (U.S. Bureau of the Census 2001b).

According to the 2000 census, primary and secondary migration of the foreign born helped offset domestic migration loss in many areas, especially the Northeast and West. In terms of population distribution, immigrants can have tremendous impact on an area's racial and ethnic makeup. Historically, immigrants settled in central cities in gateway states such as California and New York in their primary migration. A secondary migration may then ensue, often to suburbs or other states, leading to a wider spread of immigrant populations (U.S. Bureau of the Census 2003a). The 2000 census shows a new trend. While the majority of immigrants (49 percent) still migrated to the metropolitan central cities, more immigrants than in earlier censuses moved to suburbs, smaller cities, and rural areas in their primary migration. In the secondary migration of immigrants, Nevada had the highest rates of net migration (276 percent), followed by North Carolina (187 percent), Georgia (178 percent), and Arkansas (155 percent) (U.S. Bureau of the Census 2003a).

PLACE STRATIFICATION

Sociology has long focused on the problems associated with the geographic concentration of racial and ethnic groups in selected states and in certain locations within states. Geographic areas that include neighborhoods, residences, businesses, waste dumps, and environmental hazards become prized or devalued depending on their historic importance, proximity to power and influence, and quality of natural or manufactured environmental resources (e.g., forests, buildings, parks). The differential value placed on residential areas creates and fosters a spatial stratification system that often intersects with race. At various points in history, some racial groups were allowed to work but not live in select residential areas. Immigrants often began residing in certain areas of cities before they could move to other locations. It is this critical melding of space and race that still operates and has important consequences for the study of health and illness.

What is the Meaning of Residential Segregation?

One form of place stratification, residential segregation, like socioeconomic status and gender, can be considered a fundamental cause of racial disparities in health because it structures opportunities and resources that facilitate or constrain access to power, social and psychological resources, and economic capital that are linked to health and illness (Link and Phelan 1995; Schulz et al. 2002; Williams and Collins 2001). Residential segregation is far from being a problem of the past; most racial and ethnic minority groups today experience high levels of segregation from whites in cities across the United States (Iceland 2004). Residential segregation can be measured in multiple ways (Massey and Denton 1988) but generally includes: (1) unevenness or dissimilarity in the distribution of groups across an area; (2) degree of potential contact or interaction between members of different groups; (3) concentration, or the relative amount of physical space occupied by groups; (4) degree of centralization, or location near the central city; and (5) spatial clustering of group neighborhoods. These five dimensions of segregation, and the indexes commonly used to measure them, are summarized in Table 30.3. Table 30.3 also provides a comparison of the indexes for racial and ethnic groups in different regions.

African American–white segregation has declined only modestly over the past two decades, while Asian and Latino segregation from whites has increased, largely due to sustained immigration. A recent investigation into the decline in segregation among African Americans could not attribute it to any of the hypothesized sources, such as attitudinal changes on the part of whites regarding integration, the growth of the African American middle class, population shifts of African Americans to regions in the West and South with lower overall segregation, or the increase of multiethnic metropolises (Logan, Stults, and Far-ley 2004). Segregation is likely to persist because of the continued immigration of Asians and Latinos to the United States and few substantive changes in racial attitudes. Accordingly, segregation may continue to be an important setting in predicting the life chances of racial and ethnic minority group members well into the future. As the racial and ethnic minority population in the United States continues to be shaped by immigration trends in the twenty-first century, theoretical models underlying residential segregation as a fundamental cause of health and disease outcomes must account for the ways in which this phenomenon differs among racial and ethnic groups.

The literature on racial residential segregation typically rests on the premise that disadvantaged segregated neighborhood conditions explain poorer health outcomes among African Americans living in segregated neighborhoods. In place stratification theory, majority group preferences and active discrimination constrain the social and spatial mobility of minority group members, resulting in their residential concentration in poor, inner-city ghettos with limited resources. Massey and Denton (1993) contend that "white society is deeply implicated in the ghetto. White institutions created it, white institutions maintain it, and white society condones it." White preferences historically took the form of de jure discrimination in housing markets, mortgage lending, racial steering, and exclusionary zoning practices that restricted racial and ethnic minority groups to certain neighborhoods (Cutler, Glaeser, and Vigdor 1999). While legally enforced discrimination ended with the civil rights legislation in the 1960s, de facto discrimination has taken its place in the form of white preferences for white neighbors (Charles 2000) and high housing prices that effectively keep economically disadvantaged racial and ethnic minority individuals out of certain areas.

TABLE 30.3: RESIDENTIAL SEGREGATION INDEXES (WEIGHTED AVERAGES) BY RACIAL/ETHNIC GROUP AND REGION

	NUMBER OF METROPOLITAN AREAS	DISSIMILARITY INDEX[b]	ISOLATION INDEX[c]	DELTA INDEX[D]	ABSOLUTE CENTRALIZATION INDEX[E]	SPATIAL PROXIMITY INDEX[F]
American Indians and Alaska Natives						
Northeast	0	(X)	(X)	(X)	(X)	(X)
Midwest	1	0.384	0.177	0.885	0.871	1.050
South	4	0.253	0.144	0.587	0.561	1.053
West	8	0.465	0.239	0.755	0.706	1.228
Asians and Pacific Islanders [a]						
Northeast	6	0.461	0.320	0.720	0.699	1.089
Midwest	2	0.431	0.175	0.719	0.725	1.074
South	3	0.418	0.221	0.780	0.776	1.088
West	19	0.426	0.467	0.735	0.644	1.146
Blacks or African Americans						
Northeast	31	0.739	0.679	0.819	0.717	1.465
Midwest	53	0.741	0.651	0.859	0.788	1.526
South	114	0.581	0.581	0.748	0.695	1.303
West	22	0.559	0.435	0.823	0.740	1.283
Hispanics or Latinos						
Northeast	22	0.615	0.578	0.757	0.666	1.290
Midwest	13	0.567	0.449	0.765	0.710	1.328
South	38	0.461	0.601	0.736	0.706	1.182
West	50	0.514	0.597	0.791	0.695	1.261

Source: U.S. Bureau of the Census 2000, Summary File 1.

a. Asian and Pacific Islanders are grouped together to facilitate comparison with earlier versions of the census.

b. Dissimilarity Index: Measures the percentage of a group's population that would have to change residence for each neighborhood to have the same percentage of that group as the metropolitan area overall. The index ranges from 0.0 (complete integration) to 1.0 (complete segregation).

c. Isolation Index: Measures "the extent to which minority members are exposed only to one another" (Massey and Denton 1993, 288) and is computed as the minority-weighted average of the minority proportion in each area. Higher values of isolation indicate higher segregation.

d. Delta Index: "Computes the proportion of [minority] members residing in areal units with above average density of [minority] members" (Massey and Denton 1993, 290). The index gives the proportion of a group's population that would have to move across areal units to achieve a uniform density.

e. Absolute Centralization Index: Examines the distribution of the minority group around the center and varies between −1.0 and 1.0. "Positive values indicate a tendency for [minority] group members to reside close to the city center, while negative values indicate a tendency to live in outlying areas. A score of 0 means that a group has a uniform distribution throughout the metropolitan area" (Massey and Denton 1993, 293).

f. Spatial Proximity Index: Average of intragroup proximities for the minority and majority populations, weighted by the proportion each group represents of the total population. Spatial proximity equals 1.0 if there is no differential clustering between minority and majority group members. It is greater than 1.0 when members of each group live nearer to one another than to members of the other group, and is less than 1.0 if minority and majority members live nearer to members of the other group than to members of their own group.

Recent evidence suggests that the reasons for and experiences of residential segregation among other minority groups, especially those containing large immigrant populations, differ from those of African Americans along important dimensions (Zhou and Logan 1991; Zhou 1992). Asian and Latino Americans have unique residential experiences that may relate more to factors associated with recent immigration than to active discrimination by whites, suggesting that place stratification theory does not universally explain the effects of residential segregation on health status among members of these diverse racial and ethnic minority groups. Among racial and ethnic groups with large proportions of immigrants, classic spatial assimilation theory and segmented assimilation theory may be more applicable for understanding the ways in which structural and social resources are distributed and function to affect health in different types of neighborhoods.

Viewed through a classic spatial assimilation lens, recent immigrants settle in immigrant enclaves located near the inner city that can concentrate social resources but that often lack structural resources (K. Wilson and Portes 1980). These neighborhoods ease individuals' transition into the U.S. labor market and provide them with social support as they adapt to a new culture. The spatial assimilation model predicts that as individuals acculturate, become more fluent in English, and gain economic security, they and subsequent generations will assimilate with mainstream society by moving into white, suburban, and affluent neighborhoods. This decreased segregation is hypothesized to lead to better health status as individuals utilize resources located in residentially integrated neighborhoods. Socioeconomic diversity among contemporary immigrants, however, suggests that the trajectory defined by classic spatial assimilation may not apply uniformly across individuals and groups.

Segmented assimilation theory offers an alternative hypothesis (Portes and Zhou 1993). Individual attributes and group social position predict divergent patterns of spatial incorporation among immigrants and subsequent generations. If, upon settling in the United States, personal human capital attributes are low, immigrants and subsequent generations are less likely to assimilate into white, middle-class neighborhoods, instead cultivating ties within poorer, native-born coethnic or African American communities (South, Crowder, and Chavez 2005). In this case, the health effects of living in segregated neighborhoods are more likely to represent those described by a place stratification perspective.

An alternative application of segmented assimilation theory predicts that immigrants who come to the United States with high levels of human capital have more options in terms of choosing to live in communities that are not based on socioeconomic or linguistic necessity. It is plausible that groups entering the United States with many highly educated individuals who speak English well and have corresponding occupational prestige have little to gain by spatially assimilating and thus have some choice in forming residentially segregated ethnic communities (Alba et al. 1999; Logan, Alba, and Zhang 2002). Instead of being areas of concentrated poverty and structural deprivation, these racial and ethnic communities may, in fact, concentrate structural resources like supplemental education institutions that likely exert a positive effect on health status (Zhou 2007).

In summary, because of the differences in the way residentially segregated neighborhoods in which racial and ethnic minorities live are formed, the direction of association between segregation and health outcomes is likely also diverse. In the following sections, we consider the existing evidence on the relationship of residential segregation to health outcomes and the pathways through which segregation affects health status, while taking into account the complexity underlying the formation and maintenance of racially and ethnically segregated neighborhoods.

Segregation and Health Outcomes

Research on the effects of geographic context on individual health outcomes commonly conceives of residential segregation as exposing individuals to poverty and social deprivation.

A burgeoning literature demonstrates that this model works well when exploring the differences among African Americans and whites. Measured by the various segregation indexes, most evidence suggests that residential segregation contributes to inferior health status among African Americans. The effects vary depending on the dimension of segregation analyzed, however, hinting that some aspects of segregation may be beneficial to health outcomes, even among African Americans.

In a study of mortality, Jackson and colleagues (2000) found that African American men living in highly segregated neighborhoods have three times the mortality risk of African American men living in the least segregated areas. Among African American women in this study, the mortality risk for living in areas of high segregation was twice that of African American women living in areas of low segregation. Using the index of dissimilarity, LaVeist (1993) found that living in more segregated cities is associated with a rise in the African American infant mortality rate, while the rate for whites declined in such cities. In a similar analysis examining infant mortality in thirty-eight major U.S. metropolitan areas, Polednak (1991) established that the index of dissimilarity is the most important predictor of African American–white differences and that this effect is independent of socioeconomic factors. Employing a measure of spatial isolation at the census-tract level, Grady (2006) demonstrated that residential segregation predicts low birth weight for African American infants in New York City, after controlling for individual risk factors and neighborhood poverty. Concentration of African Americans in central cities is associated with increased incidence of low birth weight, somewhat influenced by exposure to older housing and less-educated neighbors (Ellen 2000). Subramanian, Acevedo-Garcia, and Osypuk (2005) established that residential isolation of African Americans from whites across U.S. metropolitan areas is associated with increased odds of their reporting poor self-rated health. In agreement with this, higher residential isolation is also associated with higher body mass index and greater odds of being overweight among African Americans (Chang 2006). One study discovered opposing effects of segregation on birth outcomes among African Americans: higher metropolitan area isolation was associated with worse birth outcomes, while higher clustering was associated with more optimal birth outcomes among African American women (Bell et al. 2006). The high contiguity between racial and ethnic minority neighborhoods may be a correlate of community attributes that are health promoting through the pathways of political empowerment, social cohesion, and protection from discrimination.

While a considerable body of research demonstrates that many aspects of residential segregation are harmful to the health status of African Americans, the findings of the limited number of studies of residential segregation and well-being among Asians and Latinos are not consistent. Among Latinos, one study showed that segregation increases the risk of tuberculosis infection (Acevedo-Garcia 2001), while others reported beneficial health effects from increased segregation: better self-rated health (Patel et al. 2003), lower disease prevalence (Eschbach et al. 2004), and lower mortality rates (LeClere, Rogers, and Peters 1997). A recent investigation reported mixed results based on the Latino ethnic subgroup under consideration, with segregation increasing the number of health problems among Puerto Rican Americans but not Mexican Americans; further, among Mexican Americans, generational status conditioned the effect: second and later generations had better health than immigrant Mexican Americans in segregated neighborhoods (M. Lee and Ferraro 2007). In the only study on residential segregation and well-being conducted among Asian Americans, Gee (2002) found that Chinese

Americans living in redlined areas of Los Angeles (areas in which banks were biased against racial and ethnic minorities in their lending practices) reported better physical and mental health compared to those living in other areas of the city. In the same study, segregation, as measured by the index of dissimilarity, did not predict health status. In sum, a complicated picture emerges: most studies show beneficial effects of segregation on the well-being of Latinos and Asian Americans, but this finding varies according to the health outcome being assessed, the racial or ethnic group under consideration, the nativity status of the respondent, and the dimension of segregation analyzed.

How Does Segregation Affect Health?

While a majority of the current research on the health effects of residential segregation has documented that a relationship exists, by examining neighborhood effects in a broad way we note that an emerging literature has also begun to explore the underlying pathways through which this relationship may operate. Residential segregation shapes access to important structural and social resources, typically measured by aggregating individual characteristics such as socioeconomic status that are seen as markers of neighborhood institutional structures and social conditions—levels of crime, community infrastructure and services, educational and employment opportunities, social integration, and exposure to discrimination. Relying largely on a place stratification perspective, a bulk of the evidence suggests that segregation is harmful to racial and ethnic minorities because features of disadvantage are clustered in segregated neighborhoods. Alternatively, the spatial and segmented assimilation perspectives suggest that aspects of segregation may be beneficial to certain minorities because structural and social resources are concentrated in the areas in which they live.

Residential segregation is often marked by institutional abandonment that has created a uniquely disadvantaged physical and infrastructure environment. Lack of political power among residentially segregated neighborhoods leads to disinvestment of economic resources and services provided by the city, such as police and fire protection, and increased exposure to higher levels of air pollution, traffic noise, and industrial contaminants (Brown 1994; LaVeist 1993). Individuals in disadvantaged neighborhoods have less access to health care and grocery stores, which can affect health outcomes directly through poor nutritional and health behavior choices (Cheadle et al. 1991). While there is increasing interest in the health impacts of aspects of the neighborhood built environment, such as housing quality, street design, and the availability of parks and recreation (Rao et al. 2007), comprehensive investigation of these pathways is still forthcoming.

Residential segregation shapes access to educational and employment opportunities, leading to limited socioeconomic attainment and corresponding poor health among racial and ethnic minorities living in disadvantaged neighborhoods (Adler et al. 1994). In most cities in the United States, residence determines which public schools students attend, and community resources determine the quality of neighborhood schools. Compared to schools in nonsegregated neighborhoods, schools that serve segregated areas tend to have lower test scores, less-qualified teachers, fewer connections with colleges and employers, more structural decay, and higher dropout rates (Orfield and Eaton 1996). Residential segregation can also systematically separate the residents of certain neighborhoods from jobs. The spatial mismatch hypothesis posits that as businesses move away from metropolitan centers and toward the suburbs, low-skilled minorities are less able to find employment due to their residential concentration in the inner city (W. Wilson 1996). Further, Tilly and colleagues (2001) find that potential employers discriminate based on the residences of job applicants. Employers were found to associate inner-city applicants with family problems, drug use, and low reading, writing, communication, and motivational skills. Lack of infrastructure, physical decay, and socioeconomic disadvantage create stressful conditions that may be expressed in terms of poor health behaviors and create unsupportive social relationships among residents in segregated communities.

Stressful social conditions in residentially segregated neighborhoods have also been linked to poorer health outcomes. Shaw and McKay (1969) argue that socially disorganized neighborhoods have fewer formal and informal types of social control and monitoring. Segregation concentrates conditions such as drug use, joblessness, welfare dependency, and unwed teenage childbearing, producing a social context where these conditions are not only common but also the norm (Massey and Denton 1993). Neighborhood safety and levels of crime may affect whether individuals engage in physical activity (Stahl et al. 2001). The perception of disorder and the resulting fear among residents in disadvantaged neighborhoods have also been shown to correlate with increases in stress and poor health (Ross and Mirowsky 2001). Disadvantaged and unstable neighborhoods may also be less able to sustain cohesive social networks and positive social norms, which have been consistently shown to be protective of health and to increase the likelihood that healthy behaviors will be adopted (Berkman 1995; House, Landis, and Umberson 1988).

While residentially segregated neighborhoods can exhibit disadvantaged structural and social characteristics, some unique features of immigrant enclaves and racial and ethnic communities may mitigate or reverse the destructive effects of residential segregation. More specifically, immigrant enclaves and ethnic communities may concentrate educational and economic resources and increase social integration and support, all of which are beneficial to health outcomes. Structural features such as educational and economic resources may be protective of health for members of these communities. Immigrant enclaves and ethnic communities often house a highly sophisticated system of education that supplements public schooling, including language schools and after-school education (Zhou 2007). These educational institutions facilitate social mobility by providing access to quality education and as settings for social support, network building, and formation of social capital for immigrant and U.S.-born children alike. Increased educational participation may be complemented by higher economic returns among participants in the enclave economy. Though controversial, some evidence suggests that returns to human capital are significantly greater among individuals employed in enclave enterprises than among those employed in businesses tied to the traditional labor market (K. Wilson and Portes 1980; Portes and Bach 1985).

Community structure can also influence social processes that are important to health status. Individuals living among others of the same ethnicity may be more likely to receive instrumental social support, be influenced by shared norms relating to health behaviors, and be more socially engaged than those living among neighbors they consider to be different from them. Strong ethnic networks can work instrumentally by providing assistance with financial needs, aid in getting to appointments, help with decision making, and informal health care

(Berkman and Glass 2000; Weiss et al. 2005). For example, the receipt of mental health care is facilitated for refugees being welcomed by a strong ethnic community, which works directly by improving knowledge of the location of services and indirectly through referral to services (Portes, Kyle, and Eaton 1992). The presence of similar racial and ethnic neighbors can also influence health behaviors (e.g., exercise, alcohol and cigarette use, and dietary patterns) through shared norms (Marsden and Friedkin 1994). Residents of racial and ethnic neighborhoods may also be more likely to have opportunities for social engagement—for example, getting together with family and friends, and participating in recreational or religious activities. Such social engagement can provide a sense of belonging, meaning, and attachment to others, which have salubrious health effects. Individuals feel that having supportive people to care for them when they are sick will increase their ability to survive health crises, and they may also feel obligated to care for themselves so they can be the provider of support for others (Ross and Mirowsky 2002).

There is some evidence that living in more ethnically dense, isolated neighborhoods reduces exposure to prejudice and discrimination. Perceptions of everyday discrimination, routine practices that infuse the daily lives of racial and ethnic minorities (e.g., being treated as if one does not speak English, is in this country illegally, or is untrustworthy), have repeatedly been shown to relate negatively to health and well-being (For-man, Williams, and Jackson 1997; Gee et al. 2007; Kessler, Mickelson, and Williams 1999). The ethnic density hypothesis suggests that living primarily among coethnic neighbors may structurally reduce the opportunities for negative encounters with whites, and thus reduce the social stress felt by minorities living in these neighborhoods by limiting their exposure to everyday discrimination (Halpern and Nazroo 1999; Hunt et al. 2007).

CONCEPTUAL AND MEASUREMENT ISSUES

The past two decades have shown an enormous increase in research that examines the effects of residential areas and health. The statistical and computer software innovations in spatial analyses have especially been useful in providing accurate means for characterizing residential areas. Despite the increase in empirical work and the solid contributions of past studies, several problems have impeded the field from making even more impressive gains. First, there is a lack of uniformity about the conceptualization of place. Several notable scholars argue that place is more than a geographic location and should be conceptualized as a socioecological force that has detectable and independent effects on social life (Gieryn 2000; Habraken 1998; Werlen 1993). If this area of study is to advance, more serious work on the conceptualization of place is needed (Macintyre, Ellaway, and Cummins 2002). Second, studies have often used different measures of place such as cities, counties, census tracts, and zip codes. When researchers show divergent findings, it is often not clear whether the differences are real or whether they are artifacts of the different measures used in the studies. Third, many studies that investigate contextual effects are actually based on the aggregated characteristics of individuals rather than of geographic areas. While the aggregate of individuals in a geographic area is important, it does not fully describe the attributes of the resources and built environment within places. Making distinctions between the compositional and true contextual effects will more clearly identify the factors that best explain how race is associated with health (Ellen, Mijanovich, and Dillman 2001).

Social environments help contextualize how race is associated with health outcomes. The current research on residential areas builds on the early work of sociologists, especially the Chicago school, who developed theories and methods to study the growth of the city and its attendant strengths and challenges. One overlooked facet of the Chicago school, especially when it comes to investigating residential areas and neighborhoods, is the social psychology of place. The social psychology of place concerns itself with how people establish connections or become disengaged with a location. Since much of the history of race and place centers on how racial groups are excluded from some geographic spaces, the social psychology of place can provide keen insights about how race is linked to health and illness.

Much of what we know about race, place, and health comes from cross-sectional studies, and longitudinal studies about place and health are essential. We lack information about how mobility, stability, and frequent moves to and from neighborhoods influence health. Studies over time can also provide insights about reverse causality; people with illnesses may move to neighborhoods that provide them with more comfort and support. It has long been suspected that immigrants who suffer from an illness, for example, may move from a predominantly white neighborhood to a racial or ethnic enclave because it provides them with social support and resources. Longitudinal designs can provide the data that can examine these types of hypotheses, which are not possible to test with cross-sectional data.

Future studies will also do well to investigate place effects in nonconventional settings. Much of the work on residential areas has focused on urban areas, and we are absent a large body of data on place and health in other geographic areas such as suburbs and rural regions. We are also absent much data on whether and how virtual places may influence health. It is possible to visit areas or to create residential areas without leaving one's computer. Since racial and ethnic groups may vary in their use of computers, and we do not know whether these virtual places have any salutary effects, this area opens up a potential area of inquiry.

In sum, the effect of place on health and health behaviors is far from uniform across population groups and health outcomes. The need, at this time, is to move toward more nuanced theorizing about the effects of place on health, and toward creating and testing hypotheses about the specific pathways by which place influences health. Accordingly, there is compelling scholarly need to make major theoretical, methodological, and empirical contributions toward understanding specifically how places promote social engagement or social estrangement, stress or security, and health or illness within and across racial and ethnic minority groups.

NOTE

1. This chapter is supported by the National Institutes of Health grants R01HD049142, U01 MH62209, U01 MH62207, and P50MH073511.

SECTION V

The Environment and Society

Whatat does the environment have to do with society? After all, we are taught through the social institutions of science, religion, and education that the social world of the human and the natural world of the animal are separate spheres. Over time, nonindigenous Western society has come to realize that we humans are very much connected to the natural world and deeply dependent upon it. What we do, in fact, does affect the natural environment, which in turn affects us. The social and the natural do not exist in isolation, but are interdependent.

The environment may not be a social institution, but it is affected by social institutions; and how the environment affects us reflects this. Unfortunately, social inequality takes on spatial and environmental characteristics. Even before there was a name for it other than racism, we can recall learning how Native Americans in the east were forced to give up their lands and move west to places like Oklahoma that were at the time considered undesirable because of their lack of natural resources—until oil was found. There is a pattern of people of color living in spaces that pose greater health risks because of environmental dumping or living in environmentally unsafe areas compared to Whites. Blacks, for instance, are more likely to live in areas near toxic waste dumps than Whites. This causes significant health consequences.

The last two readings explore the issue of how the lives of people of color are put at risk disproportionately from exposure to environmental toxins or lack of infrastructure to protect from environmental events. "Environmental Justice" by Robert Bullard introduces the issue of environmental justice as a social concept. The few pages here give a brief overview of environmental racism, its occurrence, and effects. Continuing the discussion of environmental inequality, the introduction to the book *Race, Place, and Environmental Justice after Hurricane Katrina* by Robert D. Bullard and Beverly Wright presents the effects of Hurricane Katrina as a structural one affecting different people disproportionately, as a result of the confluence of racial, class, and environmental inequalities.

DISCUSSION QUESTIONS

1. How does inequality extend to the environment?
2. How does structural inequality exacerbate how African Americans are affected during natural disasters?

ENVIRONMENTAL JUSTICE

By Robert Bullard

WHAT IS THE ISSUE?

Environmental justice embraces the principle that all people have a right to equal protection under environmental, housing, transportation, health, land use, and civil rights laws, and that no one group of people should be singled out for environmental and health hazards.

The environmental justice movement is a much-needed response to the existing environmental protection paradigm in our country, which reinforces the stratification of people according to race, ethnicity, status, place, and power. This framework also manages, regulates, and distributes environmental risks and pollution instead of preventing degradation or providing true health for all people.

These patterns have institutionalized unequal enforcement of environmental laws. Because the government has not prohibited such occurrences, it has effectively traded human health for profits, placed the burden of proof on victims, legitimated human exposure to harmful chemicals, and subsidized environmental destruction. The actions have resulted in promoting "risky" technologies, exploiting disenfranchised communities' economic and political vulnerability, creating an industry around risk management and assessment, delaying cleanup activities, and failing to develop precaution and pollution prevention protocols.

- Where Environmental Injustice Occurs
  Low-income neighborhoods, communities of color, and indigenous peoples are groups that are disproportionately affected by environmental hazards. These communities can be located

on reservations, in urban ghettos and barrios, or in rural poverty pockets in the southern United States in "colonias" (unincorporated communities), along the U.S.–Mexico border.

Polluting industries tend to "set up shop" where there is a path of least resistance. People living in low-income neighborhoods or communities of color do not usually have the economic or political resources to fend them off. Consequently, these communities are systemically targeted for landfills, incinerators, polluting industries, freeways, and other locally unwanted land uses (LULUs). They also experience unequal protection by and enforcement of environmental laws, resulting in environmental racism, classism, injustice, and degradation.

It's not by accident, for example, that the southern United States is the most polluted region of the country. The entire Gulf Coast region, especially Mississippi, Alabama, Louisiana, and Texas, has been ravaged by lax regulations and unbridled polluting industries because it's where the poor and people of color live. *Dumping in Dixie* is more than a book I wrote. It documented Louisiana's petrochemical "Cancer Alley" corridor, the area along the Mississippi River between Baton Rouge and New Orleans where cancer rates are sky high due to the chemical refineries that line the river's banks that give off high levels of industrial toxic emissions.

- Land Use Implications
  Urban planning and design decisions greatly influence the built environment, largely determining what goes in and what stays out of communities. Probably the most widely applied mechanism to regulate urban land use in the United States, zoning creates "a place for everything, and everything in its place." Theoretically, this should keep a lead smelter from being built next to an elementary school or children's playground, yet such incompatible land uses are widespread in low-income, people-of-color communities.

  Nearly half of all public housing in the United States, for example, sits within one mile of a factory that reports toxic emissions to the government. Nearly 1,200 public schools in Massachusetts, New York, New Jersey, Michigan, and California (mostly populated by low-income and people-of-color students) are located within a half-mile of federal Superfund or state-identified contaminated sites. In Camden, New Jersey, polluting facilities operate directly across from a park. In one community after another, we see schools, parks, and playgrounds that are too dangerous for kids because of their proximity to environmentally harmful industries.

- Public Health Impacts
  Clearly, where you live can impact your health. In 1999, the Institute of Medicine issued its study, *Toward Environmental Justice: Research, Education, and Health Policy Needs*, which confirmed that low-income and people-of-color communities are disproportionately exposed to higher levels of pollution in their homes, neighborhoods, and workplaces than the rest of the nation. These same populations experience certain diseases, such as cancer, respiratory infections, asthma, chronic obstructive pulmonary disease, and heart disease, in greater numbers.

  Environmental hazards such as pollution are not randomly distributed in the United States. The National Argonne Laboratory reports that 57 percent of whites, 65 percent of African Americans, and 80 percent of Hispanics live in the nation's 437 counties with substandard air quality. Ironically, millions of people who live in urban areas do not own cars, although they oftentimes breathe automobile pollution from others who commute to the city from the suburbs.

Pollution generated by motor vehicles has created over 200 nonattainment areas, or areas where air pollution levels persistently exceed national ambient air quality standards. Polluting vehicle emissions contribute significantly to illness, hospitalization, and premature death. Children are at special risk for asthma and other respiratory problems exacerbated by ground level ozone—the main ingredient of smog. For more information about pollution, see chapter 2 on air quality.

Because most metropolitan regions are designed to support suburban sprawl, we continue to mow down trees and build more highways, megamalls, and far-flung housing subdivisions, consequently requiring more use of cars, which means more pollution and possibly more illnesses. Much of metropolitan Atlanta's environmental problems and uneven growth is the result of an "iron triangle" of perverse finance incentives, poor land use planning, and an overreliance of transportation service delivery that rely upon the poor model.

Current housing infrastructure also creates disproportionate public health risks to the denizens of older urban communities. Our country's continued childhood lead poisoning problem, a preventable disease most often found in inner cities where urban or low-income kids live, is probably the most blatant example of this. Recent studies suggest that a young person's lead burden is linked to lower IQ, decreased high school graduation rates, and increased delinquency. Government and private industries, however, do not have the will or commitment to get lead paint out of older housing.

- Economic Repercussions

Transportation equity and environmental justice are intricately linked. Decisions to build highways, expressways, and beltways have far-reaching impacts on economic opportunity, the environment, and public health. Roadway projects have received over $205 billion since 1956. In contrast, public transit has received roughly $50 billion since the creation of the Urban Mass Transit Administration in 1964. This federal agency was created to offer transit assistance by providing $375 million in matching funds to cities and states for large-scale urban public or private rail projects.

The decentralization of employment centers has also had a major role in shaping metropolitan growth patterns and the location of people, housing, and jobs. Government policies have buttressed segregation and suburban sprawl through new roads and highways at the expense of public transit. Tax subsidies made it possible for new suburban employment centers to become dominant outside of cities, pulling middle-income workers and homeowners from the urban core.

- Beyond Our Borders

Most people around the world want jobs and economic development. But at what cost to their health and the environment? No global standards for environmental protection exist, making it easy for transnational corporations to flee to developing countries with the fewest environmental regulations, best tax incentives, cheapest labor, and highest profit. The result is often exploitation. This has also placed special strains (including climate change impacts) on tropical ecosystems in many poor communities and nations inhabited largely by people of color and indigenous peoples. Overall, these special strains are indicative of environmental injustice and further demonstrate the growing gap between the haves and have-nots in the developed and developing worlds.

People all over the world should understand and adhere to certain acceptable practices. Locals working for U.S. companies in Mexico, Bangladesh, or Taiwan, for example, should receive fair wages and protection from environmental and health hazards. If inhaling mercury or lead is hazardous for U.S. workers—so much that they require protective gear— the same chemicals will likely harm workers in other countries. They deserve protection against conditions that we would not tolerate here.

Furthermore, some companies are shipping chemicals, pesticides, and commercial processes abroad that have known carcinogenic, reproductive, or neurological effects. Even if these practices are legal in other countries, they have serious health impacts at home and abroad. For example, some chemicals banned here are used to grow fruits in other countries. The fruit is then shipped back to us, instigating a circle of poison by unjustly exposing both foreign workers and domestic consumers to environmental and health hazards that are outlawed here.

INTRODUCTION

By Robert D. Bullard and Beverly Wright

In the real world, all communities are not created equal. If a community is poor, black, or on the wrong side of the tracks, it receives less protection than suburbs inhabited by affluent whites. Generally, rich people take land on higher elevations, leaving the poor and working class more vulnerable to flooding and environmental pestilence.

Race tracks closely with social vulnerability and the geography of environmental risks. We saw this pattern during Hurricane Katrina in 2005 and the levee breech that flooded New Orleans. These events shone the national spotlight on government ineptness, incompetence, and severe gaps in disaster preparedness, but for decades African Americans have been complaining about differential treatment, about being left behind, and about outright racial discrimination.

Katrina raised "a new class of problems that demand rigorous analysis, prudent planning, and courageous political leadership" (Daniels et al. 2006, 4). Our analysis uses an environmental justice frame to understand factors that support and impede post-disaster rebuilding, reconstruction, redevelopment, and recovery. We examine the role of race and place and how unequal protection and unequal treatment make some populations more vulnerable in the rebuilding and recovery process. We examine how physical location, socioeconomic status, race, and institutional constraints create and perpetuate racialized place. We also explore how environmental hazards develop into public health threats and how design factors mitigate or amplify their effects.

Racial disparities exist in natural-disaster preparedness, communication, physical impacts, psychological impacts, emergency response, clean-up, recovery, and reconstruction. Disaster mitigation and investments provide location-specific benefits, restricted to populations that live or own assets in the protected areas. Thus, "by virtue of where we live, work, or own property, some members of society are excluded from the benefits of these investments" (Boyce 2000).

The disaster in New Orleans after Katrina was unnatural and man-made. Flooding in the New Orleans metropolitan area largely resulted from breached levees and flood walls (Gabe, Falk, McCarthy, and Mason 2005). A May 2006 report from the Russell Sage Foundation, *In the Wake of the Storm: Environment, Disaster, and Race After Katrina,* found these same groups often experience a "second disaster" after the initial storm (Pastor, Bullard, Boyce, Fothergill, Morello-Frosch, and Wright 2006). Pre-storm vulnerabilities limit thousands of Gulf Coast low-income communities of color participation in the storm reconstruction, rebuilding, and recovery. In these communities, days of hurt and loss are likely to become years of grief, dislocation, and displacement.

Providing a political fix for social vulnerability (improvement in the overall quality of life for low-income people) and economic vulnerability (dismantling income and wealth gaps) has proved to be more daunting than providing an engineering fix for environmental vulnerability (shoring up levees, construction of disaster-resistant buildings, changes in land use, and restoration of wetlands and floodways). It is far easier for the Army Corps of Engineers to retrofit and rebuild levees than it is for other government agencies to root out racial injustice, dismantle centuries of mistrust, and rebuild "community."

Quite often the scale of a disaster's impact, as in the case of Hurricane Katrina, has more to do with the political economy of the country, region, and state than with the hurricane's category strength (Jackson 2005). Similarly, measures to prevent or contain the effects of disaster vulnerability are not equally provided to all. Typically, flood-control investments provide location-specific benefits—with the greatest benefits going to populations who live or own assets in the protected area.

Thus, by virtue of where people live, work, or own property, they may be excluded from the benefits of government-funded flood-control investments (Boyce 2000). New Orleans' new post-Katrina levee system will not provide the same level of protection for all of that city's residents. One need not be a rocket scientist to predict who is most likely to receive the least amount of protection or which communities are likely to be left behind and left vulnerable after the flood-proofing is completed—namely, the same groups who were deserted environmentally and economically before the devastating storm.

On August 29, 2005, Hurricane Katrina laid waste to New Orleans, a city founded in 1718 and later developed largely below sea level (Regional Planning Commission of Orleans 1969; Braumbach 1981). Katrina was complete in its devastation of homes, neighborhoods, institutions, and communities. Like most major urban centers, New Orleans was in crisis before Katrina (Pastor, Bullard, Boyce, Fothergill, Morello-Frosch, and Wright 2006). The city's coastal wetlands, which normally serve as a natural buffer against storm surge, had been destroyed by offshore drilling, Mississippi River levees, canals for navigation, pipelines, highway projects, agricultural and urban development.

Over the past century, more than 2,000 of the original 7,000 square miles of coastal marsh and swamp forests that formed the coastal delta of the Mississippi River have vanished. An average of 34 square miles of South Louisiana land, mostly marsh, has disappeared each year since the late 1950s. More than 80 percent of the nation's coastal wetland loss in this time occurred in Louisiana. From 1932 to 2000, the state lost 1,900 square miles of land to the Gulf of Mexico (Tibbetts 2006).

Hurricane Katrina pushed New Orleans closer to the coast because of extensive erosion at the coastal edge. This is a national problem. Researchers, policy makers, and environmentalists are calling for restoration of wetlands and barrier islands to help protect New Orleans the next time a hurricane strikes. Reversing this deadly trend will not be easy.

Katrina was likely the most destructive hurricane in U.S. history, costing over $70 billion in insured damage. It was also one of the deadliest storms, with a death toll of 1,325 and still counting, surpassed only by the 1928 hurricane in Florida (2,500 to 3,000 deaths) and the 1900 Galveston hurricane (8,000 deaths).

Although more than 80 percent of New Orleans was underwater in the aftermath of Katrina, the hurricane, in fact, did not make a direct hit on the city. Flooding was largely from breached levees and flood walls (Gabe, Falk, and McCarthy 2005). Katrina exposed the limitation of local, state, and federal government operations to implement an effective emergency preparedness and response plan. Post-Katrina reconstruction and rebuilding efforts point to challenges that have been forgotten or ignored for decades—social inequality and racial apartheid-type systems that have operated to create and maintain separate and unequal black and white populations (Bullard 2007a, Bullard 2007b). Ignoring and/or rebuilding on long-standing inequities will only complicate the recovery process of those families most in need of jobs at a livable wage, affordable housing, quality education, health care, accessible public transit, full-service supermarkets, banking and insurance, and safe parks.

The lethargic and inept emergency response after Katrina was a disaster that overshadowed the deadly storm itself. Yet, there is a second disaster-in-the-making—driven by racism, classism, elitism, paternalism, and old-fashioned greed. Several months after the storm, "A Twenty-Point Plan to Destroy Black New Orleans" was widely circulated based on trends and observations around policy decisions on re- entry, repopulation, environmental clean-up, flood control, coastal restoration, rebuilding, and reconstruction (Bullard 2006).

Three years after the storm, it is clear that much of this "unofficial" plan has been advanced by state and federal officials and powerful local opinion leaders. Loyola University law professor Bill Quigley delineated and expanded these trends in his "How to Destroy an African-American City in Thirty-three Steps—Lessons from Katrina" (Quigley 2007). Professor Quigley states that "if there is one word that sums up the way to destroy an African-American city after a disaster, that word is delay" (Quigley 2007, 1). The contributors to this volume understand that all communities are not created equal, and thus some get more than their fair share of the benefits or residential amenities while others receive more than their fair share of the costs or disamenities. Race, class, geography, and political power mitigate the distribution of benefits and costs. Some communities become opportunity rich while others become opportunity poor. At every income level, people-of-color communities often find themselves shortchanged on residential amenities, which many middle-income white communities take for granted, such as banking, shopping, supermarkets, parks and green space, bike lanes, nature trails, and sidewalks (Bullard 2007). The events in New Orleans and the Gulf Coast exposed institutional flaws, poor planning, and false assumptions that are built into the emergency response and homeland security plans and programs. Now after three years, questions still linger: What went wrong? Can it happen again? Is government equipped to plan for, mitigate against, respond to, and recover from natural and man-made disasters? Do race and class matter? Volumes of disaster research have found racial disparities in disaster clean-up, rebuilding, reconstruction, and recovery. Race also plays out in natural-disaster survivors' ability to rebuild, replace infrastructure, obtain loans, and locate temporary and permanent housing.

CLOSED DOORS AND BLOCKED OPPORTUNITY

Generally, compared with their middle-income and white counterparts, low-income and people-of-color disaster victims spend more time in temporary housing, shelters, trailers, mobile homes, and hotels—and are more vulnerable to permanent displacement. Some temporary trailer homes have not turned out to be all that temporary. Some disaster victims wonder if they can trust the government to protect them from harm. For example, some FEMA trailers provided to Hurricane Katrina and Rita evacuees proved to be contaminated with formaldehyde. Instead of providing decent and safe temporary housing, FEMA placed storm victims' health at risk in toxic travel trailers and took more than two years to correct this failure (Babington 2007).

In December 2005, the National Fair Housing Alliance (NFHA) released a report, *No Home for the Holidays: Report on Housing Discrimination Against Hurricane Katrina Survivors,* documenting high rates of housing discrimination against African Americans displaced by Katrina (National Fair Housing Alliance 2005). NFHA conducted tests over the telephone to determine what both African-American and white home seekers were told about unit availability, rent, discounts, and other terms and conditions of apartment leasing. In two-thirds of these tests, as we have seen, white callers were favored over African-American callers.

Generally, low-income and African-American disaster victims spend more time in temporary shelters and are more vulnerable to permanent displacement compared with their middle-income and white counterparts. More than a million Louisiana residents fled Katrina, and 100,000 to 300,000 of them could end up permanently displaced. The powerful storm ravaged an eight-parish labor market that supported 617,300 jobs (Randolph 2005). In September 2005, nearly 100,000 Katrina evacuees were still housed in 1,042 barrack-style shelters scattered across twenty-six states and the District of Columbia (Frank 2005).

FEMA contracted for 120,000 mobile homes for Louisiana, Mississippi, and Alabama storm victims until they could find more permanent housing in homes and apartments. However, the pace of getting evacuees out of shelters slowed because of infrastructure problems—water, sewer, and electricity—to accommodate trailers. Six weeks after the storm hit, FEMA had placed 4,662 Louisiana families in trailers, hotel rooms, or cruise ships docked in New Orleans (Maggi 2005).

To discourage housing evacuees, some Louisiana parishes near New Orleans adopted emergency ordinances limiting the density of mobile-home parks (Maggi 2005). Some small white rural towns adopted NIMBY-ism (Not in My Back Yard) to keep out temporary housing (Chang, Soundararajan, and Johnson 2005). No one, including FEMA (which provides the trailers and mobile homes), homeowners (who are trying to protect their property values), and storm victims (who must live in the tight quarters), is served well if temporary or permanent "Katrina ghettos" are created.

Some "temporary" homes have not proved to be that temporary. Thousands left homeless by the hurricane waited for months for new or repaired housing while living in hotels, temporary trailers, and mobile homes. Mobile homes are derisively known as storm magnets because of the endless reports over the years of trailer parks being demolished during bad weather. More than 9,000 families were living in temporary FEMA housing in Florida when Hurricane Dennis slammed into the Florida Panhandle in July 2005—down from a peak of about 15,000 after four hurricanes hit the state in 2004 (Becker 2005).

African Americans seeking housing in the Deep South are routinely met with discrimination. Disasters worsen this problem and intensify the competition for affordable housing. East Baton Rouge Parish population surged from 425,000 to 1.2 million as a result of Katrina (Naughton and Hosenball 2005, 36). Katrina made Baton Rouge one of the fastest-growing regions in the country (Mulligan and Fausset 2005). The influx of these new residents to the region created traffic gridlock and crowded the schools. Many of the mostly white suburban communities and small towns are not known for their hospitality toward blacks. Thousands of black hurricane evacuees faced the added burden of closed doors and housing discrimination, while their white counterparts were given preference.

THE IMPACT ON SMALL AND MINORITY-OWNED BUSINESSES

Disasters hit small and minority-owned businesses hardest because they are often undercapitalized, vulnerable, and sensitive to even small market shifts. Blacks are a large share of the three Gulf Coast states hardest hit by Katrina—Louisiana, Mississippi, and Alabama. Blacks make up 32.5 percent of the population in Louisiana, 36.3 percent in Mississippi, and 26 percent in Alabama.

The U.S. Census Bureau reports that in 1997 New Orleans had 9,747 black-owned firms, 4,202 Hispanic-owned firms, and 3,210 Asian-owned firms; Biloxi-Gulfport, Mississippi, had 1,305 black-owned firms, 273 Hispanic-owned firms, and 1,063 Asian-owned firms; and Mobile, Alabama, had 2,770 black-owned businesses, 478 Hispanic-owned businesses, and 549 Asian-owned firms (U.S. Bureau of the Census 2002).

Katrina affected over 2,000 black-owned businesses in Mississippi. These firms generated over $126 million in sales and receipts in 2004 (Hughes 2005, 149). Katrina adversely affected over 20,000 black-owned businesses in Louisiana. These firms generated sales and receipts of $886 million. Black-owned firms and black professionals, including doctors, dentists, and other service-related businesses, have been slow to return because many lost their core customers and clientele—mainly African Americans.

Katrina negatively impacted over 60,000 black-owned businesses in the Gulf Coast region that generate $3.3 billion a year (Hughes 2005, 150). This is not a small point since most black-owned firms employ blacks. Black-owned firms have met roadblocks and have been virtually frozen out of the clean-up and rebuilding of the Gulf Coast region. The matter was complicated by the U.S. Labor Department's decision to temporarily suspend the affirmative action rule and permit no-bid contracts. Billions of dollars were spent cleaning up the mess left by Katrina. Only 1.5 percent of the $1.6 billion awarded by FEMA went to minority businesses, less than a third of the 5 percent normally required by law (Yen 2005). The Army Corps of Engineers awarded about 16 percent of the $637 million in Katrina contracts to minority-owned firms.

After Katrina, President Bush suspended the Davis-Bacon Act, passed in 1931 during the Great Depression, that sets a minimum pay scale for workers on federal contracts by requiring contractors to pay the prevailing or average pay in the region (Edsall 2005, D3). Some leaders saw the suspension of the prevailing wage combined with the relaxation of federal rules requiring employees to hire only people with proper documents as spurring an influx of low-wage illegal immigrant workers (Pickel 2005).

This has heightened tension between African Americans and Latino immigrant workers. President Bush, after mounting pressure from Democrats, moderate Republicans, organized labor, and workers in the Gulf Coast region, reinstated the prevailing-wage rule (Witte 2005). The relaxation of documents rules was designed to assist Gulf Coast hurricane victims who lost their IDs, not to be a suspension of immigration laws.

Complaints about being shut out of the Gulf Coast reconstruction were not limited to minority-owned firms. Many white Gulf Coast workers and businesses also rail about being left out, while they see out-of-state companies receiving the lion's share of the contracts. The annual payroll alone in the metropolitan areas hardest hit by Katrina, New Orleans, Biloxi, and Mobile, exceeded $11.7 billion in 2002. About 75 percent of the businesses in the disaster area were non-employer firms such as sole proprietorships. And of the remaining small businesses, 80 percent had fewer than 20 employees. Small businesses employed 273,651 workers in the New Orleans area, 54,029 in Biloxi, and 107,586 in Mobile.

FEMA and the SBA were swamped with requests for disaster assistance. FEMA doesn't offer small business loans but does provide emergency cash grants up to $26,200 per person for housing, medical, and other disaster-related needs (Abrams 2005). Some Katrina victims claim they were unfairly denied emergency aid (Sullivan 2005). They accuse FEMA of leaving them behind a second time.

After Katrina, the staff at the SBA loan-processing center in Fort Worth tripled in size. SBA disaster loans serve as the only salvation for companies without insurance, or whose insurance didn't cover all the damage. SBA offers two types of loans to small businesses, that is, firms with fewer than 500 employees: The physical (property) disaster business loan—which provides businesses, of any size, with funds to repair or replace real estate, equipment, fixtures, machinery, and inventory—and the economic injury disaster loan are available to small businesses that have suffered substantial economic injury resulting from a disaster. Both types of disaster loans are available up to $1.5 million (Rosenberg 2005).

SBA disaster loans are not just for small businesses. Homeowners and renters who suffered damage from Hurricane Katrina are also eligible for low-interest disaster loans from the SBA (Willis 2005). SBA makes the majority of its disaster loans to homeowners and renters. The loans are for repairing or rebuilding disaster damage to private property owned by homeowners and renters. Homeowners may borrow up to $200,000 to repair or replace damaged or destroyed real estate. Homeowners and renters may borrow up to $40,000 to repair or replace damaged or destroyed personal property, including vehicles.

SBA's disaster home loans have low interest rates (less than 3 percent) and long terms (up to thirty years), helping to make recovery more affordable. The federal government is expected to provide financial assistance even as private insurance companies are withdrawing disaster coverage from homeowners in hurricane-prone regions. However, most rebuilding funds after disasters come from private insurance, not the government (Comerio 1998).

Before and after disasters strike, black business entrepreneurs are significantly more likely to be denied bank credit, and when successful, receive smaller loans relative to comparable non-minority businesses. A 2005 *New York Times* study discovered that the Small Business Administration had processed only a third of the 276,000 home loan applications it received (Eaton and Nixon 2005). During the same period, the SBA rejected 82 percent of the applications it received, a higher percentage than in most previous disasters. Well-off neighborhoods like Lakeview have received 47 percent of the loan approvals, while poverty-stricken neighborhoods have gotten 7 percent. The loan denial problem is not limited to poor black areas. Middle-class black neighborhoods in New Orleans East also had lower loan rates. This trend could spell doom for rebuilding black New Orleans neighborhoods.

Katrina hit black-owned banks especially hard. In 2005, *Black Enterprise Magazine* listed Liberty Bank as the third-largest African-American bank in the United States. Before Katrina, Liberty Bank and Dryades Bank had assets of $348.2 million and $102.9 million, respectively. Liberty operated nine branches in New Orleans, three in Baton Rouge, and one in Jackson. Katrina cost Liberty an estimated $40 million (Hughes 2005). In June 2008, it dropped to fifth place with assets of $320 million.

INSURANCE TUG-OF-WAR

Disasters often set the stage for a tug-of-war between insurers and disaster victims. The total economic losses from Katrina are expected to exceed $125 billion, with insurance companies paying an estimated $40 to $60 billion. How much financial responsibility the insurance companies end up bearing will depend on how insurers handle the claims—how they determine what is "wind" and what is "flood" damage.

FEMA estimates that the majority of households and businesses in the 12 Hurricane Katrina-affected counties in Alabama, Mississippi, and Louisiana do not have flood coverage. FEMA also estimates that 12.7 percent of the households in Alabama, 15 percent in Mississippi, and 46 percent in Louisiana have flood insurance, and only 8 percent of the businesses in hurricane-affected counties in Alabama, 15 percent in Mississippi, and 30 percent in Louisiana have flood coverage.

Disasters expose the unequal treatment of African Americans and intensify long-running disputes between insurance companies and consumers who live in redlined neighborhoods—disputes revolving around where standard homeowner's insurance coverage ends and flood insurance begins. For decades, consumers, black and white, have complained about insurance companies denying their claims on the basis that damage was not wind-related but flood-related. Damage from rising water is covered only by government-backed flood insurance.

African-American households are more likely than white households to lack health insurance. The uninsured rate for African Americans is more than 1.5 times the rate for white Americans. Nearly 16 percent of Americans did not have health insurance in 2003, up from 14.2 percent in 2000 (DeNavas-Walt, Proctor, and Mills 2004).

A 2001 Commonwealth Fund survey revealed that Hispanics and African Americans were most likely to be uninsured, as 46 percent and 33 percent of working-age Hispanics and African Americans, respectively, lacked insurance for all or part of the twelve months prior to the survey (Duchon et al. 2000). In comparison, 20 percent of both whites and Asian Americans ages 18–64 lacked health coverage for all or part of the previous twelve months (Duchon et al. 2000).

African-American households are also less likely to have homeowners' and rental insurance to cover storm losses and temporary living expenses (Bolin and Bolton 1986). African Americans are also less likely than whites to have insurance with major companies as a result of decades of insurance redlining (Peacock and Girard 1997). African Americans are more likely than whites to receive insufficient insurance settlement amounts. How insurance claims are settled can impact the ability of black households and neighborhoods to recover. Ultimately, this form of discrimination harms wealth creation of individual households and siphons off investments needed to rebuild the black community.

Many white insurance companies routinely redline black neighborhoods. Although insurance redlining is illegal, it is still practiced. It is not uncommon to find African Americans who live in majority-black zip codes paying twice the insurance premium that whites pay for comparable housing in mostly white suburban zip codes (Bullard, Johnson, and Torres 2000). Race does matter in urban credit and insurance markets (Dymski 1995; Squires 1996a).

The insurance industry, like its housing industry counterpart, "has long used race as a factor in appraising and underwriting property" (Squires 1996b). In general, black neighborhoods are left with check-cashing stations, pawnshops, storefront grocery stores, liquor stores, and fast-food operations, all well buttoned-up with wire mesh and bulletproof glass (Bullard, Grigsby, and Lee 1994).

A National Fair Housing Alliance (2005) report, *No Home for the Holidays: Report on Housing Discrimination Against Hurricane Katrina Survivors,* found housing discrimination against African Americans displaced by Hurricane Katrina. In NFHA telephone tests to determine what African American and white home seekers were told about housing availability, 66 percent of these tests, 43 of 65 instances, whites were favored over African Americans. NFHA also conducted five matched pair tests in which persons visited apartment complexes. In those five tests, Whites were favored over African Americans three times.

Because of the enormity of the damage from Katrina, insurance companies tried to categorize a lot of legitimate wind claims as flood-related. This problem of white-collar insurance "looting" has hit low-income, elderly, disabled, and people-of-color storm victims hardest because these groups are likely to have their insurance with small, less reputable companies due to racial redlining. Many, if not most, Katrina victims may not have resources to hire lawyers to fight the insurance companies. In an attempt to head off a floodgate of insurance disputes, Mississippi Attorney General Jim Hood filed suit to block insurance companies from denying flood claims in cases where those floods were caused by wind. He asserted that the insurance exclusion of water damage violates Mississippi's Consumer Protection Act and "deprives consumers of any real coverage choices" (Lee 2005). The lawsuit also accused some insurance companies of forcing storm victims into signing documents that stipulate their losses were flood-related, not wind-related, before they can receive payment or emergency expenses; the lawsuit would ban such practices (Paul 2005). Such a practice is tantamount to economic blackmail.

9 781631 892998